MW00647064

LISTENING TO WAR

Listening to War

SOUND, MUSIC, TRAUMA, AND SURVIVAL IN WARTIME IRAQ

J. Martin Daughtry

OXFORD

UNIVERSITY PRESS

Oxford University Press is a department of the University of
Oxford. It furthers the University's objective of excellence in research,
scholarship, and education by publishing worldwide.

Oxford   New York
Auckland   Cape Town   Dar es Salaam   Hong Kong   Karachi
Kuala Lumpur   Madrid   Melbourne   Mexico City   Nairobi
New Delhi   Shanghai   Taipei   Toronto

With offices in
Argentina   Austria   Brazil   Chile   Czech Republic   France   Greece
Guatemala   Hungary   Italy   Japan   Poland   Portugal   Singapore
South Korea   Switzerland   Thailand   Turkey   Ukraine   Vietnam

Oxford is a registered trademark of Oxford University Press
in the UK and certain other countries.

Published in the United States of America by
Oxford University Press
198 Madison Avenue, New York, NY 10016

Library of Congress Cataloging-in-Publication Data
Daughtry, J. Martin.
Listening to war : sound, music, trauma and survival in wartime Iraq / J. Martin Daughtry.
    pages cm
Includes index.
ISBN 978-0-19-936149-6 (hardcover) — ISBN 978-0-19-936151-9 (ebook) —
ISBN 978-0-19-936153-3 (online content)   1. Iraq War, 2003–2011—Music and the war.
2. Music—Psychological aspects.   3. Iraq War, 2003–2011—Psychological aspects.   4. Music in the army.
5. Sound—Psychological aspects.   I. Title.
ML3917.I72D38 2015
780.9567'09051—dc23
2015009166

This volume is published with the generous support of the AMS 75 PAYS Endowment of the American
Musicological Society, funded in part by the National Endowment for the Humanities and the Andrew
W. Mellon Foundation.

9 8 7 6 5 4 3 2
Printed in the United States of America
on acid-free paper

To the war's many auditors.

Contents

Note on transliteration of Arabic xi

Introduction: Composing Thoughts on Sound and Violence   1
    In Lieu of an Epigraph: Sound-centered Memories of Operation Iraqi Freedom   1
    The Belliphonic   3
    Intellectual Predecessors   5
    A Necessary Detour   7
    Approaches and Challenges   12

Fragment #1: The Presence of Mind to Save an Ear: Ali's Story   27

SECTION I | SONIC MATÉRIEL
1. Belliphonic Sounds and Indoctrinated Ears: The Elements of Wartime Audition   33
    Charting the Belliphonic   33
    Listening, Structure, and Positionality   36
    Vehicular Sounds   41
    Communications   47
    Civilian Sounds   56
    Weapons   63

2. Mapping Zones of Wartime (In)audition   76
    The Audible Inaudible   77
    The Narrational Zone   80
    The Tactical Zone   88
    The Trauma Zone   92

A Complicating Factor: Iraqi Civilian Auditors   95

Another Complicating Factor: Sound and Psychological Trauma   98

Conclusion   101

Fragment #2: Stealth and Improvisation in the Desert: Jason's Story   103

*Fragment #3: Loudly Searching in the Resonant Darkness: The Anatomy
of a Nighttime House Raid*   110

SECTION II | STRUCTURES OF LISTENING, SOUNDING, AND EMPLACEMENT

Introduction to Section II: The Auditory Regimes, Sonic Campaigns,
and Acoustic Territories of Operation Iraqi Freedom   121

3. Auditory Regimes   128

Ideals of Military Audition   130

National Audition   139

Oblique Indoctrination of Belliphonic Ears   141

Situational Awareness   142

The Inclusive Auditory Regime of Iraqi Civilians   147

Auditory Literacy, Competence, Virtuosity   150

Incommensurability   151

4. Sonic Campaigns   159

Sound (and Violence)   160

Violence (and Sound)   165

The Omnidirectionality of Sound and Violence   170

Sonic Campaigns   174

5. Acoustic Territories   188

Emplacement, Displacement, Transplacement   188

Sound and Territoriality   192

The Virtual Acoustic Territory of Recorded Sound   193

The Radiant Acoustic Territories of Wartime   199

The Resonant Acoustic Territories of Baghdad   201

The Resonant Acoustic Territory of the Body   207

Life at the Intersection of Regime, Campaign, and Territory   210

Fragment #4: A Fatal Mishearing   213

SECTION III | MUSIC, MEDIATION, AND SURVIVAL

6. Mobile Music in the Military   219
  Introducing the Wartime iPod   220
  A Century of Recorded Music on the Battlefield   225
  iPods in the Iraq War   227
  Amping Up, Staying Focused, Cooling Down: iPods as Technologies
  of Self-Regulation in Combat   228
  Moving Bodies, Loosening Tongues, Adjusting Crosshairs: iPods as Technologies
  for Manipulating Others in Combat   238
  Concluding Thoughts   246

*Fragment #5: From "Hell's Bells" to "Silent Night": A Conversation about Music
  in the Military*   248

Fragment #6: Keeping the Music Turned Down Low: Shymaa's Story   254

7. A Time of Troubles for Iraqi Music   258
  Iraq's Musical Legacy   259
  Post-invasion Challenges   261
  Political Violence   263
  Sectarian Violence   263
  US Forces Targeting Music   267
  The Attenuated Acoustic Territory of Iraqi Musical Practice   269

Conclusion   271

Fragment #7: Listening as Poiesis: Tareq's Story   275

ACKNOWLEDGMENTS   279
NOTES   283
GLOSSARY   321
BIBLIOGRAPHY   325
INDEX   339

Note on transliteration of Arabic

THROUGHOUT THIS BOOK I use conventional English spellings for Arabic words that are commonly found in the anglophone press (e.g., *Saddam Hussein* instead of *Ṣaddām Husayn*) and a simplified version of the *International Journal of Middle East Studies* (IJMES) transliteration guidelines for other names and terms. When necessary, I use the diacritic ' for the glottal stop *hamza* and ' for the consonant *ayn*. When direct quotes appear in the book, the original text's transliteration is retained.

Introduction

COMPOSING THOUGHTS ON SOUND AND VIOLENCE

IN LIEU OF AN EPIGRAPH: SOUND-CENTERED MEMORIES
OF OPERATION IRAQI FREEDOM

K-k-r-r-BOOM.

—ARMOR GEDDON

The shooting started at mid-morning, ten to ten to be precise. It began as a salvo in the
distance and then spread until it surrounded us from all sides and there was no escape from
the constant sound of combat. . . . I hid at the bottom of the vehicle. I could see nothing;
the fighting was merely noise. There was no space in my brain for anything but the necessity of picking up every sound that might explain what was happening on the other side of
the metal walls in which I was encased.

—OLIVER POOLE

Zzzip.
P-e-e-e-w-w-w-w.
Crack . . . CrackCRACK.

—ARMOR GEDDON

Before the bomb drops, you can hear this horrible screaming sound. We call it 'the elephant' because it sounds like an elephant shrieking in anger.

—RIVERBEND

I heard a hiss about a split second before [the rocket-propelled grenade] hit me.
[Afterwards] I couldn't hear anything except a dull static-like humming in my ears.

—BLACKFIVE

Thump . . . . Thud . . . . BOOM.

—RIVERBEND

Glass and sound rain down on me . . . I know it was bad, I have never heard anything so
loud, and light debris is falling all around me. . . . What happened? IED? VBED? . . . .
What the fuck happened?

—THE QUESTING CAT

Dadadadadada. Dadadadada.

—AS RELATED TO TIM PRITCHARD

Whoosh.
Out of nowhere, there was a whistle and the thud of a mortar landing nearby. Captain
Scott Dyer looked around, momentarily confused. He recognized the sound of the incom-
ing shells as 120 mm mortar rounds. At the same moment he heard rounds pinging off the
tank's two-inch-thick steel ballistic skirts. His first reaction was surprise rather than fear.
So this is what it feels like to be shot at.

—AS RELATED TO TIM PRITCHARD

Last night's bombardment was very different from the nights before. It wasn't only heavier
but the sound of the bombs was different. The booms and bangs are much louder; you
would hear one big bang and then followed by a number of these rumbles that would shake
everything. And there are of course the series of deep dob-dob-dobs from the explosions
farther away. Anyway it is still early (it is 9:45pm) last night things got seriously going at
12, followed by bombardments at 3, 4 and 6am each would last for 15 minutes. The air raid
sirens signaled an attack around 12 and never sounded the all-clear signal. Sleep is what
you get between being woken up by the rumbles or the time you can take your eyes off
the news.

—SALAM PAX

Vrrrrm. Vrmmm. Vrmmm.
Ever since he'd been a kid, he'd played these games where someone would imitate the whis-
tle of an incoming shell and then it would explode and they'd fall to the ground like idiots.
Now it was happening for real.
This is scary as shit.
VRRRMMMMM.
Quirk felt warm air shoot past his ear and heard a thud about five meters in front of him.
Holy shit. He turned to Labarge.
"What the fuck was that?"
"You don't want to know, brother."
"Fuck the bullshit, what the fuck was it?"

"That was a mortar. It missed your head by about a foot and a half. It was a dud,
thank God."

"Maybe we should get the fuck out of here."

—AS RELATED TO TIM PRITCHARD

"Cotton wool in children's ears," says Rana. "When the bombs fall the explosions that
accompany them can drive you crazy. I'll stop the children's ears with cotton wool so they
won't be frightened. And I've bought sleeping pills and calming extracts so they can get lost
in dreams, away from the awful events," she says while breast-feeding the youngest child.

—AS RELATED TO ASNE SEIERSTAD

K-k-r-r-BOOM.

K-k-r-r-BOOM.

K-k-r-r-BOOM.

—ARMOR GEDDON

THE BELLIPHONIC

From the *Iliad* to *All Quiet on the Western Front,* the sounds of combat have been a prominent presence in literary depictions of war; documentary accounts and oral histories are similarly saturated with evocations of war's sonic dimension. That sound is regarded as worthy of commentary should not be surprising: armed conflict has been a noisy, grunting, clanging business throughout history. Since the advent of explosive ordnance and, later, mechanized cavalry, the sounds of modern warfare have often exceeded the range of its shocking sights and noxious smells. The distant thunder of cannon may be the only indicator that a battle is taking place beyond the next hill; the grinding rumble of tanks usually precedes their appearance from around the street corner. The 2003 US-led military intervention in Iraq was no exception; from the first sorties of the so-called Shock and Awe operation on March 21, 2003—a bombing campaign that was designed to be deafening[1]—the sonic dimension of Operation Iraqi Freedom was a source of intense preoccupation and consternation for Iraqi civilians. With time, as the insurgency gathered strength, American military service members too became aware of their vulnerability to the acoustic consequences of combat.[2] In the epigraphs above, service members and Iraqi civilians struggle within the confines of written language to evoke the urgency, indeterminacy, iconicity, and omnipresence of "the belliphonic," the spectrum of sounds produced by armed combat.[3] I introduce this term—a portmanteau that brings together the Latin word for war [*bellum,* adj. *bellicus*] and the Greek term for voice [*phone*]—in order to give us an easy way to refer to the agglomeration of sounds that are generated by (a) weaponry (e.g., small arms, improvised explosive devices, "smart bombs," cruise missiles, anti-aircraft weapons, rockets, mortars); and (b) the motorized vehicles that carry weapons into combat (e.g., Humvees, tanks, MRAPs, Strykers, Bradleys, helicopters, airplanes, as well as the cars, trucks, and other vehicles used by insurgent and sectarian fighters). But I also intend for the term to encompass sonic material that is less directly or conventionally associated with warfare: the omnipresent civilian gas generators that appeared throughout Iraq after the partial destruction of the electric grid in the wake of major combat operations in 2003; the sirens and other warning signals that punctuated life on military bases and urban areas during the war; the propaganda recordings, made by all of the major parties to the conflict, that proliferated, in English and Arabic, on radio, projected through mobile or stationary loudspeakers, and on the internet; the live human voices whose presence, substance, and style were conditioned by the ebb and flow of combat; the live and recorded music that was so actively a part of the deployments of military service members in Iraq; the Iraqi musical genres that refracted and memorialized wartime violence; the recorded devotional chants, new vocal compositions, and other utterances that often accompanied videos of IED explosions distributed by members of the insurgency; and a host of other sounds, live and recorded, that were connected, through causation or inference, to the war. In short, the belliphonic in Iraq is the imagined total of sounds that would not have occurred had the conflict not taken place.

This book charts the fraught territory upon which American military service members and Iraqi civilians encountered the belliphonic over the course of Operation Iraqi Freedom and its immediate aftermath. The terms of these encounters were various, and often overlapped with one another within the conflict's acoustic territories. The parties who actively participated in the fighting—those who, in the ocularcentric expression, "saw combat"—regularly confronted the acoustic consequences of violent acts of their own making (e.g., the explosive report of their own weapons), while simultaneously contending with the sounds of violent acts directed back at them (e.g., "incoming," or enemy fire). Civilian bystanders caught in the combat zone experienced with frightening immediacy sonic evidence of armed violence from the subject position of the potential victim. And in the time that stretched out between moments when they witnessed or participated in armed combat, civilian bystanders and military personnel alike strained to hear—or, depending on the situation, to avoid hearing—the distant sounds of combat taking place in adjoining neighborhoods. Often, the sounds of the war were valued as indices of violent acts, informationally rich signals that increased the odds of the experienced auditor's survival. In other instances, the belliphonic was received as the intermittent noise through which cherished sounds were filtered, a lamentably prominent part of the violent background against which wartime life was noisily lived. In yet other, more extreme, situations, people encountered profoundly loud or disturbing sounds that, having exited the realm of the indexical, came to constitute violent acts in their own right. Collectively, these encounters lend credence to the notion that sound is not epiphenomenal to the lived experience of war. On the contrary, as I argue throughout this book, the belliphonic is a fundamental dimension of wartime experience, and learning to contend with it is a daunting and ever-present challenge faced by service members and civilians alike. The fact that the value of belliphonic sound is ambiguous—that it can be received as simultaneously a rich source of tactical information and a profound source of trauma (in the form of hearing loss, post-traumatic stress, and other less quantifiable injuries)—both complicates and magnifies its salience. Attending closely to belliphonic sound gives one access to new forms of knowledge; at the same time, exposure to belliphonic sound can degrade or even negate the very bodily capacities through which such knowledge is acquired.

While investigating the fine-grained dynamics of sound and listening during the Iraq War is the primary purpose of the book, I also raise a number of broad questions about the intersection of sound, listening, and violence more generally. What demands do belliphonic sounds place on auditors? What are the ethical consequences of listening to violent acts? How do sound and violence move through the world? What are the limits to music's efficacy as an antidote to violence? What kinds of victims, what kinds of survivors, do belliphonic sounds create? These questions destabilize the epistemological frameworks that undergird much scholarship on music and sound, and they certainly short-circuit any lingering thoughts we might still be entertaining about there being an essential or universal relation between listening and aesthetic experience. A focus on the ground conditions of listening in wartime Iraq—on what was at stake for those who listened, and on the violent margins where listening deteriorated into pain, or deafness, or death—can lead one abductively to new vocabularies, new theoretical models, and new arguments about listening in general, both within and outside the combat zone. In turn, theorizing listening in an extreme wartime environment creates a new and productive vantage point from which to interrogate the directed but immersive nature of violence, the expansive but unequal distribution of victimhood, and the ever-present potential for violence and aggression that lurks within sound itself.

INTELLECTUAL PREDECESSORS

New vantage points never arise out of thin air, of course: they are informed by, and positioned in response to, perspectives that precede them. In this sense, *Listening to War* is most directly a beneficiary of the "sonic turn" of the 1990s that led to the burgeoning interdisciplinary rubric of sound studies. Jonathan Sterne's *The Audible Past: Cultural Origins of Sound Reproduction*[4] introduced a broad readership to the study of listening as a historically situated and technologically mediated activity, a project I continue here within a wartime context. Seminal works by Emily Thompson,[5] Bruce Smith,[6] John Picker,[7] Karin Bijsterveld,[8] Brandon Labelle,[9] and the contributors to Bijsterveld and Trevor Pinch's *Oxford Handbook of Sound Studies*[10] anticipated many of the acoustic questions that I take up here, as did Steven Connor's eclectic writings on listening and voice.[11] While my attempts to theorize violence through the prism of sound and sound through the prism of violence have no easy analogs within the sound studies literature, I share with these authors an abiding interest in the ways that sounds, environments, people, technologies, and cultures intermingle.

Equally powerfully, this book is influenced by and contributes to the wave of music scholarship that seeks to understand the relationship between music practices and the practice of violence. Recent volumes on this difficult subject include works by Bruce Johnson and Martin Cloonan,[12] John O'Connell and Salwa Castelo-Branco,[13] Eric Weisbard,[14] and Kip Pegley and Susan Fast.[15] One of the earliest scholars to focus on music and violence was Svanibor Pettan, whose edited collection, *Music, Politics, and War: Views from Croatia in the 1990s*, set the terms of debate for the field.[16] By placing music within a much more expansive field of sonic practices, my work invites these authors to re-examine the arguments for and against musical exceptionalism, and to investigate the ways that listening—to music, but also to the sounds of nonmusical events—can orient people within their environments, connect them with affective stimuli, and open their bodies up to violence and pain as well as to knowledge and pleasure.

A rare volume that blends together an analysis of sound, listening, music, and violence, albeit in different proportions than I do, is Steve Goodman's *Sonic Warfare: Sound, Affect, and the Ecology of Fear*.[17] This work outlines a "politics of frequency" that leads to an all-encompassing "vibrational ontology" that encompasses sound but also extends beyond it to "unsound" and other pre- or parasonic events. In writing this book, I have tried to give a kind of ethnographic grounding to the broad ontological formations that Goodman describes. *Listening to War* is also in direct dialogue with Jonathan Pieslak's *Sound Targets: American Soldiers and Music in the Iraq War*.[18] Pieslak's book is important for being the first (and so far only) monograph devoted exclusively to music in the context of the Iraq War. Many of the military testimonies I elicited in the context of chapter 6 complement the viewpoints of Pieslak's interviewees. Two figures, Colby Buzzell and Jason Sagebiel, are present in both books. Pieslak's book articulates a number of questions about wartime music listening that I attempt to answer more fully here. Most significantly, perhaps, for the last several years I have been in literal and figurative conversation with my NYU colleague Suzanne Cusick, whose provocative articles on the use of music and sound in interrogation during the Global War on Terror have been highly impactful throughout the humanities.[19] I draw from her work in chapters 2, 4, and 6, and adapt elements of her interpretation of acoustic violence in the interrogation chamber to fit the context of wartime listening more generally.

This volume also stages an intervention into the anthropology of the senses, whose luminaries David Howes, Constance Classen, Paul Stoller, Steven Feld, and Anthony Seeger have all made strong arguments about the cultural contingency of the human sensorium.[20] *Listening to War* is in many ways a conventional case study of the "social construction of the senses"—except that this social construction is fueled by an immersive field of armed violence that often ends up, for reasons that will be discussed at length below, privileging hearing to a radical degree.

An additional set of social scientists has made a strong mark on this text. Allen Feldman's challenging writing on violence in the contexts of Northern Ireland, South Africa, and the United States has affected my thinking at several points in the research process. I have been similarly inspired and spurred to action by the work of anthropologists E. Valentine Daniel, Nancy Scheper-Hughes, and Carolyn Nordstrom, and sociologist Michel Wieviorka, all of whom are cited repeatedly in what is to follow. My tight focus on sound and listening produces questions and insights that resonate with and extend their arguments about the situatedness of violence, in part by linking them to the sensorial anthropology I mentioned above.

Lastly, this investigation is influenced by the enormous amount of clinical and conceptual work that is often collected under the umbrella term "trauma theory."[21] Gaining traction in the immediate post-Vietnam era, and entering a new stage with the official recognition of post-traumatic stress disorder in 1980, clinical scholars of trauma assert that traumatic experience amounts to an injury, albeit an invisible one, that needs, like physical wounds, to be treated. I subscribe to the widespread understanding of trauma as an "impossible event," one that cannot be incorporated into one's ongoing self-narrative and so creates a circular temporality of flashbacks in which "the past is always present." Cathy Caruth's depiction of trauma as "less a stable object of understanding than the persistent and renewed encounter with the urgency of an event" encapsulates the slippery circularity of traumatic experience and involuntary memory discussed throughout this book.[22] While *Listening to War* is not a clinical study by any means, it does attempt to provide clinicians and theorists of trauma with a set of questions and propositions for better understanding the insidious ways in which sound underwrites trauma, along with a host of less extreme but still significant psychological injuries that take place during wartime and persist in its aftermath.

A NECESSARY DETOUR

I should mention that I didn't start out with these grand objectives and intertextual engagements when I began working on this project. My initial research questions, along with the assumptions that undergirded them, were significantly narrower, and pertained only to American service members listening to recorded music during their tours of duty in Iraq. As is often the case, the contours of my research were influenced more by a combination of serendipity, instinct, and exigency than by a systematic appraisal of lacunae within the anthropology of the senses, the interdisciplinary study of violence, or my own disciplinary home of ethnomusicology. In other words, I started out studying something small, something I thought I understood, and then found myself pulled into a broader, more unfamiliar and disconcerting subject.[23] In order to explain the conceptual territory this book covers, then, a brief autobiographical detour is necessary.

In early 2005, having spent a year conducting ethnographic research in Russia, I moved to Washington, DC (where my wife had secured a job at the State Department), and set about writing a dissertation on post-Stalinist sung poetry.[24] The contrast between Moscow, where the Iraq War was hardly a topic of everyday conversation, and the US capital, where it was the constant object of emotional discussion and anxious speculation within my social and professional circles, was, to put it mildly, striking. My life in DC was suffused with a wide range of visual reminders of the war—from the frenetic rhythms of the twenty-four-hour mediascape to the ubiquitous "support the troops" stickers that adorned what seemed to be every other bumper on the Beltway, from the frequent sight throughout the city of uniformed service members to the Pentagon looming in the distance whenever I drove on the George Washington Memorial Parkway. Within days of returning from Russia, I found myself compulsively monitoring the increasingly troubling news emanating from Iraq. By the time I finished my dissertation in the summer of 2006, I think it's fair to say that I was spending most of my spare time reading and thinking and worrying about the war.

My thoughts at that point were deeply conflicted. On the one hand, I shared the broad pacifist stance that is held by the majority of today's humanities scholars. This stance was rendered all the more acute by the frequent sight in my neighborhood of wheelchair-bound Iraq War veterans, their limbs blown off by IED explosions; these young men and women provided a somber reminder of the profound and tragic cost that war exacted on young soldiers. On the other hand, and unlike many of my colleagues in the humanities, I had had a fair amount of first- and secondhand experience with US military officers and civilian Department of Defense employees, largely during a period in the mid-1990s when I worked for a nongovernmental think tank devoted to monitoring the spread of weapons of mass destruction, but also through my wife's professional contacts at the Pentagon, where she had interned during law school. These interactions had instilled in me an abiding respect for the core competence and dedication of the people who joined the US armed forces, as well as an acute sense of the dissimilarity between the service members I knew and the caricature of the aggressively unreflective military man that has been a pop-cultural staple for decades.

My orientation toward the war at that point might best have been described as one of impassioned ambivalence. My sense was that we had made a mistake of historic proportions by invading Iraq, and that we had compounded this mistake by a string of bad policy decisions in the immediate aftermath of the war. My equally strong suspicion was that the military was not the ultimate source of the problem, and that a rapid withdrawal of coalition forces in the violent conditions of 2006 would have resulted in even more trauma for the embattled civilian population of Iraq. I was horrified by the atrocities of Abu Ghraib, but awed by the dedication of the vast majority of officers and enlisted personnel as they performed difficult and dangerous jobs in extreme circumstances. I was antipathetic to the philosophy of preventive war, but repulsed by the violence perpetrated by Saddam Hussein's regime upon the Iraqi populace and convinced that Iraq was well rid of him. I was painfully cognizant of the structural violence that accompanied America's ascendance to the status of sole global superpower and neoliberal hegemon, but unwilling to absolve the perceived victims of this historical violence of all responsibility for their own violent acts. Looming above all of these feelings was the sickening knowledge that with every day, untold numbers of innocent Iraqi civilians were dying, with no end to the killing in sight. In other words, I found myself, like many others, caught in the middle—allergic to the reductionist viewpoints of the far right (e.g., the war against terror is a manifestation of the clash of civilizations, pitting an unimpeachable secular democracy against a monolithic and inherently violent form of Islamic fundamentalism) and the far left (e.g., the terrorist attacks on 9/11 were an understandable, even justifiable, reaction to American imperialism, and the US presence in Iraq and Afghanistan was nothing more than a cynical extension of this imperialist project). I do not mean to say that all who inhabit one or the other end of the American political spectrum hold these views, nor do I mean to present my more or less centrist orientation as inherently less problematic than those at the margins. Rather, I want to point to the fact that ambivalence and contradictory beliefs of this order of magnitude frequently lead to a kind of internal intellectual stalemate—and with it, a creeping sense of apathy and, ultimately, disengagement. As someone whose research expertise lay elsewhere, the easiest and perhaps most reasonable solution to my ambivalence would have been to leave the Iraq War where it was and pick up my Russian music research where it had left off. My decision to begin investigating the sonic dimension of the Iraq conflict can be understood, in this sense, as an attempt to come up with an alternative—any alternative—to throwing up my hands in the face of the benumbing complexity of the war.

While there are certainly more obvious and consequential dimensions of warfare than the sounds that weapons and people produce and the music they consume, sound and music are, for better or worse, what I study. Abraham Maslow's famous phrase—"it is tempting, if the only tool you have is a hammer, to treat everything as if it were a nail"[25]—is more than a little bit apt here: equipped with a particular set of disciplinary tools and intellectual sensibilities, I was predisposed to approach the war as a sonorous phenomenon. Even more narrowly, as an ethnomusicologist, my attention was first drawn to musical questions: as I mentioned above, this project began as a relatively focused investigation of music-listening practices among military service members. Following in the footsteps of those who called Operation Iraqi Freedom the world's first "iPod war," I decided that it would be worthwhile to speak with some Iraq War veterans about the ways in which the advent of MP3 players had affected music-listening practices in the combat zone.[26] My initial idea was to speak to soldiers who were convalescing at the nearby Walter Reed Army Medical Center; several press stories on these "wounded warriors" had mentioned that the large population of recent amputees at the hospital was suffering from boredom and a lack of social interaction as its members spent up to eighteen months in physical and occupational therapy. It struck me that music might make for a relatively uncontroversial and diverting topic of conversation for these convalescing service members. And so, with a vague plan to write an article on iPods in the military and a somewhat better-defined hope of helping these soldiers pass the time more pleasantly, I headed down Georgia Avenue to the hospital.

It will come as no surprise to most readers—and indeed, in retrospect, was no surprise to me—that the administration at Walter Reed had a strong policy in place prohibiting any research projects dealing with its patients. My first visit to the hospital occurred in February 2007, a week or so after Dana Priest and Anne Hull's now-famous exposé of neglect at Walter Reed was published in the *Washington Post*.[27] The article, which documented the hospital's Byzantine bureaucracy and the shockingly poor living conditions that patients' family members endured, triggered a major congressional investigation as well as the resignation of the base commander and, eventually, the secretary of the army. One of the hospital administrators explained to me that, in reaction to the heightened scrutiny by the government and the press, they had become so protective of their wounded warriors that they had put a moratorium on *all* outside research on patients—including, shockingly, a request made by the designers of soldiers' prosthetic limbs to survey amputees on the limbs with which they had been fitted. In an environment of extreme caution such as this, my project was clearly destined for rejection.

When I explained that, academic interests aside, I had hoped my project would assist the hospital's wounded residents by alleviating their boredom, the administrator let me know that if I wanted to help, there was a far less problematic and more directly contributive role that I could play at the hospital: that of platelet donor. It turned out that the hospital was in acute need of platelets, the body's clotting agent, in connection with the large number of amputations they performed on service members who had survived IED explosions in Iraq. Healthy service members were regularly called upon to donate platelets, and while civilian donors were relatively rare, they were, I learned, welcomed. And so it transpired that my first conversations with active duty service members took place not within the framework of a research project, but casually, desultorily, during my monthly plateletpheresis sessions, as we lay side by side, each connected to tubes, surrounded by the soft whirring of the centrifuge, with *Black Hawk Down* or *Gladiator* playing on a TV bolted to the wall. I don't reference these casual conversations in this volume other than to say that I often found them inspiring and humbling, and to note that it was at that time that I began to pay attention to how often reminiscences about music in the combat zone ended up veering off toward other sounds—from engine noise to voices to explosions to the call to prayer—that loomed large in soldiers' memories.

Soon after I learned that a research project at Walter Reed was an impossibility, I began seeking out Iraq War veterans and active duty service members who were studying or teaching at military institutions in the United States. A colleague at the

Naval Postgraduate School in Monterey, California, mentioned my project to a class of young officers, many of whom had just returned from Iraq. They proved more than willing to talk to me. These interviews, many of which are excerpted in this volume, were remarkable for the level of precision and detail with which they described the discrete sounds of wartime life and the costs and benefits of exposure to those sounds. After a year of rich conversations with service members who had served in Operation Iraqi Freedom, I began speaking to civil servants who had spent time in the so-called Green Zone (officially the International Zone) during the war. In 2008, after taking a teaching position at New York University, I expanded the conversational pool further. That summer, I traveled to Jordan and Kuwait, where I spoke to a dozen Iraqi civilians who had fled their country after having spent several years in wartime Baghdad. In the ensuing years, I sought out more interlocutors from the US military, US civil service, and Iraqi civilian population. Finally, in early 2011, I was given permission to travel to Camp Victory and Baghdad's International Zone to record sounds for *Virtual Iraq,* a virtual-reality treatment platform created by the Institute for Creative Technologies at USC, which is used extensively for treating post-traumatic stress disorder among veterans.[28] During this trip, I was able to hear with my own ears a number of the sounds I document in chapter 1, and informally discuss sound and listening with actively deployed service members. Later, in 2012, I spent several fascinating days interviewing Iraqi refugees outside of Dearborn, Michigan. In all, I have interviewed roughly one hundred Americans and Iraqis for this project, several of whom have become long-term correspondents and friends.

In response to the direction that my first round of conversations with service members took in 2007, I began recalibrating my questions, directing more and more of them away from music and toward issues of noise, violence, ambience, and aural acuity. Music continues to be a major interest, as the chapters in this book dealing with music technologies and violence toward Iraqi musicians attest. But music and music listening are treated here as subcategories of the sonorous phenomena and situated auditory practices that are the central subject of this book. The stories my interlocutors told me indicated that, in wartime especially, music is not an autonomous world unto itself—even when that is what one desperately wants it to be. Music in wartime inflects and is inflected by violent acts and the discursive structures that enable them. And music in wartime is heard to the accompaniment of bullets, and Humvees, and helicopters, and mortars, and generators, and screams, and anxious and aggressive talk. In other words, a substantial part of wartime music's habitus consists of the interlocking matrices of violent ideologies and belliphonic sounds in which it is enmeshed.

In 2004, in response to an army specialist who asked why the army had deployed so many inadequately armored Humvees to Iraq, forcing many drivers to protect their vehicles by welding scrap metal onto their doors, Donald Rumsfeld famously replied, "you go to war with the army you have, and not the army you may want, or wish to have at a later time."[29] Given the degree to which Rumsfeld was castigated for this remark, it is with no small sense of irony that I note how perfectly it mirrors the choice that I made in 2007 to embark upon this project. As an ethnomusicologist, my choice of a project centered in Iraq would have appeared much more logical had I been fluent in Arabic and an expert on cultural and musical practices of the region. On the other hand, if that had been the case, I likely would have embarked upon a somewhat more conventional study, focusing on the effect that three decades of war have had on the Iraqi traditional music scene, for example, or on the devastatingly moving expressions of suffering to be found in Iraqi songs about the war—topics I treat only in passing here. Those books and many others still need to be written, urgently. As it stands, I have worked as best I could, with the resources at hand and the expertise I possess, to write a kind of book that, I now suspect, no author is ideally positioned to write. It is situated on the unstable ground that lies between Iraq and America, between military life and civilian life, between anthropology and musicology, between trauma studies and acoustics, between phenomenology and military history; such was the breadth of the questions that animated it. Throughout, I have benefited profoundly from the at-times-superhuman patience of my American and Iraqi interlocutors, who have explained Iraqi culture, US military structures, and wartime life to me as if to a child, from the ground up. In the end, though, I went to war with the army I had, and bear alone the responsibility for that choice.

APPROACHES AND CHALLENGES

Authors of anthropological works on violence have to address methodological problems that can be substantially more acute than those which ethnographers of nonviolent situations face. Anthropologist Jo Boyden describes some of the problems endemic to wartime ethnography, problems that extend beyond the familiar territory of "theory, conceptualisation and analysis" into high-stakes "challenges and dilemmas" concerning "practical constraints, methodology, methods and ethics." She continues:

> Personal security, access to research subjects over time and integrity of data are all threatened by armed violence. In certain cases, research is itself a major source of risk to war-affected populations. . . . During war, the researcher struggles against the odds to create the ethical and practical conditions that are normally thought of as essential to good ethnography.[30]

Often such felicitous conditions fail to obtain. War zones are commonly policed by governmental, military, or paramilitary bodies that prohibit all research that doesn't advance their own political goals. Even if permission is obtained, the constraints imposed by warring parties often make it impossible to conduct research in a robust and unbiased way. Even if these constraints are not disabling, researchers often decide that the risk to their own lives is too great to justify entering the combat zone. And even when their own security can be provisionally guaranteed, researchers often fear, rightly, that their mere presence may endanger their assistants, interlocutors, and friends in the field in unpredictable and uncontrollable ways. These conditions "are hardly conducive to sound fieldwork and commonly make participant observation, the basic tool of the anthropologist's trade, impossible."[31]

To be sure, there are anthropologists who accept these multiple risks and engage in what Boyden and others have termed "anthropology under fire" or "frontline ethnography."[32] These scholars endeavor to practice what Nancy Scheper-Hughes has called "a phenomenologically grounded anthropology, an *antropologia-pé-no-chão,* an anthropology-with-one's-feet-on-the-ground," in order to observe up close the complexity of violent situations. This kind of work positions the researcher as a direct eyewitness to violent events; it is precisely this dimension of direct witnessing that, for Scheper-Hughes, "lends our work its moral (at times its almost theological) character."[33] More often, however, it proves more viable to conduct ethnographic work in the aftermath of war, when the guns have been silenced and the population has been given the breathing room necessary to reflect upon matters other than sheer survival. Some of the most powerful and moving anthropological accounts of wartime life were produced in this way, in the wake of armed conflict, or when combat operations had attenuated to the point where the benefits of engagement outweighed the potential costs.[34] In these works, the anthropologist provides an eyewitness account of the conflict's aftermath and aftershocks that is augmented by extensive conversations with survivors about their memories of the violence in question.

This approach works well in the wake of civil war or internecine conflicts, when all parties remain more or less in the same place once the fighting stops. In international military actions such as Operation Iraqi Freedom, however, waiting until the conflict subsides generally means waiting until the foreign armies leave, which is a problem if one's research focuses in large part on the perspectives of those transient foreign soldiers. American military personnel generally deployed to Iraq for twelve to fifteen months at a time. Waiting for the war to end to begin conducting ethnographic research in Iraq would, in this case, not have created a privileged field site for conversations with soldiers who had participated in Operation Iraqi Freedom. (As it stands, more than half of the soldiers I met in Baghdad in 2011 were on their first deployment to Iraq, and so had nothing to say about the period during which combat operations were regularly taking place.) Waiting would also have allowed memories of combat, and of the sounds therein, to cool.

As it turned out, spending a sustained period in Iraq proved unfeasible for the very reasons I outlined above.[35] My persistent efforts to obtain permission from the US military to visit Iraq proved unsuccessful until early 2011, and then I was only allowed to visit for a scant week, working within strict parameters that precluded formal interviews and limited my interactions with Iraqis to those who were working in the International Zone. Even had I been granted permission to travel to Iraq unaccompanied, however, I was not convinced that the situation would be safe enough for me to make such a trip. And all the while I was receiving unambiguous signals from my Iraqi interlocutors in Jordan and the US that there would be no way to spend time with civilians outside the International Zone without increasing the risk that they would be punished by various fighting forces for collaborating with me. Given these constraints, it became clear by the end that participant-observation had never been an option, or at the very least not a good one. Instead, I cobbled together an eclectic approach that involved a number of regular activities, including surveying milblogs, Iraqi internet postings, and published firsthand accounts of the war; collecting military documents that pertained to sound and listening; viewing amateur and semiprofessional videos produced in the combat zone by military service members, Iraqi civilians, and insurgents; and analyzing music, theatrical performances, performance art, and visual art produced by Iraqis and Americans in response to the conflict. These activities proved useful, but only as supplements to my primary source for insight into the sonic dimension of the war: extensive open-ended interviews conducted with American service members, civil servants, and Iraqi civilians, and the complex of less formal conversations and correspondence that often preceded and followed them. Given that I was unable to engage in sustained periods of "being there"—unable, that is, to assume the stance of the participant-observer and eyewitness—I ended up building my arguments largely around the testimonies of military personnel and civilians who lived through the war.

Testimony

Testimony, the "autobiographically certified narrative of a past event, whether this narrative be made in informal or formal circumstances," is a concept central to the operation of trials, truth commissions, and trauma therapy, among other activities.[36] It is not coincidental that these activities are marked by their high stakes and their seriousness: this is what separates a testimony from other kinds of vocal narrative. A testimony is a special subcategory of interview. If we can say that a conversation becomes an interview when it takes on a certain structured character and the goal of eliciting information from one of the parties (the interviewee), then an interview becomes a testimony when it is marked by the solemnity that accrues around situations of vulnerability, violence, and loss. One converses about any number of topics, and one can be interviewed about any number of experiences, but one testifies about an ordeal witnessed, an injustice endured.

Testimony is also a critical element in the production of history. It is the conduit through which the experiences of the witness enter the archive. For philosopher Paul Ricoeur, the act of testimony rests upon a tripartite set of assertions: "I was there," says the witness. Then the witness assures us that the account, based on direct experience, is credible: "Believe me," she says. The witness's credibility is magnified by a final implicit offer: "If you don't believe me, ask someone else."[37] This kind of "trust but verify" structure rescues testimony from sliding into the fraught waters of unsubstantiated hearsay

or propaganda. But the fact remains that authors of works based on testimony are trust-
ing the accounts of others rather than their own eyes and ears. For this reason, a work
such as mine, based predominantly on interviews and augmented by a few brief visits
to the region, may not generate the aura of authority that a work that draws upon a
sustained period of direct observation does; it may even risk being dismissed as "parachute" or "armchair" ethnography by those who valorize participant-observation above
all other methods. But, when corroborated by multiple accounts of others, a testimony
can acquire a claim on truth. Not an absolute truth, not the truth of "how the world
is"—something that the participant-observer is also unable to achieve, by the way—but
the partial, situated truth of "how it is for him or her" (Veena Das).[38]

In his account of the role that the witness plays in the production of history, Ricoeur
acknowledges that much of what deserves to enter the historical record remains unrecorded. "There are . . . witnesses," he observes, "who never encounter an audience capable of listening to them or hearing what they have to say."[39] Thus is listening central to
this volume in two separate but conjoined senses: first, and most obviously, it seeks to
understand the dynamics of discrete acts of listening in wartime; but also, it positions
listening to witnesses as its primary methodology. As Carolyn Nordstrom, in her moving ethnography of violence during the Mozambican civil war, states, "listening is not
merely an auditory act," but a practice that is imbricated with ethics, and with obligation.[40] To elicit testimony is to pledge oneself to the witness's survival—literally, but also
figuratively, through the entry of the witness's perspectives into the archive. Listening
to war testimony becomes, for Nordstrom, "an 'art of the possible'—the possibility of
subverting the transgressions of war, of surviving, of humanity, of tomorrow."[41]

According to this line of reasoning, testimony, when elicited judiciously by a consci-
entious and committed listener, is more than historiographically useful; it can also be
therapeutic, as it provides a platform for addressing what Veena Das has identified as
the survivor's need "to talk and talk about war," and to inform the wider world of the
suffering that has taken place. In her account of anti-Sikh rioting in the wake of the
assassination of Indira Gandhi, Das describes a man who, after suffering the death of
both of his sons, talked to her in great detail about the event, and even offered to raise
money to get his account placed in the newspaper. "We discovered thus," she writes,
"that being subjected to brutal violence for two consecutive days had not been successful
in stripping men of their cognitive needs, nor could it blunt their desperate need to have
the truth recorded and communicated."[42] Many civilians and military personnel who
have lived through Operation Iraqi Freedom are similarly committed to having their
experiences heard. Their desire to speak from the subject position of the bereaved witness can be understood both in terms of publicizing tragedy to avoid its repetition—the
logic of "never again"—but it also participates in the recuperative process of speaking
(testimony) in the face of the unspeakable (trauma). As Robert Neimeyer has argued, the
narrative form of testimony is a type of meaning reconstruction, and "meaning reconstruction in response to a loss is the central process in grieving."[43]

The need to testify is neither universal nor constant, however; some people prefer not to revisit the violent events they experienced. Having come to terms with these events within a network of family and friends, they have no desire to dredge them up again for a stranger, or for an unseen audience of readers. In my conversations with civilians and service members, on rare occasions an abrupt silence, a shaken head, or a short answer in the affirmative with no elaboration would serve as evidence that there were stories—relevant, important stories—that people elected not to tell. For this reason, the sense of incompleteness that characterizes all narratives based on situated testimonies is here even more pronounced.

While testimony has proven to be crucial as a methodology here, it is decidedly secondary as a representational strategy. In other words, while eliciting testimony through interviews has been my primary method of learning about Operation Iraqi Freedom, and while the words of service members and civilians do appear, often at some length, throughout this text, I do not present the interviews here as long, uncut transcripts or "oral histories." Rather, the interviews led me to a number of conclusions about the nature of auditory experience in wartime, and these conclusions form the bulk of the work before you. Some of these conclusions amount to "bottom-up theorizing," or creating models based upon the experiences of my interlocutors. In other instances, I draw upon existing theoretical perspectives in order to show how the sonic dimension of the Iraq War is typical or anomalous in relation to observations others have made about sound, listening, or violence. I have discussed all of my arguments with a number of the people whose voices are represented in this work. Most of the arguments have emerged altered in some way as a result of these discussions. I would like to think that together we have begun to construct a grounded theory of belliphonic listening, one that pertains specifically to the Iraq War, but that could, as I mentioned earlier, serve as a starting point for the investigation of other conflicts—and of listening more broadly.

This beginning of a theory—which is most clearly manifest in the discussion of zones of audition found in chapter 2 and the tripartite theoretical model in chapters 3 through 5—highlights my general concern for the hidden and often unconscious labor that goes into the seemingly effortless activity of listening to the world. It also emphasizes the ever-present tension between the fluctuating human agency of listeners and the semi-fluid structures that shape and are shaped by their actions. As a result, my approach to theorizing sound and listening has a distinctly anti-essentialist, constructivist feel to it. I also insist on the multiply emplaced, resolutely finite, partially intersubjective, and always unfolding nature of human experience—tenets that are commonly associated with phenomenological approaches to anthropology.[44] I share phenomenology's commitment to "close examinations of concrete bodily experiences, forms of knowledge, and practice,"[45] which in this instance means a fine-grained study of the ways in which belliphonic sounds interact with discrete listeners, and how those listeners focus on one aspect or another in order to extract sense and minimize injury from them. But if phenomenology is understood to concern itself with the embodied experiences of individuals and, by extension, the intersubjective experiences of communities, then the theoretical models I build here also reach beyond phenomenology to examine broader sociopolitical asymmetries and phenomena that are too diffuse, constant, or technologically mediated to be consciously "experienced" by any one individual or cohort.

Disparate Populations, Overlapping Perspectives

One aspect of this book that deserves comment is its choice of witnesses. A prominent subset of ethnographic works on violence privileges (either implicitly or explicitly) the subject positions of victims, such as civilians in wartime Sarajevo,[46] displaced Palestinians,[47] Hutu refugees,[48] or students in Tiananmen Square.[49] This kind of project is clearly valuable, as civilian victims commonly constitute the majority of wartime casualties, and as they are precisely the populations that warring powers tend to ignore. As the editor of a recent collection of anthropological work in conflict zones argues, the paramount concerns of its authors are "the pressing realities faced by the people undergoing violence; the experiences of the anthropologist as she or he works with these people under difficult circumstances; and the implications this has for responsible theory."[50] On the other hand, an exclusive focus on civilian victims will always leave important questions about the nature of violence unanswered. Mary Louise Pratt has noted with curiosity the fact that "when intellectuals study violence we don't turn to specialists who are trained in the exercise of violence; we don't see experts in violence as a source of knowledge for us, yet we ourselves are not usually trained in the use of violence," given that "our job is to be the police of civility. So in some ways our academic discussions of violence get permeated by fear—our own fear, fear that freezes our intellect . . . and our imaginations."[51] Addressing Pratt's critique comprehensively would require engaging with all of the parties to the Iraq War, including insurgent groups, al-Qaeda in Iraq, and other antagonistic entities—an undertaking that, for reasons of access and safety, is impossible here. But by turning to American soldiers as well as the Iraqi civilians in whose name the US military has been fighting, we can benefit from the viewpoints of "experts" as well as amateurs, active participants as well as bystanders, transients as well as lifelong residents. The perspectives of these groups overlap and diverge in revealing ways, and these moments of convergence and difference are both theoretically significant and affectively rich.

How can we account for these often subtle variations in listening practices? The conventional notion of culture—as a holistic system of symbols and meanings that is broadly shared within a society and that is transmitted across generations—fails to adequately explain them. In the geographically isolated, small-scale, agrarian societies that have been the historical focus of anthropological and ethnomusicological work, one might have been able to observe differences in listening strategies that are the result of fundamentally different, relatively stable, culturally grounded epistemologies and assumptions.[52] In contemporary Iraq, however, the interpenetration of global media, technologies of all kinds, and people with experience living abroad creates a foundation of broad commonality, where unique, culturally specific practices of listening to the ambient world fail to obtain. This common ground, one of the legacies of globalization, takes on a particularly dystopian flavor when applied to the world's war zones, where weapons and battle tactics are the globalized commodities in question. "I have ... come to question traditional assumptions that people experience life in uniquely cultural-specific ways," states Carolyn Nordstrom in her ethnographic study of organized violence in Mozambique, "that what happens to individuals in World War II Europe, in Bosnia, in Mozambique, or in the Amazon Basin is fundamentally different and that these experiences are ultimately incommensurable, incomparable, unique." She continues:

> There *is* something unique about being Mozambican, Bosnian, or of the Amazon region, but there is as well a shared experience of coeval political violence. Contemporary theory, moving away from static notions of identity and culture, is recognizing the importance of seeing *people and cultures as coessentially both unique and resonating with the human condition in myriad complex ways* [my emphasis]. To give a concrete example: if military strategists share torture tactics throughout the world, then there is something victims share in the experience of torture in the most profound ways. Cultures of militarization and the ontological experiences of being victimized by military actions span cultural divisions based on national and ethnic identities to link people in warzones throughout the world.[53]

In Iraq, as elsewhere, civilians *and* military personnel found themselves in an ongoing process of enculturation into a common environment of extreme, and often extremely loud, armed violence. For this reason, many of the techniques of audition documented in this book, while reflecting the discrete experiences of service members and civilians during Operation Iraqi Freedom, will likely be recognizable to people who have endured other wars, and violent timespaces more generally. One of the most intellectually invigorating and personally humbling facets of my work over the past years has been the moment of recognition that regularly appears when I discuss my project with friends and acquaintances who served in Kosovo, or Vietnam, or Korea, or World War II, or who happened to grow up in Colombia, or Israel, or Pakistan, or even 1970s New York.

Listening to War: An Overview

Audition, like other modes of perception, requires an object. "Listening" doesn't have an independent, pre-phenomenological existence: there can only be "listening *to*" or "listening *for*." The discrete sounds available to wartime auditors, their positions in or trajectories through space, their unique acoustic properties, and the manner in which they were layered shaped to a significant degree the ways auditors would approach them. In chapter 1, "Belliphonic Sounds and Indoctrinated Ears: The Elements of Wartime Audition," I provide a detailed taxonomy of the sounds that were mentioned most often in military and civilian testimonies, along with the listening practices that emerged in dialectic relation to them. Over time, military and civilian auditors alike developed techniques for listening to these sounds, extracting tactical information from them while simultaneously striving to minimize their deleterious effects. Experienced auditors pushed the "useless" sounds of distant battles beyond the threshold of consciousness (a process I call "inaudition"), and constructed narratives of varying detail from the "useful" sounds of unseen battles. In chapter 2, "Mapping Zones of Wartime (In)audition," I envision these emergent practices as a striated topography of concentric zones that are brought into being by the positionality of listeners and the nature and depth of their experience with the belliphonic. Audition and inaudition are equally performative. They are also, equally, learned capacities that are constantly being honed. And when their object is violence, they are activities of great consequence; both have an impact on the tactical, ethical, political, and aesthetic fields of possibility within which (in)auditors are enmeshed.

This is not to say that the process of learning to listen to armed violence is absolutely uniform among Iraqi civilians and American service members. There were distinct elements to various populations' auditory experience of the Iraq War, and those differences were often consequential. However, the most profound differences were less the result of culture *qua* culture (i.e., of wholly distinct "acoustemologies" whose origins can be traced back across generations), and more the result of concrete, on-the-ground combinations of subject positions, technologies, training, conversations, regulations, and lived histories; these are the assemblages that I label "auditory regimes" in chapter 3. These regimes have their own microhistories, nestled within the broader historical trajectories that cultures follow. Some of their dynamics cut across the lines of the ethnos, joining together the hypermasculine listening practices of disparate nations, or the desperate auditory inventions of besieged civilian populations. And some are rooted in the collective lifeways of the smallest assemblages: the family, the platoon, the group of friends, the cell.

In the end, we must confront the sad fact that culture, both in the anthropological sense of a "historically transmitted pattern of meanings embodied in symbols" and in the vernacular sense of highly valued artistic works and behavioral practices ("arts and culture," "a cultured person"), is eroded under the caustic power of violent acts.[54] This fact is central to the nature of violence, a phenomenon that Nordstrom defines as being "about the destruction of culture and identity in a bid to control (or crush) political will."[55] Violence erodes culture horizontally, as the lamentably common experiences of war-torn civilian populations around the world attest. But it also does so vertically, bringing a degree of commonality to the experiences of victims and combatants alike. A consideration of the sonic dimension of warfare highlights both of these dimensions, compelling us to re-examine the conventional terminology of violence and, in particular, to recon-figure the concept of victim to include not just those who fall in the path of a bullet but all who are negatively affected by the pansensorial experience of combat.[56] I elaborate on this point in chapter 4, within the context of a broad discussion of "sonic campaigns," the concerted actions that introduced belliphonic sounds into public spaces in Iraq.

While auditory regimes provide armor against the sonic campaigns that assault them, these regimes, along with the broader cultural matrices in which they are situ-ated, are often disrupted by violence. They have to be pieced back together in the wake of violent acts; the ties that tether people to them have to be re-established. But the overwhelming sensory and symbolic intensity of some violent acts impacts people so severely that reconstituting a sensory regime or a culture more broadly proves impos-sible. This is in part due to the way that sound territorializes space, both at the macro level of the neighborhood and at the micro level, within the fluid-filled spaces of the body. In chapter 5, "Acoustic Territories," I discuss the spatial impact of belliphonic sound and the extent to which open and enclosed spaces can shape and be shaped by the sounds that pass through them. Many of these territories, particularly the fleshy ones inside the body, proved to be highly vulnerable to the sonic forces that invaded them in Iraq, a fact that makes human resilience in the face of belliphonic violence all the more remarkable.

Within this environment of vulnerability, musical sound presented yet another para-dox: it was, in its many manifestations, an effective wartime tool *and* a victim of wartime violence. In the hands of the military, with the aid of new technologies such as the porta-ble MP3 player, music was a more malleable and ubiquitous presence than ever before in the history of warfare. Chapter 6, "Mobile Music in the Military," follows iPods and the music they carried as they became integrated into the auditory regimes, sonic campaigns, and acoustic territories of the war. For American service members, music was a technol-ogy of the self that enabled them to fine-tune their mental and emotional states, while simultaneously harassing the enemy with unwanted sounds. For the Iraqi citizenry, by contrast, musical sounds, music venues, and musicians themselves became increasingly targeted by violent actors who regarded them as symbols of unacceptable religious and political affiliations. Chapter 7, "A Time of Troubles for Iraqi Music," bears witness to the shocking breadth of violent incidents directed toward music and musicians over the course of the war, and the ways in which the threat of violence was used to push music out of the civilian public sphere. Complicating the status of music further, many Iraqis admitted to reaching a state of abjection so profound that listening to music no longer made any sense to them; in the words of one Iraqi auditor, "the situation was too seri-ous for music." The kind of triple disfigurement that musical sounds endured—being radically instrumentalized by one group, literally destroyed by another, and periodically rendered moot by the exigencies of wartime—can be read as a microcosmic instantiation of the multiple processes through which affective violence permeates wartime environ-ments more broadly.

Complex Personhood

All of this is to say that life in wartime is exceedingly complex. This is, of course, true of life generally, but for those caught in a dialectical spiral of violence and vulnerability, the stakes of complexity are abnormally high. The issue of complexity returns me to the question of methodology, or rather, to the moment where methodology merges into strategies of representation.[57] The work I've undertaken does not endeavor to explain the origins of the Iraq War, propose solutions for the amelioration of ongoing violence there, or evaluate the rationale for going to war or the net effect of the war in geopolitical terms. In other words, it has almost completely bracketed out questions of "why," the questions of causality, accountability, and intention that are most common in histories of war, in favor of questions of lived experience, of "how." How have individuals and collectives dealt with the cacophony of combat? How have they been changed by exposure to the belliphonic? How have they used the materials at hand to carve out meaningful lives while surrounded by the overwhelming sensory evidence of violence? In working through these questions with American service members and Iraqi civilians, I have been consistently struck by the thoughtfulness of their accounts, and by the degree to which their stories were richer and more nuanced than I expected, given my preconceived notions of the roles they played in the war. I have thus endeavored to prevent my account of these people from sliding into the procrustean beds of familiar wartime archetypes: the inscrutable Other, the thoughtless jarhead, the noble victim, the fearless warrior, etc. In the end, I want to insist upon what Avery Gordon has called the "complex personhood" of my interlocutors, a quality that people share even when the subject positions that they occupy appear, as they often do in wartime representations, to be simply abject or simply heroic. "Even those who live in the most dire circumstances possess a complex and oftentimes contradictory humanity and subjectivity that is never adequately glimpsed by viewing them as victims or, on the other hand, as superhuman agents," Gordon states. In what amounts to a small manifesto on the concept, Gordon lists the far-reaching implications of complex personhood:

> Complex personhood means that all people (albeit in specific forms whose specificity is sometimes everything) remember and forget, are beset by contradiction, and recognize and misrecognize themselves and others. Complex personhood means that people suffer graciously and selfishly too, get stuck in the symptoms of their troubles, and also transform themselves. Complex personhood means that even those called "Other" are never never that. Complex personhood means that the stories people tell about themselves, about their troubles, about their social worlds, and about their society's problems are entangled and weave between what is immediately available as a story and what their imaginations are reaching toward. Complex personhood means that people get tired and some are just plain lazy.

Complex personhood means that groups of people will act together, that they will vehemently disagree with and sometimes harm each other, and that they will do both at the same time and expect the rest of us to figure it out for ourselves, intervening and withdrawing as the situation requires. Complex personhood means that even those who haunt our dominant institutions and their systems of value are haunted too by things they sometimes have names for and sometimes do not. At the very least, complex personhood is about conferring the respect on others that comes from presuming that life and people's lives are simultaneously straightforward and full of enormously subtle meaning.[58]

We all have our articles of faith; this is one of mine. With this in mind I have endeavored to avoid, to the extent possible, the flattening out of my interlocutors into abstractions or caricatures. Pointing to their complexity at this introductory moment is a gesture, a flag, to remind you and myself that the people whose perspectives populate this book are more real and more multifaceted than any written account can transmit.

Of course, it's easier to profess the complex personhood of one's research subjects as an introductory gesture than it is to maintain a focus on complexity and ambiguity while simultaneously drawing broad conclusions from peoples' situated accounts. Moreover, the very terminology that has accrued around violent situations undermines any effort to present one's subjects as three-dimensional, noncaricatured "complex persons." What shall we call all of the US military service members, members of the military and paramilitary forces who fought against the US-led coalition, civilians and other noncombatants who have participated in or otherwise been exposed to the war? Some have conventionally been called "soldiers" or "combatants" or, more polemically, "perpetrators," but these terms leave scant room for us to explore how the practice of (sonic) violence affects them as well as their targets. Some have been called "victims," but this term renders its designees passive objects of violence, with no obvious agency to resist it or participate in it. (In the body of this book I try to frame victimhood as a discursive category rather than as an essential identity.) The more neutral term "participant" presumes an active role taken in violent acts; the term "bystander" presumes no participation whatsoever. The term "survivor"—seemingly apt for my interlocutors, all of whom have lived through combat and are still alive as of this writing—reduces personhood to bare existence. Words matter, even when they are inadequate. In this instance, all of the conventional terms fail, as none of them allows for the mercurial shifts in perspective that individuals frequently make as they move from one category to another (e.g., from bystander to participant, from participant to victim, from victim to survivor, from survivor to critic), and none of them highlights the co-constitutive nature of violence, the fact that it shapes you as you shape it.

In what follows, I sometimes use professional designations (e.g., "service members," "civil servants") and generic categories (e.g., "civilians") to draw attention to the important differences that distinguish these groups from one another. At other times, when discussing commonalities among these groups, I resort to the term "auditor." An auditor, as its etymology (Latin *audire,* to hear) suggests, is someone—military or civilian, gun-wielding or not—who is within earshot of, and is therefore touched by, sound. Belliphonic auditors, then, are people who experience war through their ears; never exclusively, but importantly, and often, as I will argue, centrally. But the term also carries intriguing connotations from its use in the profession of accounting, in which an auditor is not a listener but a professional examiner. This, as it happens, is the way experienced civilians and service members tend to listen to combat: with the acuity, obsessiveness, and matter-of-factness of the professional. Moreover, the audit, as some of you may know from personal experience with the Internal Revenue Service, is a manner of evaluating and holding people accountable for their actions. Having heard, and seen, and felt, and smelled, and survived the war, having watched and participated in and been changed by the war, the complex persons whose testimonies inform this book all possess the right to hold the decision-makers on all sides accountable for the events they experienced. They are all auditors in this double sense of the word.

Spectacle

In the end, anxiety over the possibility of transmitting the complex personhood of my interlocutors leads us to the question of whether any group of methodologies and representational strategies can be deployed to create a fine-grained account of human lives in violent situations without having that detail turn into a voyeuristic or aestheticizing spectacle. E. Valentine Daniel memorably put it this way: "only the extraordinarily gifted or the excessively unmindful (mindless?) can write a book on violence without being troubled by the particular challenge the representational form of writing poses for the task at hand."[59] This representational challenge is multifaceted and daunting. "The point," Daniel writes elsewhere, "is this. Violence is an event in which there is a certain excess: an excess of passion, an excess of evil. The very attempt to label this excess . . . is condemned to fail; it employs what George Bataille calls '*mots glissants*' (slippery words). . . . Everything can be narrated, but what is narrated is no longer what happened."[60] We try to get it right, we try to speak the truth about violent situations, but the distance between these extreme acts and our description of them is too vast. Words—and especially the conventional, often benumbing words of our academic disciplines—fall woefully short. Vietnam veteran and acclaimed author Tim O'Brien famously wrestled with precisely this problem in his semiautobiographical war novel *The Things They Carried:*

> In many cases a true war story cannot be believed. If you believe it, be skeptical. It's a question of credibility. Often the crazy stuff is true and the normal stuff isn't, because the normal stuff is necessary to make you believe the truly incredible craziness.
>
> In other cases you can't even tell a true war story. Sometimes it's just beyond telling.[61]

In other words, in the wartime environment of *mots glissants* there is, by definition, no *mot juste*. For O'Brien, as for Daniel, the potential for speech or writing to bring clarity to scenes of mass violence is so limited as to make the true nature of war unspeakable, unwriteable, and therefore unknowable to those who did not directly experience it.

Of course, one can always adopt the poststructuralist position that presents *all* writing as slippery, and nonidentity between the "thing itself" and the written representation of the thing as the universal state of affairs within a world structured by language. The literature on this problem, the problem of representation and the limits of knowledge, is vast and interdisciplinary. Historians have grappled for decades with the fictive energy that courses beneath historical narratives;[62] ethnographers have similarly struggled with the impossible ventriloquism involved in speaking from or even about the subject position of the Other.[63] We are always going to get something wrong, even when the task at hand is simple. But Daniel and O'Brien point to the additional obstacle that war and other violent events erect. While the official goals of a particular military engagement—land acquisition, border protection, pacification, revenge—may be clear, easy to articulate, and more or less rational, the actual violent acts committed in the name of those goals cannot be so easily corralled by logic or rational thought. A child mistakes a cluster bomblet for a toy. An IED incinerates a Humvee. A woman is raped. A man is decapitated. An explosion blinds and deafens a bystander. A music store is firebombed. A "smart bomb" disintegrates a government ministry. A "suicide bomber" destroys a mosque. Living, breathing people are transformed into orphans, or invalids, or corpses, or pink mist, or ash. The strategic or tactical utility of these transformations does not begin to explain their enormity as human experiences. How does one think up the right words for representing acts of unthinkable, unspeakable violence? One could argue that the conventions of academic writing, which themselves privilege logic and rational thought, are as inadequate as the lurid language of sensationalism for accurately conveying the maddeningly opaque and illogical realities of war and carnage. O'Brien employs circular narrative techniques and detailed descriptions of events that have both factual and fictive elements in order to uncover more fundamental truths about the Vietnam War. Daniel augments his account of violence in 1980s Sri Lanka with close readings of secondary material that would appear to be of marginal significance: jokes, stories, poems, even the uncomfortable silences of his interviewees. In either case, both authors would agree that straight, dry, unreflexive, or clinical accounts of the principal events and actors often fail to capture the most important truths of violence, just as both would surely agree that their experimental techniques are not fully successful. "Sometimes it's just beyond telling."

By focusing on the invisible, ephemeral, purportedly *neutral* domain of sound and audition instead of on more obvious, dramatic, and spectacular manifestations of combat and destruction, terror and heroism, this book adopts a similar technique, a similar mode of approaching a horrifying phenomenon obliquely. While the auditory dimension of war *is* much more central than most people realize, and therefore is worthy of study in its own right, it also allows one to gesture toward the totality of the war's pansensorial onslaught and long half-life, the "excess of evil" that will always evade description. The "fragments" that I have placed between chapters involve modes of transcription and storytelling that at times depart from the academic tone of the main body of the text; they too are attempts to get at the complex affective environments that violent acts bring into being, while keeping the experiences of individuals in the foreground. In the end, though, neither the chapters nor the fragments provide any definitive answers or even much comfort, really, in the face of the violence that persists in Iraq as of this writing. The book remains vulnerable to the charge that it fails to shed much light on the root causes of violence, in Iraq or elsewhere, and that, in the absence of answers, you and I are ultimately little more than voyeurs.

In response to that argument, which has been made to me on more than one occasion during the past six years, let me bring in one last voice here, that of Allen Feldman. The author of *Formations of Violence,* a searing account of incarceration, embodiment, and political terror in Northern Ireland, Feldman has written and spoken forcefully against the idea that to write in a detailed way about the experience of violence is somehow to adopt a lurid, objectifying orientation toward it. At a round table on violence that I helped organize at NYU in 2009, Feldman had this to say about the matter:

> Since I've been writing about violence, I've been told several things: "you cannot write about it unless you can prescribe a cure for it, a resolution"; "you cannot write about it unless you enable us to take political action against it"; "you cannot write about it if you sensationalize or make it spectacular or construct a kind of voyeurism and speculum around the violent event." And finally "you cannot write about it if you aestheticize violence," which begs the question of a utopic "non aestheticized" representation of violence, which I think is an impossibility: a u-topos or non-place. These strictures reveal an iconoclastic relation to the representation and the depiction of violence in the academy. We want violence in containable, apotropaic representations that sustain our immunity to and presumed distance from violence. And if a writer transgresses that interval between writing and violence in text, then iconoclastic rules are invoked—"you're not giving us resolution or prescription, you're sensationalizing, you're amoral, you're not instigating a new political strategy nor organizing a new revolutionary organization that can interdict the violence of the world and therefore you should not write violence, you should remain silent and spare us your voyeurism." I find this a very problematic position. It originates, despite its condemnations, in an equally aestheticized censorship of violence in the academy; such iconoclasm presumes an inoffensive way of writing violence, i.e. a mode of depiction that *in not* giving offense gives the auditor/reader secret pleasure.[64]

Note that Feldman doesn't argue that writing about violence without a prescription for its resolution is an unproblematic activity; he merely states that the critique of this practice is similarly fraught. To fail to acknowledge this is to submit to a false choice: a choice between a purportedly clean activist scholarship and a fatally sullied amoral sensationalization. Scholars like Feldman and Daniel reject this choice, instead showing—imperfectly but valuably—that grappling head-on with the phenomenology of violence can produce a reaction more complicated and productive than titillation.

Nonetheless, there are steps one can take to decrease the vulnerability of the individuals whose perspectives inform a work of scholarship. With this in mind, throughout this book I refer to my interlocutors by their first names, military ranks, and occasionally pseudonyms in order to protect their privacy. (The sole exception is in the case of individuals who have already made their names public in previous published works.) At a time where Iraqis continue to be targeted for collaborating with the United States, and where Americans visiting Iraq or neighboring countries could be made more vulnerable if their participation in the war were known, a display of caution such as this strikes me as amply justified. More broadly, so as to minimize the risk of having my work cause suffering on the part of my interlocutors, I erred on the side of caution by restricting interviews to healthy adults who had not been formally diagnosed with any type of post-traumatic stress. This means that most of the stories told in this book lack the first-person perspectives on spectacular acts of violence and loss that are common in journalistic accounts of the war. But this tight focus on the more mundane, everyday experiences of military and civilian auditors making their way through wartime also helps to demonstrate one of my core arguments: that armed violence, through its sensory and affective intensity, brings injury to a far larger population than those whose bodies are penetrated by flying metal.

In the end, problems with the research and representation of violence will always linger, feeding the temptation toward avoiding the problem altogether that I mentioned earlier. If we had to solve every ethical conundrum before we could begin writing about the experiences of those who endure and otherwise participate in violent acts, there would be no anthropology of violence, no history of warfare, no study of music and conflict. I acknowledge that I haven't resolved any of the conundrums surrounding the representation of violence here. Given this fact, I will retain the right to remain troubled about these issues as we move forward. But move forward we must, for in the end, one thing is certain: the difficulties I face in writing responsibly about sound and violence are absolutely laughable when compared to the real struggle against extermination and dehumanization that my interlocutors—and their families and friends and neighbors and countryfolk—have faced throughout the war. They would want me to stop wringing my hands and get on with it. And so, dedicating this book to the Iraq War's many auditors, I'll do just that.

Fragment #1

The Presence of Mind to Save an Ear

ALI'S STORY

ALI S. IS a charismatic and good-humored young engineer who spent the bulk of his life in Baghdad.[1] He left Iraq for Amman, Jordan, in 2006, after enduring a number of close calls with sectarian fighters and losing members of his social circle and extended family to wartime violence. Adjusting to life in Jordan was a challenge. By 2006, the Iraq War had produced a full-blown humanitarian crisis, unleashing the world's fastest-growing refugee population on Jordan, Syria, and other nearby countries. The Jordanian government allowed several hundred thousand Iraqis to enter its territory, but they had no legal status there, as Jordan was not a signatory to the UNHCR Refugee Convention. This made the most rudimentary activities—settling down, finding work, gaining acceptance in the community—extremely difficult for large numbers of displaced Iraqis. Still, when compared to the situation in wartime Baghdad, the peaceful streets of Amman must have felt like a gift.

My friend Ammar introduced me to Ali in Amman in the summer of 2008. Midway through a multihour, free-ranging conversation, I asked him if he remembered the moment he found out that the war had started. Did he see explosions? Hear a report on the radio? How did it happen? Ali recalled that, on March 20, 2003, he got a phone call from his girlfriend, who lived near Saddam Hussein's primary palace, in what would soon become the International or "Green" Zone. She told Ali that she could hear the anti-aircraft guns stationed around and atop the palace firing their large-caliber exploding rounds into the sky. Ali had heard these guns before, in 1998, when the American armed forces bombed Baghdad during Operation Desert Fox. Each round made a double report: once when released from the muzzle, again a few seconds later upon its detonation in the air. But both of these sounds also created their own echoes, doubling the number of muffled cracks and deep thuds each round produced. When all of this was multiplied by the large number of guns surrounding the palace and the large number of rounds each gun fired, the acoustic effect was arresting. The knowledge that this rhythmic banging signaled the beginning of the widely anticipated war surely amplified its impact on the tens of thousands of Baghdad residents who were within earshot.

The booming report of the anti-aircraft guns didn't reach Ali's neighborhood, Zayouna, east of the Tigris, but a few minutes after putting down the phone, the telltale sound of Baghdad's air-raid sirens—their slow glissandos pushing the pitch up and down, up and down—began to echo in the distance. These same sirens had announced air attacks during the Iran-Iraq War during the 1980s and the first Gulf War; tested regularly during air raid drills, they were familiar to everyone. The sirens' ascending wail removed any lingering doubt in Ali's mind that the war was starting out there in the darkness.

Zayouna was spared the brunt of the Shock and Awe bombing, but a week into the campaign, a pair of cruise missiles hit an Iraqi ministry building a few blocks away from Ali's family's apartment. Ali recalled walking down the hallway with his father, carrying a glass of water, when he heard a strange sound approaching from outside.

> It was like '*shhhhhhhhhhhh*'—something like an airplane, but like a slow airplane.
> The speed of the sound was like a train.

This, he explained to me, was the sound of the first cruise missile, flying low to the ground, parallel to the third-story window of his apartment. Later, with experience, Ali would learn how these missiles behave:

> The cruise missile flies horizontal, [at a] maximum [height of] 20 meters . . . And then it goes up, and then it [*he uses his hand and makes the* shhhhhhhhhh *sound with his mouth to indicate that the missile ascends sharply; then he falls silent and tilts his fingers downward to show how it cuts its motor, and, in freefall*] hits the building from above. So you can hear the sound of the missile coming [horizontally] . . . .

And once you start *not* hearing the sound, it means it's coming down. . . . When it goes down, there is no sound. So after you hear the *'shhhhhhhhhhh'* you have two seconds to . . . predict that there's gonna be an earthquake. [*He chuckles at this turn of phrase.*]

At the time, this being Ali's first encounter with a cruise missile, he didn't have the archive of belliphonic knowledge necessary for making such a prediction. But his father did; having served in the Army during the Iran-Iraq War and witnessed the bombing of Baghdad in 1991 and 1998, he was well acquainted with the acoustic signatures of missiles, mortars, and gunfire. As Ali stood, uncomprehending, still holding his glass of water, his father's reaction was as instantaneous as it was surprising: he yanked his hearing aid out of his ear.

Ali's father had damaged his hearing while serving in the Army during the Iran-Iraq War. His affliction, asymmetrical noise-induced hearing loss, is common throughout the world's war zones. We would call it "shooter's ear": if you are right-handed and aiming a rifle, your left ear is directly exposed to the barrel, whereas your right ear, pressed against your shoulder and partially falling into the "acoustic shadow" of your head, is slightly better protected.[2] He wore a hearing aid in his left ear, turned to a high volume so he could make out his family members' voices.

As the missile passed their window, Ali's father realized two things. First, he could hear that the missile was headed away from them, meaning they probably weren't in mortal danger. Second, with its flight path as close to them as it was, it was probably heading for the nearby ministry building, meaning that the detonation would likely be deafening. In the second after he made those calculations, he managed to remove his hearing aid. A split second later, the missile exploded. Ali vividly remembers what this felt like:

[This was] the first time I heard this kind of bombing. I thought, "it's *really* close to our house," because it was *huge!* I could feel it, and even the ground started to shake, and *I* shook, in the middle of the corridor.

The explosion produced a ringing in his father's good ear that lasted for hours. Ali, standing closer to the window, was temporarily deafened. As a result, he didn't hear the noisy approach of the second cruise missile, a second *"shhhhhhhhhh"* headed toward the same destination as the first. The explosion it caused took him completely by surprise, and made his body shake again. It was so loud that he could hear and feel it above the muffled drone of his temporary deafness.

The angle of Ali's family's windows prevented them from seeing the weapons meet their target. Their encounter with the cruise missiles was not visual but vibratory: their ears, their skin, their apartment building, Ali's glass of water—all were equally the recipients of the explosion's waves. But these recipients (the human ones, anyway) were not equally prepared to receive and make sense of the vibrational invasion of the missiles. They interpreted these sounds variously, and some of their interpretations were judged to be more virtuosic than others; years later, having heard and seen and smelled and felt the sensory consequences of the protracted conflict, Ali's family still speaks admiringly about his father's quick reaction to the sound of the missile outside their window.

SECTION I
Sonic Matériel

POP. POP POP POP. BRRRRRRPPP. POP.
POPPOPPOPPOPPOPPOP. BOOM!! BOOM!!
POP POP POPPOPPOP. BRRRRRRRRRP. BRRRRRRPP.
Automatic gunfire pierces the spring morning, sending the birds of southern
Kirkuk skyward with a start, and my crew to a bit higher alert level.
My squad had just dropped some medics off at a training location
so they could educate the Iraqi Army. It was mid morning, but the mercury
was already becoming unkind. We were swigging water
and having a smoke break before returning to the FOB.
That day, I was in the vehicle commander's seat,
for my squad leader was home on leave.
"Whoa, that sounds close," says 'Little Man', my 5'3" driver.
"That sounds like Aidalla Police station," says Jones, my gunner.
"Yep, sounds like rifle, machine gun fire, and maybe RPG's,"
I said. "Sounds like a firefight."
. . .

—"MA DEUCE" MILBLOG
Monday, February 27, 2006

1

Belliphonic Sounds and Indoctrinated Ears

THE ELEMENTS OF WARTIME AUDITION

CHARTING THE BELLIPHONIC

To witness war is, in large part, to hear it. And to survive it is, among other things, to have listened to it. Or better: to have listened *through* it. The auditors of wartime Iraq learned to listen through the war in three senses, all germane here. First, they were compelled to listen to the sounds of everyday life—voices, music, sounds produced by the natural world, sounds produced by electronic media—*through* an intermittent scrim of belliphonic sounds: the vehicular, weapon-related, and other sounds that armed combat produces. The belliphonic in this scenario was coded as noise, as something to be "tuned out" to the extent possible. As we will see below, remaining sane in wartime depended in some measure upon one's ability to turn the mind away from the invasive and enervating sounds of military traffic, helicopter flybys, and distant gunfire, and toward more meaningful sounds, or sights, or smells, or bodily sensations—or the silent, internally voiced monologues that constitute thought.

However, this mode of "listening through war" by tuning out the belliphonic could be jettisoned instantly when people deemed the sounds of armed conflict to contain useful information. Here, the figure and ground of the previous scenario were reversed, and the sonic dimension of violent acts was taken very seriously. Belliphonic sound in this scenario was regarded not as noise but rather as a valuable signal, albeit one that needed to be decoded in order to be fully understood. People who spent a sustained period of time in wartime Iraq gradually developed the ability to draw an amazing amount of tactical information from the sounds of battle that surrounded them. *Through* the war—*by means of* the war—witnesses were transformed into diagnosticians, expert listeners, urban auscultators assessing the health not of a patient but of a neighborhood.[1] If, upon hearing the passage of a bullet, one could identify its caliber and draw some rough conclusions about its proximity and trajectory, and if one was able to combine this auditory knowledge with a detailed understanding of the surrounding populace, one could make educated guesses about battles taking place within earshot but outside one's field of vision. Those who learned to listen through the war produced rich narratives of unseen action. This was a valuable, even life-sustaining, skill.

At the same time, in a temporal sense, to listen *through* the war was to have experienced its evolution and fluctuations. Like most armed conflicts, the Iraq War had a discernable circadian rhythm, as evidenced by the US Army's standing orders to maintain heightened vigilance at dusk and dawn, when fighting tended to be heavier.[2] For those who spent protracted amounts of time in the combat zone, like war correspondent Oliver Poole, sounds became familiar presences that moved in tandem with the cyclical rhythms of combat:

A year [after taking a position as war correspondent for the *Daily Telegraph*] I could tell the time of day in Baghdad by the nature of the explosions. I was living there full time by then and it had quickly become a familiar routine. The early mornings were the busiest as roadside bombs buried during the night were set off by the first patrols. It would be a fresh dawn introduced by a dull pop, a finger of smoke rising into the still subdued sky and the knowledge, even as I waited for the kettle to boil, that someone was already having a really bad day.

The suicide bombers liked to strike in the mid-morning. I could often hear the blast in my room in the Hamra [hotel], sometimes even feel the vibrations, and I would rush up onto the hotel's flat roof to try to pinpoint its location. . . .

Afternoons were favored by the mortar teams. A few rounds thrown into the Green Zone at tea time to make sure no one was too relaxed. Then, after sunset, came the machine gun fire. Most military operations and extrajudicial killings occurred at night. There would be the controlled phat-phat-phat of the disciplined bursts from American M-16s or the torrent of flat pings that marked the splurges from Iraqi Kalashnikovs. Neither would go on long. Ten seconds, twenty seconds maximum. I never knew why it was taking place or exactly where. It was only sound, a jarring out there in the darkness.[3]

Cyclical motions such as these were nested within longer-term unilinear change. The belliphonic sounds of the Iraq War mutated over time, rendering audible the emergence of flare-ups and ceasefires, the introduction and discontinuation of military technologies, the erection and partial removal of blast walls in Baghdad and other cities, the abrupt rise, gradual reduction, and subsequent surges of IED explosions, the destruction and partial reinstatement of the electric infrastructure, the reintroduction of formerly prohibited vocal forms of sectarian expression and the introduction of new forms of mass dissent. In short, the belliphonic changed in concert with the changing strategies and tactics of insurgents, sectarian fighting groups, US-led forces, and civilian populations; the war sounded different in April 2003 than it did in May of that year, or than it did in 2004, or in 2010. The vast majority of Iraq's civilians were in Iraq when the war started and are still there as I write this. This population "listened through the war" for a period unmatched by military service members on a standard twelve-month tour of duty. At the same time, the exigencies of extended tours, "involuntary mobilization," the "stop loss" program, and multiple deployments created the conditions for sustained, comparative listening experiences for many service members as well.[4]

All of these modes of listening involve movement—and this is not surprising, as movement is at the core of listening and sound alike. Auditors are constantly shifting the sounds they hear from one conceptual category to another as they identify them, bring them into the foreground, relegate them to the noisy background, or push them out of consciousness altogether. At the same time, the natural and architectural environments that absorb, reflect, amplify, and distort sounds are in a constant state of flux, even though their movement is often too slow to be readily perceived. Many belliphonic sounds cause people to lurch into movement, both voluntary and involuntary. (The sound of a gun battle slowly approaching can convince one to seek shelter; the unexpected sound of a nearby explosion can force one out of one's seat and into the air.) And of course it is in the nature of sound itself to be always on the move, always appearing and disappearing, brought about by attack and then existing in a constant state of motion, of ascent and descent and timbral shifts and crescendo and decrescendo and echo and, in the end, decay. Except that its eventual decay doesn't mean it's gone for good: sounds, as we know, are often recycled. Through technological means, sounds can be recorded, replayed, stretched, compressed, edited, recomposed. Likewise, through the less predictable channels of human memory, sounds can be captured, processed, and looped, and looped, and looped, and looped again, variously enchanting or haunting their human hosts depending upon the qualities of the events remembered, the vagaries of the hosts' emotional states, and any number of other arcane factors that complicate the interactions of the brain, the ear, and the resonating body.

War too is all about movement. From slow-rolling vehicles to supersonic projectiles, from troops on the march to flying shrapnel, in attack and retreat, even in siege and the supposed stalemate of trench warfare—matériel, vehicles, service members, and civilians alike become meaningful wartime actors by being set into motion. The movement of people and things in wartime is often anxious, often aggressive, sometimes linear, sometimes Brownian, but always present as one of war's defining characteristics. More generally, war itself is often described as a kind of violent motion or spasm, a disturbance, an abrupt perturbation of social, political, and ethical relationships. The fact that even in the best and most peaceful of times those relationships are never static does not rob war of its exceptional turbulence. Compared to combat, the "peacetime" world appears to stand still: war is, in Paul Virilio's formulation, a timespace in which "the static sense of the world [comes] to an incomprehensible end."[5] If a theoretical model for belliphonic sound is to do justice to the complex and kinetic listening experiences that people have accrued during the Iraq War, then, it will need to be similarly kinetic. Models that rely upon stasis will be inadequate to the task of describing the moving targets of sounds, and listening, and wartime. Belliphonic structures exist, but they do so fluidly.

LISTENING, STRUCTURE, AND POSITIONALITY

The obverse of that last sentence is also true: the slippery kinetics of the sounds of war present a challenge to those auditors who encounter the belliphonic, but not so insurmountable a one that people fail to discern patterns within them. Like hearing people everywhere, war's auditors hear continuity amidst the cacophony that surrounds them. Or perhaps it's more accurate to say that they *create* continuity through listening to the sounds that surround them. This sense of continuity or structure is thus a construct, but an important one that people hold onto as tightly as they hold onto their sanity. Before we attempt to grapple with the belliphonic's unpredictable fluidity, then, we will need to examine a few of the aggregations of recurring sounds that gave structure to people's lives in the war zone. But given that these sounds were themselves perceived by local residents to be interruptions of the situation that preceded their appearance, we need first to listen backward, back to before the war started. It is important, I think, to gain a general sense of the relative normalcy that has been so thoroughly erased by a decade of uninterrupted bloodshed before turning to focus on that bloodshed and the sounds that accompanied it.[6]

Civilians who spent their lives in Iraq carry memories of what their neighborhoods looked, smelled, sounded, *felt* like before the onset of war in 2003. Ali A.,[7] a thoughtful, soft-spoken architect in his thirties who emigrated to the United Arab Emirates after a sectarian group murdered his uncle and organized an attempt upon his life, recently recalled for me the feel of Zayouna, his Baghdad neighborhood, in 2002. Before the onset of Operation Iraqi Freedom, Zayouna was one of the capital's more affluent residential neighborhoods, known for its gardens and plant nurseries, with a mixed population of Shi'a, Sunni, and Christian residents. Much of life was lived outside in prewar Zayouna, and this resulted in a vibrant social scene populated by a multiplicity of voices. From his family's house, near the popular Maysaloun Square, Ali was able to hear the voices of playing children against a backdrop of civilian traffic noise and chirping birds. Street vendors calling out to potential customers from a nearby market could be heard throughout the day. A walk around the neighborhood would bring him into contact with more sounds and sights and smells of commerce, as neighborhood residents circulated through coffee shops, restaurants, Internet cafes, and boutiques. Popular music—of the Iraqi, non-Iraqi Arab, and western varieties—emanated from radios and tape cassette and CD players in many of these storefronts. In addition to well-known Iraqi singers such as Kazem al-Saher and Hussam al-Rassam, Ali loved the American singers John Denver and Michael Jackson; he regularly played all of these artists on his car's cassette deck with the windows rolled down. Five times daily, with absolute regularity, the call to prayer rang through the neighborhood in its Sunni and Shi'i iterations. And on Sundays, Ali could hear the bells tolling from a nearby Assyrian Christian church. On the occasion of a funeral or on religious holidays, he would hear amplified voices reciting passages from the Quran in the neighborhood. During weddings, music—usually live, usually amplified—and brief bursts of celebratory gunfire echoed down the streets. All in all, in Ali's reminiscence, Zayouna was a pleasant, bustling neighborhood, where sound was most frequently the result of normal, everyday civilian activities: commerce, conversation, motorized movement, worship, play.

Ali's remembrance points to a partially vanished sonorous world that American service members never experienced, but that lingered in the memories of Iraqi residents of the city and inflected their experiences of the unfolding conflict. Unlike the military forces that occupied the city in the wake of the 2003 invasion, whose first impression of Baghdad was that of a city already abuzz with the cacophony of combat, long-term residents were able to listen to the war with a *comparative* ear, contrasting their memories of prewar Baghdad with their ongoing, daily experiences of the war. From their vantage point, the belliphonic was not the normal state of affairs but an invasion in its own right, competing with, drowning out, and in part replacing the sounds of peacetime civilian life. If we were to express this most fundamental difference between the foreign military and local civilian population, we might draw a pair of Venn diagrams such as those seen in figure 1.1. For foreign troops who arrived in Baghdad with or after the commencement of hostilities, there is a perfect overlap between one's first impression of the city and one's

IMPRESSIONS OF BAGHDAD   IMPRESSIONS OF WAR IN BAGHDAD

U.S. SERVICE MEMBERS

LONG-TERM RESIDENTS

FIGURE 1.1 Transient and Long-term Experiences of Operation Iraqi Freedom

first experience of the city at war. For long-term residents, by contrast, the experience of war, and of the belliphonic in particular, is formed against the memory of what existed before 2003.

What these two diagrams illustrate is the fact that, even at the level of the most simplistic abstraction, we cannot talk in an unproblematic way about "the sounds of war." A sound's salience and emotional charge depends upon the life histories of the people who hear it, and upon the comparative backdrop against which they listen to the sounds that are emplaced in a particular time and location.

Of course, the comparative backdrop is more complicated than my diagrams indicate. For one thing, almost all of the Iraqis with whom I spoke mentioned that Operation Iraqi Freedom was not the first war they had experienced. All but the youngest residents of Baghdad carry vivid memories of Operation Desert Fox, the four-day bombing campaign that US President Bill Clinton initiated in December 1998. Most people over twenty-five years old can easily recall the first Gulf War, and the sounds of the hundreds of air sorties that were directed at Baghdad in January 1991. And many of those who are over thirty-five recall the air and missile campaigns in the early stages of the devastating Iran-Iraq War, which ran from 1980 to 1988. An entire generation of conscripted soldiers served in the trenches of that war, and were thus exposed, for prolonged periods, to the sounds and sights and smells of combat. (Figure 1.2 presents these conflicts in a timeline.) These broadly shared experiences gave people a rich, if troubled, archive of sensory memories with which to contextualize the unfolding events of Operation Iraqi Freedom.[8]

In a comparable way, American service members who served in Kosovo, or Rwanda, or the first Gulf War, or Vietnam were able to process the experience of Operation Iraqi Freedom as one conflict in a string of others. But the vast majority of American service members, who fall between the ages of eighteen and twenty-five, experienced war for the very first time in Iraq, and never at home in the United States.[9] For these service members, the sensory experience of combat could not be comparative in the same emplaced sense that it was for most Iraqi citizens. In any case, with the exception of

IRAN-IRAQ WAR	GULF I	DESERT FOX	OIF (and its successors)
1980–88	1991	1998	2003–

FIGURE 1.2 Timeline of Iraqi Wars

service members who served in the first Gulf War, any combat memories that they had acquired prior to their deployment originated not in Iraq but elsewhere. As a result, the sounds that struck Iraqis as unnatural and unwelcome (if not unprecedented) additions to their acoustic environment may have struck the other group as organically tied to the site of their resonance. Service members who spoke of Iraq as "an uncivilized country" or as inherently "filthy," "violent," and "noisy" were in this sense mistakenly extrapolating their personal experiences of an anomalous period in Iraq's history to encompass its national character as a whole.

Indeed, as any long-term Iraqi resident will tell you, the country looked and felt different during the war than it did before the war started. It also sounded different. Some of these differences were manifest in the contemporary acoustic environment of the country; others are the result of the acoustic memories of its inhabitants, memories that continue to inflect and infect the ways civilian auditors hear the present. To visit contemporary Zayouna, Ali's old neighborhood, in 2011 was to visit a place that had been changed from years of armed violence. Formerly well-kept streets were more likely to be marked by the sound, sight, and smell of burning garbage than by the susurrus of leafy trees. With the emigration of the majority of the city's Christians, the church bells fell silent. The disintegration of municipal services, along with the continued threat of terrorist and sectarian violence, combined to create a far less hospitable environment for public recreation. This meant there were fewer children on the street, and thus less of their shouts and laughter. Urban residents in 2011 were much more reluctant to play Western or Arab popular music in the streets than they once were, as these sounds were widely known to incite retributive attacks.[10] Moreover, the proliferation of noisy generators throughout the neighborhood meant that it was much harder to hear birdsong in Zayouna.

Along with these sonic absences and new presences, Zayouna's wartime residents had to contend with memories of recent violent acts and the sensory experience of those acts. Those who were in the neighborhood on March 19, 2003 carried around memories of the astonishingly loud sounds of the Shock and Awe bombing campaign, in which the roar of cruise missiles and other heavy weapons exploding throughout Baghdad was accompanied by the loud and persistent response of Iraqi sirens and anti-aircraft guns. In the subsequent years, according to the Iraq Body Count, over 280 people were killed in the neighborhood, due mostly to sectarian violence.[11] Gunfire, car bombs, roadside bombs, magnetic bombs, mortars, drive-by shootings, and suicide bombings echoed through Zayouna's streets in those years. Seven large bombings in the neighborhood killed more than a dozen people each.

Forty-three bombings had multiple fatalities. Seventy-nine bombings killed one person each, and an unrecorded number of bombings wounded passersby and caused property damage.[12] All of these explosions were heard by thousands. All formed links in a chain of events that continue to be remembered primarily for the lives they took, but are often remembered *through* the loud sounds they produced, sounds that regularly washed over residents, causing their startled bloodstreams to become suffused with cortisol, adrenalin, and other chemicals. From his house in Zayouna, Ali heard and even felt the truck bomb that exploded outside the UN Headquarters on August 19, 2003, killing UN Ambassador Vieira de Mello and twenty-two others. This attack symbolized for the international community the violent instability of the post-Hussein era and the magnitude of the task of nation-building that lay before them. For Ali and his neighbors, however, it was first experienced as a shocking acoustic event, a huge boom in the middle distance, long before it coalesced into a symbol.

Ali was also a participant in, and later wounded by, shooting in his immediate neighborhood. Once, three cars full of Shi'i fighters from Sadr City pulled up outside the house of his neighbors across the street. Knowing that the retired military officer who lived there had been captured by the Americans, they burst into the house to loot it. The man's wife and daughters barricaded themselves into a second-story room and began screaming out the window for help. Hearing them, Ali grabbed his Kalashnikov[13] and ran up to his roof, where, along with some other neighbors in adjoining houses, he began shooting at the fighters and their cars until they sped off, leaving his neighbors behind. Several months later, as he was pulling out of his garage, a car pulled up, blocked him from behind, and showered his car with bullets. This time it was his next-door neighbor who heard the shots and ran up to his roof. The neighbor directed several bursts from his Kalashnikov toward the shooters, causing them to screech off down the street. Ears ringing from the gunfire and body bleeding from shrapnel, Ali was taken to the hospital. A month later, he left the country for good. Years have passed since then, but Ali still gets anxious when he hears fireworks, or a car backfiring, or a tire exploding.

Sound is ephemeral, or so we are told. It is true that gunfire is no longer a daily occurrence in Zayouna, and bombings are relatively rare, though they have increased over the course of the past few years to rival wartime levels. Nevertheless, at the moment I write these words, Zayouna sounds more like a peacetime neighborhood than it did during the hottest years of the war. But sound lives on in human memory far after its physical vibrations die away. The sounds of bombings and gun battles, the screams of victims and the wailing of the bereaved continue to haunt Ali's memories of his life in the neighborhood. Multiply Zayouna by the number of neighborhoods in Iraq, and multiply Ali's experiences by the number of people who witnessed the war, and you begin to get a sense of the immense scale and lingering power of the war's auditory dimension.

The crude diagrams above and the stories accompanying them point to a simple yet profound fact: listening is not merely a biological activity but also a sociocultural one. Each individual act of listening is informed by a host of factors, some of which are predictable and knowable (such as the experiential differences that separate transients from long-term residents) and others of which are not (such as the emotional states of individual auditors; the specific fusion of visual, haptic, olfactory, and other stimuli that help constitute their experiences; and the individual half-lives of the memories of similar experiences that haunt each act of audition). Any discussion of "the sounds themselves," then, needs to make room for the empirical, emotional, and interpretive variations that exist within the heterogeneous groups of auditors who encounter, process, and are altered by those sounds. In the taxonomic section that follows, I gesture toward some of the most fundamental variations, the broad differences that the location and background of the auditors can engender. In subsequent chapters, I will add more nuance to these general observations. But for now, I concentrate on the basic, "operational" differences that obtain in the combat zone—for what matters most, in the end, in terms of sound *and* survival, is whether you hold the keys to the Humvee or are out on the street; whether you are the shooter or the target; whether you are the active participant or the potential "collateral damage" observing the war as it erupts into your neighborhood. What matters also is whether you grew up in Iraq or elsewhere, and whether you speak Arabic or English, or both, or neither. In other words, in combat there are moments where structural difference trumps individual agency, and these moments tend to insert distance between service members and civilians, Americans and Iraqis. The following section endeavors to highlight a number of these moments within the context of a selective taxonomy of belliphonic sound.

VEHICULAR SOUNDS

Service members blazing down open highways or negotiating the tight corners of city streets in High Mobility Multipurpose Wheeled Vehicles (HMMWVs, or Humvees, in the vernacular), Bradley fighting vehicles (Bradleys), Stryker interim armored vehicles (Strykers), the newer Mine-Resistant Ambush Protected vehicles (MRAPs), and, more rarely, M1 Abrams battle tanks always had to contend with the distinct background noise of their engines. An up-armored Humvee can generate 95 decibels of engine noise for its passengers; a tank's engine is significantly louder. A tank's engine noise combined with its thick hull renders all but the loudest explosions inaudible from inside; it creates, through noise and steel, a nearly impermeable "auditory bubble."[14] Bradleys, Strykers, and MRAPs also block out street sounds, though to a lesser degree. However, gunners and scouts, who commonly stood in the hatches of these vehicles with their heads and upper bodies exposed, heard much more than their comrades inside, and were expected to report on sonic and other events when the situation demanded. Unlike those inside the vehicles, however, their auditory awareness was complicated by the persistent sound of wind.

None of the ground vehicles currently used by the US military were designed for stealth. In addition to their loud engines, drivers and passengers during Operation Iraqi Freedom endured a chorus of other sounds, including a penetrating high-pitched creaking from the shock-absorbing springs beneath the vehicle's seats; the loud staccato knocking sound of vehicular components being jarred, metal on metal, by bumps and holes in the road; the white-noise drone of a fan system so loud that it could drown out the sound of the vehicle's idling engine; and the vehicle's siren, used liberally to disperse traffic. When on bases, these vehicles were driven slowly. (The speed limit on Camp Balad, for example, was a strictly enforced 10 miles per hour.) But "outside the wire," on open roads, where "combat driving" was prescribed to minimize the likelihood of an ambush, drivers gunned their engines and drove as fast as traffic and road conditions allowed. In these situations, the sound of the high-revving engine rose to compete with the other loud sounds the vehicle produced. To be inside a vehicle in such circumstances was to be enclosed inside a vibrational cocoon; with limited visibility through dusty, double-paned armored windows, the sensory input from the sounds of the vehicle and the full-body thrum of the engine could draw one's attention inward, away from the roads and their unpredictable hazards and toward the microworld of the cabin. Major Aric Bowman, who escorted me on a number of military vehicles in Iraq in 2011, mentioned that the engine noise and rocking motion of the Humvee made him want to fall asleep whenever he got in one.[15] Inexperienced passengers could have the opposite reaction, as it turned out. When I first arrived in Iraq, a Humvee engaged in high-rpm combat driving sounded to me like a vehicle in an acute state of emergency. It sounded to me like a vehicle in fight-or-flight mode, in the middle of an escape or an attack—and that engine sound caused a visceral reaction of panic on my first few anxious rides. With time, I might have been able to teach my body what my mind already knew, that the extreme sound of the gunning engine was a preventive measure to forestall the onset of an actual emergency, and so was actually the normal state of affairs. Experienced service members had already learned this lesson, and so could find themselves lulled to sleep by what for me were terrifying sounds.

Helicopters frequently accompanied US ground troops throughout the Iraqi theatre, and contributed substantially to the auditory experience of those inside them or on the ground beneath them. The massive twin-propeller CH-47D Chinook, a version of which has been in military service since the Vietnam War, produces a piercing, high-pitched whine from its turbine engines, along with a number of variously pitched engine drones and the deep rhythmic beating of its rotors. The percussive sound of the rotors is so powerful that it enters far into the realm of the haptic: as it approaches, it is deeply felt as well as heard. Other, smaller helicopters—Apaches, Black Hawks, Kiowas, the MH-6 "Little Bird"—all have their own signature sounds. As they approach, the low percussive roll of the rotors can force one's chest cavity to vibrate in concert with its pulses. This sensation abates by the time the helicopter is overhead; once it begins moving away, the sound of the rotors is thoroughly mixed with the sound of the engine, and no longer feels like fists beating on one's chest.

For service members who could distinguish one helicopter from another, the sound of the Apache, an attack helicopter, meant that missile fire could be on the way. The sound of a Chinook might signal that supplies were forthcoming. Medical evacuations took place on Black Hawks or Chinooks, so those sounds could trigger sympathy if you were not wounded, relief if you were.

Inside helicopters, all sounds are drowned out by the persistent arcing whine of the engines. In my one flight on a Black Hawk, this whine was composed of several distinct, high-pitched drones, the highest of which appeared to be at the upper threshold of human hearing. No one but an inexperienced passenger (such as myself) would ever invite this painfully layered screech into the ears unmediated, however. Hearing protection, in the form of over-the-ear headphones, was mandatory in helicopters throughout the area of operations, and communication with other crew members took place through them, with the aid of small microphones attached to the headsets. Crewmembers did their best never to take their headsets off mid-flight.

The post-Hussein-era Iraqi army and police were the other major militarized presence in Iraq, and they too filled the streets with loud vehicular sounds. In addition to Humvees, MTVR trucks (a.k.a. "7-tons"), M113 armored personnel carriers, and other vehicles procured from the United States, the Iraqi army made use of a large collection of fighting and logistical vehicles produced in the former Soviet Union, the United Kingdom, France, Brazil, South Africa, Poland, and Pakistan. Many of these vehicles left an even larger acoustic imprint on their surroundings than the Humvee and MRAP. But engine noise, loud as it was, wasn't always the dominant sound that wartime vehicular traffic generated: members of the Iraqi police and army were widely reported to fire automatic weapons into the air in order to clear traffic at intersections. While this was not a standard practice for the US military, there is ample evidence that US military contractors, including those working for the well-known Blackwater firm (renamed Xe Services LLC in 2009), also engaged in this loud and dangerous activity. And so it is that we must add the sound of machine guns to the roster of vehicular sounds that ground their way into the daily lives of troops and civilians alike.

Throughout Operation Iraqi Freedom, support troops and civilian contractors, counted together, outnumbered combat troops by nearly three to one.[16] These groups included thousands of drivers, mechanics, and convoy security personnel, for whom the sustained sounds of vehicles constituted an ongoing condition, not to mention an occupational hazard. But most of the rest of these service members and third-country contractors—the American logistics forces filling the administrative ranks, the thousands of Filipino and Bangladeshi service employees who staffed the dining and laundry facilities, the legions of Ugandan and Peruvian guards providing security at checkpoints—spent very little time in vehicles, and virtually no time outside the bases where they were stationed. For them, as for most Iraqi civilians, the sounds of military vehicles emanated from the street, sometimes up close, often at a distance. Pedestrians, civilian motorists, and other bystanders grew accustomed to the frequent passage of military convoys. All auditors who found themselves outside a passing tank or MRAP or Humvee or other vehicle experienced a familiar yet distinctive acoustic event, with a constantly shifting timbre or tonal color and a predictable structure of crescendo, followed by a decrescendo combined with the smoothly falling pitch of the Doppler effect. This structure was frequently punctuated with other, less predictable sounds, from the siren to the sound of music emanating from on-board speakers to amplified warning messages to the aforementioned gunfire.[17] Some of these sounds were loud and invasive enough to be heard *and* felt, even by passersby. If one was outside the vehicle but very close to it, vehicular force in the form of sound, a sound that one hears and feels and at times fears simultaneously, could compel the auditor into involuntary motion—an unplanned leap onto the curb, out of harm's way, for example. This kind of automatic reaction was pre-reflective, and not unlike the automatic defensive crouch I find myself making in New York City when a nearby fire truck uses its air horns to clear people from an intersection.

But most vehicular sounds reached auditors from greater distances than this, and these distances allowed them the split second needed to interpret the possible meaning of their arrival. For a pedestrian allied with the armed forces—an on-base contractor, say—the sounds of military vehicles approaching and passing would likely fail to arouse an emotion more extreme than mild annoyance at the creation of dust and decibels. Within the local civilian population, however, the very same sounds were capable of producing an acute sense of anxiety ("What are their intentions?" "Are they coming to search my house?" "Are they coming for one of my neighbors?" "Does their approach mean the shooting is going to start up again?"). For those who were in a position of vulnerability, the sounds of military vehicles were perceived as a more distinct and fraught event than for those who were not threatened by their approach. This anxiety of the vulnerable is palpable in the published account of "Riverbend," a young Iraqi woman who blogged about the unfolding war from her house in Baghdad. On September 19, 2003, she posted an account of troops conducting a search of her neighbor's house. Her auditory acuity warned her of what was coming:

> At around 3 am, I distinctly heard the sound of helicopters hovering not far above the area. I ran out of the room and into the kitchen and found E. [her brother] pressing his face to the kitchen window, trying to get a glimpse of the black sky.
> 'What's going on?!' I asked, running to stand next to him.
> 'I don't know . . . a raid? But it's not an ordinary raid . . . There are helicopters and cars, I think . . .'

I stopped focusing on the helicopters long enough to listen to the cars. No, not cars—big, heavy vehicles that made a humming, whining sound. E. and I looked at one another, speechless—tanks?! E. turned on his heel and ran upstairs, taking the steps two at a time. I followed him clumsily, feeling for the banister all the way up, my mind a jumble of thoughts and conjectures.

Out on the roof, the sky was black streaked with light. Helicopters were hovering above, circling the area. E. was leaning over the railing, trying to see into the street below. I approached tentatively and he turned back to me, 'It's a raid . . on Abu A.'s house!' He pointed three houses down the road. . . The armored cars were pulling up to Abu A.'s house, the helicopters were circling above, and the whole area was suddenly a mess of noise and lights.[18]

For Riverbend, anxiety preceded, but was then exacerbated by, identification of the vehicular sounds on her street. As civilians, she and her brother avoided the streets when they were filled with military vehicles. Additionally, a citywide curfew, in place for much of the war and subsequent occupation, kept them and other civilians indoors throughout the evening and night hours. As they took shelter in their homes, often finding themselves confined to them, the sights of military movement were much less common than the sounds, which penetrated walls and windows, announcing the conflict's arrival in their neighborhood. When asked, military and civilian listeners alike most frequently spoke of vehicular sounds as noise, and therefore, it would seem, as devoid of meaningful content. At the same time, as Riverbend's descriptions and dozens of other testimonies of civilians and service members indicate, people living through war regularly read the sounds and sights of military vehicles indexically—as indications that, variously, support had arrived, wounded were being transported, supplies were being hauled, surveillance was being undertaken, or aggression was imminent. Experienced auditors (both Iraqi and American) did not always need to see the vehicles in question in order to identify them and make an educated guess as to their purpose. But if an Iraqi civilian auditor and an American military auditor might both have been adept enough to distinguish the sound of a Humvee from an MRAP or a Chinook from a Blackhawk, they wouldn't necessarily have assigned the same symbolic value to these sounds. As symbols, sounds (of weapons and more generally) are inherently polysemic and audience-dependent. Tareq, an Iraqi dentist, read the sound of the Chinook as a troubling symbol of American panoptic control over Baghdad, a constant reminder that the occupying forces ruled the skies, and were always watching.[19] This was a symbol whose affective force was multiplied by the vibrational invasion that accompanied the sound of the rotors. Living on a flightpath, and enduring multiple low-profile flyovers daily, he complained that the sound of the Chinook constituted a regular invasion of his house, one that "would make the plates vibrate off the table." By contrast, Tracy, a former civil servant in the International Zone, had offices near a busy helipad. Bombarded by the same loud drumming that Tareq was, Tracy had the opposite reaction. She was happy to hear the helicopters, and regarded the sound of their beating rotors to be "the sound of freedom."[20] Years after leaving Baghdad, she was still emotionally moved by the memory of the sound of Chinooks and Black Hawks taking off and landing, carrying troops, diplomats, supplies, and wounded.

The symbolic valence of "the sounds of freedom" was widely espoused within the US forces, and was offered to the Iraqi civilian population as a way of rendering belliphonic sounds less disruptive and traumatizing. Take for example the widely discussed 2004 presentation by Brigadier General Mark Kimmitt, deputy director of operations for the Coalition Provisional Authority, in which he suggested that his Iraqi questioner recalibrate the symbolism of the sounds of helicopters:

QUESTION (Through interpreter): "[I am] Ibrahim Hasan, from an organization of Faily [sic] Kurds. A group of families have recommended me to give you a message that is in form of a question, so please be so honest in answering this question.

The helicopters who are flying a low profile in the areas where they are fully populated, in different times and different circumstances . . . has just scared the children and the innocent people and the families, and also . . . some of those members of the families have been inflicted and they just were scared, and there have been so many diseases—psychological diseases, skin diseases also, due to these, I mean, illegal flying low profile helicopters in those areas. So they are just seeking for a solution. If it is possible, please find a solution to save the lives of those people who are—who were harmed and inflicted with harm because of these actions.

GEN. KIMMITT: Yeah, number one, the low-profile helicopter flights have a purpose. It allows our helicopters to fly low and fast. It allows them to conduct their operations to provide security to the people of Iraq.

Having spent most of my adult life either on or near military posts, married to a woman who teaches in the schools, you often hear the sounds of tank firing. You often hear the sounds of artillery rounds going off. And [my wife] seems to be quite capable of calming the children and letting them understand that *those booms and those bangs that they hear are simply the sounds of freedom.* If you can take this message back in the form of a statement, that if you tell your families and you tell your children and you tell your wives that there is nothing to fear from those helicopters—in fact, much of the peace you enjoy and the fact that the children can go back to school, the children can go out to play, the children can enjoy a free life—is because of those soldiers that are inside those helicopters out there, protecting their freedom and protecting their future.[21]

This exchange illustrates a number of the complexities of the Iraqi civilian–US military relationship, not least of which is the incommunicability of vulnerability—the difficulty civilians had in transmitting how it feels to be at mortal risk. Mr. Hasan was attempting to do just this, to communicate the persistent state of fear, psychological trauma, and even physiological damage that exposure to the sounds (and fumes) of low-flying helicopters produced. General Kimmitt's answer, which relied upon an epistemology of stability rather than one of vulnerability, presented the flyovers as an antidote to fear, a loud thing that must be done in order to keep Iraqis safe. But it also highlighted the moment of choice that lies at the heart of listening as a hermeneutic act: once identification has been accomplished ("that's definitely a Chinook overhead"), auditors must choose how to interpret the value of the sounds to which they are exposed ("Chinook sounds herald increased safety" vs. "Chinook sounds herald the presence of aggressive forces"). To say that we are always free to choose how to interpret these sounds, however, is to ignore the structural impediments that a state of profound vulnerability creates. There are times when one's ability to choose how to frame a sonic event is compromised by the helplessness one feels in relation to that event. Decibels notwithstanding, vehicular sounds may feel more invasive if you aren't sitting in the driver's seat, with the ability to turn the engine off. And if the sound of an approaching vehicle presages a potentially violent altercation between you and its passengers, it will always be less open to free interpretive play than if it doesn't.

COMMUNICATIONS

Amplified and Unamplified Voices Inside Vehicles

Voices frequently penetrated the noise of vehicular engines. Service members in vehicles often found themselves in a state of almost constant conversation, trading barbs and stories, commenting on traffic and events seen through their windows, and exchanging tactical information related to the mission at hand. Humvees are relatively small vehicles, with two rows of seating and a gunner standing or crouching between the driver and the truck commander (TC);[22] it is possible to have an unassisted conversation inside a Humvee, although one has to speak forcefully to overcome the chorus of sounds the vehicle produces. In larger, louder vehicles, crew members were required to wear headphones under their helmets that both shielded their ears from vehicular noise and served as communications systems, projecting the voices of their fellow crew members as well as more distant interlocutors into one ear or another. The microphones that transmitted voices often picked up background noises as well, as Irvin, an Army major who served in Iraq in 2003 and again as a company commander in 2006, describes:[23]

> The one vehicle that I could distinguish with the headphones was if someone was talking to me from a tank, because I would hear the whine of the M1 [Abrams tank] while they were talking. As soon as they would cue the mic, I could hear the "wwwoooo" and so I knew, you know, even if I didn't know who it was, if I had

a tank out doing whatever, I knew, "OK, it's coming from one of my tank crews somewhere," because I would hear that whine and I wouldn't hear it on a Bradley, Humvee, helicopter, even when I talked to the aviator, it was only the M1 where I could hear that in the background all the time.

As opposed to their comrades in ground-based vehicles, aviators, who were safely out of the range of most hostile weapons, generally displayed a cool calmness that was audible in their voices. Irvin and a small group of Army majors who had recently returned to the United States after a deployment to Iraq recalled the particular characteristics of voices coming from different vehicles:

ERIC: You also knew when it was an aviator 'cause they would come in so clear.

IRVIN: And they're always calm!

ERIC: 'Cause that's like a phone call, it's very, very clear.

IRVIN: Yeah, they're always talking.

ERIC: Perfect calm: you know, they're up in the air.

MARK: Yeah. I mean I recall that with a Humvee, I don't remember talking to Bradleys or tanks much, but you could definitely discern between talking to a helicopter versus a Humvee, cause the Humvee has got that same thing, it's got that kind of choppy, bubbling "bur bur bur bur bur," whereas the helicopter is usually quiet. You generally can hear the blades, [though]. I remember hearing rotary blades on the helicopter.

ERIC: [The aviator] sounded like an airline pilot.

KEVIN: Yup.

ERIC: You know, talking to everyone in the cabin, telling them what to do. "Time traveling to Dallas . . ."

IRVIN: "We're fine!" [laughter]

KEVIN: "It's nice."

MARK: "It's cold and wet." [laughter]

The broadcast of an utterance on a military communications network ("net") was preceded by a click, a short beep, and the onset of a soft stream of static. Like comm systems everywhere, military-grade microphones and headsets favored midrange and high frequencies, accentuating the voices they projected, but leaving them sounding somewhat tinny and strident. Despite this, the voices on the net were generally intelligible, and enjoyed a far greater degree of clarity than the voices that emanated from headphones during the Vietnam War, or even Operation Desert Storm. The comm system allowed truck commanders and other crew members to maintain visual awareness without having to shout or turn their heads to be heard. They listened to voices of people in and outside their vehicle while their eyes scanned the environment for targets or hazards.

TCs would often monitor two nets simultaneously—one with each ear. As Eric, who commanded a Bradley fighting vehicle, explained:

> Basically, you're wearing a helmet with a set of headphones and ... on top of that ... I would stuff another microphone in one ear, and I don't know if this is even possible, but I feel like ... you learn to listen independently with each ear and, so, you're literally talking to your own crew, your own driver and gunner and loader, you're attempting to listen to all the various reports that are going on out there, and then you're also listening to your higher headquarters ask you questions, and so, I have very few distinct memories of hearing anything other than my own machine gun in the background because I'd say that 90% of my time there I was trying to understand what was going on out there [by listening to radio communications].

The headset that Eric used was called the CVC—the Combat Vehicle Crewman Headset. It was developed by the Bose Corporation, and intended specifically for tracked armor such as the Bradley. Equipped with full-spectrum noise reduction, the CVC attenuated engine noise, although not completely, while amplifying the voices of Eric's crew members and a fluctuating group of unseen people with whom he consulted during his missions. Noise reduction notwithstanding, the auditory situation in the Bradley remained highly challenging, with many layers of sound that had to be "listened through" in order to hear what mattered. But with practice, Eric learned to tune out the drone of the engine and the other ancillary vehicular noises that made it through his headset:

> You got really good at focusing on the reports that were coming in, and as time went on, the outside sounds of helicopters and your tank running—I can remember as a Bradley lieutenant ... you could barely hold a conversation with another guy in your tank because it was so unnerving to have all of these different sounds and it just drove you, kind of drives you nuts. But by the time I left Iraq, it seemed as natural as talking to somebody on the phone.

The central importance of communications compelled Eric to concentrate all of his auditory awareness on the chorus of voices that were delivering potentially vital information to his ears. Over time, he attained a kind of virtuosity as an auditor in the high-stakes arena of the combat zone:

> I guess if something, if my hearing evolved over time, I became much better at listening independently with each ear, maybe immediately sensing when somebody was in trouble by the tone of their voice, being able to connect different people sounding differently at different times to help me understand the circumstance, so

[I wasn't focused] so much on [the sounds of] different weapon systems or what-ever, but really dialing in on, you know, 'I hear what this guy is saying, but the *way* he is saying it leads me to believe this is kind of what it looks like on the ground'.

As a technology of combat, service members valued their communication links almost as much as they did their weapons. Being in auditory contact with headquarters gave Army infantry constant access to the commanders who could authorize and otherwise guide their actions. Being in contact with personnel monitoring the video feed from a drone flying overhead gave them access to people with a bird's-eye view of the battle-field. In this sense, radio communications enabled listening to serve as a surrogate for sight and distance as a simulacrum of presence. These two substitutions in turn allowed service members to engage in truly distributional warfare: the "brains" at distant head-quarters and the "eyes" in the sky exchanged auditory signals with the "boots on the ground." Marines, while similarly distributed, tended to work in a bottom-up fashion, with missions planned by combat troops on the ground to conform with commanders' general "intent," and most intelligence coming directly from scout-snipers in the field. The members of the insurgency and other anti-US factions engaged their own kind of distributional warfare, with the cell phone acting as both an instrument of communica-tion and a popular long-distance detonation device. But their consumer-grade commu-nications technology, though highly effective, could not be compared to the elaborate communications networks that the US military enjoyed.

The sophistication of military communications by no means guaranteed clear transmission of a message, however. Even in the best conditions, coordinates and instructions could be misheard or misunderstood. General fatigue, which was com-mon on motorized patrols, increased the likelihood of a mix-up. The chaotic sonic environment inside Humvees and other vehicles—engine noise, ambient noise, conversations inside the trucks, the sounds of gunfire, static on the line, and the possibility of multiple communications at one time—amplified the danger of mis-communication further. And although it continues to be a difficult topic to research, evidence is coming to light that the early generations of radio-controlled IED jam-mers "seriously degraded" or even prevented communications within motorized convoys in Iraq.[24] It was in these senses that "noise," from the cognitive variety to the technological kind, constantly threatened to inhibit the reception of the signal, rendering communicating while on missions a more complicated activity than one might initially think. It took an enormous amount of labor, in the form of individual practice (i.e., learning to listen binaurally, through a scrim of ambient sounds, to comm transmissions) and technical re-engineering (e.g., developing a new generation of jammers that didn't interfere with on-board radio systems) to attain and maintain a state of effective communication along the many nodes of the military communica-tions network.

Amplified Voices and Other Signals Outside of Vehicles

While the voices and beeps and clicks of communications were a constant presence inside military vehicles, outside them, in the open spaces of military bases and civilian neighborhoods, amplified communication was sporadic, unpredictable, and often tied to violent events that were imminent or ongoing. Civilian and military testimonies alike point to the messages, sirens, and warning tones of Civil Defense and military information systems as a memorable part of their experience of the war. American military bases throughout the theater were equipped with powerful loudspeakers that broadcast voices and a rhythmic warning tone alerting all within earshot to take cover in advance of a mortar or rocket attack.[25] On Camp Victory in Baghdad, a brassy five-shot burst of tones tuned to a major second and repeated at regular intervals, often interspersed with the words "incoming, incoming, incoming," signaled an impending attack. In the International Zone, attacks were preceded by two tones, spaced a perfect fifth apart, alternating in ten-note cycles. A recorded male voice would then proclaim: "Duck and cover. Get away from the windows. Stay covered and await further instructions." On other bases these tones were a tritone apart. Other warning alarms would ascend a perfect fourth, then slowly fall back to the original pitch. One base's alarm was pitched high like a whistle, ascending and then descending a major seventh, cycling in that manner for several seconds, after which a male voice would command, "Attention, attention, attention. Alarm red! All personnel seek shelter in a bunker." All of these alarms were extremely loud at their points of origin, and they all emanated from multiple speakers simultaneously. Often the alarms would begin sounding after the attack had commenced. Thus one loud series of events (i.e., the attacks themselves) would be accompanied by another (the sirens) that warned, belatedly, of their arrival. A single mortar lobbed onto a base had a destructive ambit that could be measured in square meters; the alarm system it triggered would be audible over a square kilometer or, in the case of the larger bases, much more. Gavin, a civil servant who served in the International Zone during a period when mortar attacks occurred nearly every night, surmised that insurgents were well aware of the prolonged chorus of alarms that their mortar and rocket attacks triggered:

> Actually it was the Duck and Cover that kept me up at night during bad periods—and not the explosions. You know, the *"DEE-dee-DEE-dee-DEE-dee-DEE-dee:* Attention in the compound: duck and cover, duck and cover!" from our Peruvian guards. And you know that would keep you up all night, cause when they're shooting at you every 15 to 20 to 40 minutes, they'd hit the "Duck and Cover" and wake you up, and whether you responded or not you were awake. . . . In 2008 in April around Easter, I actually thought that Muqtada al Sadr's way of torturing us was to keep us up all night, keep us awake all night.[26]

Communication also took place between service members and the local populace, but within fairly tight parameters, and seldom with the uninhibited flow of a casual conversation among equals. The most noticeable and public mode of one-way communication between US troops and Iraqi civilians, and the one that is most commonly mentioned in civilian testimonies, was the informational/warning message projected through loudspeakers by PSYOPS (psychological operations) units and troops at checkpoints. Using powerful loudspeakers mounted on Humvees and installed at checkpoints, smaller "man-pack" speakers carried on foot patrols, or, more rarely, the truck-mounted "Long-Range Acoustic Device" or "LRAD,"[27] these troops disseminated messages, in English and Arabic, throughout the streets of Baghdad and many other Iraqi cities and towns. The advantage of this practice over the dissemination of written materials was articulated in detail in a document describing "psychological operations, tactics, techniques, and procedures," produced at the Department of the Army Headquarters in December 2003. Here, communication with the enemy and with local citizens is described in the zero-sum language of the battlefield:

> The loudspeaker can be directed to be broadcast at opponent forces that have been cut off, urging them to surrender or cease resistance. Loudspeakers can also be used to issue instructions to persons in fortified positions and locations, and used for deception operations by broadcasting sounds of vehicles or other equipment. Loudspeakers can also be employed to control the flow of refugees and DCs [dislocated civilians], and to issue instructions to reduce interference by civilians on the battlefield. *During loudspeaker broadcasts, the TA* [target audience] *becomes a captive audience who cannot escape the messages being delivered.* In addition, if the message is properly tailored and has been well conceived, *the TA will not be able to escape the psychological impact of the message.* Loudspeakers can be used to exploit any opportunity that suddenly arises, and can reach the target faster than other media do.[28]

In engagements throughout Operation Iraqi Freedom, traditional loudspeakers and, more rarely, LRADs, were also used to communicate with members of the insurgency, as this description from a 2005 study for the National Defense University illustrates:

> In recent fighting in OIF, Iraqi insurgents hid among women and children while engaging in combat operations with coalition forces. In order to cull out the insurgents, *the U.S. military broadcast loudspeaker messages denouncing the insurgents as cowards.* Often the insurgents responded by emerging to fight more directly. It is possible that they felt trapped and were moving to extricate themselves or for some other reason. However, the extremely close proximity between the loudspeaker broadcasts and the dramatic change in the target audience behavior suggests a strong correlation between the two.[29]

After major combat operations ended, as attacks from the insurgency began to mount, the American armed forces increasingly used loudspeakers to communicate with the civilian population at large. PSYOPS loudspeaker teams were deployed in conjunction with leaflet distribution and radio broadcasts to disseminate propaganda-driven announcements about, in the language of another Army manual: "what PRC [populace and resources control] measures are in effect; when certain PRC measures are no longer in effect; what civic action projects are being conducted in the area; [and] what other programs are available for their benefit."[30] Troops and contractors also used loudspeakers on vehicles and at checkpoints to issue loud warnings for vehicles to pull to the side of the road as convoys passed, or stay a certain distance away from a vehicle or checkpoint. In all of these cases, from commanding belligerents to surrender to broadcasting warnings to advertising the successes of the post-Hussein Iraqi government, the voice over the loudspeaker enunciated its messages with amplified force and strident timbre, booming authoritatively over the largely unamplified populace, leaving no room for response or question, clearly and forcefully articulating the official line of the occupying forces.[31]

Except when it didn't. The authority of the amplified and disembodied voice was frequently compromised by distortion, static, background noise, repetition, poor translation, or the lack of translation altogether. These factors often combined to render the loudspeaker's message unintelligible and effectively moot. The frequent, unannounced, and undesired arrival of loud, commanding voices whose semantic content was occluded by static and accompanied by piercing electronic sounds elicited a range of reactions among auditors, from curiosity to frustration, confusion to exhaustion, anger to derision to bemusement. As a technology of pure communication, the loudspeaker was imperfect. But as a generator of sporadic, emotionally cathected sonic events, it left a deep imprint on the memories of civilian and military auditors alike.

The military was not the only entity in Iraq to possess amplification devices, of course. Loudspeakers atop the minarets of the country's mosques were regularly used to broadcast sermons and sacred recitations, and were also employed in disseminating political speeches, tactical instructions, and propaganda to followers. Muqtada al-Sadr's headquarters in Sadr City featured "seven agitprop-style [loudspeakers] clustered on the roof," which were regularly used to broadcast messages to the surrounding neighborhoods.[32] And in mass demonstrations that were held throughout Iraq over the course of Operation Iraqi Freedom, protestors, using their own megaphones to coordinate mass chants, occasionally drowned out the US military loudspeakers in the area. In these situations, amplified communication could be framed both as transmission of a message and a zero-sum competition between antagonists, held within the noisy field of combat.

Unamplified (but not Unmediated) Military-Civilian Vocal Exchanges

One other type of transmission bears mentioning here: the troubled and often inter-rupted attempts at two-way, real-time military-civilian communication, attempts that were mediated not by amplifiers or radio waves but by human interpreters on the ground. Service members who patrolled Iraqi cities on foot regularly found their own voices mixed with the voices of local residents, speaking primarily in Arabic, but also in Kurdish, English, and other languages, and in multiple dialects. Some—though far from all—units that regularly engaged with Iraqi citizens traveled with a "terp," an Iraqi or third-country native-Arabic interpreter working as a local contractor for the military. Over the course of the war, tens of thousands of men and women worked as interpreters in profoundly challenging conditions.[33] Most of them, while bilingual, had not been professional interpreters before the war, and so hadn't received formal train-ing in simultaneous interpretation. Very few interpreters had worked with Americans before, which meant they were not attuned to the multitude of accents, colloquialisms, and frank slang that characterized service members' speech. Their lack of formal train-ing and imperfect knowledge of English made their jobs difficult, but these difficulties were minor compared to the existential threats that interpreters, one of the most vul-nerable populations in the country, faced. A *New York Times* report from 2008 enu-merated some of these dangers:

> Those [interpreters] who work for the Americans are often accused of being apos-tates and traitors. Their homes are bombed. Death threats are wrapped around blood-soaked bullets and left outside their homes. Their relatives are abducted and killed because of their work. And of the interpreters themselves, hundreds have been killed.[34]

For this class of professional listeners and speakers, the moment of risk involved in listen-ing to belliphonic sound (here in the form of voices speaking about war-related matters) had less to do with the immediate physical and psychological traumas that are discussed elsewhere in this volume, and more to do with the increased odds of becoming a target of violent retribution for allowing meaningful communication between US forces and the local population to take place.

Beginning in 2004, it became a common practice for interpreters to wear face masks in order to shield their identities and in so doing reduce the risk of sectarian retaliation for their collaboration with US forces.[35] On house patrols, service members strained to make sense of the masked interpreter's voice as it overlapped and alternated with the foreign voices of their true interlocutors. Their heavily mediated conversations took place in a fraught auditory space, one often filled with a multitude of vocalizations that were triggered by the troops' forced entry: crying, supplication, and angry shouts from the civilians, instructions hollered from one unit member to another, along with instructions coming over the comm systems, the growl of nearby generators and vehicles, and, occasionally, gunfire in the background. The stakes of accurate communication, which, in many instances, could not be higher, only added to the challenges that service members, Iraqi civilians, and interpreters faced. And the politics of a situation in which heavily armed service members gave instructions and asked questions of unarmed (or disarmed) Iraqis, often at gunpoint, surely inflected how words were received and responses given.

Most of my Iraqi interlocutors had come into personal contact with US service members during Operation Iraqi Freedom. The vast majority of these interactions took place during searches of their houses. Ammar, who speaks fluent but not idiomatic English, ended up serving as his family's ad hoc interpreter during a search of their Baghdad home in 2004. He described a tense scene in which belliphonic noises and voices blended together with the imminent threat of violence:

> Once, they jumped on our house—it was really scary, I think it was 2004. My father and my brother were in Egypt. I was with me and my mother and sister and my grandmother and aunt. So I got scared because they almost broke down the door, our door. They were kicking it with a very loud sound. The generator was on so I didn't notice them at first and they just entered the house, spread out in the house. When they saw me speak English, the Lieutenant showed [he makes a thumbs-up gesture], as a gesture from him to show me that he is here in peace. He told me that 'I won't enter your house, I will stay here and let the guys go inside and please I am sorry to come to you in such a late time of the day' . . . . That was a really good picture for me, the guys who came in the house.
> . . . So I walked upstairs with one of the soldiers and he [was] showing me that I have a computer and he said to me the first time I hear "internet" in the American style: "innernet." I told him "what?" He said, "innernet, you have innernet?" I said yeah.
> *JMD: So did you understand what they were looking for?*
> They searched only our house, but he said it is a random checkup. But we didn't think it was random, maybe because my father had been [a minor Hussein-era] official, or maybe because our house has the only power in the street. But they were respectful guys.[36]

Several months later, a more aggressive search proved more nerve-wracking:

> The [next search], it was scary. I was staying at my aunt's house in Adhamiya, it is on the airport highway, it is very busy with American Humvees, because it is on the way to the airport. Every five minutes you see three Humvees passing or a tank passing. So we were sleeping, me and my uncle. They start kicking the door, just a few seconds from using those knock-knocks.

JMD: Battering rams?

Yes. So I was very scared. They came in a combat theme, they just spread out in the house and they sat on their knees with [flashlights on their weapons, training them on Ammar and his family]. I went to talk to [the officer in charge] in English, and he yelled at me. The Iraqi translator told me to be quiet, be quiet. I remember that the first [time] we saw American troops coming to our house, [I had conversed with them], so I wanted to talk with this lieutenant or something, but he started yelling at me. I wanted to show them the rooms—he almost hit me. So I was very scared and when he almost hit me and the other one pointed the M4 on me, I was really scared that he was going to shoot me, because it happened: once they wanted to enter [my friend's] house and the family didn't pay attention to them, so when they entered they pushed out [my friend's] father. . . . They pushed out her father and her brother starts yelling at them and they shoot him immediately. So I just remember that and I was very scared. They found the safe, they couldn't open it, they started yelling to open the safe, so it was totally different from the first time.

As with so many situations that are described in this volume, challenges to listening which in other environments would have been simply frustrating are here pushed into the realm of the terrifying. Unable to understand the foreign-language utterances that surrounded them, or trust that their interpreter had translated a particular sentence accurately, or hear distinctly through the surrounding cacophony, service members found their agency as interrogators severely hampered. This, it would seem, rendered them more vulnerable to violence, *and more liable to use violence,* than they would have been if they had understood all of the nuances of their vocal exchanges with civilians. Meanwhile, robbed of the ability to control a makeshift interrogation taking place at gunpoint in their own homes, Iraqi civilians found themselves in situations where a misplaced word could lead to indefinite detention or immediate violence.

As Ammar's story illustrates, cross-cultural communication during the war was consistently confounded by technological problems, acoustic challenges, human fallibility, linguistic incompatibility, acute fear, entrained aggression, and the general aura of precarity that enveloped most encounters between service members and civilians. These factors combined to make communication a deeply fraught activity in both auditory and existential terms, and to make miscommunication one of the hallmarks of the war.

CIVILIAN SOUNDS

Even in peacetime, urban life is noisy. Urban life in wartime, as I hope to have demonstrated, is ineluctably noisier, even before we begin to talk about the profound sonic intrusion of explosions and gunfire. Wartime urban life in places where the centralized electricity source has broken down can be noisier still. With the disruption of local fuel production and distribution in the wake of the 2003 invasion, and with the physical degradation of the power grid through targeted insurgent and sectarian attacks, electricity plants throughout Iraq were forced to radically cut back on the production of power. As a result, Baghdad and other cities throughout Iraq witnessed a proliferation of noisy gas- and diesel-powered generators—both small units supplying electricity to individual homes, and larger units parked on neighborhood streets from which groups of residents drew power.[37] According to civilian testimonies, the hundreds of thousands of generators that ran in Baghdad from 2003 to 2009 (the number has since decreased somewhat, although power problems persist as of this writing) produced a noisy environment of layered machinic growls, which often drowned out the quieter ambient sounds of the city. In this rumbling environment, the insect, avian, and even canine populations were muted, often to the point of inaudibility; and casual conversation felt more like work than it had previously, as people learned to holler over the generators' sounds. Smaller towns and military bases were similarly marked with the sound, smell, and subtle vibrational "feel" of gas and diesel generators. Chris, a civil servant who served in Baghdad for two years as an embedded advisor to the Iraqi National Parliament, described the sound that these generators produced:

> Generators. The sound of generators everywhere. You know, generators that are on their last legs, generators, like back-up generators that have to kick in when the primary generators are off. *That seemed to drown out almost everything else.* . . . just this awful clanking sound of generators in the background is what I associate the soundscapes of the IZ [International Zone] with. . . . They drowned out all these sounds that you associate with culture . . . like conversations, the sounds of birds, or wind blowing through palm trees. It's like you don't hear a natural soundscape anymore. . . It's much more of an industrialized soundscape.[38]

When I visited Baghdad in 2011, I found this "industrialized soundscape" to be significantly more invasive than my own (extremely loud) neighborhood in lower Manhattan. Every Baghdad neighborhood I visited was marked with the loud hum of multiple generators. This hum, filling in the space between helicopter flybys and vehicular passages, was too loud for me ever to ignore. On one occasion, the sound of the generator that powered a small Iraqi shop was so pronounced that I couldn't hear people talking just a few feet away from me. Yelling in my ear, an Iraqi interpreter who was with me explained that this was still a common phenomenon in the city, and that it was widely regarded as the audible legacy of the war: it was the sound, he said, of "a failed occupation."

Listening to the Adhan

Punctuating the growl of generators and civilian traffic, more predictable than the chorus of voices uplifted in the occasional mass political protest, more emphatic than the murmur of voices speaking on the street or the increasingly rare sound of festive outdoor weddings, two genres of sacred vocal performance regularly made deep impressions on military and civilian perceptions of the acoustic environment of wartime Iraq. The first of these, the adhan or Muslim call to prayer, figured centrally in service members' reminiscences. Bathing American military installations and civilian neighborhoods alike in the ritualized sound of a human voice five times daily, the adhan was, for most of my military interlocutors, the most striking and memorable non-weapon-related sound they recalled from their tours of duty in Iraq.

For observant Muslims the adhan resonates within a powerful cultural matrix of temporality, theology, and topography to structure diurnal, spiritual, and social life; in the words of ethnomusicologist Tong Soon Lee, the call does nothing less than "produce Islamic space," marking, for auditors of all faiths, the territory as a zone of Muslim devotion.[39] As in other countries with large Muslim populations, it is also an aesthetic phenomenon, the beautiful delivery of which is cherished by those who have the critical apparatus to discern the specific virtuosities and idiosyncrasies that separate one muezzin's call from another.[40] Divorced from its religious context, however, as it is for the majority of US troops,[41] the call to prayer is subject to other, less homegrown aesthetics. While some of the service members with whom I spoke praised the adhan for its haunting beauty, others Orientalized, objectified, and at times even denigrated it as the sonic embodiment of an Arab world that is for them relentlessly foreign, threatening, uncultured, and unknowable.

Operating outside of the spiritual community that has assigned the adhan its rich historical and symbolic resonance, non-Muslim American service members were left to approach it on their own terms. As a musically inclined Army captain described it, the adhan is

> sung, it's almost Gregorian. And of course musically I always thought it was interesting because they have quarter steps in their notes: quarter pitches, most people don't care, but I'd always be amazed at the tonal quality of these. You know they're just preachers, the imams, but they have this amazing voice control, cause he's working all kinds of quarter steps, [when] most people [in America] don't even know the difference between a sharp and a flat.[42]

Although he mistakenly conflates the imam with the muezzin who delivers the call, the captain accurately pinpoints the sophistication with which the voice is deployed in the adhan and Quranic cantillation, and expresses amazement at the voice's virtuosity in this context. He answered the adhan with an appreciation for its beauty, a foreign beauty that he learned to cherish over the course of his deployment.

An Air Force major who served in Kirkuk in 2006 arrived in Iraq with a general awareness of the call to prayer's significance within Islam. With time, however, he also came to assign the adhan a significance that was purely tactical:

Something else unique about the Middle East is prayer time, you would hear the mosques, and you knew that, OK, all the Muslims are going to be praying, so, one, no one's gonna be shooting at us for the next two minutes, and two, we gotta watch out because people will pull over, and stop what they're doing and start praying and we don't need to run anybody over or get in the middle of an accident because folks are stopping to pray. . . . If it was prayer time it was very convenient, and we would whip right through, and be out of their way in no time flat.[43]

In the Major's case, recognition of the adhan's surplus tactical significance did not prevent him from acknowledging its primary function for its intended community, or from regarding it as beautiful. But as I mentioned earlier, other military auditors appear to have heard nothing beautiful in the adhan, and to have regarded it as little else than a sinister signal of Islamic aggression and unbridgeable cultural difference. To their ears, the amplified voice of the muezzin sounded like a sonic incursion that helped to produce an "Islamic space" that was inherently hostile to the troops and their mission. In these circumstances, it is perhaps not surprising that some service members treated the adhan with derision, shouting vulgar parodies of "Allahu akbar" through handheld megaphones for the entertainment of their platoon or the perturbation of local civilian auditors, and, in some cases, posting videos of these performances on the internet. One such video, titled "American Call to Prayer," features a muscular soldier in PT gear (shorts, Army T-shirt, reflective belt) standing atop an MRAP in what looks like a motor pool.[44] A caption underneath the video offers an explanation: "While in Iraq I was able to come up with a few call to prayers on my own, So I led my platoon in the prayers." As the video begins, the soldier raises a megaphone, hits it a few times to deal with what appears to be a short in the wiring, and to the bemusement of his unseen audience, chants, in a strident sing-song voice, a crude improvisation that begins:

Allah, somebodygotitoo, allah, alloo, Alexisabutthead, Allah. . .selam.
Hola, como esta, IdonotknowhatamIsaying. . .bee-bap. . .

This kind of caricature—the result of a culturally constrained listening that is simultaneously a *mishearing* or failure to listen—is indicative of a general process of denigration that is common in wartime. Informal acts such as these help set one of the necessary preconditions for organized violence: dehumanization of the enemy.[45] The "American call to prayer" is one small iteration of a broader ad hoc process of wartime dehumanization, whereby symbolic violence (here in the form of acoustic vandalism) serves to render corporeal violence both thinkable and desirable. Of course, it stands to reason that this process was reciprocal, and that antagonistic shouts, public chants, and other critical vocalizations directed toward the US military presence in Iraq were undertaken with similar goals.

If the American reception of the call to prayer involved a broad spectrum of reactions—ranging, in the few examples above, from aesthetic enjoyment to tactical redeployment to parodic defacement—it does not follow that Iraqi reception was uniform, or static. The only thing we can say with relative certainty about the adhan as an interpretable text for Iraqis is that, having been a relatively steady presence in Iraq for centuries, it would not have sounded as exotic, mysterious, or strange as it did for the vast majority of service members. In the terminology of R. Murray Schafer, the adhan is a "soundmark," a sound that, like a landmark, "is unique or possesses qualities which make it specially regarded or noticed by the people in that community."[46] But it, like all soundmarks, remains a site of polysemy for any population, particularly one that is as diverse in faith and degree of devotion as contemporary Iraq.

Some Iraqis who spoke to me about the adhan mentioned, unsurprisingly, the profound spiritual significance of a ritual act that dates back to the Prophet Muhammad. Others pointed to the aesthetic beauty of a perfectly delivered adhan, recordings of which they loaded onto their cell phones and MP3 players. But several mentioned that the call has taken on a political dimension in the years following the invasion. After the fall of the Hussein regime, as tensions between Shi'i and Sunni sectarian groups began to increase, the adhan—whose Shi'i and Sunni versions audibly differ—took on an additional significance as a barometer of demographics, and of sectarian tension.[47] As once-mixed neighborhoods became dominated by one sect or another, the shift in populations was registered publicly, vocally, in the concentration of loudspeakers amplifying one call to prayer or another. This distinction, inaudible to most American service members who were unable to discern the Shi'i call from its Sunni counterpart, was fundamental to Iraqi auditors.

Lastly, it is important to remember the fact—once obvious but now, with the postwar emigration of a large number of Christians, less so—that not all Iraqis are Muslim.[48] So while the call bathed auditors with its vibrations indiscriminately, at the level of interpellation it reached out to and hailed members of the local population selectively. Of course, this selectivity was itself in flux, as the war forced millions of Iraqi citizens and residents to flee densely populated areas for the countryside, and often to leave altogether and seek refuge in neighboring countries.

These nuances notwithstanding, it would be irresponsible not to acknowledge the broad differences that separated the overwhelmingly non-Muslim foreign troops from the overwhelmingly Muslim local civilians as they listened to the adhan. In fact, it was precisely at moments like this when listening practices encouraged and enacted by US military service members appeared to diverge most radically from those of the Iraqi civilian population. The act of creative misprision that allowed the major to read an expression of religious observance as a barometer of insurgent violence, or the more extreme act performed by the soldier atop the MRAP, points, emphatically I think, to the discursive horizon beyond which the intersubjectivity of listening reaches its limit. It is highly likely that a person for whom the adhan is a symbol of the presence of Allah and his blessing might refuse or otherwise be unable to occupy a stance from which the adhan is read as a marker for a narrow window of tactical opportunity. And it is almost inconceivable that such a person would be able or willing to direct his or her empathic reserves toward someone as they desecrated the adhan in the way described above. One does not have to essentialize difference to acknowledge, within these stories, at least the possibility that some practices of listening may be simply incommensurable, some interpretations mutually exclusive. Here, as elsewhere, the antagonistic forces of armed conflict are duplicated and reified through something as invisible, ubiquitous, and seemingly benign as the act of listening.

Listening to Ashura

The efflorescence of the Ashura ceremony throughout Iraq after the fall of Saddam Hussein's regime produced another instance of divergent listening practices that reinscribed and deepened tension between communities of auditors.[49] Ashura, the tenth day of Muharram, the first month of the Islamic calendar, is the most sacred day of the year for Shi'i Muslims. On that day in the year 680 C.E., Husayn ibn Ali, the grandson of the Prophet Muhammad and the third Shi'i Imam, was killed at the Battle of Karbala (an Iraqi city on the banks of the Euphrates) by troops loyal to Yazid I, the second caliph of the Umayyad Caliphate. The "battle" amounted to a massacre, as Husayn was beheaded, along with the men in his entourage of less than one hundred friends and family members, by troops numbering roughly 100,000. The spot where Husayn's body was buried in Karbala became a site of pilgrimage within several years of his death. For well over a thousand years, Shi'i faithful have commemorated Husayn's martyrdom by attending mourning ceremonies and poetic recitations. Some Shi'a in Iraq and elsewhere have also engaged in re-enactments of the battle of Karbala, accompanied by long processions that take place in the ten days leading up to Ashura. During these events, male pilgrims of all ages flagellate themselves with chains or cut their foreheads with knives and swords, while marching to the rhythmic accompaniment of drums and chants. This practice symbolizes sorrow at the death of Husayn as well as penance for being absent at the battle of Karbala, and thus failing to defend him and his family. There are no easy analogues to this ceremony within the Sunni population. As a result, more than any other day, Ashura crystallizes the distance between the practice of Shi'i and Sunni Islam.

For the two decades preceding Operation Iraqi Freedom, as part of a program of containment and subjugation of Iraq's Shi'a majority population, Saddam Hussein's government prohibited public Ashura processions and self-flagellation rituals. In 2004, the year after his ouster, public Ashura ceremonies were reinstated on a massive scale.[50] Each year, from 2004 to the present, thousands of men and boys in Baghdad's Kadhimiya neighborhood, and pilgrims in Karbala ranging from several hundred thousand to well over one million, have processed to the chant of "Ya Husayn!" and "Haydar! Haydar!" (a title of Husayn's father, Ali ibn Talib), while huge crowds of women have wailed in a ritualized expression of sorrow for the martyr's death. In recent years in Baghdad, a canal has been tinted red to symbolize the blood of Husayn that was spilled.

Arakel, an Iraqi Christian who left Baghdad in 2006, explained how the postwar sounds of Shi'i vocalization mark territory along sectarian lines:

> When you walk into a Shi'i neighborhood [during the period surrounding Ashura], you can hear the tone of these songs playing. After the war they're . . . loud—and if you have a shop, you have speakers outside your shop playing. . . you can't talk to each other in a public street because that's how loud it is. So you can tell, 'I'm definitely in a Shi'i neighborhood.' Before the war . . . you couldn't tell, walking down the street, what kind of neighborhood this is without having prior knowledge.[51]

The return of Ashura ceremonies to Iraq after their long absence sparked a tragic wave of violent reactions from Sunni groups and counterreactions from Shi'a.[52] For both populations, however, the sound and sight of this once-prohibited ceremony provided breathtaking, incontrovertible sensory evidence that Saddam Hussein's government was no longer in power. For auditors who lived through the Hussein era, regardless of their religious affiliations, the ceremony demanded to be read as a metonym of a post-regime-change Iraq in which the political agency of the Shi'i population is ascendant.

Ashura was a noteworthy event for military service members as well, with most of their attention drawn to the shocking sight of pilgrims hitting their foreheads with knives, which causes blood to stain their white robes. However, having spent the Hussein era outside of Iraq, several of my military interlocutors admitted that they initially failed to grasp the significance of this event. When speaking with service members who served in the early years of the war, the reaction I commonly received to questions about Ashura was that they remembered it as simply being emblematic of "Iraqi music" or "Iraqi chant." Service members who served later in the war, or those whose missions entailed regular interaction with the local citizenry, were more likely to know that Ashura was a type of Shi'i devotional performance, and that it was a practice that Operation Iraqi Freedom had rendered possible after many years of prohibition. This gradual acquisition of locally inflected knowledge points to the broader fact that, over the course of the war, some service members attempted to listen to their environment *as if they were* Iraqis. Similarly, civilian testimonies are rife with evidence that Iraqis often worked very hard to learn to listen *as if they were* American service members. Though these two disparate communities of auditors were separated by ideology, history, culture, demographics, training, and technology, their listening practices and interpretations of began to bleed into one another over time.

Relative Quietude and Natural Sounds

One last thing needs to be said about the sounds of civilian neighborhoods in wartime. It is tempting, given the extreme nature of belliphonic sounds—and given the hyperreal depiction of combat in popular cinema—to imagine that war zones are filled to bursting with violent noise at all times. While this chapter highlights a number of the invasive sounds that were prevalent in wartime Iraq, it is important to stress that the belliphonic did not and indeed could never completely drown out the sounds of human life and the natural world within Iraq's vast topography. War is a noisy phenomenon, to be sure, but Iraq is a big place, a place that was able to absorb a great number of sporadic belliphonic vibrations. Even Baghdad, the noisiest and most densely populated of Iraqi cities, contains open spaces that presented military and civilian auditors alike with moments of quiescence, in which the soft calls of birds, the distant barking of dogs, the Tigris lapping up against its banks, or the low sound of the wind in one's ears could be apprehended. The persistence of natural sounds and the sounds of "normal" civilian life within the patently unnatural and abnormal environment of war always provides a strong foil to the caustic energy of belliphonic sound. And it is against that foil of normalcy that the most aggressive sounds, the sounds of weapons and explosions that I endeavor to describe in the next section, must be measured.

WEAPONS

Vehicular sounds, the sounds of communications, and the sounds of urban life occasionally leapt to the forefront of service members' consciousness. A Humvee engine made a strange noise, and its driver listened intently to it to discern its condition. The sounds of angry civilian crowds—or, conversely, an eerie reduction of the ambient sounds of the street—caused experienced service members to prick up their ears as they scanned their surroundings for evidence of an impending attack. The click and beep that preceded communications resulted in a conversation inside an MRAP being cut off as all ears turned toward an incoming message. And of course even people in the most war-torn environments remain capable of being transfixed by the things that once caught their attention in peacetime: a call, a cry, a laugh, a snippet of a song, a dog's bark, the howling of the wind. But service members most frequently referred to these sounds as the sonic background *through which* they were actively listening for another set of sounds. The crack of bullets, the low boom of the IED, the whoosh of the rocket-propelled grenade, the arcing whine of the mortar—sounds that heralded the nearby presence of violent acts, sounds that at certain volumes became a form of violence in their own right—were, for obvious reasons, of intense interest to service members in Iraq. These sounds were of such importance that apprehending them took precedence over nearly all other activities.[53] For all parties, the anticipation, experience, and retention of weapon sounds were central activities within the phenomenology of combat.

As weapons technologies have evolved, so have the sounds that accompany them. Belliphonic sound in the Civil War initially involved cannon fire and the ragged sound of the single-shot musket, and was dramatically expanded with the introduction of the Gatling gun soon before the war's end. By the time of World War I, automatic weaponry and howitzer fire had become so common that they served as sonic icons for war generally. Operation Iraqi Freedom was marked by some weapons technologies that had been around since the Vietnam era, as well as others that were developed and introduced after 2003. The sonic signature of its arsenal thus overlaps with but is distinct from those of other wars. While a complete taxonomy of the weapons used in Operation Iraqi Freedom would be unfeasible here, I want to single out a number of the most common weapons in order to provide a sense of the range of sounds they produced and the opportunities and liabilities they presented for those within earshot.

Small Arms

Small arms fire was extremely common during Operation Iraqi Freedom, as insurgent groups battled with US and coalition forces, sectarian groups battled largely with one another, police and contractors used automatic weapons in combat situations and to clear paths through crowded intersections, civilians occasionally took up arms to defend their homes, and Iraqis continued the prewar practice of marking major events and sports victories with celebratory gunfire. For auditors who lived through the peak years of the war, the sound of small arms rattling away at various distances was a daily presence.

The sounds that bullets make depend on a wide variety of factors. Some of these have to do with the source—the weapon's model and barrel length, and the projectile's caliber, powder charge, and grain. Other factors are external to the weapon and cartridge: a shot's trajectory, its proximity, and the acoustic environment in which it is fired all affect the sound that reaches the ear. The initial report, the sound of the explosion that releases the bullet, is generally followed by the sound of its impact; when a bullet strikes a surface, it causes that surface to sound as well, adding the hard knocking sound of wood, the less resonant smack of concrete, the sharp pang of metal, or the duller thud of flesh to the mix. In between the moments when these sounds are created, projectiles produce a great number of sounds as they displace air during their flight. Bullets traveling at supersonic speeds announce themselves with a whiplike crack as the sound barrier is broken. When they slow down to subsonic speeds, a bullet displacing air can create any number of whizzing and hissing and buzzing and twanging sounds, depending on a large number of variables. In the words of a captain in the Army infantry who served in Iraq in 2005:

> The gun being fired near you is . . . very loud, I mean there's almost a pain sensation involved . . . and that's probably within about fifty feet. Outside fifty feet, that's where the sound really changes depending on what direction it is, if it's being fired away from you or towards you and how close the bullet passes. If you can hear a "phiff" noise or a "zing," in and around you, the bullet probably passed within a few feet of you, probably about ten feet at the limit. And that's really nerve-wracking. Also, ricochets off your vehicle or anything near you—you know you hear it ricocheting and you usually get a "zing" noise like in the Western movies, and those aren't loud at all, sometimes you can't even—and then you're like "What was that?" and then you're like, "Oh crap, we're getting shot at" and everybody hits

the ground, because somebody just heard a "ffft," you know, a "phip" or a "fff." If they're shooting away from you, and you're away from the fire as well, you usually can't hear the bullet as it travels, but if it's being fired toward you, as it passes you or after it passes you, you can certainly hear the air being displaced.[54]

At close distances, a bullet displacing air sounds louder, but proximity is not the only factor governing these sonic shifts. A company commander who served in Mosul in 2005 and 2006 recalled:

> I had a bullet go by my head that rang my ears for about two days. That was shot at me from maybe 100 meters or so, so fairly close, but that was not quiet at all. . . . At long distance, you might hear the splash on the Humvee or whatever, and then if it's really long, it's like [the snapping of] a high-tension wire. It's like a zip, I can't make the noise, but either it's like a zip, or, if it ricochets off the ground next to you, you can hear that, but you don't hear the report. And then different caliber weapons displace different amounts of air, but I think the range matters a lot, and the caliber, but [also] where it hits: does it ricochet or does it hit the Humvee or does it go over your head? All of these things have different sounds, but some are soft and some were really, outrageously loud.[55]

Iraqi civilians tended to be slightly farther removed from gunfire, and so had less frequent experience with the hissing, zipping sounds of bullets displacing air on near trajectories. Unlike combat service members, whose mode of operation rendered them simultaneously shooters and potential targets in battles with insurgents, civilians were often able to take cover in their houses or other locations that afforded some protection from speeding bullets. Many testimonies describe civilian auditors watching engagements from their roofs, ducking down behind walls if things got too close. And yet, living in the combat zone for longer than any single military deployment, absorbing the sounds of small arms fire for years as the war dragged on, Iraqi civilians—many of whom had experienced Operation Desert Storm in 1991 and the Iran-Iraq War in the 1980s—became highly adept at discerning one firearm from another. As one civilian auditor explained: "I learned to distinguish between these voices [i.e., the sounds of different weapons]. I learned to distinguish between the sounds [due to] the large number of wars we have endured for so many years." This auditor recalled that, even as a child, she would always ask her parents about the types of weapons she heard from inside their apartment, drawing on their expertise to become a more highly trained auditor herself.

In 2007, before he emigrated to Jordan, my long-term interlocutor Saif participated in *Hometown Baghdad*, a web documentary shot in the city in 2007 by an all-Iraqi crew.[56] One episode of *Hometown Baghdad* was devoted exclusively to the sounds of small arms fire. Titled "Symphony of Bullets," it was based on interviews given by Saif, Adel, and Ausama, three young and charismatic upper-middle-class Iraqi men in their 20s. The episode begins with Adel adding an entry to his video diary with a small handheld video camera. With the camera trained on his beleaguered face, he says, in a resigned voice:

> I was going to meet my friends in college, to prepare for exams but . . . I couldn't get out today. And the reason is, uh, well, why don't you just hear for yourself?

At this point, Adel swivels the camera and its highly directional microphone to the window of the second-story room. The sound of small arms fire, which had been audible underneath his voice, grows louder as a hail of unseen bullets echoes down his street. With the sound of the gun battle persisting, Adel leans back on his couch and says:

> So [I had] just better lay down and listen to the—[and here he pauses, searching for the right phrase, which he quickly finds]—"symphony of bullets."

Over a series of shots taken from the window at different times of day and night, and with one of Bach's unaccompanied cello suites placed incongruously in the background by the series editors, we hear long streams of small arms fire recorded from Adel's house. Based on their volume and echo, the shots appear to be coming from the middle distance, several blocks away. In any event, the shooters are nowhere to be seen. But the sounds of the shots bespeak an intense battle, involving lots of indiscriminate gunfire, taking place in the neighborhood.

In the next scene, Ausama, folding laundry in his bedroom, hears a single shot ring out in the neighborhood beyond his open window. "That was a bullet," he says with a bashful smile:

> I think a sniper shot. Now we recognize the bullets—if it was AK bullets or a sniper, or we can say if it is an American bullet or Iraqi bullet.

Later in the episode, Adel shows the filmmakers the pistol that he carries to protect himself and his family. The scene shifts to Saif's house, where he pulls a large pump-action shotgun out of a wardrobe and demonstrates the act of pumping a cartridge into the chamber. Two of his friends enter the room and Saif, with a large smile on his face, pumps the shotgun again for their benefit. They love the iconic sound and Saif's cinematic bravado as well. One of the friends is carrying a small umbrella, and he, laughing, grabs it as if it were a shotgun and, saying "check this out!" mimics Saif's pump action. All three erupt in laughter. While likely staged, the scene reminds me of a fact that bears mentioning here: by the time the war started, a large portion of the civilian population in Iraq had armed itself for defensive purposes. Indeed, Iraqi civilians are generally much more closely acquainted with firearms than the American readership of this book. More than one generation of Iraqi boys received rudimentary training on AK-47s during high school, and most Iraqi men underwent a program of indoctrination and weapons training after being conscripted into the Hussein-era military. Drawing upon their firsthand experience with firearms, not to mention their prolonged exposure to hostile fire, nearly all of my Iraqi interlocutors claimed to be able to tell the difference between the (largely Russian-designed) firearms favored by the insurgency and the US military-issue M4s, M16s, M9s, M249 machine guns, M2 50-caliber machine guns, sniper rifles, and other arms that constituted the most arresting element of the belliphonic background during the hot years of the war. They had become, by their own accounts, virtuosic auditors, and they understood that their ability to listen acutely was a skill that increased their likelihood of survival.

Mortars and Rockets

If small arms fire was a common, sustained presence in the active combat zones of Iraq, other weapons made their appearances more sporadically, and spectacularly. The flights and detonations of mortars and rockets commanded attention across a more expansive ambit than bullets possibly could. Mortars, the lower-tech of the two weapons systems, constituted a minor part of the US arsenal in Iraq. By contrast, the forces battling against the United States and its allies used mortars incessantly, directing thousands of them at military and civilian installations, both within the International Zone and throughout the country, from the first year of the war right up to the moment when the last troops were withdrawn in December 2011. US service members worked hard to become attuned to the sounds of mortars, while also being moved, and shaken, and exhilarated by these sounds, and the haptic sensations that accompanied them.

In 2007, a major mortar attack was carried out on Camp Echo in central Iraq. A few dozen of the eighty-one mortars that detonated during the attack were captured on an audio recording that was subsequently posted online.[57] Initially, when the mortars were at some distance, no flight sounds preceded their explosions. Later, when the mortars' trajectories brought them closer to the recorder, the ballistic paths they traced through the air became audible. The mortars' flights created a strangely melodic cooing sound, very close to a sine wave, with a distinct, identifiable pitch that smoothly descended nearly two octaves before ending in detonation. The mortars that detonated closest to the recorder produced additional sounds in flight, such as a pitched buzzing that resembled an airplane's jets, or an additional cooing pitched nearly an octave lower. The recorder captured these sounds, along with the voices of a number of service members who, it appears, had taken shelter in a bunker. Their talk, mostly produced in reaction to the largest explosions, demonstrates the extreme nature of the experience:

[cooing, then explosion] "Everybody OK?" . . .
[cooing, then explosion] "Fuck." . . .
[cooing, then explosion] "Goddamn!" . . .
[cooing, then explosion] "Wow."

Other utterances point to the extent to which the service members, in their windowless bunker, experienced the attack as an auditory event. Unable to see what was going on, they could nonetheless determine whether an unseen mortar had landed on the ground or on a building (e.g., [explosion] "Another hit"); attempt to identify the location of particular explosions (e.g., [explosion] "That sounds like [indecipherable]'s compound"); and calibrate the sounds they were hearing with their memories of past mortar attacks (e.g., [explosion] "That sounded weird").

The sonic particularities of mortars attracted the attention of J.C., a captain in the Army infantry, who described his experience hearing and *not hearing* them in Iraq in 2005:

> Mortar rounds are weird. . . . I've been a hundred yards or further away from a mortar round impacting, and it sounds less like whistling but more like a car that's screeching to a stop and its wheels are skidding. For maybe half a second you hear this *"reeee—boom."* [That's if] the round is far away. All of the close, like, under fifty meters impact—and I don't know if I'm a magnet for mortars or what—but . . . I had one hit, it was about seventeen feet from where I was laying, we were getting hit further away and then one of them just got closer, enough to throw dirt on me and everything, and there was nothing before the explosion. Zero sound. It was awesome, just a big explosion. So then I initially thought, "man, I can't believe I lay down that close to an IED that went off," cause it was along a road, and lo and behold it was just one more mortar.[58]

In contrast to the strangely melodious sound that ballistic mortars can produce while falling to earth, rockets, propelled by hot gases, are accompanied by an extremely loud and invasive barrage of white noise throughout their flight paths. The intense sound of the AT4 shoulder-fired rocket favored by the US military is a case in point. In one instance documented by a military study, a soldier in training who fired an AT4 without donning hearing protection suffered immediate "vertigo, tinnitus, and hearing loss so severe that he had to communicate by writing during the audiometric examination the following day." The soldier's hearing loss was permanent, resulting in his release from active duty.[59]

For those who witness a rocket's flight overhead, the sounds may not immediately deafen, but they are arresting nonetheless. An Army major who served in Baghdad, Haditha, Mosul, and Ramadi on two deployments in 2003 and 2004–5 recalled the disquieting sound of the Russian-made rockets favored by the insurgency:

> One of my most vivid auditory memories is . . . in Amadiya they fired lots and lots of mortars, but they also really liked the 122-millimeter rockets and I distinctly remember the sound of those as being a ripping noise, where it sounded as though,

man it's weird to describe, but it's literally like they're kind of ripping through the sky. . . . I just remember the first time hearing that being such a unique noise and kind of wondering, you know, "what is that?" You clearly knew it wasn't good! [laughter] I mean not really understanding what it was and I'm sure it has to do with the aerodynamics of a rocket versus something that travels ballistically as opposed to under its own power, but yeah, the 122-millimeter rockets were very distinct and you picked up on that very quickly.[60]

A civil servant who lived and worked in the International Zone was similarly struck by the sound of rockets:

The first sounds that I remember being aware of other than just generally noisy things was the sound of . . . rockets going overhead, which was, you know, *vvvvv, vvvvv, vvvvv,* um, flying over fairly low. I didn't ever see them, but you could hear them pretty clearly and [you knew] those were headed toward the palace [where the US Forces in Iraq headquarters was located].[61]

In many situations, one would be unable to "get a visual" on a speeding rocket, and so would base one's speculations purely on the sounds one heard. Even if the telltale "*vvvvv*" of a rocket in flight was inaudible (as when a rocket detonated in the distance without passing overhead, for example), many people claimed to be able to identify it from the distinct sound of its explosion, a "sharp, flat *crack*" that was louder than a mortar, and more acute than the rolling thunderous sound of the IED, the final class of weapons to be discussed in this chapter.

Improvised Explosive Devices

If there was such a thing as a signature weapon of the Iraq War, it would surely be the so-called improvised explosive device, or IED, made from artillery shells, pipes, or other containers, packed with military-grade or homemade explosives, and triggered by inexpensive but often inventive detonators. Insurgents and sectarian fighters deployed tens of thousands of IEDs over the course of the war, hiding them in animal carcasses, burying them beneath roadside rubble, loading them into car trunks (these were called "vehicle-borne IEDs" or "VBIEDs"), and strapping them to suicide bombers. Estimates for the number of IEDs detonated during the war vary significantly, but it appears that roughly half of all US military casualties in Iraq were the result of IED explosions.[62] As with the explosions produced by rockets, the close experience of an IED detonation could be deeply, often paralyzingly, intersensorial: survivors of IED attacks describe the experience as one of visual, auditory, haptic, thermoceptive, and proprioceptive intensity. At a distance, as with other weapons systems, sound predominates. Below, three auditors attempt to describe the distinctive sound of IEDs:

[Auditor #1, a civil servant]:

A mortar or a rocket coming in—the best I can describe it is that it sounds like something is hitting the ground and going up; [whereas if the explosion is] something that is already on the ground [i.e., an IED], it's a different sound *pushing* up. I don't really know how to describe it, but you just know that it wasn't something that came in and landed and exploded, it was on the ground, it's a more earthy tone—I don't know, how would you describe it?[63]

[Auditor #2, another civil servant, a colleague of auditor #1]:

A car bomb is a low loud boom, even if it's far away or it's very close. It's a low-frequency boom and a mortar is a crack, like an airburst crack, and a higher pitch. A rocket is like a much louder version of that, but it's a crack, you know it's a crack [followed by] a "whooooommmm."[64]

[Auditor #3, an Army major who served in Baghdad]:

A mortar . . . it sounds like almost any kind of indirect fire, a howitzer. When it lands there's a [makes two sounds, one short, one long like a double clearing of the throat], it's almost like the blast is somewhat controlled, because it is. You know, it's not going everywhere, its generally going up and so there's like a [makes the same sounds], but with an IED the blast goes everywhere and it goes in all directions, versus generally going up and out. It's going out everywhere and so you can tell where; and there's also, in terms of numbers, I mean cause typically IEDs, we usually would only have one go off at a time, where mortars would be, you know, there would be two or three rounds that they would fire. So, it just sounds different. I was a mortar platoon leader when I was a lieutenant, and so that sound of the mortars, it just sounds very different from these IED blasts that are not necessarily artillery rounds or mortar rounds, but they can be, you know, Semtex, you know, whatever explosive, you know, fertilizer, whatever it is, it just, the makeup really makes the sound distinct.[65]

One other important sonic detail separates IED explosions from the explosions of rockets and mortars: IED explosions are not preceded by the crescendoing sound of a projectile in flight. The nature of the weapon enables the IED attack to occur suddenly, with no warning. People reacted in different ways to the IED's combination of surprise, volume, and physical disruption. Sometimes the reaction was one of shock, with all of its clinical attributes: dizziness, disorientation, nausea. At other times, particularly among the young males who formed the overwhelming majority of the US troop presence in Iraq, the reaction was one of exhilaration. The following is a transcript of the most-watched internet video of an IED attack. Titled "I Get Blown Up!," this amateur video documents the reactions of a four-member marine crew when their Humvee runs over an IED in downtown Ramadi in 2006:[66]

TABLE 1.1

"I Get Blown Up!" [transcript]

Apparent proximity to the recorder

near   far

Scene #
[Time elapsed, min:sec]:

1. [00:00–01:35]
   [*The Humvee drives through the town, the second vehicle in a convoy. Filmed from the rear seat of the vehicle, so that one mostly sees the backs of the driver's and vehicle commander's heads and the lower body of the gunner, who is standing just behind them in a hatch that is open to the air. The crew member who is filming swivels the camera left and right, zooming in and out to try to capture one visual detail and then another. The crew banters calmly. The laboring engine provides the most prominent sound in the recording.*]

2. [01:36–01:39]
   [*The driver accelerates as the Humvee passes a gas station on the left. One of the crew exclaims:*]

                                                    Gas station!

3. [01:40–01:44]
   [*The EXPLOSION occurs, a loud thunderous, rolling boom. It momentarily blackens the screen and creates profound distortion and clipping on the audio track, causing the sound to briefly cut out altogether at one point. When the audio and video resume, the crew is coughing from the smoke and debris that entered the vehicle through the gunner's hatch. The driver continues to maneuver the Humvee down the road, peering through the cracked window as the crew reacts to the attack.*]

4. [01:44–02:04]
   Fuckin' shit!
        Damn!   Everybody good?
                              We're good.
   Aw, shit! [coughs]
              Hey, check yourselves.
              [*And to the gunner, who was semi-exposed when the explosion occurred:*] You good, De Kitko?
              [coughs] Naw.   You alright?
        Holy *shit* I got that on tape!
   [*The vehicle commander exchanges some indecipherable words with a voice on the comm system.*]
              Ha ha!

5. [02:04–02:17]
        Hahahaha!   Fuck yeah!
              [*De Kitko, the gunner:*]
              Ha ha, my ears are ripped!

(continued)

TABLE 1.1 Continued

Oh!		Fuck that!
Oh yeah—that was super!		Oh. . .

6. [02:17–02:25]

   [*The driver pats what may be an image of the Virgin of Guadalupe taped above the windshield, and says:*]   Baby, my baby!

Whoo!	Guadalupe!	Fuck! You alright, De Kitko?

   I'm good.

7. [02:25–02:35]

   Damn!

   [*De Kitko:*]

   I got shit all over me.

   I can't—my ears are fuckin' done!

   It's on tape! Ha ha ha ha! Whoo!

8. [02:35–02:51]

   [*The driver exclaims that he will simply*] keep pushin' before my shit just gives out, motherfuckers!

   [*Out of the kill zone, the Humvee rolls to a halt, and one of the crew members matter-of-factly says:*]

                                   Well, I guess we're done for the day.

For these marines, the IED's explosive sound was no longer an index of violence; having crossed from the realm of the purely sonic into a blend of sound and haptic pulsation, it constituted a violent force in and of itself, one that the poor-quality digital recording cannot begin to replicate. Temporarily deafened by the blast despite the headphones he was wearing, the gunner shouted louder than his fellow crew members. His vocal reaction to the blast ("My ears are ripped!" "I can't [hear?]—my ears are fuckin' done!") illustrates the extent to which this attack constituted an assault on the senses, and on the faculty of hearing specifically. Even in a case where their proximity to the explosion enveloped the crew members in smoke and cracked their windshield with shrapnel, it was the deafening nature of the blast that first warranted comment.

The more troubled reaction of an army captain who served in Iraq from 2005 to 2006 stands in stark contrast to the adrenalin-enhanced euphoria of the marines. In his testimony, the captain recalled the number of IED attacks he endured while serving in the area that soldiers dubbed the Triangle of Death:

There were these three towns. . .they form a triangle: Yusufiya, Latifiya, and Mahmudiya. And the three roads that make three sides of this triangle are just notoriously hit by IEDs. I mean, it's. . .it's. . .some parts of the road are almost impassable due to craters. So all throughout the day, every few hours, somebody hits an IED. And it all was in about a fifteen to twenty kilometer circle. So it's all audible. . . . Even if it's five kilometers away, you can still feel the ground shake. You hear this deep boom, like this: "BOOOOOM!" And after that you go to the radio and sit back and listen, trying to determine if it was a US unit [or] an Iraqi unit [that was hit]. . . So, that sound—a few times a day, we would just, we would hear it, everybody just stopped what they are doing [and would] kind of go to the radio room and just listen [for the report on the explosion's consequences]. Or I'd just pick up a cell phone and call the Iraqi colonel, or if I was with them, I would be like "Hey, get on your radio, and call your checkpoint and let's see if we can figure out who's hurt." So that sound became—if I have any form of PTSD, loud, not percussive noises, but deep booms . . . far away, from construction sites or something like that. . . any time that happens, I don't dodge or hit the floor, but I stop and I'm like "whoo, I wonder who's hurt?" You know, my head just gets that thought instantly.[67]

Combat troops who served in Iraq during the years of peak violence generally have many stories like this to tell, stories in which belliphonic sound creates a sense of exhaustion, anxiety, vulnerability, and dread. Iraqi civilians have remarkably similar stories about the emotions aroused by the sound of IEDs. It needs to be noted that, while many of these explosions were aimed at US troops, many others were specifically intended to wreak havoc on the civilian population; as sectarian violence increased in 2006 and 2007, an alarming number of Iraqi civilians fell victim to improvised explosive devices on roads, along with smaller "sticky bombs" thrown into shops or placed on cars and suits of explosives being carried by suicide bombers. On several occasions, IEDs planted at the sites of funerals killed civilians who had come to mourn friends and relatives who had themselves been killed by IEDs days before. The telltale sound of an IED did not provide auditors with any conclusive information about the identities of its victims. It simply informed those within earshot that the insurgent and/or sectarian forces were still alive and active, and that somewhere in the invisible distance, some number of unsuspecting people were likely dead, or maimed, or traumatized, or deafened.

The growl of the Humvee engine. The *thump-thump-thump* of the approaching helicopter. The drone of the generator. Human voices shouting, crying, asking questions in a foreign tongue. *"Allahu akbar!"*: the call to prayer. *"Down on the ground!"*: the shouted command. The *dadadadadada* of automatic weapon fire. The *shhhhhhhhhhhhh* of the rocket in flight. The *fffft* of the bullet displacing air. The sharp *k-k-k-k-r-boom* of the mortar. The rolling *BOOM* of the IED. These were a small number of the urgent sounds that inscribed themselves into the archive of collective memories of Operation Iraqi Freedom. Sources of tactical information, affective intensity, and physiological and psychological damage, they created formidable challenges for military and civilian auditors throughout the war. Together, they transformed the war zone into a complicated belliphonic mise-en-scène within which the relative position of sound and auditor radically affected the auditor's perception of violent acts. The next chapter seeks to clarify, to the extent possible, the complex dynamics of these perceptual transformations, as sounds and auditors moved back and forth across the war's terrain.

FIGURE 1.3 A US Marine lance corporal covering his ears after throwing a fragmentation grenade into a back room in Fallujah in 2004. (Photo by Scott Peterson/Getty Images)

FIGURE 1.4 An Iraqi girl plugging her ears as a Bradley fighting vehicle carrying members of the US Army 3rd Infantry passes by her Baghdad street in 2005. (Photo by David Furst/AFP/Getty Images)

Things change after our first direct encounter
with small-arms fire. We're back with an artillery
unit, just getting settled, and when we first hear it,
I don't register immediately what it means. *Pop,
pop, pop!* My first thought is: That sounds like
the firing range. Then it clicks in my mind: They
sound like gunshots because they *are* gunshots.
The guys in the artillery unit take cover behind
their vehicles.

—KAYLA WILLIAMS

2

Mapping Zones of Wartime (In)audition

THE DEGREE OF attention people gave to the sounds of weapons was radically
dependent upon a number of factors, the most important of which appears to have
been the proximity of the sound's source. In examining the importance of location to
the perceived salience and character of weapon sounds, we might profitably imagine,
as a heuristic exercise, a striated landscape consisting of a number of roughly concentric zones that surround each auditor (see Figure 2.1). These zones, I hasten to state, are
not part of military or civilian discourse, but represent my attempt to synthesize the
testimonies of service members and civilians regarding their common-sense assumptions about their listening experiences in Iraq. What follows is a description of how
these zones are configured by service members' experiences. Iraqi civilian listening
practices involve a slight reconfiguration of these zones, which I describe at the end of
this chapter.

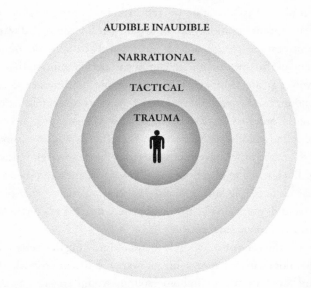

FIGURE 2.1 Concentric Zones of Wartime (In)audition

I. THE AUDIBLE INAUDIBLE

Distant gunfire was such a constant presence during Operation Iraqi Freedom that experienced service members regularly claimed to "no longer hear it." Only green troops new to the theater commented upon the frequent popping sounds of distant weapons. Their more seasoned comrades teased them about their overly acute hearing. In the words of a soldier stationed in a small Forward Operating Base outside Baghdad:

> You hear it so often it becomes background noise. It's different than the IEDs exploding or mortar hitting—you just don't even care about the shooting unless it's sustained or you can tell it's people actually shooting at each other back and forth. That background noise became inaudible to us almost. New units would show up, a visiting team of investigators, or somebody would show up, and they'd be like "Ooh! Didja hear that?" and you're like "What?" and they're like "That shooting!" and, "Oh, yeah, yeah, that's probably, you know, this neighborhood because they always shoot at noon, who knows?"[1]

Distant gunfire became part of what I suggest we call the zone of the *audible inaudible*: a conceptual space that housed sounds so distant and/or ubiquitous that they ceased to draw the attention of the experienced auditor. To locate a sound in the audible inaudible is to say that it was no longer fully "there," no longer available to the auditors whose unconscious or, at most, quasi-conscious alteration of perceptual priorities created the zone in the first place. This alteration or "redistribution of the sensible" occurred over time.[2] Prolonged exposure to the sounds of distant gunfire compelled wartime auditors to develop cognitive filters that separated "meaningful" belliphonic sounds from those that contained no useful information. In contrast to the assumption that "expert listening" always involves greater acuity than "naive listening," auditory expertise in wartime Iraq did not amount to an overall sharpening of the ears but a combination of sharpening and dulling; in order to be effective fighters, service members needed to become inured to some sounds and hyperattuned to others. In this way, over time, experienced auditors came to embody the concept of an acoustic filter: through repeated acts of listening their bodies learned to effectively amplify some sounds and silence others. Their common experience of failing (unconsciously) or refusing (quasi-consciously) to register some sounds *as* sounds points to the distance between hearing as a physiological capability and listening as an intentional act.

We can imagine the zone of the audible inaudible growing in size as auditors became habituated and indoctrinated into a life of wartime listening: with the passage of time, fewer and fewer distant belliphonic sounds would trigger an adrenaline- and cortisol-fueled "fight, flight or freeze" response; with more time, some of these sounds would no longer rise to the level of consciousness. But we can also imagine wartime experience resulting in a gradual deterioration or thinning out of the inner reaches of this zone, as combat sounds previously thought to be meaningless were found to contain useful intelligence. If one learned that the persistent sounds of small arms fire were coming not from an undifferentiated distance but from a particular neighborhood in which a new Forward Operating Base had recently been established—and therefore that the gunfire is not "directionless" or "in the background" but aimed at fellow soldiers whom one knew personally—these sounds could attain an importance that pulled them out of the audible inaudible and into a zone of active attention, even preoccupation. For each of the war's auditors, then, the audible inaudible was in a constant state of flux. The mutable character of the zone didn't prevent it from being a formidable place, however. For those who learned how to *not hear* the distant sounds of the war, the audible inaudible amounted to a portable audiotopia, a tantalizing zone of imagined silence where experienced ears could rest and jangled nerves settle. It was also a badge of honor; nearly all of my interlocutors took great pride in their ability to desensitize themselves to the belliphonic in this way. They regarded it as proof that they were no longer "green" but "battle-hardened."

In some instances, the capacity to tune out gunfire created a kind of perceptual inversion in which sonic absence became more noteworthy than sonic presence. Mary, a civil servant stationed in the International Zone for several years in the middle of the war, recalled the distant noise of the belliphonic becoming "a part of your life until you don't almost hear it anymore, for me. You hear the silence more than you hear the noise."[3] With this statement we encounter another belliphonic paradox, in which persistent noise becomes more peaceful, more "quiet," more unremarkable than silence. In an atmosphere where a sharp drop in background noise was frequently the result of the departure of local bystanders who knew an attack was coming, some silences were considered to be a sinister presence portending immediate "action." Distant gunfire, by contrast, was a sign that the "action" was taking place somewhere else.

Of course, one can easily argue that the tuning-out process I have been describing is hardly unique to wartime; people in all environments develop the ability to ignore sounds that are a constant presence and that don't appear to be freighted with urgent significance. When I first moved to Greenwich Village from suburban Maryland, the late-night sounds of Harley-Davidsons and honking horns and drunken tourists outside my fifth-story window kept me awake and aggravated; I now sleep peacefully through this nightly acoustic invasion of my space. However, the kinds of sounds that I push out of consciousness in my small, peaceful corner of the civilian world generally strike me as being, for lack of a better term, "ethically innocuous": they index behaviors that, while annoying to me, exist within the spectrum of normal, peaceful human activities. (When they don't, my ears tend to perk up.) In wartime, by contrast, the sounds of distant gunfire are connected in a concrete, isomorphic sense to the act of killing. No matter how distant or diffuse, these sounds are evidence that people are shooting and, in all likelihood, being shot. And this shooting is not a mere abstraction or statistic, unmarked in space and time: it is taking place *now*, and *within earshot*. This fact alone raises the stakes of the acts of psychoacoustic erasure that are collected under the term "audible inaudible."

To acknowledge the ubiquity of this moment of nonlistening or *inaudition* is not to condemn people for allowing their zone of the audible inaudible to flourish in wartime, nor is it to ignore the extent to which the cultivation of such a zone is important for staying sane, for staying *alive*. It is merely to note that the zone of the audible inaudible is one of the places where sound, listening, and ethics are most tightly intertwined. In violent timespaces, fluctuations in the audible inaudible are signs that auditors' perceptions of their ethical obligations are similarly in flux. Prolonged exposure to the belliphonic resulted in a reduction of auditors' capacity to register (a) the presence of ongoing violent acts, and (b) the existence of the people who were perpetrating and enduring these acts. Such an acknowledgment or recognition of the Other is, I want to argue, a necessary precondition for the establishment of ethical relations. One must first know that other humans, other subjects, exist—and not just in the abstract but concretely, at this moment, here and now—before one can begin to decide how, or whether, to approach them. The point is not that ethics demand that one leap into action whenever one hears someone in distress; the point is that, if one no longer *recognizes* that moment of distress, the question of choosing how or whether to act is moot.[4] Of course, one could argue that military command structures and communications systems effectively create a radically distributed macro-sensorium, within which individual auditors understand themselves to be responsible for only those acts that take place nearby.[5] From the standpoint of tactics, the US military in Iraq functioned in exactly this way. But in phenomenological terms, the conundrum remains: how can ethical decisions be made if the sustained exposure to violence degrades one's ability to perform the act of recognition that sets the ground conditions for such decisions? The creation and cultivation of the audible inaudible is more than a natural process or survival technique. It is both, but it is also a process that shrinks the field within which ethical calculations take place. And this is one of the subtle ways in which belliphonic sound incrementally dehumanizes its auditors: they must create a zone of the audible inaudible in order to survive, but in doing so they move themselves into an ethically impoverished space, a world of ethical deafness.[6]

"Didja hear that?"
"What?"

2. THE NARRATIONAL ZONE

When gunfire got closer, however, experienced ears perked up; it was in the middle distance that belliphonic auditors began to pay acute attention to the unique sounds and approximate locations of particular weapons. Visual obstruction from buildings and topographical features, along with the small size and high speed of bullets in flight, often rendered it impossible to observe the details of an urban firefight with the eyes. The ears, by contrast, had less trouble determining that shots had been fired. Having learned over time to decode the acousmatic sounds of battle, experienced auditors were able to construct rich and detailed narratives of battles that were fully within earshot but were not, or were only partially, visible. They became, in this situation, virtuosic hermeneuts, cultivating and taking pride in their ability to identify sounds, interpret their significance, and map them onto their knowledge of the neighborhoods from which they emanated. We might thus imagine a second conceptual zone, more proximate than the audible inaudible, a zone in which gunfire was close enough to attract the attention of experienced auditors but still too far away to pose a physical threat. In this *narrational zone,* experienced auditors took note of belliphonic sounds, identified the weapons that likely produced them, located these sounds in space, and used these observations to create a *belliphonic audionarrative*: the story of an unseen battle unfolding before one's ears.

The stories that emerged from within the narrational zone acquired greater accuracy and hermeneutic richness as auditors' combat experience increased. An army captain who served in Iraq in 2003 and 2004 explained that his audionarratives got more detailed as his knowledge of the surrounding neighborhoods, and the different fighting groups in those neighborhoods, grew:

One of the things that we started noticing [after some time in the combat zone] is we could tell if a police station was being hit or if they were shooting at the government building downtown, or if it was at the propane distribution spot, or wherever, based on where the stuff was coming from. Not necessarily whether it was incoming to us, but you could just tell, kind of what part of town, where it was hitting, and it helped us determine which little FOB [forward operating base] or mini-enclave of troops we had to send out [a radio call to] and say, "Hey, what's going on?"[7]

Some gunfire could be differentiated by the distinct report of particular weapons. The M2 50-caliber machine gun was singled out by a number of military auditors as having a "distinctive" or "commanding" sound. In other cases, the identity of a weapon couldn't be based on volume or timbre alone. For example, the AK-74, a popular firearm within the insurgency and sectarian militias, and the U.S. military M4 carbine both use similar rounds (5.45 caliber for the AK, 5.56 caliber for the M4); as a result, the report of a single round of these firearms would sound almost identical, particularly at a distance. However, experienced auditors knew that M4s are designed to fire no more than three-round bursts, and that most service members are trained to fire single shots on the semiautomatic setting.[8] Fighters using the AK-74, by contrast, commonly shot in fully automatic mode. With this knowledge, an experienced auditor could easily discern the one weapon from the other. Two army majors who served in Iraq in the early years of the war described the difference between AK and M4 fire to me:

MAJOR 1: I guess one of the things about it, if you're talking what differentiation there is, [is] the rhythm of the sound. Where if it's like an American firing, usually it's semiautomatic, so even if the guy is firing, you know, pulling [the] trigger insane, it's still, he's still, it's not the same as automatic fire, whereas if it's an AK, like even to this day I don't think I can distinguish between the two, like between an M4 and an AK, cause the M4 is so loud, but the *rhythm* of who is firing is really, that's how I could tell who's shooting and what's going on.

JMD: *Because the insurgents would just hold down the trigger?*

MAJOR 2: Well, usually they would fire automatic. The AKs typically aren't the most accurate and they're not, I mean, you're not dealing with special operators [i.e., snipers or highly trained military personnel—JMD] or anything like that. So, it's just spray, and I guess that was the difference in hearing the sounds. . . . That was how I could tell: it's the rhythm of the sound versus just the sounds [themselves].[9]

The centrality of sound to memories of warfare is partially accounted for by the radical degree to which the identifiable sounds of battles such as these occupied the sustained attention of experienced auditors.

Many of the most detailed audionarratives of the Iraq war were recorded in milblogs—publicly available online journals written by active-duty service members. Accounts of combat action were often published on the same day that an incident occurred, while the authors' impressions were still fresh. I reproduce three at length here that are emblematic of this kind of vivid writing. In each, descriptions of auditory phenomena are given special emphasis. These accounts show how listening to belliphonic sounds within the narrational zone can produce extremely detailed stories of unseen action.

Hearing the Violence, Seeing the Tree

On December 12, 2005, a post appeared on the milblog "One Marine's View" that began with the following description of a typical morning on his base in central Iraq:

It's a nice peaceful morning. *You hear the surrounding city traffic and movement, birds, fresh air and distant 50 cal opening up off base.* I'm finished working out now and I will enjoy the remaining peaceful morning and a cigar. *Fifty cal rings out again off base at a local check point.* I eyeball our humble 4ft Christmas tree which is a representation of this place. Lacking ornaments for the most part, we used bullets, cigars, Marlboro packs and other things we like and hung them on the tree. *(There goes a large explosion detonates off base/IED most likely).* The tree looks like a freaking train wreck but it's our train wreck. Above it a piece of paper size cardboard box flap that reads "Merry Christmas-USMC-Iraq 2005" in permanent marker duct taped to a cami net pole. *Now multiple deep thump explosions off base characteristic of a MK19 grenade launcher. . . . friendly.* Today feels like when you're about to take a test you have been dreading and are nervous about but you know you're ready, you've done other tests just like it and you've done all you can for this one however, you will be relieved when it's over. *More MK 19 impacts. Marines must have some enemy off site and engaging them.* "Surreal." That's the word for this place. As I smoke the nice stoag I scratch my head and listen to the impacts getting closer and think, I need to reshave my head. As my peach fuzz hair is growing on my grape. *The sound of snipers firing on a makeshift range nearby continues as they dial in their weapons. They are practicing long range shots as you can hear the shot then a full second later hear the impact. Dozens of carefully aimed shots perfectly executed as they hone and use their weapons like surgical tools. The MK 19 gunner is talking to us. Not with words but with rounds. Initially fast furious rounds were fired telling us he has the enemy in sight and is engaging to kill. Then a couple sporadic rounds telling us here is some icing for their cake to finish them off and I think I got them all.* I draw a few more puffs of the even burning stoag, it's a good one a (PUNCH) Gran Puro 48 ring. Big beastly cigar. Like many things, size matters.[10]

Beneath the swagger and bravado of this entry, we can see an experienced auditor virtuosically interpreting the belliphonic sounds that surrounded him. New arrivals to the area of operations, confronted by the same sounds, would be ill equipped to tell a story more detailed than "I think we're under attack!" The author, by contrast, wove an extremely detailed audionarrative into the fabric of his observations of his immediate surroundings. In so doing, he demonstrated how rich and generative the narrational zone can be for ears attuned to the belliphonic's semiotic potential. For him, the sounds of unseen action took on some of the immediacy and specificity of spoken utterances. ("The gunner is talking to us. Not with words but with rounds.") At the same time, he captured one of the core dynamics of intersensoriality: the way in which our different sense organs provide us simultaneous access to disparate environments, tethering us to multiple actions and places at once. At the moment that I type these words, for example, I am looking at my keyboard, hearing the traffic outside my window, and smelling the scent of pot roast wafting into the living room where I sit; my senses furnish me with clues as to the dimensions of three separate events (typing, driving, cooking) in three distinct locales (living room, street, kitchen). This is our universal condition, although it is surprising how infrequently theorists of the senses grapple with it.[11] The condition amounts to intersensoriality *as* phenomenology: in life, the senses apprehend multiple events that are unfolding variously, at different speeds in different spaces. These events are often separated by space and by the independent causal chains in which they are enmeshed. This condition is exacerbated in war zones, where the extreme loudness of the belliphonic can draw one's attention to events taking place miles away, *and* where the violent nature of these events often sharpens the disjuncture between what we see and what we hear. Seldom is the contrast between the heard and the seen more acute than it is for a person whose ears witness an explosion while his eyes contemplate a Christmas tree.

Conjectures and Assurances

The narrational zone was the place where sounds were crafted into stories. Some of these sounds—such as the report of the C-RAM, a weapons system with no analogue on the other side—were instantly recognizable and unequivocal; most were less so. Experienced auditors made educated guesses, stringing them together into narratives whose plausibility was commonly evaluated by their coauditors—those who are also listening. In this second milblog post, the author of "One Marine's View" attempts to piece together the details of a complicated action taking place outside his living quarters in 2005:

Silent, dark. . . . . . . a bit chilly, then the most annoying sound you can imagine blaring in my ear. The alarm clock! Strategically, I smack it down but its china made plastic makes it durable as only for it to roll under my rack and continue to blare its annoying noise. I get moving stand up. . . . . Crump! A single mortar round impacts close enough to rattle my hooch, with the glass rattling. Silence . . . . maybe it was a single round as they like to shoot and scoot and I'm counting seconds to my self to measure flight time, one thousand one one thousand two. Perhaps it was a single . . . . . . Crump, Crump two more impacts hit. Freaking great we are being bracketed. Sound of friendly fast movers gets louder as counter artillery responds and wakes everyone up that may still be asleep. Crump, crump, crump, more impacts, GRAND! They are firing for affect but not hitting a damn thing because they hear the jets and aren't firing accurately because they are trying to run away (typical). Small arms fire erupts off in the distance. Possibly eyes on the mortarmen. Distinct AK and RPK Russian machine gun is heard. Thumping American 50 caliber is answering back. Now two 50 Cals begin their supportive firing suppression. A distant explosion of an IED is heard as US troops are obviously in pursuit of the insurgents and they try to kill us with left behind IEDs. Jets still swarming up above. 50 cal is sporadic now, no more foreign machine gun fire is heard. Most likely eliminated. I go outside to evaluate the nearby gunfight and see a great sunrise, it's amazing how this place can be so attractive yet so dangerous.[12]

Here, the audionarrative, while extremely detailed, is expressed in language that points to the indeterminacy of many of the sounds that penetrate walls of the author's quarters. Even the most experienced auditors battled with opacity and confusion when trying to decode the sounds of complicated combat action; in this post, the variable difficulties were expressed through a spectrum of speculative terms. The author's interpretations ranged from tentative ("maybe," "perhaps," "possibly") to more assured ("most likely," "typical") to unequivocal ("obviously," "we are being bracketed," "American 50 caliber is answering back"). The story that emerged highlighted both the informational richness of the belliphonic in the narrational zone *and* placed a limit on that richness, a limit that the faculty of sight yearned to fill ("I go outside to evaluate the nearby gunfight . . .").

The Attenuating Sensorium

In addition to relying on ambient belliphonic sounds, military auditors drew extensively on information gleaned from comm systems as they constructed their audionarratives of violent events. Military regulations and informal practices alike demanded that earwitnesses get on the radio and communicate with their comrades in the immediate aftermath of an attack. On August 5, 2005, the author of the milblog "A Day In Iraq" recorded his impressions of an IED attack on his convoy. His account stresses the centrality of radio exchanges with unseen coauditors, adding an important technological dimension to the narrational zone. It also describes a situation in which intent listening,

listening for news of the condition of one's comrades, swallows up the intersensorial world and distorts one's temporal apprehension of it:

> During bad or uncertain times, time itself doesn't stand still or slow down, it's more like it spreads out, like each minute has its own personality and some of those personalities really want you to get to know them. That happened with me today, probably with a few of us.
>
> We were out in the city, the filth evident in the open sewage flowing into the streets, creating small puddles and ponds of shit water. Trash, wet decaying trash, with vehicle parts thrown in, form little islands in these puddles. It's not uncommon to see dogs, cats, and even cattle feasting on these piles of filth and lapping up the black liquid surrounding them. It was just another hot day in the cradle of this uncivilized world. A couple of trucks full of Iraqi soldiers were with us as well, putting a local face on this global war. We'd been out about three hours with no contact, a somewhat noteworthy achievement given the experiences of the past week or so.
>
> After sitting in one place for a while, letting the IA [Iraqi army] soldiers search the area and pass out some leaflets, we began to move again. The Humvee I was gunning in brought up the rear, with me facing our six, looking back over the area from which we came. I was busy moving around in my seat, looking left and right and to our rear, smelling the black shit water and trash, scanning windows and rooftops, trying to consume as much water as the amount that was quickly leaving my body, and BOOM!
>
> The sound of the explosion doesn't affect me so much as the thought of what produced it. It was another IED, and a cloud of smoke and dust began rising over some buildings around the corner.
>
> I immediately realized that some of our Humvees were around that corner, the same corner from which the smoke cloud now floated over like some evil spirit. That's when time started spreading out, forcing me to come to know it intimately. I needed a ticket for the train that would take me to the next station, the next minute, to get back to the present that was leaving me behind. The radio became my ticket.
>
> "Red 3, this is Red 4 over" "This is Red 3" "Is everyone okay?" Short pause, "Roger, it was in front of us, over" I knew there was another Humvee in front of Red 3. Our platoon sergeant called over the radio again, "Red 2, this is Red 4, is everyone okay?" Silence. I've now stopped chewing my gum. Silence. Silence. "Red 2, this is Red 4, is everyone okay?" Silence. I do a mental list of who all was in that Humvee. Sgt. B, Ray, Farrell, Rob, and Hogan. Ray is going home on leave soon to see his wife. They're going on a cruise somewhere in the Caribbean. Silence. Before we left, Rob and I were acting like we were getting pumped up by the loud music coming from someone's computer. It was AC/DC, and everyone

in our room was mockingly throwing fists in the air like we were about to run out onto the field before the biggest game of our life. Someone joked that the terrorists were probably listening to some music as well, preparing themselves to meet us on the battlefield. Silence. This minute is spreading thin. I borrowed a movie from Hogan the other day and need to return it. Silence. Farrell couldn't stop smiling the other day after getting a letter from a girl back home. Silence. Sgt. B has a son that looks just like him.

I'm now looking down at the radio as if looking at it will make them answer. Answer the damn radio. Out of the corner of my eye I can see little beads of sweat running down the cheek of Sgt. P. "Red 2, this is Red 4, is everyone okay?" Still staring at the radio, the run down, slum-like buildings, trash, car parts, car frames, cats, dogs, goats, people, shit smell, sewage puddles, heat, and the sun no longer exist, only this green radio that looks like a brick.

In his high pitched, one of a kind, can only be Sgt. B voice, Sgt. B brings the little brick to life. "This is Red 2, roger, we're fine, the IA truck took most of the blast!" My train has safely reached the next station and I'm reunited with the present. I turn away from the radio and continue looking back to our rear, my mouth again chewing the spearmint gum. I became aware of the hot sun, the shit smell, and the feasting felines lapping up sewage water.

The radio speaks again, but I barely hear it, something about a medevac for some of the IA soldiers. I later felt bad for my relief in knowing that it wasn't any of our guys that got hurt. It's not that I don't care about the Iraqi soldiers, I do, but they aren't family. Three or four of them got loaded on the back of the meat wagon, and our Humvee and another escorted them back to our outpost. Able to stand up now that we were back in a safe area, with no threat of snipers, I could see the wounded getting out of the back of the truck. The most serious, the one with a bandage over his head, got off the truck without any help and walked inside with the others. All of them are walking wounded, and I again feel relieved, just not as relieved as I did before. The fact that no one was seriously injured is no mystery to me. I attribute it to God's presence and protection, even on these shitty streets.[13]

The author of "A Day in Iraq" described the everyday experience of his urban patrol in emphatically intersensorial terms: sights, smells, and heat combined with the sounds of urban life to create a synesthetic swirl of impressions of the neighborhood. But the unseen and unexpected "BOOM" of the IED thrust the author into a kind of sensory funnel, in which the full spectrum of stimuli that preoccupied him a moment before attenuated, leaving only those that mattered—the sound of the detonation and the sight of the smoke cloud—in the perceptual foreground. The author mapped his auditory experience of the detonation onto the location of the smoke cloud and his knowledge of the convoy's personnel, creating a terrifying hypothetical narrative of the unseen event, a narrative in which his comrades were injured or dead. Seeking to refute this story, the author then went further down the funnel, redirecting all of his attention to the radio in his truck. Everything else—"the run down, slum-like buildings, trash, car parts, car frames, cats, dogs, goats, people, shit smell, sewage puddles, heat, and the sun"—was bracketed out in the prolonged period of suspense that preceded the news that his comrades were uninjured. With this news, time resumed its habitual pace, and the sensory funnel reversed itself, letting in the sights, smells, and temperatures that constituted the author's normal, everyday experience.

If the characteristics of the zone of the audible inaudible are such that they prevent the (in)auditor from acknowledging—and therefore entering into ethical relations with—people who are in harm's way, then the narrational zone is its affective and ethical opposite. Within its confines, belliphonic sounds are meticulously, ferociously analyzed and mined for information—information about the identity of unseen others and the nature of the violent events they are experiencing.

What auditors do once they have identified these events and their victims and perpetrators is another matter entirely, however. The author of "A Day in Iraq" expressed guilt for his initial feeling of "relief" upon learning "that it wasn't any of *our* guys that got hurt." Indeed, in talking to people who have spent protracted amounts of time in the combat zone, I have been struck by the frequency with which they speak of a kind of emotional roller coaster: initial surprise at the sound of an attack in the middle distance is often followed by a chain of reactions including (1) fear that the violence is moving closer, (2) relief when this turns out not to be the case, (3) guilt for feeling relief that one's distant comrades may be undergoing an attack, (4) despair if sonic evidence confirms that this is the case, elation if one's enemies turn out to be the targets, and, occasionally (5) guilt for feeling elation at a violent death, regardless of the affiliation of the victim. All of this commonly occurs within the space of the narrational zone, where sounds serve as building blocks for stories that are freighted with emotional and ethical significance.

Just as we found analogues to the audible inaudible within peacetime civilian life, we can easily draw lines connecting our own capacity to create audionarratives with the acts of interpretation that take place within the wartime narrational zone. I am now in my office in the NYU music department, and I know with utter certainty that my colleague Mike Beckerman is in his office, with which I share a wall. He—and it could only be he—is banging out a raucous, jazz-inflected piece by the Czech composer Jaroslav Ježek; his muffled voice tells me that there is someone else in the office to whom he is explaining Ježek's charms. A chorus of shouts from beyond my office window tells me that a crowd has gathered across the street to watch the UEFA Cup match through the large window of Murphy & Gonzales, the Irish-Mexican pub on the corner. And so on, and so on: hearing people are all virtuosic creators of audionarratives within their home terrain.

The difference between my act of interpretation and those of wartime auditors in Iraq is twofold. First, the high stakes of belliphonic listening regularly compelled auditors to listen with an adrenalin-infused concentration that is not nearly as widespread in peacetime life. As a result, conversations about weapon sounds during Operation Iraqi Freedom had a ubiquity and intensity that are seldom matched by people who are not confronted with the sonic evidence of extreme violence. People in Iraq listened to the belliphonic as if their lives depended upon it. At times, this was indeed the case.

The second characteristic that distinguishes wartime audition has to do with the fact that listening is simultaneously safer and less avoidable than looking. As I mentioned earlier, looking at an unfolding combat scene involves risking being seen, whereas listening poses no such inherent risk. In Iraq, people in bunkers and trailers and other buildings often listened to attacks without being able to see them. Service members in combat situations looked as much as they could, but they commonly did so quickly, furtively, taking cover between glances around the corner of a building, peeking up from behind a barrier and then ducking back behind it. This practice of intense but constricted looking was drilled into them by military training. During and between these fraught acts of looking, however, they were constantly listening.

Perhaps this is why listening is so central to memories of wartime: people were always listening, even when it was too dangerous to look. Throughout most of the narrational zone, however, the action was far enough away that one didn't need to worry about the exposure and vulnerability that looking affords. Listening trumped looking only when the firefight was so close that being hit was a real possibility—and this possibility placed considerable constraints on the stories people told themselves about unseen action. At the inner reaches of the narrational zone, then, we need to sketch in another striation, one in which narrative, while still present, is severely affected by the proximity of bullets.

3. THE TACTICAL ZONE

The sounds of weapons took on a much greater urgency when they signaled the imminent presence of projectiles or shrapnel in the spaces where service members found themselves. When gunfire was nearby, the richness and detail of the audionarrative collapsed into the briefest tactical assessment: run *this* way; shoot in *that* direction. Close in, in what I'll call the "tactical zone," listeners trained their skills of echolocation to determine the proximity of explosions, the trajectory of bullets, and the locations of shooters. As an air force major who served in Iraq in 2006 described it:

> Beneath the engine sounds, transmission sounds, road noise, static over the radio . . . and ambient noises [over microphones] . . . everybody is very much in tune, listening for gunfire or rocket fire—and we had incidents of people firing rockets or mortars at us, and it was very much like the movies, cause you'd hear the whistling sound that goes by you and the first thing that pops in your mind is "Oh

my god, somebody's shooting at us!" Secondly you say, "Ooh, I heard the whistling sound, and that means they missed, and it already went by us," and the third thing is "OK, where is that clown that just shot at me?"[14]

In 2006, a Sergeant stationed in Baghdad wrote a milblog post describing an attack he had survived earlier that day. In it, the sonic dimension predominates, the assessment was brief and to the point, and the reaction to the belliphonic was instantaneous:

No sooner had [my Platoon Sergeant] finished yelling at me, than there was an almighty BOOOOOOM, immediately behind us, followed by a deep, basal WHHHHOOOOOOOOSSSHHHHH, right over our heads. Clearly we were under attack, it was close, and more was coming in on top of us. I did the usual crazed-dog-chasing-his-tail 360, located the nearest bunker, and took off for it, leaving a dust trail behind me while simultaneously yelling for my soldiers to follow me. Later SFC Y. commented, "If I could get you to run that fast on a Physical Fitness Test, you would have one of the best scores in the company." I was convinced that the rushing noise of the round overhead meant that it was coming straight for us, and, in fact, there were a series of deep WHUMMP-WHUMMP-WHUMMP explosions nearby, fortunately heard by us from inside the dark, fetid safety of the bunker.[15]

The urgency of the assessment here is the distinguishing factor of the tactical zone, as are the existential stakes for auditors. A misinterpretation of belliphonic sounds in the narrational zone would result in an inaccurate story; a misinterpretation in the tactical zone could result in immediate bodily harm, death of the auditor, or death of an innocent the auditor mistakenly targeted. In the combat environment, many auditors gradually developed the ability to forestall panic, which enabled them to act quickly and rationally on the sounds they heard.

Listening to Incoming

Unlike the sensory vortex of gun battles, which demanded immediate action on the part of the combat service member, mortar and rocket attacks on bases placed most of the base population in a reactive stance: the entire base population was on the receiving end of these attacks, while only a very small subset of troops were charged with returning fire. On large bases such as Baghdad's Camp Victory, it would be possible to miss the sound of a mortar impact on the opposite side of camp amid the white noise of generators and traffic. But on smaller bases, mortar and rocket attacks were absolutely synchronizing moments, where the entire population was transfixed by the sounds of incoming rounds. In some instances, sustained experience with the sounds of mortar rounds and the chorus of alarms and warning messages that accompanied them led to a kind of fatalism, where military regulations to don body armor or run to a bunker were ignored by experienced auditors unless the attack appeared to present a clear and imminent danger. The degree of danger was determined almost exclusively by listening.

The following conversation among army majors at West Point who had recently returned from deployments to Iraq is emblematic of the jaded attitude of seasoned troops who had learned how to determine when an attack was truly dangerous:

KEVIN: I thought we had developed a pretty good sense of, "that's far away, we've got some time to get to the bunker," or, "we better hurry up." It got to the point where, for us it was [in a disinterested voice:] "oh, there's incoming [mortars]."

MARK: Yeah, we didn't even do [i.e., report to] bunkers.

KEVIN: We stopped doing bunker drills. It was like, "OK, here it comes, hope it doesn't land on me this time."

MARK: Yeah, we didn't even have them [bunker drills].

KEVIN: We became very nihilistic.

MARK: I mean I can remember specifically standing outside of our, having a conversation with my boss outside of our TOC [tactical operations center], hearing the ripping noise and just not doing anything and then, I wish I could recall for you what auditory trigger it was that said, "that's coming right at us"—

KEVIN: You knew.

MARK: —And we jumped inside and literally the thing landed like 15 feet from where we were standing. Fortunately, we went into a semi-, one of those hurricane shelter types, semi-concrete building, but, yeah, I can't remember what triggered it, but you just knew. Maybe it was just volume.

KEVIN: "This one sounds different, and I haven't heard this before. I'm not dead yet, so it probably can't be good." You go into deductive logic really quick.

MARK: We continued to have a conversation and then realized, you know, "oh, OK."

KEVIN: "This sounds different to me and I haven't heard it before. I'm not hurt yet, so it's something different."

MARK: You can definitely tell, I don't know about you guys, but I think with mortars, with mortars it was much easier to tell distance because, with the rocket you didn't get the feedback of the launch, so the rocket, I don't generally remember hearing the launch of a rocket. Whereas a mortar, you get that real muffled "thum" noise [when they are launched], and so that, you could hear that and you knew, that was feedback: "OK, it's far away, it's close, you know, we've got time, we don't have time" kind of a thing. I distinctly remember with mortars, kind of being able to judge that. With rockets it seemed like maybe that was part of the scary part of that too, it was that rockets you didn't hear until they were literally kind of, whatever it was, halfway there kind of a thing.[16]

Sometimes this training worked. At other times it was overwhelmed by the intensity of the sensory barrage, allowing panic and confusion to dominate.

The Fog of War

In close combat, this jaded attitude was one auditors could scarce afford. In situations where sounds and projectiles overlapped in the immediate space surrounding them, the overwhelming consideration was for self-preservation. When bullets whizzed by them, service members did their best to suppress panic in the face of the "phiff" or "zing" or "phip" or "ffff" of nearby projectiles and figure out, through a combination of listening and looking, what they needed to do in order to protect themselves, and, secondarily, where they should aim to kill the shooters. These decisions had to be made instantaneously, and service members made them while being bombarded by a host of new visual and acoustic stimuli informing them that more shots were being fired, that one of their comrades had been killed, that civilians had been wounded, that support was arriving, or that a retreat had been called. In a firefight, many things clamored for service members' attention, and this noisily dangerous environment posed a major challenge to anyone trying to make a calm, measured decision. Service members who found themselves in these situations often talked about their experiences in terms of sensory overload. A battalion commander who served in Baghdad and Diwaniya in 2006 and 2007 described the chaotic environment in which troops encountered close fire:

> One of the things about sounds on the battlefield is that sounds oftentimes create more confusion than they do clarity, and the problem is, particularly leaders, they're listening to multiple things at once. You've got all of these ambient noises that are going on; conversations on the street, generators, cars honking, any day-to-day activities. If you're on a vehicle and you're plugged in to our vehicle radios, I mean, in my situation I was listening to TacSat,[17] two nets, two radio frequencies, and my crew, because you have to tell the driver to turn left, turn right, stop and someone is giving a spot report. So, you're trying to sort out between four or five conversations. Then you've got, maybe you're linked in to an Apache [helicopter], trying to call an Apache, so linked in through and trying to listen to what's important and disregarding what's not important is one of the biggest challenges with sound. .... I mean, at the same time you're taking in all of this stuff visually, with other senses, whatever may be going on. But, from the perspective of managing sound on the battlefield, the hard part was trying to differentiate between what was important and what was not.[18]

Military training, informal conversations, and the accumulation of combat experience were all brought to bear on these moments saturated with aural and other stimuli. But when the sounds of armed attack were added to this mix of urban ambience, white noise, and military communication, service members were often pushed beyond their abilities to maintain what the military calls "situational awareness." Several "friendly fire" incidents can be traced back to the sensory, and specifically auditory, confusion that is a common feature of the tactical zone. Among them is this report of a 2005 action that hinged on an act of mishearing:

> When a unit from the 502nd Infantry Regiment came under small arms fire in Baghdad on 4 November 2005 they assumed they were being attacked by the enemy. Five men were injured and another, Staff Sergeant Joseph Fegler, 24, was killed. Two hours after the engagement it emerged that the damage had been done by the rear gunner of another US convoy up ahead. *The first shots the victims heard had been warning shots fired to get them to keep their distance.*[19]

Stories of fatal misprision such as this are common, and are generally understood to be inevitable. No amount of training, no new auditory technology, no single set of human ears can create conditions of absolute clarity within the noisy chaos of battle. The decisions military auditors made in Iraq were often imperfect—sometimes fatally so. Sound in the tactical zone was a valuable resource, but amid the fog of war it often proved an inadequate one.

4. THE TRAUMA ZONE

In the tactical zone, people listened with their ears—but also with their skin, their chest cavities, the hair on the back of their necks, their viscera. The loud sounds of weaponry regularly bled into the realm of the haptic when they were this close up. When they were even closer, and even louder, these sounds lost their capacity to serve as a resource, a text to be interpreted, an illuminating index of a nearby violent act; at the closest distances, the loudest sounds assaulted bodies, and they often did so before any tactical judgment or meaningful interpretation could possibly be made. We thus need to distinguish one more zone, even more proximate than the zone where sound acquires immediate tactical significance, the space in which belliphonic sounds produce physiological damage—the trauma zone.

The physical injuries created by the loud sounds of weapons begin with tinnitus and hearing loss. Department of Defense regulations stipulate that all service members in the field wear in-ear hearing protection if they are exposed to continuous sound levels of 85 decibels and/or impulse sounds of more than 140 decibels.[20] Given that an up-armored Humvee can produce as much as 95 decibels of background noise, a burst from a 50-caliber machine gun is 160 decibels at fifty feet, and an IED, the most common weapon used in Iraq, could be literally deafening, most of the service members patrolling Baghdad and other cities fell under these regulations. While army audiologists claim that the current military-grade earplugs do not significantly impair one's ability to hear soft sounds, and in some cases actually enhance this ability, none of the combat service members I met wore them consistently, fully inserted in both ears, when conducting foot patrols.[21] They preferred to risk their ears in order to *feel* unencumbered as they tried to discern the subtle sounds of bullets, footsteps, and distant voices that surrounded them. Their stories all deal with deviation from the regulations, not out of laziness but out of a desire to maintain auditory vigilance:

[Auditor #1]

On dismounted patrols if I wore an earplug I'd usually wear it in my right ear because that's where my rifle, if I'm shooting, is right closest to, but . . . as company commander I did not enforce that rule because I felt that my soldiers' ability to hear things when walking through fields or along canals or down city streets is more important than the possibility of hearing loss. You know, it's better to have some hearing loss than get shot and not have a chance to react.

[Auditor #2]

There were some times that I would take one earplug out because I was having difficulty listening to the radios and we would have something [e.g., an IED] go off, and I'd get a good ringing in my ear. We had some guys, their vehicles got directly hit, and even with the earplugs they would hear ringing for quite a while. A lot of the army guys, they wouldn't wear hearing protection when they were out maneuvering on foot, so if they were close to an IED they could have some permanent damage to their ears. They could also get damage from just shooting their guns without hearing protection and that's an occupational hazard.

[Auditor #3]

This is always one of those hilarious things. The standing order for the 101st Division, which, you know that's 20,000 guys, is earplugs on all missions. And inside the trucks I'd usually wear at least one, just cause it's just noisy, and getting hit by an IED is—that's the only thing that's gonna save your ear. Gunfire right next to you when you're outside—it's one thing to have a shot or two within a couple of feet of your head, but I'd run over to where an Iraqi soldier is, you know, trying to hit somebody, and he just wails off with fifty shots on a machine gun, you know, feet from your head, and you're just instantly deafened for a few hours. It was the ringing. And then if someone's saying something to you and you can't see them, you might not realize that they're talking to you. You could still hear sounds but . . . your ability to hear clearly was reduced.[22]

This Odyssean bargain—trading ear protection for the unfettered ability to hear one's surroundings—surely accounts, at least in part, for the fact that tinnitus and hearing loss were the most common injuries among service members who served in Iraq.

At very close distances, the loudest belliphonic sounds overpowered even the most robust military-grade earplugs.[23] According to a 2005 study conducted by the *American Journal of Audiology*, soldiers deployed to Iraq between April 2003 and March 2004 were more than ten times more likely to suffer noise-induced hearing loss than soldiers who didn't deploy, with over 15 percent of soldiers sampled reporting ringing in the ears.[24] More recent studies confirm the link between exposure to action in Iraq and noise-induced hearing injuries.[25] In fact, tinnitus and hearing loss have been a problem throughout the era of modern combat. The US military's statistics as of 2011 indicated that 745,000 veterans (of all wars) are receiving compensation for tinnitus, more than for any other war-related injury. As always, hearing loss occupies the second place, with 672,000 veterans receiving aid.[26] For members of the Iraqi army, who have little to no hearing protection, fire significantly louder Russian-made weapons, and have been victim to as many if not more IED attacks, the rate of hearing loss is likely greater than that of their American and coalition comrades. Lastly, while no statistics exist, civilians, although generally more distant from the sound of gunfire, surely are physically affected by the militarized noise in the city.[27]

Service members suffer hearing loss from repeated exposure to the sounds of their own weapons. (This well-documented phenomenon, known colloquially as "shooter's ear," has decreased somewhat over the course of the twentieth century as American weapons have become quieter and effective hearing protection on firing ranges has become common.) But the most serious cases of hearing loss, involving punctured eardrums and the risk of permanent deafness, involve exposure to IEDs and exploding ordnance. Those who survived the nearby explosion of an IED were often left with permanent damage to their hearing, on top of the more visible injuries they may have sustained. An Associated Press story from 2005 captured this problem:

> For former Staff Sgt. Ryan Kelly, 27, of Austin, Texas, the noise of war is still with him more than four years after the simultaneous explosion of three roadside bombs near Baghdad.
> "It's funny, you know. When it happened, I didn't feel my leg gone. What I remember was my ears ringing," said Kelly, whose leg was blown off below the knee in 2003. Today, his leg has been replaced with a prosthetic, but his ears are still ringing. "It is constantly there," he said [of the tinnitus—JMD]. "It constantly reminds me of getting hit. I don't want to sit here and think about getting blown up all the time. But that's what it does."[28]

At the heart of the zone of physical trauma, when one is exposed to a nearby detonation of an IED or other explosive device, the distinction between the sound of the explosion and its destructive force breaks down completely. The detonation of an IED generates an irregular, supersonic blast wave of compressed air that, at a distance, slows down and regularizes into a configuration that we perceive as sound. For those nearby, however,

TABLE 2.1

Zones of Wartime (In)audition and Ethics

Zone	Audible Events	Listening Stance	Ethical Possibilities
"audible inaudible"	distant gunfire	inaudition	ethical vacuum
"narrational"	unseen combat in the middle distance	hermeneutic listening, auscultation	ethical thought is possible
"tactical"	nearby combat	constrained hermeneutic listening	ethical thought is possible
"trauma"	nearby sounds that incapacitate	inaudition, exposure	ethical vacuum

this very wave of acoustic energy is experienced as physical force. While medical studies are not yet conclusive, a growing body of evidence suggests that this wave of atmospheric pressure is one of the leading causes of traumatic brain injury or TBI, the signature injury for the ongoing conflict.[29] The lasting damage to the brain caused by a blast wave that, with distance, degenerates into an audible explosion can in this sense be understood as a sound-related wound. It is here that the contention of music scholars such as Suzanne Cusick and Jenny Johnson—that the aural and the haptic are often experienced in a synesthetic fusion that can be both viscerally thrilling and deeply traumatizing—is given its most frighteningly literal dimension.[30] Overwhelmed by the immediacy and materiality of *sounds which cannot yet be heard*, of waves of pressure that act violently on passive bodies, auditors became inauditors once again: the waves constituted them as victims before the victims could constitute themselves as listeners. In this situation, as in the zone of the audible inaudible, the minimum conditions necessary for ethical calculations to take place failed to obtain. Knocked unconscious, deafened, concussed, and otherwise damaged by explosive sound, *traumatic inauditors* were rendered, if only temporarily, incapable of meaningful thought or action. (Table 2.1 elaborates on these points.)

A COMPLICATING FACTOR: IRAQI CIVILIAN AUDITORS

I began thinking about concentric zones of wartime audition in conversation with military service members, largely before I began speaking with Iraqi civilians in 2008; consequently, I have used military experiences to structure and illustrate the four zones of audition above. Iraqi civilians adjusted their listening stances as well, of course, and they did so, I was to discover, in ways that were roughly commensurate with the zones I outlined above. My Iraqi interlocutors spoke with some pride of their ability to filter out the sounds of distant gunfire, creating a haven of inaudition within the audible evidence of war. And, like their counterparts in the US military, they placed great stock in their ability to distinguish one weapon or vehicle from another. In a narrational zone that was commonly anchored by a lifetime of experiences in the same neighborhood, the Iraqis I spoke with had become masterful at crafting accounts of violent events that happened, repeatedly, within earshot of their homes. Basma, a young woman who lived in Baghdad until 2006, recalled how her quiet, out-of-the-way street became a site of repeated carjacking in 2004:

> For a while it was so common that taxicabs get stolen. So probably the thieves and all of those people just take the cab and they tell [the driver] to go to that street which is easier for them to run away and they just tell him to stop with a gun and they shoot him in his leg so he can't . . . they don't usually kill them. Some [drivers] get killed—it depends on if they fight, for not giving up the car. So because my house was on the corner, we always heard the gunshots, and we knew directly that someone got shot, a taxicab outside. That was for a while in 2004 and 5. That was so common. We had a lot of [cab drivers] to take to the hospital. . . . We heard that—we knew the gunshots and that it's not in the air, and it usually came at a quiet time in the afternoon, like 3:00 or 4:00. It was very common, it was so common in my area.[31]

On multiple occasions, after hearing these telltale sounds and waiting for the requisite silence that indicated the carjackers had left the scene, Basma and her family would rescue the wounded drivers and take them to a nearby hospital.

Arakel, who also lived in Baghdad until 2006, painted an even darker scenario, explaining that in his neighborhood, sectarian fighters targeted the Iraqi intelligentsia—not for their cars, but in order to execute them. This was a common enough occurrence that he knew what to listen for:

> When you hear loud gunshots and then tires being smoked [i.e., screeching], there's something wrong going on: somebody got killed. Ninety-nine percent of the time if you hear "taf-taf," and then "eeeee," smoked tires, somebody got shot, because that's the way it is, hit and run. . . . By default, if you hear two gunshots and smoke, a doctor, a lawyer, an engineer, or a previous Saddam loyalist got killed.[32]

Unlike combat troops, whose mission was to engage in fighting, civilians rarely sought to place themselves in what I have called "the tactical zone" of belliphonic audition. Instead, they spent long stretches of time confined to their houses, seeking the protection that their walls could provide them from the violent action outside. Deprived of visual cues or the detailed intelligence that radio communications provided of ongoing action, they were captive audiences to the "symphony of bullets" that Adel mentioned in the *Hometown Baghdad* segment: the overwhelming majority of their witnessing took place with their ears and not their eyes. In this sense, the narrational zone of audition was even more acutely demarcated and experienced for them than it was for their counterparts in the military, whose duties regularly (albeit erratically and furtively) placed them in the sight line of violent acts.

While civilians may not have actively sought positions within the tactical zone, the threat of being swept up into an attack or gun battle was ever-present whenever they left their homes. Unarmed (or at most lightly armed), without body armor or armored vehicles or air support, Iraqis nonetheless left their homes and entered public spaces to go to work and school, to go shopping, and to tend to family and other social obligations. Within this sphere they were vulnerable, and the sense of vulnerability encouraged a stance of hypervigilance that itself bred anxiety, exhaustion, and its own kind of fatalism. Tareq and Ammar spoke about this feeling of vulnerability and stress:

> TAREQ: I feel, after these four years, that I'm not secure. . . . It is a painful feeling when you leave your home [in the morning] and you don't know if you will come back alive or not, it is not an easy thing, especially to a civilian. Because I am a civilian, not a soldier. [If I were a soldier] it is my job to go and fight, and maybe I die, I know that, but I am a civilian. It's a bad thing when you go outside your home to go your college or work or to meet a friend and you don't know if you will come back to your home alive or not. It's so painful a feeling and—[his friend Ammar interjects]
>
> AMMAR: If you surrender to the idea of getting killed, sometimes you start thinking, how am I going to die? Is it by a roadside bomb, is it by AK bullet, is it by a US bullet, is it by Iraqi army bullet, is it by thieves on the road? . . .
>
> TAREQ: [And then you think, I might die here] but I wish if I die, I hope my body will still be intact so my family can still recognize me in the medical forensic department.[33]

My Iraqi civilian interlocutors occasionally encountered loud belliphonic violence firsthand. One spoke of being temporarily deafened by a car bomb that detonated 150 feet away from him. Another found his ears ringing when a soldier in an Iraqi army vehicle next to his car fired off several rounds of its machine gun to clear an intersection. While their status as civilian bystanders allowed them to avoid combat situations whenever possible—and thus minimize their involvement in tactical and trauma zones—we know that hundreds of thousands of Iraqis were exposed to gunfire, mortar fire, car bombs, and ambulatory suicide bombers. By the most conservative mainstream account, over one hundred thousand died in this kind of violence. Belliphonic sounds reached out and pulled exponentially more civilians into stances of tactical and traumatic audition.

There are of course profound cultural differences that separate Iraqi civilians from American service members. But as I mentioned earlier, there is no evidence that "culture," conventionally framed, enabled Iraqis to listen to the belliphonic in a fundamentally different way than their counterparts in the American military did; they did not inherit an exotic, antimodern Arab "ear" from their forefathers. The differences that existed between Iraqi civilian and US military listening practices can be traced instead to concrete distinctions between the vicissitudes of individual lives, the technologies and training available to one group or another, and the positions individuals occupied in the temporary social structures of wartime. These distinctions, while crucial, are not embedded in the web of multigenerational continuity that continues to characterize mainstream notions of culture. And the distinctions that do exist are blurred by the fact that all hearing people, civilians and troops alike, were to a great extent enculturated into a common wartime habitus. Anthropologist Steven Feld has defined the term "acoustemology" as "an exploration of sonic sensibilities, specifically of ways in which sound is central to making sense, to knowing, to experiential truth."[34] Life in wartime places constraints on this kind of exploration, but radically increases the salience of sound for those who are struggling to make sense of their surroundings. The constant presence of armed violence forces civilians and service members into a common, caustic wartime acoustemology, evoked here by the concentric zones of audition. Within the homogenizing pragmatism of what literary scholar Patrick Deer has termed "war culture," groups are armed differently and given different tasks, but their general listening strategies, and many of their wounds, are comparable.[35]

ANOTHER COMPLICATING FACTOR: SOUND AND PSYCHOLOGICAL TRAUMA

Although most of the acts of listening to the war in Iraq can be conceptualized in terms of the four zones of increasing proximity that I just outlined, these distinctions of distance lose much of their relevance when the discussion turns to psychological trauma and the various conditions that have been gathered, since the Vietnam War, under the label of "post-traumatic stress." The psychological wounds inflicted at the nexus of sound and violence are profound, albeit poorly understood. What does seem clear is that, for tens of thousands of Iraq war veterans, sound serves as a powerful trigger for post-traumatic stress, and distant sounds as well as close-up sounds can have this effect. The published account of First Sergeant Russell W. Anderson Jr. describes this acute situation:

The anxiety attacks—[they're] unbelievable. Loud noises. I'm a hunter and I was on the gun range with my younger son and these people next to us started firing in rapid succession. I dove under the truck. I was so embarrassed. At least my son didn't see it. Anything can trigger [PTSD].[36]

A 2008 RAND report, which concluded that 20 percent of veterans returning from Iraq and Afghanistan display symptoms of PTSD, explained how the state of hyperalertness that is so valuable in combat becomes dysfunctional in civilian life, when veterans cannot turn it off. Anxiety over this situation then leads to a state of "avoidance," in which veterans go to great lengths to minimize their exposure to loud sounds and other stimuli:

> Hyperalertness was explained as being part of the job when in Iraq or Afghanistan. One Marine (NCO/officer) participant found himself outside patrolling his yard in the middle of the night in pajamas with his weapon. Others spoke of needing their weapon by them when they sleep. The adrenaline is so high for returning military that they avoid situations that drive it up. For example, we were told by several Marines that situations such as amusement parks and driving are difficult for the first few months. Symptoms of anxiety also make loud noises (including those from small children) difficult to take. One Marine summed it up: "4th of July will never be the same again."[37]

While sound is one trigger among many, it is often singled out as a primary stimulus of traumatic stress. An article published on July 2, 2011, in the *Chicago Tribune*, urging readers to consider the implication of lighting off fireworks in neighborhoods where Iraq war veterans live, is a case in point. The article related several stories of veterans reacting strongly to "the random pop-pop-pop of firecrackers," including this one:

> Former Navy Seabee John E. Baker spent parts of two years in Iraq manning a mortar, launching shells and ducking small arms fire from insurgents. For weeks Baker's South Side neighborhood has been filled with festive explosions, and the crackle of a string of firecrackers outside his apartment sets off the same reflexive adrenaline surge as the enemy fire he faced some six years ago.
>
> "You figure out what it is real quick, but you get the tingling, my heart starts racing fast," said Baker, 30. "It might just be for three seconds but it feels like 10 minutes. It can take you away, and you're not there anymore."[38]

Stories like this are legion. All point to the capacity of belliphonic sound to live on as a ghostly resonance, haunting those who have been exposed to the toxic nexus of sound and violence.

Some Iraq war veterans developed the symptoms associated with PTSD after experiencing a single traumatic event. Others found themselves dealing with PTSD's depression, anxiety, hyperarousal, and aggression after enduring weeks or months of entrenched violence. The volume *Fields of Combat* contains the testimonies of a number of service members who were diagnosed with PTSD upon returning home; one veteran, "Jesse" (a pseudonym), related the exhausting state of affairs on a base in the Sunni Triangle:

> They started mortaring us, and I heard these sounds . . . we were running with this colonel. . . . I'd been on the phone with my mom when they started mortaring us. I had to get off the phone and she was crying . . . running with this guy and hiding behind this concrete wall. We didn't have our body armor so [the colonel] gave us his, and we were like, 'Who is this guy?' He was one of the commanders, but we were like 'Holy shit!' And they were firing on the runway, and the radio was blaring, and I remember that after one hit I couldn't remember for a few seconds what had happened. I was dazed and confused. They kept mortaring us, and we called it 'Mortaritaville'.[39]

Prolonged exposure to belliphonic sound regularly produced exhaustion, depression, and other lingering effects associated with post-traumatic stress. Jesse's PTSD developed after a long string of acoustic and other sensory experiences, among which were those that he jokingly characterized as "wasting away in Mortaritaville."

While none of my primary interlocutors had been officially diagnosed with PTSD, most of them did describe symptoms that resemble those associated with the disorder, including hyperalertness in the wake of sounds that resemble those heard during deployment, and strong, anxious reactions to those same sounds. A common refrain during military testimonies was "I don't have PTSD, but—" followed by an account of panic or anxiety after a low boom from a construction site, or a burst of lightning, or a slammed door. Their stories indicate that, even for the very large population that doesn't suffer from full-blown post-traumatic stress, sounds, along with other triggers, continue to pose challenges and obstruct the return to normal life.

That return has been fraught for many. After relocating back to American cities, Iraq War veterans were confronted with many urban sounds that resembled those they had heard in Iraq, rendering the possibility of flashbacks, anxiety, and stress all the more likely. Beyond the obvious sounds that resemble weaponry (firecrackers, backfires, slamming doors, construction site noises, etc.), other more subtle sounds can trigger panic or an unwanted memory. Something as ubiquitous and seemingly innocuous as a car accelerating to pass you on an American highway can sound a lot like the beginning of a vehicle-borne IED attack in Iraq, for example.

Despite a large number of well-funded investigations, the depth and breadth of the PTSD problem—and the significance of acoustic stimuli for PTSD—remain poorly understood.[40] At the same time, it does not diminish the profundity of this problem to acknowledge that, for Iraq's permanent residents, a "post-traumatic" situation continues to be a distant dream; for the majority of Iraqis, the trauma of living in a combat zone, while somewhat diminished since the peak years of civilian violence in 2006 and 2007, continues.

CONCLUSION

> This is a lifelong thing. Every veteran I've ever met has been like, "this is, you know, this is here
> for good, I mean, this is not something that you are gonna be able to ever wish away. You are
> part of this club, and that shit never washes off."
>
> —from *On the Bridge,* a documentary film by Olivier Morel

For people new to the experience of combat, there is initially no space in which weapon
sounds are ignored, no space where rich narratives are constructed, no space where educated guesses are instantly made to help people avoid injury. The inexperienced start out
with a vast zone of indeterminacy, a place where belliphonic sounds tend to provoke
fear and anxious questions ("What was that?!" "What should I do?") but provide few
definitive answers. With time, most auditors begin to discern the informational content
of belliphonic sound, and learn to adopt different modes of audition accordingly. For
those who had learned how to coax this information from belliphonic sounds, to listen
through a violent timespace such as Operation Iraqi Freedom was to slide unpredictably
from one fluctuating zone of audition to the next, and, as a consequence of this movement, to be interpellated into one listening stance after another. One moment you are
tuning out the sound of gunfire on the horizon. A second later, you hear something
that causes your ears to prick up. Another second passes, and a sound sends you running for a bunker. Several minutes pass, the all-clear siren sounds, and you are back to
ignoring the soft pops in the distance. All the while, you are, in the words of anthropologist Thomas Csordas, "synthesizing the immediacy of an embodied experience with the
multiplicity of cultural meaning in which we are always and inevitably immersed."[41] In
other words, you are grappling with layers of sound, adjusting the foreground and background relations, contending with multiple sonorous ambiguities and illusions—all
while emplaced within a fluctuating matrix of (war) culture, all while accessing different
aspects of your own history as a (belliphonic) auditor. In this way, you are always, always
moving—throughout time and space, across zones of audition, and among possible listening stances. This movement, this affective hermeneutic dance, is simultaneously the
product and the source of experience: to listen is to live, and to know how to listen is a
skill that is developed through living. People moving within the audible-inaudible, narrational, and tactical zones in Iraq were, in this sense, doing in an extreme environment
that which all hearing people do. The differences between their situation and those of
people living in peacetime arise from the fact that in combat zones sounds command
extreme attention—not solely because of their volume, but also because of their intimate
connection with violent acts. The fusion of sound and violence in Iraq created new sonorous objects to be dealt with, and the ubiquity of these objects made the zones of audition there a topography of precarity. Within this vulnerable space, people learned how
to listen and how to not listen to violent acts, simultaneously. Their acts of audition and
inaudition placed them in situations within which they acted ethically, or unethically,

or simply failed to engage with ethical questions at all. Throughout, belliphonic sounds exacted their toll on auditors who were often listening through fear, exhaustion, heat, rage, the danger of impending violence, the exhilaration of survival, and the stench of death.

The movement from zone to zone that we can recognize as the auditory aspect of wartime life was only brought to a halt when sounds got so loud and so close that they could no longer be apprehended as sounds—when a close impact left one deafened, or severely concussed, or knocked out. At this moment, the hermeneutic dance abruptly ended, and the auditor became a passive body upon which sound acted not as interpretable text but as brute force. The exigencies of modern combat thus stretch the activity of listening to its twin breaking points, from the imagined silence of the audible inaudible at one extreme to the enforced silence of irrevocable physical trauma at the other.[42] In this situation, when people were confronted by audible sounds that were ignored and unhearable sounds that deafened, "listening," as a theoretical concept, broke down completely. In its place was a strange collection of shards of audition and inaudition—moments when people strained desperately to make sense of sound and moments when they were exposed to sonic violence, moments when sound escaped conscious attention, moments when sound infiltrated the memories of traumatized auditors, and moments when the physical processes that resulted in sounds exacted punishment upon bodies pushed past the conventional limits of audition.

Many of these intense moments were forced upon belliphonic auditors by the violent ecology of the war zone. Civilians and service members who were exposed to combat during Operation Iraqi Freedom all had to contend to one degree or another with the sounds of distant gunfire, the more proximate belliphonic sounds that bespoke violent acts, and the potential physiological and psychological damage that sonic violence could produce. It would seem here that the severe and unforgiving structure of the war wholly determined the listening practices of those who were enmeshed in it. We will see, however, that this is not exactly true—idiosyncratic acts of audition, acts of listening against the grain, did take place throughout the war. We will also see that the structure of the war zone was itself mutable: auditors listened through changing topographies of violence and precarity, topographies to which they often contributed. More specifically, they listened *to* an environment that they helped, fractally, to produce, and they listened with bodies that were indoctrinated into, and helped to support, a distinct but evolving auditory habitus. The relationship between sound, space, violence, and audition is thus a co-constitutive one. This relationship—the roiling dynamics that underwrite the "soundscape of war"— is the subject of the next three chapters. Before that, the following fragments provide two discrete vantage points on belliphonic listening. The first tells the story of a Marine scout-sniper who learned, over the course of his deployment, how to draw a great amount of information from belliphonic sounds. The second, a transcript of a nighttime house raid, documents an acute form of inaudition that took place at close range.

Fragment #2

Stealth and Improvisation in the Desert

JASON'S STORY

THROUGHOUT THE MODERN era, warfare has been associated with loudness. But loudness is not a universal attribute of war. Indeed, fighters from the prehistoric era to the present have understood the value of stealth, and therefore of quiet. In any engagement, combatants implicitly weigh the costs and benefits of noise (e.g., no secrecy but lethal firepower and the sonic intimidation that accompanies it) with those of quiet (e.g., lower lethality but greater stealth). On the ground in Iraq, tank commanders occupied the noisy end of the belliphonic spectrum, as their vehicles and weapons systems made stealth impossible. At the other end, snipers and scouts worked on creating conditions of near-inaudibility so as to conduct their missions undetected. What follows are four short sound-centered stories told to me by a person well versed in belliphonic quiet, a retired scout-sniper who served in Iraq from March to October of 2003.[1]

Jason Sagebiel grew up in south Texas, the eldest of three siblings. His father was in real estate; his mother worked a variety of jobs over the years, from German professor to bed and breakfast owner. Jason was a soft-spoken, good-natured kid. In high school, he spent his free time playing music and sports, and he showed a talent and enthusiasm for both. After graduation he tried to enlist in the army, but was rejected for bursitis he had developed running track. Several years later, after Jason's sister Ann joined the Marine Corps, her recruiter convinced Jason that he could probably get a medical waiver if he was still serious about enlisting. After some time, the waiver was granted, and in the summer of 1999 he joined the Marine Reserves. (Soon after, his youngest sister Amanda, not to be outdone, joined the marines as well. Both sisters are on active duty as of this writing.) At the time, Jason had just finished his sophomore year at Loyola University in New Orleans, where he was majoring in music composition and classical guitar.

His official duties in the Reserves were relatively light for the next few years while he was in college, although he did volunteer for extra training whenever he had the time. But at the beginning of his senior year, in the wake of the 9/11 attacks, expectations for reservists intensified. Jason's unit was activated one year later, and sent off to California for formal training. The transition from one life to the other was abrupt: Jason literally put down his guitar in New Orleans one day and picked up a rifle at Marine Corps Air Ground Combat Center in Twentynine Palms three days later. After three months of training, he shipped out to Kuwait; three days after arriving there, his four-man scout-sniper team was sent across the border as part of an advance party into Iraq.

Though trained as snipers, Jason and his team ended up working largely as scouts, tracking down and observing the behavior of "high-value targets," reporting their whereabouts back to command, and sometimes providing supporting fire when Special Forces came in to extract or kill them. His team was initially sent to conduct operations in an area to the southeast of Baghdad, near the Tigris River. They ran one mission after another, without a break, for the first sixty days of their deployment. In order to be as mobile as possible, they only carried equipment of "operational significance": their firearms, ammunition, scopes, and enough water to avoid dehydration. (Jason didn't see a toothbrush during those sixty days; he took his first shower on day sixty-four.) During that period, he and his team members honed their skills in the field, becoming more observant, and more lethal, with each engagement.

1. STOP, LOOK, LISTEN, SMELL

Given the nature of his missions, Jason's memories of combat didn't involve the constant belliphonic cacophony documented in the previous chapters of this book. On the contrary, his team was trained to be so quiet that the sounds they made seldom rose above the ambient noise of their surroundings. When I asked him about his most prominent sonic memories, he outlined a collection of soft, half-whispered belliphonic sounds that were all the byproducts of the team's stealthy operations: the cooling fan on the CLU (command launch unit, a 10× thermal imager that they used for night vision), which reminded him of the soft whirring sound produced by the title character of the movie *Robocop*; the sound of his own heavy breathing, which he constantly fought to suppress; the memorable, albeit exceedingly soft, sound of his attempts to walk noiselessly on sand. He and his team wrapped their gear in electrical tape to prevent metal elements from bumping noisily against one another, so he never heard the clicks and clanks one associates with handling firearms as they were walking or crawling into position—only the soft sound of packs and other gear rubbing against clothing, and of clothing making contact with the ground. They had been trained to understand that making sounds—even these barely audible ones—could give their position away to the enemy. Even these soft sounds, then, provoked anxiety: they were sounds that could get Jason and his team killed, and as such, they commanded the team's attention and respect.

Listening was a central part of a formalized regime of sensory awareness that Jason and his team had internalized in training. Whenever they were inserted into a new area, they would take cover and spend from fifteen to over ninety minutes conducting a procedure they called SLLS (pronounced "sills"): Stop, Look, Listen, Smell. The goal of SLLS was to get a sense of the environment and to set a baseline of sights, sounds, and smells against which they would compare the rest of their time there. Any deviation from this baseline would cause them to stop, look, listen, and smell again.

During the SLLS exercise, the team paid great attention to any manmade sounds that were present. But they also listened acutely to the animal world:

> You listen to patterns of bugs. They make certain noises unless they're aggravated, and then they make a different sound. If you get into an area, birds will chirp, animals will make sounds, insects will make sounds, and then after you sit still for a while they quit making those sounds. And so if you started to hear those sounds again but you're not moving, then someone else is, or something else is. . . . Animals have much less cognitive skill but much better sensory ability than humans. So a lot of times if animals were available we would rely on their senses, on their reactions to fill us in.

Recruiting the animal world to act as listening surrogates was one of several auditory procedures that they regularly performed on missions. Hypervigilant listening for them was a matter of training, but with time it became absolutely second nature to the members of the team. It was a reflex, an automatic thing that they were constantly doing: listening to the environment for the presence of others, while at the same time listening to themselves so as to police the sounds they were making.

Jason remembers one mission particularly vividly, and as it happens, sound played a central role in it. It was the first time he and his team members were in serious danger—as he put it, it was "my first perilous shoot-'em-up." Their objective was to observe the security headquarters of a hostile group, in a neighborhood that was so dangerous that army MPs were reluctant to patrol it, even in tanks. After dark, they headed out across an open field to a bombed-out building that their contacts in Military Intelligence told them was empty. Their plan was to use the abandoned building as an observation point for the group's headquarters across the street and the heavily armed guards that the group had patrolling throughout the neighborhood. As they reached the fully exposed middle of the field, a pack of wild dogs approached them and started barking. While they were concerned that the noise would attract the guards' attention, they had no other option but to keep moving forward: "we just let them bark, because if we shot them, people would hear the shots." The team reached the building without being detected, slipped through the door, and lowered their packs to the ground. Looking around the room, they discovered that it wasn't abandoned. The house was filled with Kalashnikovs, RPGs, land mines, and IED components: they had stumbled upon an active weapons cache. A collection of weapons this big would seldom be left unguarded, so the Marines decided that they needed to quietly move from room to room, "clearing" each one to make sure no one was in the two-story house. Jason and one of his team members took the stairs up to the second floor, and found themselves in a bombed-out room that was missing its front wall and part of the ceiling. As they moved across the rubble-strewn floor, his partner tripped on a small piece of rebar jutting up from the concrete.

His foot slams against the concrete floor, and [as the room is open to the street because of its missing wall and ceiling] . . . it's like an upside-down bell. And it just echoes, echoes, echoes. It was probably much less loud than I thought at the time, again, because things were really quiet. Yeah, I mean whispers sounded like shouts at that time, now that I think about it. [So] it makes this huge, huge noise, and—I pull him back, we're sitting there, we're just waiting, and about ten seconds after this happens . . . they open up on us, they started firing. . . . People were patrolling the area, so one of these patrols was now firing.

In response to the sound of a misplaced foot, the guards unleashed a barrage of fire. But the echo of the foot alone wasn't enough to allow the guards on the street to determine the scout team's location, as Jason quickly learned:

I was getting ready to fire back and my team leader, who was more experienced, thank God for that—he was like, "don't." Because his observation was "some of the rounds are hitting our building . . . but some are not," meaning if they knew exactly where we were, and they were actually trained, all the rounds would be hitting our building. Which meant to him they didn't know exactly where we were at. "So if we shoot back . . ."—and as soon as he said this, [I remembered that] this was something we learned in squad leader school, it's what we call "recon by fire": they shoot, you shoot back, and there you are [having given your position away]. So they were reconning by fire. So we didn't shoot back, and now they were left basically to have to go house to house to find us.

The team sat silently for hours, watching the patrol look for them, and then watching them give up. They continued waiting, silently, until dawn, when help arrived and they were extracted.

3. IMPROVISATION

In between missions, Jason's team would redeploy to a nearby Forward Operating Base to clean their weapons, write up their reports, and catch sometimes as little as a few hours of sleep and relaxation before heading out again. After the initial sixty-day rash of missions, though, things calmed down, and the team enjoyed longer stretches of inactivity for the next month or so. It was during one of these that Jason attempted to regain a sense of himself as a musician:

> They—whoever "they" is—say war is 90 percent boredom and 10 percent sheer terror. I would like to amend that to 99.9 percent boredom, and .1 percent *absolute fucking sheer terror.* That's how it is. And in one of these 99.9 percent boredom phases [one of his platoon members who was a musician and he] started doing guitar together. Just being bored one day we found over by Supply a bunch of these pallets, and just with nothing better to do we were like "well you know, we can at least practice our technique even if it doesn't make any noise." So we . . . went over and broke off some pieces and we used our fighting knives to carve them, we built saddles and bridges, and put them on this long stick.

They found some parachute cord and sliced it open to expose its constituent strings. Then they bored holes into the sticks with the pointed end of a knife, wrapped five courses of the nylon strings around them, pulled them tight, tied them off, and grinned at each other over their new makeshift guitars. Jason and his friend began working on right- and left-hand technique, playing arpeggios for hours as they whiled away the day. Occasionally, they thought up pieces as well:

> I couldn't play anything I knew because it wouldn't sound right. So we'd make little songs on these incredibly out-of-tune, distuned, quarter-tuned,

whatever-you'd-call-them instruments. And we came up with some wacky shit. Which I imagine is probably how music started, you know, before they had defined instruments, it was just like, "here's all this weird stuff . . ."

Their instruments didn't have sound holes or hollow bodies, so they were exceedingly quiet, but that didn't bother them. They were just happy to give their fingers something to do, and give their ears some low-decibel "wacky shit" to listen to.

4. JACK JOHNSON

Aside from his makeshift guitar, Jason's team had one other musical outlet: the music of Hawaiian folk-rock singer Jack Johnson. This was, it must be said, not the music most people on their Forward Operating Base were listening to. The preferred genre there was death metal, which the infantrymen on base would listen to in order to "pump themselves up" before going out on mission. Jason explains that their musical differences were the result of differences in their combat profiles:

Most of these guys were inside the wire [i.e., on base] for the whole time: they'd pump themselves up [by listening to metal], they'd go on patrol, then come back. [By contrast] we were *outside* the wire all the time. We'd come back, we'd have like three hours to recover before we had to go right back out.

In other words, they didn't need music to "get pumped up"; they needed it to "chill out." The team members pooled their money and bought a portable CD player, but they had no CDs to listen to. The girlfriend of one of them burned four CDs worth of Jack Johnson songs and mailed them to the base; for the length of their tour, this was the only recorded music they possessed. They had no speakers, so they broke the headpiece of the earphones in two and lay down on the sandy floor in pairs: two placing their ears as close as possible to the left channel, two doing the same to the right, all breathing as quietly as possible so as to catch Johnson's barely audible strains. It was a surreal microculture of quietude in the middle of a war zone: heads together, gazing at the ceiling, the Marines strained to hear the Hawaiian-born folk rocker sing "Bubble Toes," filling in with their memories of the song the decibels and frequencies that the tinny headphones denied them, doing their best to relax before going back out to shoot, and be shot at.

Johnson's music helped him stay sane at the time, but the solace that it gave him turned out to be perishable. The singer's voice ended up fusing so tightly with Jason's experience of combat that he can no longer listen to it without being swamped by unwanted memories of his deployment:

I have not been able to listen to Jack Johnson since I came back. It's just like too much of an experience for me. You know people talk about gunfire and all this other stuff [triggering traumatic memories]? For me, it's Jack Johnson. That's the thing that triggers all the shit from Iraq. So, I go to parties and Jack Johnson plays—I walk outside. I go to [a department store] and it shows up on the radio—I walk outside. Jack Johnson is for me symbolic of Iraq.

What is it like to listen for the enemy with a body suffused with adrenalin? What is it like to know that making a single sound could result in your immediate death? How valuable is music as a tool for calming down in the face of violence and vulnerability? How insidiously powerful is music as a carrier of traumatic memory? These questions link Jason's unique experiences to the broadly intersubjective field of contemporary war culture, the violent habitus into which fighters and bystanders are indoctrinated, largely against (or at least independent of) their wills. In places where sound and violence intersect, people around the world find themselves similarly compelled to listen, and to strive to remain silent, and to struggle with the fact that they are troubled by much of what they hear.

Fragment #3

Loudly Searching in the Resonant Darkness

THE ANATOMY OF A NIGHTTIME HOUSE RAID

AS I MENTIONED IN the previous chapters, one of the primary sites of encounter between US service members and Iraqi civilians was the home: US forces conducted tens of thousands of house raids and other "cordon-and-search" operations over the course of Operation Iraqi Freedom, entering homes with or without their owners' permission to search for "weapons caches, explosives, contraband, evidence, [and] intelligence" and capture "insurgents, sympathizers, or criminals."[1] House raids generally took place between midnight and 5 a.m., in order to catch their targets while they were sleeping.[2] While this kind of forcible-entry operation did result in major victories for US forces (including, most notably, the capture of Saddam Hussein), the vast majority of the houses raided belonged to innocent civilians.[3] But whether they were combatants or merely bystanders mistaken as such, one thing remained constant: as one vet who regularly conducted raids attested, "we scared the living Jesus out of them every time we went through every house."[4] At the same time, although they tried not to show it, the assault teams were also beset by the fear, magnified in their pre-mission briefings, that the houses they raided likely contained dangerous, heavily armed insurgents who were ready to kill them as soon as they came through the door.

Raids typically began with the assault team loudly battering down the front gate and door; the sound of forced entry would wake most residents of the darkened house. Team members would flick on the lights, or if there weren't any, aim their flashlights (and with them, the rifles to which they were attached) in residents' faces, while shouting commands at them ("Don't move!" "Get down on the ground!"). Once they were located, women and children would be quarantined in one room, while men were lined up outside, often kneeling, often facing a wall.

Spreading out into the house as they searched, the service members wouldn't be able to maintain visual contact with one another, so they would shout back and forth. When they moved from one room to another, they would yell "coming in!" or "coming out!" to lessen the odds that they would be accidentally shot by a member of their team. At the same time, one or more service members would be directing instructions and questions at the house's residents, sometimes with an interpreter, sometimes without, often at a shout. If men of military age were found, they would be pulled aside, asked questions separately, and in some cases handcuffed, hooded,[5] and taken away for a full interrogation elsewhere. If nothing suspicious was discovered, the troops would leave, often with a quick verbal apology, and move on to the next house. Throughout the noisy operation, listening—on the part of service members and civilians—was a central, if anxious and exceedingly complicated, activity.

What follows is a transcript of a soldier's video recording of one such night raid, on an unspecified night in an unspecified town in Iraq.[6] In this recording, even though no shots are fired, the aggression, confusion, anxiety, and terror that are the hallmarks of the belliphonic encounter are clearly audible. The transcript renders visible a particular kind of "close inaudition" that structures many interactions between service members and civilians. In order to complete their mission, the soldiers ignore the repeated screams of an Iraqi woman in the house. Her scream, it appears, is relegated to an atemporal space of irrelevance: whether it is the first or the hundredth scream matters not at all. Meanwhile, the soldiers hold an operational conversation, shouting orders and observations to one another in a businesslike manner. The choice to ignore the woman's scream is understandable from the standpoint of the soldiers involved. At the same time, it represents yet another moment in which the specific exigencies of combat combine with sound and listening to create an ethical crisis without a single shot being fired.

TABLE 2B.1

Transcript of a Nighttime House Raid. [Fragment #3]

Apparent proximity to the recorder

near   far

Scene #
[Time elapsed, min:sec]:

1. [00:00–00:01]
The recording of the house raid begins in darkness. The image coming from the portable video camera mounted on one of the team members' vests is almost completely black. A distant porch light, visible here as a small wavering point of light several pixels wide, is the only evidence that there is video to go with the sound. The soldiers preparing for the raid could surely see much more than we can here, but it is a very dark night nonetheless. As their raid depends on the element of surprise, they keep their lights off, their vehicles quiet, and their voices at a whisper.

The recording begins on the street outside the house, one second before the raid commences. The camera was turned on mid-utterance: over the drone of an idling Humvee engine in the distance, we hear the soldier/videographer softly conclude a phrase that presumably begins like this:

[Here it] fuckin' goes.
It is unclear whether he is speaking to himself, to his comrades, or to the unseen future audience of the video. Regardless, with this phrase, the soldiers spring into action.

2. [00:01–00:18]
[bang]
A soft metallic banging in the dark indicates that the front gate has been forced open. A voice calls out, softly but urgently:

    Door's open,
        door's open!
        Go!

Another urgent voice appears to be softly hailing a comrade, after which more banging on the gate ensues:

    Bob, Bob,
        Bob, Bob,
        Bob!—

[BANG bang bang]
[bang BANG bang BANG bang bang]
We hear more and louder banging of the perimeter door as the soldiers break it down to enter. There is no more time for stealth now: two voices shout, with increasing volume, pitch and urgency, building up to an aggressive yell:

            Go go go go GO!
            Go go go!

And amid the sound of equipment rubbing against uniforms as the team breaks into a jog, another voice curtly addresses a soldier who, apparently, is not storming the house as quickly as the others:

> [What are you doing]
> fuckin' standin' there?

3. [00:18–00:34]

[bang]

The voices from here to the end of the recording are nearly constant, one on top of another. As they approach the house, a porch and the front door, lit by a fluorescent bulb, lurch into view.

Hey where's that
fuckin' door knocker
[i.e., battering ram]?

> Right here.
> > Over there.

Alright.
Here's the door knocker.

> Got it. Got it.

Alright. There's a door
right up there let's go let's go.

> The door's right up here
> Let's go let's go let's go.
> [bang]

Goin' straight for the door.

> Go.
> > Go. Go.

Multiple jogging footsteps and heavy breathing are audible as they approach the door.

4. [00:34–00:39]

A pause, and then the videographer says:

Ready?

Another pause, nervous breath is audible, then the loud sound of the metal door being battered in.

[BANG]

5. [00:39]

Light pours from the open door, and with it, the high-pitched screams of a woman within. She may be screaming someone's name, or simply screaming without words—it is impossible to tell, as the resonance of the house (along with the lo-fi sound of the recorder) reduces her voice to an echoic blur. She screams each time she takes a breath. She sounds terrified.

The screaming woman is never seen by the soldier wearing the camera. She is in another part of the house, but her voice is clearly audible through to the second half of the recording. At no point do the soldiers appear to acknowledge her screams or entreaties: they are preoccupied with their task, and talk right over her vocalizations.

(continued)

TABLE 2B.1 Continued

Having breached the doorway, the soldiers find themselves in a concrete room with bare floors and walls. Portable gas lamps on the floor are the only furniture. Sound bounces off the room's walls as the woman's screams and soldiers' shouts persist, creating disorienting echoic effects.

The soldiers fan out, each checking a different room. While the large room they initially entered is well lit, the others are dark, illuminated only by the tight circle of light from the flashlight attached to each M4 rifle. Within this beam of light we see a lacquered wardrobe, a carpet on the floor, curtains in the window. The videographer is confronted with multiple doors that he needs to open and check.

6. [00:39–00:53]

[bang]

[scream]

Go go go go go!

[scream]

[scream]

Hey!

[scream]

I got multiple doors!

[scream]

Comin' in, comin' in!

[Indistinct yelling from soldiers.]

Hey Lee!

[scream]

You comin'?

[scream]

The sound of doors being slammed open.

[bang BANG]

[bang BANG]

The soldier with the cam checks a darkened room while his team members talk on top of one another in the hallway.

[Indistinct talk from soldiers.]

[scream]

[scream]

[scream]

There's nobody.

[scream]

[scream]

It's good. It's clear.

[scream]

Let's go.

Let's go this way.

[scream]

[Indistinct yelling from soldiers.]

7. [00:53–01:04]

Some team members have reached another part of the house. Their shouts are coming from farther away now. The soldier with the cam continues checking rooms.

On the ground!

Get on the ground!

Get on the ground!

[scream]

This one?

[scream]

Get on the ground!

[scream]

Hey!

There's a bunch of them up here.

Yalla![7]

[scream]

Yalla!

Hey!

[Indistinct yelling from soldiers.]

Hey!

[Indistinct yelling from soldiers.]

Go go!

We got another fuckin' door!

8. [01:04–01:09]

Deep inside the house, a soldier's voice shouts with high-pitched intensity. The resonance of the house muddies his words, but his shouts are among the loudest voices thus far, competing only with the woman's initial screaming:

Hey sir!

Hey sir, come on in!

Hey sir!

[scream]

[Indistinct yelling from soldiers.]

9. [01:09–01:29]

The woman's screams are losing steam: she has exhausted herself through screaming. Her screams are now more like moans, with a single moan following every breath that she takes. The soldiers continue their room-to-room search.

[moan]

Hey Lee, you got anything?

[moan]

No. They're all on the roof.

Lock this room, pull up tents.

[moan]

We gotta walk along the roof.

[moan]

(continued)

TABLE 2B.1   Continued

Hey, what's goin' on?
Hey. He's got the roof.
We're goin' to the roof.
We're upstairs and out.
Let's go!   [moan]
                                                              [moan]

Hey, there's that other door
back there we have to clear.

                                                              [moan]
                                                              [moan]

Hey, Larry, Larry!
[indistinct]

10. [01:29–01:53]

The woman's moans have turned into sobbing and pleading, presumably in Arabic. Her words are swallowed up by her distance from the camera and the reverberating noises in the house. The banging of doors slamming and boots on stairs continues.

Ready?
[bang]
                                                              [pleading]
[bang]
                                                              [pleading]
Comin' in!
[bang]
Comin' in!
                                                              [pleading]
for a tac.
                                                              [pleading]
                                                              [pleading]
Does that open out or in?
In.   [pleading]
Alright. Just watch that right now.
That goes to the outside, watch that.
I know.
Who touched this, did he have priorities?
Yeah.
                                                              [pleading]

11. [01:53–02:12]

The woman's voice dies away. Soldiers' voices emanate from farther inside the house, with more echo than before.

Room's clear.

Room's clear? Alright we're going to go and move outside, [indistinct]. Hey look over there in that room and make sure, [someone interrupts, indistinct] hey look over there in that room and make sure there's no more breezeways and hurry up. [The same voice interrupts again, indistinct.] Hang on we're just makin' sure makin' sure this door doesn't go anywhere.

12. [02:12–02:25]

Hey, I got lights outside!

The woman's voice returns, and her intonation is clearly one of pleading. It is unclear whether her pleas are addressed to the soldiers, or to an unseen interpreter, or whether they are offered up in prayer. She is still too far away from the recorder for any words to be intelligible.

> [pleading]
> [pleading]

I got people out here!

> You got people?

I just saw lights outside!

> Oh they're searching
> right now from the roof.

Alright.

13. [02:25–02:38]

The video has been dark for the last 30 seconds, with the only light coming from one soldier's flashlight aimed near the ground.

> Hey [indistinct]? I'm comin' out!
> Hey listen up, there's nothing happening, let's forget
> about it, alright?

> Alright.

> Comin' out! Comin' out!

14. [02:38–03:06]

The military-age male fighters that their briefing had clearly led them to expect are nowhere to be seen. It dawns upon the videographer that they have raided the wrong house. The team packs up and prepares to leave.

There ain't any males here.

[We] hit the wrong house!

> Huh?
> Whad'you say?

Wrong house.

> He go upstairs?
> > Yeah.

We're outta here, Milton.

> Jason clear?
> > Yeah!

> We're all clear.

(continued)

TABLE 2B.1   Continued

Alright. Sir!

Yeah.

Building's clear.

Building's clear?

OK [indistinct].

[pleading]

The recording stops abruptly amidst the sound of the soldiers leaving and the woman sobbing and continuing her pleas. Three minutes and six seconds have elapsed from start to finish.

Structures of Listening, Sounding, and Emplacement

Introduction to Section II

THE AUDITORY REGIMES, SONIC CAMPAIGNS, AND ACOUSTIC TERRITORIES OF OPERATION IRAQI FREEDOM

HAVING SKETCHED OUT a number of wartime Iraq's regularly occurring sound events, and gestured towards some of the modes of audition that grew up in response to them, I want to pause here and reflect in greater depth on the ways in which listening and sounding were emplaced within the war's fluctuating territories. This reflection is animated by a number of interlocking questions: What are the overt and hidden forces that structure the act of listening, both within the fractured timespace of war and more generally? What manifestations of human agency enable auditors to escape the gravitational pull of these forces? What entities are responsible for the introduction of sounds into a given timespace? What are the political, ethical, and aesthetic implications of these acts of sounding? How do places prolong, curtail, enhance, and distort sounds? How are places transformed by sounds, and by listening? These and other questions are posed in service of a single broad question, which, in its most blunt formulation, sounds like this: *what is the nature of (wartime) auditory experience?*

Somewhat more polemically, I ask these questions in order to encourage a slight recalibration of one of the more prominent terms within contemporary music and sound studies. The term is *soundscape.* Coined in the 1970s by Canadian composer and theorist R. Murray Schafer, "soundscape" has come to signify the totality of sounds in a given environment, or, more precisely, the sounds available to the ear in a given place.[1] One of the founders of acoustic ecology and a committed critic of noise pollution, Schafer imbued the term with a negative teleology of contamination, in which "hi-fi" (i.e., natural, rural) soundscapes were gradually transformed into "lo-fi" soundscapes by the incessant march of industrialization and the noise that came with it:[2]

> The lo-fi soundscape was introduced by the Industrial Revolution and was extended by the Electric Revolution which followed it. The lo-fi soundscape origi-nates with sound congestion. The Industrial Revolution introduced a multitude of new sounds with unhappy consequences for many of the natural and human sounds which they tended to obscure. . . . Today the world suffers from an over-population of sounds; there is so much acoustic information that little of it can emerge with clarity.[3]

By this measure, the sonic environment of modern war represents the bottom limits of "lo-fi," an abject space that so assaults the world of natural sounds that it barely qualifies as a soundscape at all.[4]

Recent work on soundscapes[5] has detached the term from this value judgment, deploying it without prejudice in a variety of urban contexts, from factories to office buildings. But the nature of the relationship between the sound wave and the receptive ear remains less than transparent. David Samuels, Louise Meintjes, Ana Ochoa, and Tom Porcello assert:

> Like landscape . . . [soundscape] contains the contradictory forces of the natural and the cultural, the fortuitous and the composed, the improvised and the deliber-ately produced. Similarly, as landscape is constituted by cultural histories, ideolo-gies, and practices of seeing, soundscape implicates listening as a cultural practice.[6]

While sound-centered scholarship has been probing the cultural dimensions of listening for decades now, the interconnectedness of listening, sounding, the body, technologies, and the environment remains a rich topic demanding further exploration. As Samuels and his writing partners contend, the general "assumption that sound is only a matter of the vibrations of the source" leaves "undertheorized the social, ideological, or political positionalities of listeners."[7] Unless these positionalities are made explicit, the sound-scape concept ends up strangely both presuming and *erasing* the listener: it cannot be constituted without an ear, but it offers no framework for understanding the processes through which a listener becomes a listener, or the distinctions that separate one listener from another, or the factors that enable idiosyncratic listening acts. All too often, the "ear" that constitutes the soundscape remains an abstraction, a mute and essentially pas-sive recipient of waves, the enabling fiction of an idealized sonic environment.

If the soundscape concept is to be brought into alignment with the most incisive new work on sound and listening, we will need to reattach its abstract ear to a historically and culturally inflected body; conceive of that body as one that sounds while listen-ing, listens while sounding, and learns while doing both; and emplace that body within an ever-changing series of overlapping vibrational environments. In service of that goal, I have reconfigured the soundscape as a tripartite system of "auditory regimes," "sonic campaigns," and "acoustic territories." While my wartime subject matter has compelled me to adopt this overtly militaristic set of terms, they are intended to have a broad application both inside and outside the war zone.

TERMINOLOGY

Let's begin by defining the terms I'm putting into play here and sketching out the connotative fields that surround them. While "auditory," "sonic," and "acoustic" are frequently used as rough synonyms, treating them with some definitional precision will increase their usefulness as theoretical devices in the chapters that follow. The *Oxford English Dictionary* defines "auditory" (from the Latin *auditorius*) as "pertaining to the sense or organs of hearing; received by the ear."[8] The word thus points most directly not to sound but to the act of hearing. Additionally, "auditory" frames hearing—and, by implication, the more intentional act of listening—as a physiological act, one involving an anatomical apparatus (minimally: ear, auditory nerve, brain) and, by implication, a sentient body.[9] The intuitive model of listening that the term "auditory" projects looks something like this:

sound + receptive body = audition

In other words, audition (the act of listening) is the process that takes place when a receptive pair of ears (as well as skin, the chest cavity, and other bodily zones[10]) comes into contact with sounds.

Pairing "auditory" with the term "regime," however, puts significant pressure on the left side of the above equation. A regime, whether it is Napoleonic or Foucauldian or fitness-oriented, necessarily involves discipline. Regimes exert power over their subjects: through the threat or exercise of force, through overt appeals to ideals, through subtle influences that operate subconsciously—or through a combination of the three. The model of listening that the term "auditory regime" projects, then, introduces another element to the equation:

sound + receptive body + power (largely in the form of "culture") = audition

In other words, as I've stated elsewhere in this volume, listening to the world is not an innate, universal capacity, the logical result of ears encountering sound waves. Rather, it is something that we learn how to do, and *we learn how to listen in an environment that is already shaped by and coursing with power.* This contention has a rich intellectual history.[11]

Nowhere are the levers of power that shape listening more robust than within a wartime military operation. In chapter 3, which follows this introduction, I will argue that service members' acts of wartime audition and inaudition took place within the context of an unspoken and evolving but nonetheless powerful "military auditory regime." This extreme listening habitus can be defined as the agglomeration of technologies, regulations, formal and informal training exercises, casual conversations, and shared life histories that shaped service members' listening practices in Iraq. These elements helped give service members a collective sense of what it means to be an effective listener, which sounds are beautiful, which sounds are dangerous, what kind of listening to undertake in a given timespace, and what kinds of vocal and bodily reactions (or, better, "performances") are appropriate in the wake of belliphonic events. The regimentation of the armed forces notwithstanding, the military auditory regime was not all-powerful: service members were often able to engage in idiosyncratic or even transgressive acts of audition. Rather than a listening diktat, then, what the regime provided was a ready set of "scripts" (in Schank and Abelson's sense[12]) outlining behaviors that would be deemed appropriate.

In contrast to "auditory," with its emphasis on listening, we can use the term "sonic" to point to the nature of sounds themselves and the act of sounding. Defined by the *Oxford English Dictionary* as "of or pertaining to sound or sound waves," "sonic" as a term remains silent on the complicated topic of audition. Instead, it emphasizes sound's physical dimension, and presents sound as a force with measurable effects. The equation implied by "sonic" in this sense is the inverse of what we had before:

$$\text{audition} - \text{bodies} = \text{sound}$$

In other words, if you bracket out the listening body at the moment of audition, you are left with a surplus of sound, moving through the available medium according to the laws of physics.

The term "campaign," however, pulls us out of the realm of physics and into the realm of social (and more specifically, political) science—and in so doing, it reinserts bodies into the equation. "Campaign" (from the French *campagne*, "country, 'the field'") has been "applied to any course of action analogous to a military campaign, either in having a distinct period of activity, or in being of the nature of a struggle, or of an organized attempt aiming at a definite result." Campaigns are organized by people, and they are organized around a goal, and they are implemented with the help of technologies and training. They involve struggle, or even conflict, and as such they necessarily involve the exercise of power. The term "sonic campaign" conjures a model of sound and listening that is likely to contain these elements:

$$\text{bodies} + \text{technologies} + \text{actions} + \text{power (a.k.a. "culture")} + \text{audible vibration} = \text{sounds}$$

Of course, not all sounds can be traced to human actions: the natural world is a sonorous world, a world of crickets chirps and wind and thunder. But human actions almost inevitably result in sounds, and those sounds are often subject to structures and agendas not unlike those that shape listening. Just as people learn how to listen within an auditory habitus, they learn how to sound within a cultural field of sonic discipline. The difference is that while listening is a semiprivate activity that seldom draws attention to itself,[13] sounding is by its nature public, and therefore subject to coordination. This contention, too, has its precedents.[14]

Nowhere is the public, intersubjective dimension of sound as invasive as it is in wartime. In chapter 4, I examine the sonic campaigns of the Iraq War's principal antagonists, campaigns in which individuals learned to produce and curtail particular sounds within a semistructured field of technologies, regulations, objectives, procedures, training, and informal conversations. The Iraq War, we shall learn, was partially fought along sonic lines.

If "auditory" draws attention to the physiological act of listening and "sonic" homes in on the physical act of sounding, the term "acoustic" has acquired a connotative field that emphasizes the relationship between sound, listening, and place. Although its etymology (from the Greek ἀκουστικός, "of or for hearing") places it as an apparent synonym for "auditory," its usage has tended to foreground the way sounds resonate in and are shaped by particular environments. When we remark upon the "acoustics" of a concert hall, we are listening not to sound qua sound but to the fusion of sound and a built environment. "Acoustic," therefore, gives us a third perspective on sound, which can be distilled as follows:

audible vibration + place = sound

In other words, sound only becomes perceptible—and therefore, from the perspective of the listener, sound only becomes *itself*—when it moves through a particular medium, in a particular place. From the vantage point of acoustics, therefore, the minimal unit of analysis is the fusion of sounds and environments.

When added to "acoustic," the term "territory" further amplifies the central role that the environment plays in our perception of sounds. But "territory" also introduces yet another vector along which power is exerted: a territory is not just any place, but a special area that is "selected . . . and defended against others," an area that is held "under jurisdiction." A territory is a place that has been conquered, a place whose identity is maintained by force or threat of force. And so the connotative field that "acoustic territory"[15] produces is one in which sounds become a perceptual reality only when they make contact with places and the power relations that inhabit them:

audible vibration + place + power (a.k.a. "culture") = sound

At the same time, "acoustic territory" hints at the ways in which our understanding of the places in which we live and move is structured in part by reverberating sounds and acts of listening. Listening to the sounds that share space with you is one of the "cultural processes and practices through which places are rendered meaningful—through which, one might say, places are actively sensed."[16] Sound and listening together can thus create a territory defined by audibility. In this sense:

sound + power (a.k.a. "culture") + location + listening = place

Accordingly, we can define "acoustic territories" as the shifting environments, structures, and other absorptive and resonating elements that enclose, modify, and otherwise mediate the sounds in a given timespace, *and* the distinct places whose boundaries and characters are constituted by sound and listening. There is ample precedent, too, for this line of thinking.[17]

Nowhere are acoustic territories as dangerous or potentially damaging as they are in wartime. In chapter 5, I look at the spaces in Iraq that have been most thoroughly territorialized by belliphonic sounds. I also analyze a number of the ways in which built structures in Iraq distorted auditory perception, creating confusion and alarm among auditors. Lastly, I consider the corporeal spaces in which belliphonic sound resonated, and the deleterious effects of those vibrations. Framing the ear canal, cochlea, chest cavity, and neurocranium as acoustic territories gives us, I argue, a new and productive vantage point from which to examine all of the varieties of sound-induced trauma.

These, then, are the three analytics that will be deployed in the following triptych of chapters: "auditory regimes," which point to the complexities of listening; "sonic campaigns," which emphasize the labor and agendas that underlie sounding; and "acoustic territories," which show how listening and sounding are shaped by the environment, and how, at the same time, they create understandings of place. All three of these frameworks are linked by a number of commonalities: each involves human and nonhuman actors[18]; each is ephemeral, tactical, and dynamic; each involves overt and hidden strata of labor; and each, significantly, can be a site for violence. (Table 2c.1 charts out some of the common ground among them.) Shared attributes such as these knit the three frameworks together into a co-constitutive whole: each one can only come into existence in the presence of the others.

Coursing with movement, dense with people and objects, and in a constant state of evolution and decay, auditory regimes, sonic campaigns, and acoustic territories coalesce to form the anatomy of a dynamic and inherently combative soundscape, a vibrant vibrational environment created through the interplay of sound, listening, and emplacement—an environment within which questions of politics, aesthetics, and ethics demand to be addressed.

Common Attributes of Auditory Regimes, Sonic Campaigns, and Acoustic Territories.

1. *All involve people:*
   - Auditory regimes are populated by auditors, and the legions of people who influence the act of listening (by writing regulations, training people, designing listening technologies, etc.).
   - Sonic campaigns are populated by people who are responsible for sounding. In musical spheres, these people are commonly called "performers"; in the combat zone, they are shooters, drivers, propagandists, demonstrators, vocal bystanders, and others. Sonic campaigns also include sonic planners. These are "composers" in the musical sphere; generals and other strategists, insurgent leaders, PSYOPS commanders, and other decision-makers in wartime.
   - Acoustic territories are populated by people who design and build elements of the environment that affect sound: e.g., architects, landscape designers, construction workers, blast-wall installers. They also involve people who alter and destroy these elements: e.g., pilots, tank commanders, IED planters, suicide bombers. At the same time, given that our very bodies are constantly serving as resonating chambers and sound-absorbing structures, the frame of the acoustic territory involves every person whose body comes into contact with a given set of sound waves.

2. *All involve objects:*
   - Auditory regimes make use of objects that mediate sound for listeners, including earplugs, cotton balls, microphones, computerized echolocation devices, sedatives, stimulants.
   - Sonic campaigns employ sounding objects ranging from musical instruments to voices to loudspeakers to vehicles to weapons.
   - Acoustic territories are made largely of architectural and naturally occurring objects (e.g., trees, sand, geological formations, and, again, bodies and their internal resonating cavities).

3. *All are impermanent and dynamic:*
   - Within an auditory regime, priorities, restrictions, technologies, and tactics are in a state of constant evolution until a new set of organizing principles places the regime in a state of crisis. Like political regimes, all auditory regimes ultimately fall and are replaced by others.
   - The tactics and technologies of sonic campaigns are in a similar state of flux—and the people who organize to make sonic incursions into a particular environment are always on the move. Like military campaigns, sonic campaigns end, in victory, defeat, or stalemate.
   - Despite the appearance of permanence, architecture and other structures in the natural and built environments are constantly subject to decay and change. In the combat zone, the acoustic territory's built environment is under literal attack, with old structures destroyed and, eventually, new structures built on the ground from which the rubble has been cleared.

4. *All involve labor:*
   In wartime and peacetime, people are constantly working. They work to contend with the sounds that surround them, they labor to produce sounds, and they struggle to occupy and give shape to the territories in which they find themselves.

5. *All involve the potential for violence:*
   Sound carries the potential to damage the ears and/or psyches of all within earshot. Sound can be the vehicle of symbolic violence. Territories (acoustic and otherwise) can be sites of violence, or subjects of violence themselves.

"Today's epistemologies of listening are not part of a pre-meditated advancement but rather the results of cultural and social habits formed in immense fragmentary fields of interaction."

—RAVIV GANCHROW[1]

3

Auditory Regimes

DURING OPERATION IRAQI Freedom, a vast assemblage of training, techniques, pre-scriptions, objects, and discourses shaped the way that service members listened during their deployments. Beginning in basic training, they learned through exposure to weap-onry how to recognize weapon sounds and how to function within a loud belliphonic environment. Once deployed to the Area of Operations, they found themselves subject to written regulations and oral orders to maintain "situational awareness," wear earplugs in loud situations, and confine recreational listening (to music, to radio programming, to audiobooks) to certain times and locations. They availed themselves of sophisticated technologies that increased and even replaced the aural acuity of their ears. And, per-haps most importantly, they regularly engaged in casual conversations about belliphonic sounds, conversations that amounted to informal auditory training. Drawing upon the above, they cobbled together semi-improvised tactics for contending with belliphonic noise. Many of these tactics were not unique to the Iraq War; rather, they were part of the collection of auditory acts that has accrued over centuries of warfare. Others were keyed to terrain or technologies that were specific to Operation Iraqi Freedom and the generations of service members who served in it. Collectively, these shared tactics tended to maximize the information extracted from the sounds that surrounded them and minimize the trauma that those sounds could cause—although, as we will see, their effects were not always straightforward, and their powers to decode and pacify the belliphonic were limited.

The military does not officially recognize this assemblage, or conceptualize it as a unified regime. While some of its elements (e.g., regulations) were part of official doctrine during the war, and some of its technologies (e.g., noise-canceling headphones) were specifically designed with the importance of listening in mind, other aspects occupied the realm of "common-sense" techniques stemming from the prereflective sense of "the way things are" that French sociologist Pierre Bourdieu labeled "doxa."[2] No regulations stipulated that service members hold detailed discussions in order to determine the identity and trajectory of mortars being lobbed over their heads—but they talked about this anyway, regularly, because that felt like the only reasonable thing to do. And they tended to talk about belliphonic sounds in a conversational style that also felt natural and reasonable.

From this vantage point, then, the regime was a classic Bourdieusian habitus, the "durably installed generative principle of regulated improvisations" that "makes it possible [for individuals] to inhabit institutions."[3] The embodied knowledge of the habitus is, in the words of Craig Calhoun, the manner in which each individual "connects with the sociocultural order in such a way that the various games of life keep their meaning, keep being played."[4] However, in a combat environment where violent death was an ever-present possibility, the stakes of these games were so high that the habitus took on a special kind of regimentation, both from without, in the form of institutional policing of listening practices, and from within, in the form of an extreme embodied hypervigilance. During combat situations, listening was a means of survival, and developing an intuitive "sense of the game" of listening—with the aid of technologies, training, talk, and other resources—was a matter of life and death. The learning curve for developing the proper auditory sensibility was necessarily steep, with much of the most valuable conversation-based training taking place within the first few engagements for combat troops. Service members whose work profiles kept them on base (or "inside the wire") had fewer opportunities for learning how to listen to the full range of belliphonic weapon sounds. Nonetheless, over time they too learned how to identify the weapon sounds they regularly encountered, as well as how one was expected—by commanders and by comrades-in-arms—to act in the presence of those sounds.

For service members, the zones of wartime audition discussed in chapter 2 were, we are now in a position to say, produced within and inflected by the fraught environment of the military auditory regime: they were learned capacities that became embodied knowledge as service members interacted repeatedly with belliphonic sounds *and* with the discursive streams and technological mediations that accompanied them. The feats of identification, echolocation, and interpretation that I pointed to in chapter 1 are similarly entwined in this prereflective, unspoken habitus: they were shaped by it, and once enacted, they became a part of it. They were public performances that helped to entrain other auditors into a synchronized, intersubjective experience of combat. Green troops heard a noise and said *what the fuck was that?* Seasoned troops calmly explained, *that was a mortar, and it sounds like it hit near the PX. We've been getting mortared from that neighborhood at the same time of day for a week now.* The next time the same sound occurred, the now-not-quite-so-green troops said *ah yes, another mortar, just like yesterday.* These semi-improvised, semi-scripted performances, along with the technologies and bureaucracies and life histories that accompanied them, emerged from and contributed to the self-reproducing cultural matrix of wartime.

IDEALS OF MILITARY AUDITION

The zones of wartime audition were thus not self-evident but learned. Some of this learning took place in basic training, as service members were exposed to different weapons systems and the doctrine of "situational awareness." Much learning took place, as described above, after deployment, on the ground, in the direct experience of combat. But most service members arrived in the war zone and even in the military already equipped with a powerful set of listening stereotypes to emulate. These ideals of military audition had been prefiltered through lifeworlds and mediascapes, and so arrived in Iraq, once again, as unquestioned doxa or "common sense." Together, they formed the conceptual foundation upon which the military auditory regime of Operation Iraqi Freedom rested. All of them can be traced deep into the history of warfare, and so are not unique to the Iraq War, but their character was subtly inflected by the Iraq War and the generation of service members who formed the bulk of the troops. We could label them the ideals of (1) expert masculine auscultation, (2) hypermasculine inaudition, and (3) euphoric auditory hypermasculinity. Or we could be more attentive to the conversational style of the military and call them the ideals of (1) "being a professional," (2) "staying cool under fire," and (3) "feeling the rush."[5]

You have no doubt noticed the presence of the terms "masculine" and "hypermasculine" in each of the formal descriptors above. This should not be surprising. To assert that the US military—a fighting force that still restricts women from serving in most combat positions and prohibited uncloseted gay people from serving until several months prior to this writing—has a lot invested in a rather potent and aggressive stereotype of heteronormative masculinity is to indulge in understatement. The question is not *whether* the military's symbols, rituals, and behavioral models emphasize conventions of masculinity, but *how* something as seemingly passive and innocuous as listening aids in the construction of the military subject (whether male or female) as masculine. To code the first listening ideal "masculine" is to assert that the behavior embedded within it is widely read by the military (and more broadly) as emblematic of so-called "manly" traits: objectivity (as opposed to empathy), rationality (as opposed to emotionality), toughness (as opposed to delicacy). To label the second two ideals "hypermasculine" is to point to an expanded constellation of traits that includes a high level of comfort with violence and a visceral attraction to dangerous situations.[6] In reaching toward these ideals of audition (or, depending on one's outlook, in falling into these pernicious stereotypes), service members ended up unconsciously rehearsing and re-presenting a kind of (hyper)masculinity that helped them fit into the military community and propagate its ethos.

Being a professional

Military service members are expert auditors. They transform sound into actionable intelligence; with great precision, they can determine what's happening by tuning into the sounds that surround them. They calmly assess the situation, as a doctor would, discerning, through listening and looking, the sonic and other pathologies in the neighborhood. They act bravely when they encounter sonic evidence of danger, and maybe even crack a little joke to demonstrate their sangfroid.

This doesn't always happen, of course. Exposure to the belliphonic can produce confusion, fear, and ambivalence in the most seasoned service member. But it is, unambiguously, an ideal to which military auditors aspire. Calm professionalism has been valorized throughout the history of the US military; to this day it is encoded in the central lines of the Soldier's Creed:

I am disciplined, physically and mentally tough, trained and proficient in my warrior tasks and drills./I always maintain my arms, my equipment and myself./I am an expert and I am a professional.[7]

Representations of military auditors "being professional" and performing acts of expert masculine auscultation are legion. Let's look at two archetypal examples, found in popular films to which active-duty service members drew my attention:

Casablanca (1942)
Rick Blaine (Humphrey Bogart) is a nightclub owner in Casablanca in December 1941. Currently a civilian, he was once a soldier, fighting on the side of the Loyalists in the Spanish Civil War—and it's clear by the film's end that he is headed back into the fight. A flashback to 1940 finds Rick and his young lover Ilsa Lund (Ingrid Bergman) in a small café in Paris at the start of the German invasion. They stand at the café window, kissing, when they are interrupted by the distant boom of cannons. Ilsa breaks off the kiss and looks out the window, frightened.
ILSA, looking up into Rick's eyes:
"Was that cannon fire?"
She drops her head onto Rick's shoulder
"Or is it my heart pounding?"

RICK, unfazed:
"Ah, that's the new German 77.
And judging by the sound, only about thirty-five miles away."
Rick nonchalantly picks up a champagne glass and directs Ilsa to a seat at a table.
More cannon fire echoes in the distance.

RICK, amused:
"And getting closer every minute."
Handing Ilsa a glass of champagne:
"Here, drink up, we'll never finish the other three."

Concise, confident, and impeccably cool, Rick effortlessly decodes the sounds of the German cannons, and refuses to allow them to ruffle his feathers.[8] His performance of masculine auditory prowess contrasts starkly with Ilsa's more emotional, troubled, questioning—in other words, "feminine"—reaction to the same set of belliphonic sounds.[9]

That same kind of unflappable acuity is deployed in a more aggressive context in a war film some four decades later, directed by and starring Clint Eastwood:

Heartbreak Ridge (1986)
    Marine Gunnery Sergeant Thomas Highway (Clint Eastwood), a veteran of the Korean and Vietnam wars, has been tasked with training a reconnaissance platoon during the buildup to the US invasion of Grenada. Nearly every word out of the seasoned sergeant's mouth is profane. (When introducing himself to the platoon, for example, he growls "My name is Gunnery Sergeant Highway, and I've drunk more beer and pissed more blood and banged more quiff and busted more ass than all you numbnuts put together.") The platoon is undisciplined and disrespectful, but eventually warms to his harsh tactics. Early on in their training, Highway leads them on an extended jog through territory that ranges from dusty fields to dense woods. In the woods, as they round a path that opens out onto a small clearing, Highway veers off the path and the Marines, oblivious, jog on. Highway reappears at the tail end of the jogging formation, an assault rifle in his hands.
    As the last Marines enter the clearing, Highway opens fire on them. He shoots approximately thirty live rounds at their feet, while the Marines scream in terror and fall over themselves in a panicked attempt to flee.

PLATOON MEMBERS, screaming:
"Shit!" "Fuck!" "Get out of my way!" "What the hell's goin' on, man?"
    As the mayhem subsides, and the Marines look, bewildered, in Highway's direction, he explains the point of this unorthodox exercise:

HIGHWAY, angrily, through gritted teeth a la Dirty Harry:
"This is the AK-47 assault rifle, the preferred weapon of your enemy.
And it makes a distinctive sound when fired at you. So remember it."

Later in the film, the Marines have an opportunity to demonstrate that their ability to act as auditory professionals has improved. The platoon's commanding officer—a young, effete, glasses-wearing, college-educated lieutenant—and the rest of the platoon have begun walking through a small settlement of wooden structures on a training exercise; Highway emerges from one of them and unleashes another barrage of live AK fire. As the enlisted men scramble for cover (without the screaming and confusion this time), it is the lieutenant's turn to be overwhelmed:

LIEUTENANT *(sprawled behind a barrier, screams):*
   "Good Lord, what was that?"

ENLISTED MAN #1 *(calmly, with a slightly pedantic tone):*
   "Sir, that's an AK-47 assault weapon."

ENLISTED MAN #2:
   "The preferred weapon of our enemy."

ENLISTED MAN #3:
   "It makes a very distinctive sound when fired at us, sir."

LIEUTENANT *(still breathing heavily, but impressed, and bemused):*
   "Yes it does, doesn't it!"

Here, the imperative to develop what Trevor Pinch, Karin Bijsterveld, and others have called "diagnostic listening" skills is so intense that the gunnery sergeant resorts to violent tactics to instill it in his charges.[10] Auditory training is presented as a life-saving technique, and those who have acquired the skill of auscultation are equipped for victory. The expert masculine auscultator is the ideal that lies at the center of the narrational zone of audition that was discussed in chapter 2. People develop this kind of listening skill through training and experience, but they join the armed forces already understanding that it is an important virtue. War culture, as transmitted from one generation of soldiers to another and as idealized in films such as the ones above, thus establishes the ideal of expert listening as something that makes one an effective warrior and a bearer of valued traits: competence, bravery, rationality.

Nearly every one of the male and female service members whom I interviewed appeared to implicitly understand and emulate this ideal, standing ready with stories of their experiences as expert auscultators in the narrational zone. Civil servants (e.g., USAID workers, embassy staff) also tended to take pride in their ability to discern the distinct sounds that weapons make, and be able to identify them calmly, without leaping into their body armor or diving under their beds. At the same time, their adoption of the ideal of expert auscultation was nowhere near as complete or intense as that of their counterparts in the armed forces. This does not mean that the ideal was less universally recognized—only that civil servants felt less constricted by it. One USAID employee who worked in the International Zone in 2006 admitted that she was unable to listen to weaponry with the acuity of the experts. She framed this inability in explicitly gendered terms:

> I would be with military people and they would say, "well this is a 50 caliber" or "that was this" or "this was that." I never got attuned to that. I'd say, "how do you know that?" Well because they're in the military and they're used to it or the security detail or *maybe because I'm a girly-girl.* I mean I could tell if it was something loud, bigger was loud, then smaller, if it was small arm fire, you just get to know that. How you instinctively get to know that, I don't really know. [my emphasis]

Military proficiency and masculinity are performed in part through feats of expert audition. The better one is at decoding belliphonic sounds, the larger and more reliable his or her narrational zone becomes. And with the expansion and refinement of the narrational zone, the military auditor is regarded as a bigger expert, a better warrior, and a more masculine, macho presence on the battlefield.

With an understanding of the importance of "being a professional" now in place, we are able to discern additional dimensions within pronouncements such as the one below, which was first discussed in chapter 1:

> The gun being fired near you is . . . very loud, I mean there's almost a pain sensation involved . . . and that's probably within about fifty feet. Outside fifty feet, that's where the sound really changes depending on what direction it is, if it's being fired away from you or towards you and how close the bullet passes. If you can hear a "phiff" noise or a "zing," in and around you, the bullet probably passed within a few feet of you, probably about ten feet at the limit. And that's really nerve-wracking. Also, ricochets off your vehicle or anything near you—you know you hear it ricocheting and you usually get a "zing" noise like in the Western movies, and those aren't loud at all, sometimes you can't even—and then you're like "What was that?" and then you're like, "Oh crap, we're getting shot at" and everybody hits the ground, because somebody just heard a "ffft," you know, a "phip" or a "ffff." If they're shooting away from you, and you're away from the fire as well, you usually can't hear the bullet as it travels, but if it's being fired toward you, as it passes you or after it passes you, you can certainly hear the air being displaced.

Apprehended from the standpoint of the auditory regime, it is clear that this display of auditory virtuosity is about much more than simply "the sounds themselves." It is a description of sounds that is simultaneously a performance of the military values of competence, rationality, and toughness in the face of violence. Not unlike doctors, for whom the stethoscope and the act of auscultation it enables are hallmarks of the profession, the battlefield auditor above diagnoses the "patient"—a violent timespace—while at the same time publicly demonstrating his own professional qualifications. However, in contrast to the act of placing the stethoscope to the patient's chest, the auditory event described above is simultaneously an act of diagnosis *and* an act of treatment—not for the patient, but for the doctor himself. In diagnosing belliphonic pathologies with a professional's ear, expert auscultators shield themselves from the sheer terror of the *violent auditory unknown*. This is one of the moments in which *listening* differs most greatly from *hearing*: when one has (or cultivates, or even imitates) the presence of mind needed in order to truly listen to sounds and then identify them, the sounds emerge from this operation of identification somewhat pacified. Perhaps this is one of the reasons that the doctrine of "being a professional" is so deeply ingrained in the practice of wartime audition.

Staying Cool Under Fire

Military auditors stay cool under fire. They don't freak out, they don't cry, they don't panic, they don't scream or even flinch when a bullet whizzes by their heads. They are stoic masters of their own bodies. In fact, they are so self-possessed, so in control, that they appear not to notice the loud sounds of bombs exploding near them. They walk through violent timespaces utterly unperturbed. Oblivious to the dangers that surround them, they exude an aura of invincibility.

This doesn't always happen, of course. There are sonic events in wartime that cause everyone to flinch. But it is, unambiguously, an ideal to which military auditors aspire. Along with the virtuosity of their acts of decoding the sonic environment, military auditors strive to master their bodies, to rein in the chemicals that course through their veins in situations of combat or attack, to stay cool when the action gets hot. Modeled in lived experience, reinforced in cinema and folklore, the auditor who keeps cool under fire performs an ideal of inaudition that bespeaks an almost superhuman comfort with the immediacy of extreme violence. An exemplary representation of this kind of selective deadening can be found in one of most famous scenes of one of the most widely referenced war films ever released:

Apocalypse Now (1979):
  Lieutenant Colonel Bill Kilgore (Robert Duvall) commands a squadron of attack helicopters. The scene in question finds him on the ground, in the middle of an intense battle near the Vietnamese coast. After inexplicably stripping off his shirt, the bare-chested Kilgore, still wearing his cavalry Stetson, leaps out of his foxhole and walks through the battlefield, accompanied by a soldier carrying the squadron radio unit. Shouting over the gunfire, Kilgore calls in a massive napalm air strike on enemy positions at the treeline, telling the pilot to "Bomb them into the Stone Age, son." The planes make a low pass of the tree line, drop their napalm canisters, and fly off as a line of orange-flamed explosions lights up the forest. As the oily mushroom clouds rise up

and subside, Kilgore stands up, hands on his hips, and shouts a question over the din to one of the enlisted men:

<u>*KILGORE:*</u>

"Smell that? You smell that?"

<u>*LANCE*</u>, *crouching in the foxhole:*

"What?"

<u>*KILGORE:*</u>

"Napalm, son. Nothing else in the world smells like that."

Kilgore calmly lowers himself into a squatting position, resting his forearms against his thighs, fingers interlaced. His voice takes on a contemplative tone. It's as if he's not on the battlefield but kneeling by the edge of a peaceful stream. During his speech, helicopters fly by, mortars explode, bullets zip in the background, but Kilgore doesn't appear to hear any of them.

<u>*KILGORE:*</u>

"I love the smell of napalm in the morning. You know, one time we had a hill bombed, for twelve hours. When it was all over, I walked up. We didn't find one of 'em, not one stinking dink body. The smell, you know that gasoline smell, the whole hill . . . smelled like—"

and here, he pauses for a full five seconds, staring off into the middle distance as he searches for the appropriate word. When he finds it, his voice lowers in pitch and volume as he utters:

"—victory."

A helicopter flies by, and a mortar explodes roughly ten feet behind Kilgore's back. The two infantrymen who are crouched nearest him flinch, but Kilgore doesn't appear to notice. He continues:

"Someday this war's gonna end."

And then walks off calmly amidst the cacophony of battle, as if walking through a quiet forest.

Moving through a combat environment calmly, without flinching at belliphonic sounds, is a feat of mind over body, and it is one that must be learned. The traits associated with the ideal of hypermasculine inaudition are more volatile than those linked to the universally privileged stereotype of auditory professionalism, however. Unlike the auditory professional, whose prestige grows in tandem with his listening prowess, the auditor who has attained perfect nonchalance under fire is regarded as flirting with irrationality, and even madness. While admired and useful in moderation, when taken to the extreme, hypermasculine inaudition becomes pathological: at its most complete, it is marked by the thousand-yard stare and the loss of the inherent human fear of death—traits that can render the combat-weary soldier a liability to himself and to his comrades. Still, dialed back to an acceptable level, the ability to display hypermasculine comfort in the face of painfully loud and invasive violent acts remains a badge of honor among service members.

We are now equipped to see that this ideal of auditory jadedness is the force at work in what I called the zone of the audible inaudible in chapter 2. The soldier who claimed to "hear it so often it becomes background noise" was exhibiting pride in his ability to maintain that ideal within the operational limits that allow the audible inaudible to yoke up with the narrational zone into a unified practice of efficient listening. His body has been trained to ignore those sounds that carry no actionable content, and to remain hyperaware of sounds that do. While presented in that quote and elsewhere as the natural result of exposure to the belliphonic, it is clearly a balancing act: military auditors must not let their zone of the audible inaudible disappear, lest they go crazy from the constant sound of distant gunfire. Nor must they allow the audible inaudible to swallow the narrational or tactical zones, as this would entail their transformation into the ranks of those zombified by war, and therefore into a trauma patient unfit to serve. Maintaining this balancing act requires training and support; the auditory regime represents precisely the institutions, conversations, and listening habitus that provide them.

Feeling the Rush

The combat service member isn't just brave in the face of danger; he loves danger. He is intoxicated by combat, and feels a rush of energy when he's surrounded by whizzing bullets, exploding mortars and other belliphonic sounds. These sounds, so intimately connected with death, make him feel truly alive. *He whoops with euphoria amid the thunder of battle, and spurs his comrades on to ever greater feats of victory.*

Once again, it will come as no surprise to learn that this doesn't always happen. Belliphonic battle sounds and the violent events that accompany them cause bodies to be flooded with cortisol and adrenaline, but the reflexive actions that those chemicals trigger can tilt in the direction of retreat as well as attack, terror as well as euphoria. All the same, it is, yet again, an ideal to which military auditors aspire. In the intersubjective experience of battle, service members listen to the sounds of weaponry, but they also listen to one another as they react to those sounds. This reaction, this vocal performance, can channel the adrenaline away from the urge to flee or freeze and toward a hypermasculine display of bravado and aggression. And just as the other ideals find themselves modeled in cinematic depictions of war, Hollywood provides many representations of combat troops "feeling the rush" in the wake of loud military events, both incoming and outgoing: from the cathartic whooping when Tom Cruise's character buzzes the control tower in *Top Gun* to the ecstatic screaming that greets the alien ship's explosion in *Independence Day,* cinematic models of euphoric reactions to spectacular scenes of loud military aggression are extremely common.

A filmic model that is more relevant to my specific purpose here is the iconic *Red Badge of Courage*, shot in 1951 and starring WWII Medal of Honor recipient Audie Murphy.[11] Based on Stephen Crane's classic Civil War novel, Murphy plays the role of a young Union infantryman who flinches at the sound of the cannons and flees the battlefield during his regiment's first altercation with the Confederate army. The next day, disgusted by his cowardice, he finds himself reacting differently to the chaos of rifle shot, cannon, and the battle cry of the advancing enemy:

The Red Badge of Courage (1951)

Fleming (Audie Murphy) crouches in a battle line next to his friend Wilson (Bill Mauldin) as the Confederates mount a charge. Smoke from the big guns obscures the figures of the advancing army, rendering the visual field of this black-and-white battle scene almost abstract—clouds of grey on grey. In contrast, the belliphonic noise is immediate and almost overwhelming, with Union cannons firing right over the soldiers' heads from about twenty feet behind them, the high-pitched "rebel yell" of the advancing Confederates building in a slow crescendo, and the periodic crash of forty Springfield rifle muskets being fired simultaneously by the Union troops. When one of his comrades falls down wounded, Fleming takes his place, and finds himself next to Wilson.

WILSON, somewhat diffidently:

"[They're] comin' right at us."

FLEMING, with newfound and undisguised aggression:

"They'd better watch out. By jiminy, if they keep on hittin' at us, well—they'd just better watch out, that's all I say!"

WILSON, circumspect:

"[If] they keep on hittin' at us they'll knock us into the river."

FLEMING, impassioned, shouts:

"The devil they will!"

The explosions build to a climax, at which point Bronislau Kaper's musical score kicks in with intensity: strings attack a single high-pitched figure while a chorus of low brass moves urgently upward. These musical gestures lead the ear to a second climax as they transform into a recapitulation of "The Battle Hymn of the Republic," which serves as the film's principal leitmotif. Amid this loud fusion of diegetic and nondiegetic sounds, something snaps in Fleming, and he leaps over the berm and begins charging through the open field toward the enemy. Taking some cover behind an abandoned hayrick, Fleming stuffs another ball in his musket, and continues to race toward the Confederates, completely unprotected. The narrator's voice appears as Fleming is in mid-charge:

NARRATOR:

"The youth was not conscious that he was erect upon his feet. He lost every sense but his hate. For the first time in his life he was possessed by a great passion: the passion to destroy the enemy. He felt the power of an army in himself. He was a battle cry, a bullet, a sword."

No longer flinching when the cannon roar, Fleming is spurred on by belliphonic sound and the other stimuli of combat to leap into the fray, risk his life, and unite his stunned comrades in their admiration of his bravery. In the film's final scenes, he greets the thunder of the rebel cannon with his own battle cry as he screams for his fellow troops to follow him.

In Iraq, combat service members worked to master their adrenalin-infused fear and rechannel it as aggression and euphoria—"the passion to destroy the enemy," or simply the joy of survival mixed with a contemptuous "fuck you" to the instigator of the failed attack. In the homemade video titled "I Get Blown Up" (transcribed in chapter 1), the full-spectrum sensory experience of surviving an IED attack, an experience that temporarily deafened the gunner, afforded the marines in question the opportunity to perform for themselves and one another a kind of toughness and excitement that is thoroughly hypermasculine in its presentation. Let's look at this transcript again, this time through the lens of the auditory regime. (The transcript can be found on pp. 71–72.)

Through a mixture of studied nonchalance ("Well, I guess we're done for the day"), bravado ("Fuck yeah! Oh, yeah, that was super!"), and expressions of imperturbability in the face of physical trauma ("Haha, my ears are ripped! . . . My ears are fuckin' done!"), the Marines seamlessly incorporated the explosion into their ongoing auto-narratives of sangfroid and toughness. Like the Italian Futurists who preceded them a century ago, they treated the explosion as an exhilarating performance of "the Art of Noise": a thrilling, aestheticized spectacle.[12] Of course, they could do so because they reflected on the explosion from subject positions that were not already fatally fractured; we can easily imagine the same explosion triggering a wholly different reaction in a service member who was already traumatized by previous exposures to violent acts. But it is the potential for the explosion to create physiological and psychological damage that makes this performance of hypermasculine euphoria so important. From the vantage point of the marines in the Humvee, "feeling the rush" can be understood as a tactic for scripting behavior within the unstable inner zones of wartime audition characterized by the ever-present possibility of violent death.

NATIONAL AUDITION

As I mentioned in the introduction, when discussing the auditory tactics of the military I have concentrated my attention on the American armed forces rather than the multinational coalition that the Bush administration formed before invading Iraq. A brief deviation from that pattern will prove useful here as an illustration of the degree to which indoctrination into an auditory regime allowed service members to develop very specific embodied reactions to belliphonic sound. These reactions were so deeply ingrained that they felt instantaneous and precultural to the auditors who performed them. But they were taught, and that teaching sometimes varied within the "coalition of the willing."

Here is a case in point, involving a distinction between British and American military tactics for dealing with belliphonic sounds, as observed from the vantage point of a civilian auditor whose informal training placed him between the two. Gavin, a civil servant who is mentioned elsewhere in this volume, lived and worked in the International Zone during a period when it was the target of frequent mortar attacks. In a tense environment such as this, where the sound of an incoming mortar or rocket attack could precede detonation by a few seconds or less, auditors had to learn to make quick decisions:

> Well, you'd have to decide. I know something's gonna hit, so do I drop, British style, just drop where you are? Because . . . you know, our walls were covered with impacts from mortars and rockets, and [the impact scars] were all above three feet maybe. . . . You all talk about this, when you're out on a FOB or something: the British, the British just drop. If you hear something, just lie down. Cause you're probably not going to get hit unless it hits exactly where you are. And the American thing is to decide, where are you going to run? Where is the nearest duck-and-cover bunker and can you reach it in ten seconds? And if not, where's the next best place, but if you're running, you're completely exposed. The upper half of your body is gonna get hit by anything that hits within your line of sight, which is a lot less safe. So you go through a complex calculation, and I tended to, I mean I got caught outside in that housing complex a lot. We had [covered] porches, [and] I would tend to just run into somebody's porch. . . . There was a wall there that you could duck behind and get down, which seemed to me to be kind of a reasonable compromise. If you were hearing impacts, you would have to judge: you needed to know how close that was. Should I just drop or, you know, if you hear something far away, you know it's a mortar but it's like within a mile, then OK I've got time to get on a porch or I've got time to get to a duck-and-cover bunker. But I can remember like serious adrenalin one time, walking back from lunch with three or four people, and we hear: "BOOM!" one crack, you know, then "BOOM!" closer and then it was just like "shit . . ." and that was one of those days when we got hit pretty hard. So you do have a very quick visual reconnaissance and calculus [to determine] where do I go from here?[13]

Gavin's experiences with mortars took place within a tactical zone of audition, the space of compressed hermeneutics where split-second decisions are made. But they are not made from a position of tabula rasa. The military auditors around him had to train their bodies to react to sound and other sensations in order to maximize their chances for avoiding injury. Here, in exclusive areas within their broadly overlapping auditory regimes, they trained themselves to be British (and drop) or American (and run for cover). In his moment of indecision, when he had to consciously choose how to act, Gavin found himself in the gap between two versions of the military auditory regime—which, he learned, was an inherently dangerous place to be.

OBLIQUE INDOCTRINATION OF BELLIPHONIC EARS

Beyond the military tactics described above, the catharsis experienced by service members who regularly listened to metal and other "extreme" musics at loud volume also helped to script culturally appropriate responses to loud violence. The sonic onslaught of metal, arguably the most popular genre among US troops, felt liberatory and transgressive, but also safe: it was predictable, rhythmic, "noise"-infused music, performed aggressively, composed with catharsis in mind—and remaining at all times under the listener's control.[14] In deploying this music as part of a public performance of socially acceptable rhythmic and timbral aggression, service members unconsciously trained themselves to react to belliphonic sound as they would to metal's headbanging throb: "fuck yeah! Oh, yeah, that was super!"[15]

The tight relation between the catharsis afforded by music and that afforded by combat is rendered explicit in George Gittoes' documentary *Soundtrack to War*, filmed at the beginning of Operation Iraqi Freedom, in the spring and summer of 2003. In it, Gittoes comes upon a two young soldiers sitting outdoors, their M16s propped up against a wall. One of the soldiers is practicing a metal lick on an electric guitar plugged into a cheap amp. He explains for the camera:

SOLDIER #1: That was some music I've been working on for the past three days, a riff that came into my head, um, for me, I'm gonna put some gore metal lyrics to it, I think that'll sound the best. And uh, to me, war *is* heavy metal. [*Somewhat self-consciously he flashes the "devil horns," pinkie and index fingers extended upward, tongue out.*]

His friend then elaborates:

SOLDIER #2: War is heavy metal: it's fast-paced, heavy, and emotional. [It] gets your adrenaline goin', it helps you feel what you got to feel, and get it out of the way . . .

Later in this volume I will explore at some length the complicated ethical terrain upon which service members in Iraq drew this kind of equation between war and music, and the ways in which that equation feeds into the aestheticization of violence. For now, though, I'll simply suggest that the blurring of music and combat in the phrase "war *is* heavy metal" provides yet another conceptual template for the mode of hypermasculine euphoric listening to belliphonic sound.

The tension between the power of belliphonic sounds and the interpretive practices and coping mechanisms that emerge in reaction to them was played out within the boundaries of an inherently masculinist military auditory regime that relies in part on widely traded stereotypes such as these. Auditors in Iraq took for granted that the auditory techniques of "being a professional," "staying cool under fire," and "feeling the rush" enabled them to perform—and in performing acquire—valued traits such as bravery, toughness, and competence. In addition to experiencing combat firsthand (like the Marines who survived the IED explosion) and being steeped in cultural products (such as the well-known films above), inexperienced service members engaged in a host of informal interactions with their seasoned comrades, interactions that helped to solidify these privileged ideals of auditory awareness.

These interactions took many forms. In a self-taped video made in a drab office trailer on Loyalty Base near Ramadi, an unnamed military contractor plays a practical joke on his colleague, who, it appears, is a third-country subcontractor.[16] After setting up the camera, the American contractor calls his colleague in, ostensibly to give him some clerical training. Unbeknownst to the trainee, he has loaded a recording of the "incoming" alarm on his computer, and turned his speakers up to maximum volume. With an inconspicuous keystroke, the alarm is triggered: eight loud blasts of the siren, followed by a recorded voice shouting "Incoming! Incoming! Incoming!" and more siren blasts. The unsuspecting trainee leaps off the chair and onto the ground, lying face down as the alarm continues to sound. The contractor, who has also dropped to the ground, then slaps the trailer floor hard with the flat of his hand, roughly simulating a mortar's impact. Groaning "Oh, shit! Aggh! Aaaghhh! Oh, shit!" he then lurches to the door, his hand held to his stomach as if he's been hit by shrapnel. The trainee stands up, dumbfounded, until the contractor comes in, doubled over in laughter, and retriggers the alarm, revealing its artifice. The clip ends with the contractor giving his exasperated trainee a hug. Was this "false alarm" a simple, juvenile, frat-house-style prank? Yes. Was it also an exchange that solidified the centrality of "being a professional" and "staying cool under fire" within the military? Absolutely. We can profitably imagine the auditory regime of Operation Iraqi Freedom as being made up of countless microinteractions such as this.

SITUATIONAL AWARENESS

By now it should be abundantly clear that service members were listening not from a position of tabula rasa but from within what John Mowitt, with a nod toward Raymond

Williams, calls a "structure of listening,"[17] or employing what Jonathan Sterne has called "audile techniques."[18] In other words, they were never "simply listening," but were always listening within the regimented environment of a military that formally endorsed the stance of "situational awareness" and informally cultivated the overlapping ideal stances mentioned above. Evidence of the labor the military expends on disciplining listening can be found in a broad array of regulations and training manuals, beginning with the army field manual titled *The Warrior Ethos and Soldier Combat Skills*.[19] The most recent edition, published in January 2008 and reflecting four years of the Army's combat experiences in Iraq, emphasizes the importance of the SLLS (stop-look-listen-smell) maneuver that Jason Sagebiel, earlier in this volume, described as central to his training as a marine scout-sniper. In a chapter revealingly titled "Every Soldier is a Sensor," the relationship between individual soldiers' senses and the chain of command is explicitly prescribed:

> Every Soldier, as a part of a small unit, can provide useful information and is an essential component to the commanders achieving situational understanding. The task is critical, because the environment in which Soldiers operate is characterized by violence, uncertainty, complexity, and asymmetric methods by the enemy. The increased situational awareness that you must develop through personal contact and observation is a critical element of the friendly force's ability to more fully understand the operational environment. *Your life and the lives of your fellow Soldiers could depend on reporting what you see, hear, and smell.*[20] [my emphasis]

Soldiers in Iraq were instructed to keep their ears attuned to the presence of "running engines or track sounds; voices; metallic sounds; gunfire, by weapon type; unusual calm or silence; dismounted movement; [and] aircraft." They were encouraged to count the time between seeing a weapon's flash and hearing its report, and then to multiply by three to determine its distance in hundreds of meters. And they were taught to recognize certain sounds and react instantaneously to them. When moving through enemy territory at night, their ears needed to be particularly acute and their reactions quick, as this injunction from the field manual indicates:

> If you hear the firing of an aerial flare while you are moving, flip up your [night vision device] and hit the ground (behind cover if possible) while the flare is rising and before it bursts and illuminates.[21]

Throughout the process of training and indoctrination into military norms, the sustained emphasis on situational awareness placed listening, along with looking and smelling, at the forefront of the sensory tactics of the Iraq War. According to the military auditory regime, an effective listener was one who paid attention to sounds and other stimuli, quickly ascertained their significance, and then acted judiciously upon the information that they yielded.

In order to do so, however, the military ear had to be in good working condition. In other words, in war, as elsewhere, listening as an intentional act is forever subordinate to and dependent upon hearing as a biological feat. Just as a Humvee engine is only useful if it is in good operating condition, the instrumentalized ear of the military "soldier-sensor" could only be regarded as an asset if it was not damaged. A 2009 article on the importance of audiology to the Army's effectiveness warns:

> Poor hearing jeopardizes the unit mission and increases the likelihood of a serious mishap due to a soldier's inability to hear verbal orders, understand radio communications, localize the direction of sounds, gauge distances accurately, and have good overall situational awareness.[22]

An official statute regarding the Army Hearing Program makes the case even more forcefully:

> Hearing is a critical sensor used by Soldiers that increases their survivability and lethality. . . . Good hearing can mean the difference between life and death in combat, as well as in training.[23]

In addition to proclamations such as these, we can ascertain the importance of belliphonic listening by examining the lengths to which the military went to protect service members' ears from the extremely loud belliphonic sounds that often surrounded them. While military technology in general has been steadily developing from decade to decade, the US military only recently began making major advancements in hearing protection. During Operation Iraqi Freedom and the ongoing war in Afghanistan, the problem of hearing loss was attended to as never before. Early statistics indicated that the rates of tinnitus and permanent hearing loss among troops in Iraq and Afghanistan were exponentially higher than those from nondeployed troops—so high, in fact, that they constituted the two most common injuries in those wars. Military strategists voiced alarm that tinnitus and hearing loss threatened situational awareness and degraded the ability of troops to communicate while on mission.

Over the course of the war, audiological research confirmed this fear. One study, published in 2008, examined the time that it took for tank crewmen to act correctly upon spoken orders in combat situations. Those with "poor word intelligibility" (i.e., hearing loss that prevented them from hearing more than 50 percent of what was said to them) took 90 seconds to identify a target, whereas those with "good word intelligibility" (i.e., the ability to discern more than 50 percent of spoken orders) took only 40 seconds. More distressingly, 37 percent of those with poor word intelligibility heard the command incorrectly, as opposed to only 1 percent of the other group. These incidents of mishearing resulted in crewmen with substantial hearing loss "engaging incorrect targets"—in other words, firing a 120 mm explosive cannon round at the wrong people or structures—8 percent of the time. These potentially tragic incidents did not occur at all among the troops with undamaged hearing who were evaluated. This study points to the obvious fact that, in combat, the stakes for accurate communication could not be higher. In combat, hearing loss is not merely inconvenient; it is a disability that can easily produce unwanted, unnecessary deaths.

I will return to the subject of hearing loss in chapter 5. For now, it is enough to stress that hearing loss during Operation Iraqi Freedom was a problem of staggering proportions,[24] and that the military deployed a large number of audiologists and introduced a number of new technologies to address it. The most widespread of these technologies was the Combat Arms Earplug, distributed to soldiers and marines when they first deployed to Afghanistan in 2001, and standard issue to combat troops throughout the Iraqi theater. As described by a team of military audiologists:

> The device allows soft sounds to flow unimpeded through a filter but blocks loud impulse sounds, such as an explosion or a rifle discharging. This allows effective communication, enables situational awareness, and provides protection from hazardous weapons firing and explosions. With units' strength decreasing because of hearing loss, commanders began to recognize that hearing readiness is an extremely important factor of a unit's performance in combat. All deploying soldiers were therefore issued the earplugs in 2004. In fact, the US Marine Corps was so convinced of the effectiveness of the combat arms earplug that it ordered over 20,000 pairs, thereby temporarily depleting the entire national stock in 2003.[25]

One of the virtues of the combat arms earplug was its low cost: the unit price of the reusable plugs was roughly $10 per pair. Complementing this low-cost, low-tech measure were more sophisticated noise-reducing technologies. The Combat Vehicle Crewman Headset (CVC), manufactured by Bose, featured full-spectrum noise reduction and noise-reducing microphones, which attenuated engine noises in order to improve the intelligibility of oral communication. CVC headsets were widely distributed among "mounted" troops, those who served in tracked vehicles such as Abrams tanks and Bradley Fighting Vehicles. Loud impulse noises such as explosions activated an internal circuit that instantly triggered robust noise reduction in the CVC. Similarly, military-grade headsets manufactured by Peltor attenuated loud sounds down to 82 decibels. Unlike the CVC, however, Peltors also amplified soft ambient sounds up to 18 decibels.

Peltors were so effective at blocking out the noise of an explosion that they gave one of my interlocutors a scare after his first close-up experience of an IED explosion:

I was hit by an IED, a very, very large IED, very, very close. And when I woke back up I thought I had lost my hearing—I mean I couldn't hear anything at all, but I could see people talking to me. And it wasn't until [then that] I realized that there is an emergency cutoff on the Peltor where it just completely shuts everything off! [laughter] Oh yeah, I was yelling, "Hey! Can you hear me?" But yeah, it just shuts off when a really large explosion happens.[26]

QuietPro, a set of in-the-ear plugs connected to a pocket-sized control unit, was yet another device developed specifically to help infantry "maintain situational awareness . . . in noisy combat situations." Manufactured by Nacre, a Norwegian company, QuietPro sets feature a digital processor that samples incoming sound waves 64,000 times per second. Like the Peltor sets, the instant an explosion or other loud event occurs, ambient amplification is turned off and active noise cancellation is turned on. Unlike the Peltors (or at least the generation that the soldier above used), QuietPro immediately restores the previous settings as soon as the sound has passed.

If these technologies rendered their wearers auditory cyborgs of sorts, with ears more robust and sensitive than those of unassisted auditors, other technologies were designed to supplant human hearing altogether. In response to the extreme challenges the noisy background posed to military auditors, the US military began supplying some troops with artificial gunfire detection devices in 2008. One such device, the Boomerang, developed by BBN Technologies, consists of an array of seven microphones protruding from a metal pole and hooked up to an onboard computer. The Boomerang was mounted onto Humvees and other vehicles that patrolled Iraqi streets. When a bullet passed within fifty feet of the device, the computer recorded the moment its passage was detected by each microphone; based on the trajectory of the shock wave and the time elapsed between the shock wave and the muzzle blast, it calculated the azimuth, range, and elevation of the shooter. Azimuth and range were delivered to the driver by a computerized male voice (e.g., "shot, three o'clock, one hundred twenty meters"); these two statistics plus elevation data were also projected on a small screen on the dashboard. According to a BBN spokesperson, Boomerang-assisted retaliation for insurgent sniper fire became so accurate that snipers began avoiding vehicles that sported the telltale array of fingerlike microphones (see figure 3.1). Insurgent forces gave the Boomerang a colloquial name that evoked both its shape and its efficacy: "the death octopus."[27]

Beginning in 2011, with the deployment of the Individual Gunshot Detector, a smaller device that a foot soldier could wear, the technological augmentation of human hearing became even more sophisticated.[28] Augmenting the listening skills service members acquired over the course of their tours of duty, high-tech devices such as these radically reconfigured the sensory range of the US military, rendering it distinct from that of all other parties to the conflict.[29] This assemblage—an evolving collection of

FIGURE 3.1 Humvee with Boomerang gunfire detection device attached, Baghdad, Iraq, 2011. (Photo by the author)

common experiences, binding regulations, unexamined doxa, and readily available technologies—helped military auditors determine which sounds were deemed valuable and which were not, which sounds were freighted with meaning and which were insignificant, and, literally, which sounds crossed the threshold from inaudibility into audibility and vice versa. A consideration of these factors demonstrates that there were areas within the military auditory regime that were in every way inaccessible to Iraqi civilians. At the same time, the omnidirectionality of sound and of violence ensured that, to a significant degree, Iraqis and Americans were all enculturated into a broad intersubjective space within which belliphonic sounds resonated with intensity. In the next section, I will try to lay out some of the convergences and divergences between the military auditory regime and the less regimented set of listening practices to which Iraqi civilians had access.

THE INCLUSIVE AUDITORY REGIME OF IRAQI CIVILIANS

The US troop presence in Iraq numbered 157,800 at the peak of the "surge" in 2008.[30] Contractors came close to doubling this number, and coalition troops extended it by another 9,000 or so at their peak.[31] As a result of mandatory training, uniform rules of conduct, and the centripetal force that military culture and "the warrior ethos" have exerted historically, the US military is characterized by a homogeneity unmatched in other institutions. It is in fact an icon of the synchronization of bodies and affect, one in which soldiers *literally* march together in lockstep. It should come as no surprise, then, that the auditory regime of the military is extremely well-defined relative to that of other populations.

The Iraqi civilian population, by contrast, is exponentially larger and more diverse in terms of age, education, professional training, material wealth, and political orientation than the US military. When comparing members of an authoritarian institution such as the military with a large multicultural population such as that of Iraq, we immediately run into a problem of scalability, and, to some degree, incommensurability. The strict listening habitus of any disciplined, top-down organization will in many senses be incomparable with the massive constellation of unregulated listening practices found within an entire nation of people. And yet the extreme exigencies of combat ensure that some entrainment, some synchronization of listening practices, always takes place. As a result, in wartime Iraq, civilians reacted to loud belliphonic sounds in ways that significantly overlapped with the reactions of service members.

Evidence of this overlap can be found in the videotape from a press conference held in Baghdad in 2007. On March 22 of that year, United Nations Secretary General Ban Ki-Moon stood at the tall podium of the press room in the International Zone with Iraqi Prime Minister Nouri al-Maliki.[32] Flagpoles bearing the Iraqi and UN flags had been placed behind the two men on either side of the podium; they stood out against the dark blue cloth and large potted plants that formed the rest of the backdrop for the televised event. As the cameras rolled, Secretary General Ban spoke of the commitment the international community had made to the establishment of a free and democratic Iraq. The next moment, while Ban was waiting for a question from an Arabic-speaking journalist to be translated, a large explosion took place outside the building. The force of the explosion knocked loose small pieces of plaster from the ceiling and caused the flags behind the podium to flutter. The explosion's sound was so powerful that it overwhelmed the capability of the TV cameras to capture it: video footage of the event was accompanied by a loud roar profoundly distorted by the digital "clipping" of the recorders. (That there was clipping was understandable, given the magnitude of the explosion; they would later discover that a rocket had landed a mere fifty yards away, carving out a large crater one meter deep and throwing shrapnel throughout the courtyard.)

Confronted by irrefutable sensory evidence of the explosion, Mr. Ban reacted instinctively. His body immediately pulled down into a protective crouch, his eyes darting right and left to try to catch a glimpse of what had happened. Ban's encounter with the belliphonic surely caused cortisol and adrenalin to shoot into his bloodstream; his wide-eyed, open-mouthed crouch would have been accompanied by the fast pounding of his heart, a flush of perspiration, and a surge of "fight, flight, or freeze" energy. His reaction to the sonic and haptic intensity of the unseen explosion was, in other words, precisely the one that humans evolved in order to survive in the face of danger. That this reaction was not accompanied by a startled scream (as it would have been, I imagine, had I attended the press conference) was a testament to Mr. Ban's relative composure in the face of an extreme event.

What is remarkable about the video recording of the press conference is not how Mr. Ban reacted, however, but rather the fact that Mr. Maliki, standing at the same podium, managed *not* to react in any visible way. As Ban was heading into his crouch, Maliki stood erect. He didn't scream, didn't crouch, didn't look around, didn't flinch—he barely even *blinked* in reaction to the explosion. His aides ran up to him within seconds, only to hear the Prime Minister calmly dismiss the event with a short Arabic phrase meaning "it is nothing." The extreme disparity between the two men's reactions to the same set of sound waves not only received mention in the news stories about the substance of the press conference, it *became* the story. CNN, BBC, and other news outlets throughout the world broadcast the tape without a single audible line from the press conference other than the explosion and Maliki's stoic "it is nothing."

Maliki's performance—for listening here is precisely that—presented him to the public as a hypermasculine strong man so inured to belliphonic violence that he could withstand it and remain unaffected by it. His act of calm audition, audition that was so unperturbed that it resembled inaudition, presented the attack to the public as an interruption, an inconvenience—as inconsequential. The similarity of this actual performance to Colonel Kilgore's tranquility on the battlefield in *Apocalypse Now* is striking. But in this instance, the similarity bespeaks less the global reach of American cinema and more the coincidence across cultures of locally inflected archetypes of hypermasculine inaudition.[33] Indeed, Maliki's performance resonated deeply with conventional representations of masculinity and leadership in Iraq—including, but certainly not limited to, the stoic public face of his predecessor, Saddam Hussein. His unflinching body was evidence of his virtuosity within a local auditory regime that valued self-control over emotion, imperturbability over bodily reflex. This performance was enabled by decades of unofficial "training" in the form of repetitive attacks during the three wars and numerous smaller actions that took place in Iraq over Maliki's adult lifetime. Of course, the sustained experience of violence is always unpredictable in its outcomes, underwriting a spectrum of reactions ranging from hypermasculine inaudition to the terrifying flashbacks associated with PTSD. But some reactions produce more cultural capital than others, and Maliki's ability to remain "cool under fire" was given fulsome praise by the Iraqi media.

This well-publicized performance was hardly the only moment of overlap between Iraqi civilian and US military listening practices; many features within the general topography of belliphonic listening were held in common by both groups. All of my Iraqi interlocutors were able to place their own listening experiences within the concentric zones of wartime audition that I outlined in chapter 2, for example. Virtually all of them recognized establishment of a "zone of the audible inaudible" as being a salient part of wartime life. And like their military counterparts, many Iraqis, particularly young ones, took pride in their ability to tune out distant gunfire. Iraqis from all backgrounds had acquired the skills necessary to discern AK-47 from M4 fire, or distinguish a large explosion far away from a smaller explosion closer in.

Also, tragically, there is compelling anecdotal evidence that some portion of the civilian population suffered hearing loss and tinnitus that can be traced back to exposure to loud belliphonic weapon sounds. As I mentioned in chapter 2, an Iraqi otologist reported to me that incidents of hearing loss due to barotraumas (i.e., the pressure change that accompanies a loud weapon sound) surged at his clinic in the weeks after the US invasion. Exposure to the belliphonic is damaging, whether you are civilian or service member, American or Iraqi.

AUDITORY LITERACY, COMPETENCE, VIRTUOSITY

The examples above would appear to indicate that Iraqi civilian and US military auditors all operated within a common system of what cultural historian Robin Bernstein has termed "performance competence." Adapted from Jonathan Culler's concept of "literary competence," Bernstein's competent performer "understands how a book or other thing scripts broad behaviors within her or his historical moment—regardless of whether or how the performer follows that script." Competence—whether among readers, performers, or, in this case, auditors—involves a level of mastery beyond that of mere literacy. Bernstein elaborates:

> A reader who possesses literacy but not literary competence might read a novel and a scholarly monograph and understand each individual sentence while failing to understand the conventions and functions of the respective genres. In parallel, a person who possesses performance literacy but not performance competence would understand that a chair exists, literally, as an object to accommodate sitting, but would not understand that a beanbag chair and a Hepplewhite, as things, prompt different styles of sitting and that each of those practices of sitting is embedded in a system of culture, a habitus.[34]

We can easily translate Bernstein's model into auditory terms, where "literacy" amounts to the ability to identify a sound's source, and "competence" involves understanding the scripted behavior embedded within that sound. But if the testimonies of service members and Iraqi civilians have taught us anything, it is that, within the extreme environment of the combat zone, mere competence is often inadequate. With the stakes of listening immeasurably high, the Iraq War's military and civilian auditors worked hard to attain a level of *virtuosity* that enabled them to react quickly and in a nuanced way to sounds—or, conversely, to choose *not* to react to them and reap the benefits of inaction.

One can identify a cruise missile as a cruise missile (literacy); hear that it's approaching and take cover (competence); or predict based on its trajectory and your knowledge of the neighborhood that it will detonate close enough to deafen you, and so quickly pull your hearing aid out of your ear as you head for cover (virtuosity). One can recognize gunfire as gunfire (literacy); discern the subtle sonic differences that distinguish one type of firearm from another (competence); or learn to push the sounds of gunfire out of consciousness when they are too distant to be of narrative value (virtuosity). One can realize that a siren is a siren (literacy); understand that the siren is hailing you to take cover (competence); or deduce that it is senseless to run to safety because in the last months the mortar attacks in your area have actually *preceded* the onset of the siren (virtuosity). Acts of virtuosic audition and inaudition such as these regularly took place among Iraqi civilians and coalition service members throughout Operation Iraqi Freedom. And their ubiquity is further proof that "war culture," the radically pragmatic quasiculture of organized aggression, systematically degrades the cultural matrices that have built up around each population over generations and replaces them with the mind-numbing homogeneity of the cost-benefit equation.

INCOMMENSURABILITY

To say that Iraqi civilians and American service members both strove to attain a level of auditory virtuosity is not to say that they inhabited the same auditory regime, however. In a number of important ways, the assemblage of objects, tactics, conversations, and expectations that characterized civilian listening practices differed from the more narrow and regimented approach to listening found in the military. Some of these differences were occupational in character. Combat service members, as their designation indicates, engaged in combat, and hence were regularly exposed to painfully loud belliphonic sounds—of their own weapons, and of weapons directed towards them. As such, they tended to spend a significant amount of time in what I have termed the "trauma zone" of audition, the zone in which belliphonic sounds can cause physiological damage. Many Iraqi civilians had brief encounters with sounds loud enough to damage their hearing, with the consequence being the noticeable increase in hearing loss that I mentioned above. Nonetheless, as civilians, they were under no compulsion to remain in a combat situation when one arose around them. Unlike service members—and insurgents, and sectarian fighters—civilians could retreat to safety when shooting began; while this kind of retreat didn't pull them out of earshot of these sounds, it did tend to remove them from the kind of proximity that causes permanent damage to the ears. My Iraqi interlocutors, for example, were all familiar with the sounds of weapons, but with the exception of the initial bombing campaign in 2003 and sporadic exposure to nearby IEDs in subsequent years, none of them regularly found themselves so close to loud weapon sounds that their ears rang as a result. What was for combat troops a regular occupational hazard was for civilians a rare, violent eruption of a terrifying cloud of sound that betrayed the proximity of projectiles and shrapnel and heralded the imminent possibility of death.

With this difference, coalition military and Iraqi civilian auditory regimes are at their most distinct: if the quintessential military response to the sound of incoming fire was to return it, answering deadly noise with deadly noise, the quintessential civilian experience of combat involved seeking shelter from battle. This act tended to protect bodies and ears from damage, but it also rendered the experience of war less intersensorial and more purely auditory than it was for combat troops. As a mother who fled Baghdad with her children in 2006 recalls, her memories of the war are overwhelmingly sound-related:

> We weren't able to see things outside because we were afraid [and stayed indoors]. That's why we don't have a memory of what we *saw*.[35]

While positionality in this tactical, occupational sense is important to consider, it is equally important to note that life histories converge with spatial politics over longer time periods as well, in ways that powerfully inflect listening practices. To wit: in Iraq, as my interlocutors pointed out time and time again, violence and privation have formed the constant backdrop of everyday life for several decades. As I mentioned in chapter 1, Iraqis who are my age and older remember their devastating war with Iran that brought millions of Iraqi soldiers into direct contact with weapon sounds and produced roughly 375,000 casualties in a country of 16 million.[36] During the Iran-Iraq war, the sounds of gunfire and explosions were drilled into the ears of a large percentage of the population. Less than three years after the war's end, the first Gulf War brought the sounds and shrapnel of combat to the nation's capital—and thus to its women and children and elderly as well as to its soldiers. For four days in 1998, Operation Desert Fox acquainted a new generation of Iraqis with the sounds of cruise missiles and anti-aircraft fire. Moreover, a longstanding culture of domestic gun ownership was amplified by Hussein-era policies that resulted in high school students receiving formal AK-47 training in the 1990s and early 2000s. As a result, Iraqis of all ages and backgrounds were exposed to belliphonic sound and the violent acts that accompany it long before the initiation of Operation Iraqi Freedom in 2003. In testimonies about the most recent war, references to these prior experiences are common, as in this conversation between me and Ammar:

> JMD: *How long did it take you [after the war started] to begin to learn the differences between the sounds of different weapons?*
> It didn't take me much because most of the Iraqi youth had learned to use automatic weapons. If I'm not saying 90 percent, let's say 80 percent.
> JMD: *Had been trained?*
> Trained to use AK.

JMD: And when did that training occur? Was that in high school, or . ?.

Yeah, it was in high school in 1997. And also another one in 2000, and 2001. In 1997 the training was called "Nahwa Day." *Nahwa,* in Arabic, [is a word you use] when I am in trouble and you [instinctively] run . . . to help me. Without [me] asking you. That's the close meaning of *nahwa.* And in 2000 and 2001 it was called the Kurdish Army, the Jerusalem Army. [Saddam Hussein] created an army from graduates, high school graduates, and from college students and also from old men. [It was understood that] this army is the army he will take to Palestine to raid Jerusalem from Israel. He was saying that this army [comprised] about 5 million people—because everyone had training in the Kurdish Army, in the Jerusalem Army.

JMD: So, literally, every male high school student—

Every male high school student, after he finished the baccalaureate exam.

JMD: And how long was the training?

A month [for the Jerusalem Army]. It was not like Nahwa day. [On] Nahwa day, the training was in the schools after the studying hour, a single hour of training explaining the light arms, the guns, the pistols, and the AK and how to . . . assemble them. Everyone should learn how to assemble them and also how to disassemble them in a quick time, in a short time.

JMD: Girls too?

Not like us, no. . . . Maybe only a few high schools [trained girls in this way].[37]

Adult Iraqi ears were thus seasoned by a combination of training and direct experience of gun battles and bombing runs. Iraqi children, most of whom were born after Operation Desert Fox, literally grew up in an environment coursing with belliphonic sounds, as the "major combat operations" of Operation Iraqi Freedom gave way to years of counterinsurgency and sectarian violence. The effects of prolonged belliphonic noise on young children is an urgent topic that is as yet poorly understood.

Iraqi civilians used a number of technologies to mitigate the deleterious effects of belliphonic noise—but those technologies were decidedly "lo-fi," the result of improvisation and desperation, and in no way comparable with the military-grade earplugs, sophisticated noise-canceling headphones, and other devices issued to service members. Mothers spoke to me of stuffing their children's ears with cotton balls, or administering cough medicine to make their children drowsy, in an attempt to lessen their terror during the initial bombing campaign. Sleeping with pillows over one's head was common, as was covering windows with blankets. Cobbling together sound mediators from the materials at hand, civilian auditors fought their own metaphorical battles against the traumatic effects of belliphonic sound.

These battles were often lost. And acknowledgement of that loss constitutes another of the principal differences between military and civilian auditory regimes. While Iraqi civilian listening practices were to some degree structured around the ideal of hypermasculine inaudition that we witnessed in Nouri al-Maliki's performance at the press conference, they extended far beyond the narrow band of listening norms that the military auditory regime ratified. Among the civilian population—and particularly among women and children—listening to the sounds of war was understood to involve fear, as well as the urge to protect the weak from belliphonic-induced terror. A listening conditioned by fear is one that is located at the periphery of the auditory regime, where the embodied pragmatics of "war culture" are occasionally overwhelmed by biological responses. But a listening conditioned by a desire to shelter others points to the existence of a powerful alternative auditory ideal that is readily available to Iraqi women (and to Iraqi men, in a slightly attenuated fashion); we might call it the ideal of "empathic maternal audition."

In 2012, during a trip to the greater Detroit area to meet and converse with recent Iraqi immigrants, I met woman whom I'll call Noor. On the eve of the Shock and Awe campaign, after George Bush had announced that military action was imminent, Noor gathered her extended family, including her grown children and several young grandchildren, in her house. In recounting the beginning of the war, she spoke of the visceral fear brought on by exposure to belliphonic sound, but also of the protective instinct that allowed her to partially overcome that fear:

> The [air raid] sirens would make us more terrified than the rockets themselves. All the kids would come running to their parents. Everyone was scared. The elderly people were more scared for the kids than for themselves. The first thing I did was embrace the children, gather them up in my arms to protect them.[38]

Lacking the technological means to quiet the siren or the bombs that followed, Noor used the affective technology at hand—her arms—to create a microenvironment for the children in which sound became marginally less frightening. Although scared herself, she had the presence of mind to project herself into the subject position of the terrified children and to act to mitigate their fear—fear that, unchecked, could have allowed the siren to slip easily from an index of impending violence into the realm of a violent act in its own right.[39] In doing so, she acted in accordance with an ideal of selfless maternal audition that, while locally inflected, is transculturally valorized. Needless to say, this was an ideal, and her embracing arms a technology, that would not have been readily available to a military auditor seeking to calm the frazzled nerves of his troops.

Fear and empathy were hardly the only culturally sanctioned reactions to belliphonic noise, however. The sounds of combat also produced frustration, defiance, exhaustion, anger, protest, acceptance, and many other intelligible states and logical reactions within the civilian populace. At the same time, a number of Iraqi civilians with whom I've spoken—almost invariably young men—remember experiencing exhilaration and "feeling the rush" upon hearing and feeling a nearby explosion in a way roughly commensurate with the euphoric reactions among troops that I discussed earlier.

The Iraqi civilian auditory regime staked out its most exclusive territory when it encountered language in the form of speech. In this multilingual country of 27 million, Arabic was by far the most commonly encountered language, the native tongue of the majority of the population and a suitable lingua franca for most others. Additionally, English has been the dominant foreign language in the country since the 1970s; one of the principal languages of higher education, it was spoken, with varying degrees of proficiency, by the Iraqi intelligentsia.[40] Even among monolingual Iraqis, though, the vast majority of speech encountered on the street would have been intelligible. This fact necessarily inflected the act of listening, lending it the naturalistic aspect that characterizes the domestic sensory regimes many of you who are reading this book no doubt inhabit.

In such a setting, the speech centers of the brain tend to seek out the human voice, and pay singular attention to it when it is close enough and distinct enough to be intelligible. Together, the ear and brain strain to pull voices into the field of intelligibility. (Think about the so-called "cocktail party effect" in which you are able to tune out a large amount of ambient noise in order to focus on something being said nearby.) Vocal encounters with occupying troops were few and far between for most Iraqi auditors, whose attention normally drifted casually toward and away from the talk of local passersby over the course of the day, much as yours probably does at home. But when they did occur, at checkpoints or during house raids or in other precarious exchanges, civilian auditors strained to understand the foreign speech idioms of heavily armed soldiers who by definition held the power of an interrogator—the power to detain and question at will. Conversations such as these were tense activities. Civilians unfailingly discussed these encounters with one another, often using them to hone tactics for performing the dutiful, innocent listening subject the next time: *don't make sudden moves, look them calmly in the eye, nod your head, keep calm.* These and other pieces of advice were currency within an auditory regime that valued human survival more than conversational parity; in other words, performing "hearing" was often more important than being heard.

Contrast this listening stance with that of the overwhelmingly monolingual US troops: surrounded by people speaking a language they could not understand, service members regularly found themselves swimming in a sea of unintelligible voices. Their condition was one of constant semiotic inadequacy. The feeling of vulnerability that this condition engendered was only intensified by their awareness that any crowd could contain members of the insurgency, any voice could be communicating information through channels they could not access. Heavily armed, they spoke to locals with the aid of a live interpreter or other device,[41] but even the best interpreter could only translate one voice at a time. During these interpreted conversations, the voice of their true interlocutor, the person with whom they strove to communicate, was routinely coded as noise, as it interfered with their ability to understand what the interpreter was saying. In these and other complicated ways, the politics of intelligibility made different marks within the auditory regimes of Arabic-speaking civilians and their English-speaking military interlocutors.

These were some of the overlapping contours and exclusive regions of the Iraqi civilian and US military auditory regimes in wartime Iraq. Both regimes situated belliphonic sounds along a striated topography within which similar acts of inaudition, hermeneutic listening, tactical listening, and traumatic exposure take place. But the relative thickness and malleability of these zones often differed. Both presumed certain privileged positions for auditors within their topographies—but the locations of those positions diverged at crucial points. Both drew upon listening stereotypes and lived histories to give shape to an auditory habitus—but the character of those stereotypes and length and depth and detail of those lived histories did not perfectly align. Both availed themselves of technologies that mediated sound for auditors—but the listening acts that those technologies afforded were grossly imbalanced, and the technologies themselves were often incommensurable. Both assigned great importance to the speaking voice—but the linguistic abilities each regime presumed were largely exclusive, and exclusionary.

At times these differences were significant enough that they actually helped determine *what was heard*, in addition to providing blueprints for the interpretation of sonic events. The distinct contours of the sensory regimes of service members and civilian bystanders—not to mention those of the insurgency, about which we can only speculate—helped create a fundamental disjuncture that put distance between their very perceptions of Operation Iraqi Freedom. It was not simply that the political stances of these groups led to different interpretations of the war as good or bad, liberatory or harmful. This may also have been true, but, due to differences of positionality and technology and life history and embodied knowledge—in other words, due to the differences in the character of their auditory (and scopic and other sensory) regimes—the war was, quite literally, *sensed* differently by these groups. Belliphonic and other sensory stimuli had to travel to distinct locales, overcoming distinct obstacles along the way, to reach the variously constituted subjects who formed these groups. A single sonic event, reaching differently enculturated ears through different channels of mediation, splintered into different "sounds" at the moment of audition.

This sensory disjuncture may have acquired its greatest potential for damage in the moments when a monolingual service member was confronted with unintelligible Iraqi speech, for these were moments where an activity as innocuous as "listening to a human voice" could work in the direction of dehumanizing (or even demonizing) the Iraqi Other. The sensory disjuncture that governed this precarious moment placed the Arabic-speaking Iraqi in what philosopher Jacques Rancière has called "a space separated from public life; one from which only groans or cries expressing suffering, hunger, or anger could emerge, but not actual speeches demonstrating a shared *aisthesis*."[42]

The auditory chasm separating Iraqi locals and American service members extended well beyond the realm of language into less obvious situations of auditory incommensurability that were similarly resistant to all attempts to overcome them. Recall Brigadier General Mark Kimmitt's press conference, discussed in chapter 1, in which he urged Iraqis to hear the invasive vibrations of helicopter flybys as "the sounds of freedom." We are now in a position to say that General Kimmitt was, in essence, asking Iraqi civilians to subscribe to the military auditory regime, or at least to adopt the hermeneutic stance that it encouraged. However, now that we have catalogued some of the elements of that regime—from training to technology to conversations to media representations to relative degree of vulnerability—it becomes clear that throwing off one regime for another is hardly a simple matter in which one simply *decides* to hear a helicopter as symbolizing one thing or another.

There are, we can now conclude, moments when the distance between auditory regimes is unbridgeable. When one population has recourse to sophisticated listening devices and the other doesn't, or when one is fluent in the dominant language and the other isn't, a strict "partition of the sensible" (Rancière)—a border separating what is audible from what is not, or what is understandable from what is not—obtains. More subtly and more often, though, the distance between regimes creates conditions in which some listening acts that feel authentic and good to one population feel uncomfortable and embarrassing to another. When, as in the helicopter scenario above, one group is encouraged to listen according to a privileged archetype, and the other group's archetypes discourage auditors from listening in that way, the pressure for each party to conform to its norms can be intense. This is not to say that idiosyncratic or iconoclastic acts of listening aren't possible, however. Opportunities for transgressive audition are ever-present. But to choose to listen "against the grain" is to engage in a kind of labor, and risk incurring a kind of cost.[43] The presence or constant threat of violence often multiplies the labor and amplifies the potential costs of transgressive audition.

At other moments, belliphonic subjects tried but failed to perform the feats of audition prescribed by the regimes in which they were enmeshed. Service members who were unable to adopt the stereotypical stances of wartime audition and inaudition found themselves in positions of extreme stress and anxiety. Very little empirical data on the narrow question of audition and combat stress exists, but it is not unreasonable to ask if the large number of service members who sought out or were directed toward treatment for anxiety disorders in theater may have been related, in part, to an inability to listen to or otherwise sense the combat environment in the ways that were valorized by the military's auditory (and other sensory) regime(s). If all of the sounds of combat retain a hot, screaming, terrifying quality, preventing the auditor from entering the cool hermeneutic space of the narrational zone; if one constantly flinches at frequent detonations and gun reports rather than developing an armor of hypermasculine inaudition; if one is unable to focus on a sound's indexicality and location, and instead experiences it as a direct assault of belliphonic violence—serving as an effective combat service member would be virtually impossible. The experience of combat would, in this case, be one of unmitigated sensory terror.

If failing to join a wartime auditory regime can result in severe anxiety and stress, succeeding may create its own set of challenges. A mountain of research and testimonial evidence has demonstrated that, for troops who sustained acute psychological trauma while in theater, the transition back home to the United States has proven exceedingly difficult. Among the symptoms that service members diagnosed with post-traumatic stress disorder experience are uncontrollable hypervigilance and hyperaggression. Sounds often serve as triggers for these behaviors. Of course, during combat deployments, hypervigilance and hyperaggression are not treated as pathologies—quite the contrary: they are survival skills. In a wartime atmosphere, the ability to pay acute attention to the acoustic environment and respond aggressively to the sensory assault of an attack are appropriate responses, ratified by injunctions to maintain situational awareness, conversations about belliphonic sounds, and shared experiences of combat. In this sense, the armoring of the sensorium that wartime auditory regimes demand amounts to a kind of adaptive scarification or self-injury, where the richness of sensory experience is stripped away until little other than pragmatics remains.

It is only when service members re-enter a civilian world where sound is not the constant partner of aggressive acts that this learned behavior becomes maladaptive. Could some part of post-traumatic stress be understood as the inability to exit wartime auditory (and other sensory) regimes and enter the more relaxed regimes of "peacetime?" If so, we can say that, for the American military population, one of the primary challenges has been not only to deal with traumatic memories of the war, or with the loss of loved ones, or the physical destruction—but to coax their bodies out of the wartime sensory regimes in which they were, by necessity, locked. Along the same lines, we can note with sadness that, as of this writing, hypervigilance and hyperaggression remain highly adaptive behaviors for many Iraqis, who continue to be immersed in an atmosphere of persistent violence.

For those who are caught in the cruel dialectic of wartime structures and agencies, the sensory regimes of war must be understood as something more—and more sinister—than a standing resource. They are undeniably that, but to the extent that they adhere unnecessarily to those who have trained their bodies to their strict and unforgiving rhythms, they are also a liability. For service members and civilians, then, interacting with them always means work: wartime auditory regimes, having been laboriously constructed, must at war's end be laboriously overcome.

"The practice of violence is highly visible to the senses."
—DAVID RICHES

4

Sonic Campaigns

IF THE LAST chapter illuminated the complex regimes that affected listening and rendered it tactically useful within the spheres of military and civilian wartime life, the present chapter returns to the phenomenon of *sounding*, armed with new questions about the many structures and agencies that enable, shape, and constrain it. Chapter 1 provided an introductory catalogue of prominent belliphonic sounds, along with a discussion of how the subject positions from which people listened to them affected their perceptual appearance. Retaining the sonic particularities of that chapter as a baseline for further discussion, I now want to back up somewhat and interrogate the concepts of sound and violence and their interrelation more broadly. In doing so, I want to put forth the following proposition: that sound and violence can be productively imagined as essentially commingled terms, with each manifest within the other as constant potentiality and structural analogue. To approach sound and violence in this way is to estrange each of them from the contemporary discourses that surround them, and in so doing, open them up for fresh consideration and possible retheorization. After adjusting the theoretical background in this way, I will discuss a number of instances in which combatants on both sides deployed or forcibly curtailed sound, and examine the consequences these acts of sounding and silencing produced. Focusing on the "sonic campaigns" of the US military and the Iraqi insurgency in this way will enable us to trace new, occasionally erratic and surprising, lines of responsibility through the timespace of the conflict.

SOUND (AND VIOLENCE)

What is a sound? Is it a thing or a process? An instrument or an event? An immaterial quality, a property of an object, or an autonomous entity itself? These are more complicated questions than they might appear at first glance, and are in fact the subject of ongoing philosophical debate.[1] As with all good debatable topics, it is easy to marshal anecdotal evidence depicting sound as one type of entity or another. For example, we often treat sounds as if they were physical things, things that stand out against the general acoustic background as a painting stands out against a wall; things that command our attention; things, like texts, that reward close reading. Moreover, we commonly speak about sounds as if they were discrete objects with material characteristics: sounds can be *brassy*, or *gravelly*, or *sharp*, or *bright*, or *soft*, or *smooth*. At the same time, when pressed, we understand that this talk is metaphorical. Our common sense generally recognizes a fundamental difference between sounds and material objects. Unlike a painting, which is tangible and persists through time in a stable state, a sound would seem to be immaterial, ephemeral, in flux. If I were to speak aloud the sentence I'm writing now, my words would cease to exist soon after they left my mouth. And yet physicists describe sounds as having a certain materiality—if by materiality we mean a measurable configuration in the physical world. In this sense, sounds are things, albeit temporary ones.

Steven Connor has argued in favor of the event-like nature of sound, contrasting this with the thing-like nature of visual objects:

> When we see something, we do not think of what we see as a separable aspect of it, a ghostly skin shed for our vision. We feel that we see the thing itself, rather than any occasion or extrusion of the thing. But when we hear something, we do not have the same sensation of hearing the thing itself. This is because objects do not have a single, invariant sound, or voice. How something sounds is literally contingent, depending upon what touches or comes into contact with it to generate the sound. We hear, as it were, the event of the thing, not the thing itself.[2]

Casey O'Callaghan, an analytic philosopher who recently devoted an entire monograph to the nature of sound, agrees that sound is best characterized as an event. Additionally, he holds that while we may intellectually grasp the lessons of acoustics—that what we conventionally call sounds are produced by compressions and rarefactions that move outward from a vibrating source through the surrounding medium—we don't actually experience sound in this way. He argues that the human experience of sound belies the physics of sound propagation; the waves set in motion by a distant voice may move through space, physically entering our ears along the way, but we *hear* the sound of the voice as existing somewhere way over there, by that guitar, that car horn, that open mouth.[3] In O'Callaghan's treatment, a sound is a constituent part of a localized incident of vibration (what he calls, significantly, a "disturbance event"). Under "normal" conditions, this proposition appears self-evidently true; in fact, it is precisely our understanding that sounds emanate from and are to some degree tethered to discrete vibrating objects that renders the crucial human process of echolocation possible. But does it hold in the more extreme belliphonic cases that I have been cataloguing here? And if, as I will argue, it doesn't, what implications does this conceptual breakdown have for our understanding of sound generally?

The intimate connection I want to draw between sound and violence rests in part on the premise that, regardless of where we take its source to be, we are all aware when we are in the *presence* of a sound. Sound's diffuse and immersive presence is, we have already seen, one of its most salient characteristics—it is the source of the ontological difference between the unidirectionality of a speeding bullet and the expansive and variegated sonic envelope of its report. The dynamism with which sounds spread through space is such that we can experience most of them as "big," as bigger than we are. If again I were to begin reading this sentence to you aloud, you could walk around in the cloud of sound that is my voice and experience it as bigger than you; it would remain recognizably itself as you maneuvered about the room. The "size" of most of the sounds we encounter—by which I mean the area over which they are identifiable as sounds, as themselves—marks them as inherently intersubjective phenomena, phenomena that are accessible not just to you but also to those around you, and therefore as "events" (or temporary objects) whose ontology is expansive and dispersed.

This is, admittedly, a counterintuitive way to think about sound. When you hear the barely detectable drone of a voice in the distance, you are more likely to equate its low amplitude "softness" or "faintness" with "smallness." But if you consider the area over which that sound is perceptible, you will have to admit that its size is much more formidable than its volume at any single point of reception would suggest. Projecting this insight forward into the realm of the belliphonic, we can say that most weapon sounds (gun reports, rockets in flight, detonations, etc.) are not just big but absolutely vast, commanding attention, intimidating, shocking and aweing large populations dispersed over large areas. We aren't talking about the softball-sized sonic ball of a mosquito's whine here. We are talking about enormous sonic spheres (when airborne) and hemispheres (when originating on land), massive domes of vibration enveloping a landscape that is itself trembling, sonorous domes with fuzzy boundaries within which the concentric zones of audition are constructed by the individual auditors who are caught within them.

In addition to size, we can experience sounds as having mass. Or, more accurately, we can experience this as occasionally being the case. Most "normal" sounds that we encounter are characterized by their phenomenological *weightlessness*. Again, if I were reading aloud to you, the sounds I would be making with my voice would wash up against your body as waves of compressed and rarefied air, putting measurable pressure against your skin—but you wouldn't be able to sense this; your body wouldn't perceive the sound of my voice as having any materiality at all. O'Callaghan's argument above is strongest when dealing with these kinds of everyday sounds.

But those of us who frequent dance clubs or battlefields know that sounds *can* be "heavy," heavy enough to push up against you, or weigh you down. A close encounter with the twin air horns on New York fire engines leaves me with the impression of something like a thin sheet of corrugated tin being dragged over my body, and I *leap* out of the intersection—in fact, the sound appears to *propel* my body out of the intersection, without my thinking about it. Similarly, the report of a large number of M4s on a firing range in Iraq in 2011 generated a sharp pain in my unprotected ears and caused my body to involuntarily flinch as I simultaneously heard the sound, felt it hit my body, and experienced the muffled buzz and high-pitched whine of temporary hearing loss. On Camp Victory in Baghdad, an encounter with a C-RAM (Counter-Rocket, Artillery, and Mortar system), a large computer-controlled Gatling gun that fires a fast stream of thousands of large-caliber exploding bullets into the air to destroy incoming airborne weapons, caused my knees to buckle; even though I was wearing state-of-the-art sound isolating headphones at the time, and so experienced no discomfort in my ears, and even though I had been given a countdown to tell me when the weapon was going to be fired, the overwhelming presence of the sound hitting my skin and rumbling inside the cavities of my body literally *felled* me. In an even more extreme vein, Jason Sagebiel told me of moments when he was thrown a distance by the blast wave of an explosion, the very wave that turned into the explosion's rolling boom for more distant auditors. Moments like this, in the street or near powerful loudspeakers or amid gunfire or near explosions—moments when sound acquires the appearance of mass and texture, of being big and heavy and rough, of being both an acoustic and a haptic event—these moments compel us to acknowledge that sound is not only a text for us to interpret, but a force for us to reckon with.

In recent years, a growing number of theorists in and outside music studies have begun attending to sound as force. Steve Goodman, in his provocative volume *Sonic Warfare,* discusses instances when sound is used "to modulate the physical, affective, and libidinal dynamics of populations, of bodies, of crowds." [4] He argues that "before the activation of causal or semantic, that is, cognitive listening"—in other words, before sound acquires the status of text, or before our brains recognize it as such—"the sonic is a phenomenon of contact and displays, through an array of autonomic responses, a whole spectrum of affective powers." Jenny Johnson's work on sound and traumatic memories of sexual abuse focuses on these affective powers by documenting the ways in which music and other sounds that accompany violent events such as sexual abuse can fuse with embodied experience to produce involuntary somatic "sense-memories." These traumatic synesthetic events, triggered by sound, mark one of the many pathways by which sound can short-circuit conscious thought to act upon bodies and alter subjectivities. Less concerned with the human psyche, Curtis Roads charts another trajectory for sonic force in his discussion of "perisonic intensities," his term for extremely loud and invasive sounds whose presence is literally "destructive to the human body."[5] These works all point to the fact that the semantic richness of sound—sound's intelligible, interpretable dimension—can at times be complicated, if not eradicated, by its overwhelming materiality. As actors in the world, some sounds assert themselves so forcefully that they preempt the human act of interpretation. Sounds can be bigger than us, and they can be heavy, and sometimes that size and weight are directed onto bodies that reveal themselves as frail, as vulnerable—physically and psychologically vulnerable—to the violence with which they resonate.

What this means is that, in combat situations, the loudest belliphonic sounds are not experienced as events occurring at or near their vibrating sources. Pace O'Callaghan, many of these loud (or to use my synesthetic terms, *big* and *heavy*) sonic events engender an immediate experience of sound as bodily invasion or assault. Sounds of this magnitude have a distinct material presence, and with it, a kind of intrusive agency: they rub up against the body, punch the chest cavity, pierce the eardrum. Moreover, and perversely, these aggressively intimate acts of invisible sonic touching frequently foreclose the faculty of hearing altogether. Some of the testimonies in chapter 1 point to this fact. In his semiautobiographical novel *Yellow Birds*, OIF veteran Kevin Powers chillingly describes the sensation of creeping deafness caused by the sound of his protagonist's own firearm in a firefight:

> The [sound of the enemy] bullet came so quickly that the time it took to push [my thoughts] out of my head was imperceptible, so that before I even noticed, the other boys were firing back. I began to fire, too, and the noise of the rounds exploding in the chamber pushed in my eardrums and they began to ring and the deafness expanded as if someone had struck a tuning fork at the perfect pitch, so that it resonated and wrapped everyone in the orchard in his very own vow of silence.[6]

Power's protagonist experiences a more extreme and instantaneous deafness when his platoon stumbles upon a "body bomb," an improvised explosive device concealed in a corpse. The unexpected detonation of the bomb temporarily deafened them all:

> The lieutenant stood and turned to us, but before he could utter a word we were overtaken by blindness, as if the sun had fallen out of the sky. We were covered in dust and deafened before any sound could reach us. I lay groggy on the ground and my ears rang and buzzed loudly and as I looked up I saw the rest of the platoon

moving on the ground, trying to get their bearings. . . . The buzz in my head was oppressive, and I couldn't hear the bullets as they passed, but I felt a few as they cut the air. The fight was hazy and without sound, as if it was happening underwater.

In these descriptions, as in the testimonies of service members and civilians who experienced temporary deafness and ringing in the ears in the wake of belliphonic activity, the common-sense understanding of sound as a localizable event fails to obtain. We can no longer speak of sound as existing phenomenologically at or near the source of vibration. Instead, the event feels like it is taking place *right here*, on the surface of the auditor's skin, or inside the body's cavities. These extreme events illustrate the principle that we know from acoustics to be empirically true: sound is always a combination of *sonance* and *resonance*: a sound is never a single vibration at the source, but a symphony of dispersed sympathetic vibrations that we tend to perceive as a single entity.[7] If this variable complex of resonances is understood to comprise the event that is sound, then the eardrum and skin and vibrating surfaces within the auditor's body partake in that event. And they do so involuntarily.

Let's retreat from the belliphonic back into "normal" sonorous life for a second. Think of the complicated and sometimes unpredictable ways that you—and by "you" I mean *all* of you: your thoughts, your heart rate, the hairs on the back of your neck, your gut—think of all the ways that you react to a wistful melody, or a military march, or a throbbing beat, or a bump in the night, or the caress or sucker-punch of a well-timed word. Our bodies are uniquely attuned to sounds. Sounds send our bodies into altered sensuous states. Under normal circumstances, we listeners have cobbled together a fair amount of agency, however, and so we can train ourselves to react, or not react, to sounds in unique or culturally resonant ways. Even in wartime, the effects of the tactical habitus of audition in which service members (and civilians) find themselves are evident, as the previous chapter demonstrated. But any acts of entrainment or interpretation that we might attempt take place within a vibrational field of sounds that are constantly forcing our bodies into sympathetic movement. Before we can decide how to react to a sound, we are subtly swaying to its rhythm, like a marionette on a string. Suzanne Cusick has written that "we live immersed in a vibrating world that keeps us all always already in constantly re-sounding touch with every other vibrating entity." And she pointed out that this state of sympathetic vibration can take on "decidedly dystopian political possibilities" when the power of sounding is controlled by one party absolutely. Here's what she had to say about the practice, widespread throughout the Bush years, of bombarding shackled prisoners with loud music for hours on end:

Always compelled by the physical properties of sound to vibrate in their very bones with those sounds, the prisoners subjected to the music program have no choice but to *become, themselves, the characteristic sounds of their captors.* This is, I argue, an ultimate violence that batters prisoners' bodies, shatters (however temporarily) the capacity to control the acoustical relationality that is the foundation of subjectivity, and blasts away all sense of privacy, leaving in its place a feeling of paradoxically unprivate isolation.[8]

In situations of acute violence or duress such as these, sound becomes not just instrumentalized, but *weaponized*. It acquires the capacity to injure with the intensity of a sharp instrument puncturing your eardrum or a blunt instrument concussing your brain. It can injure with the insidiousness of encroaching psychosis, infecting the mental space in which subjectivity is constructed and maintained. Like a bread knife, whose sharp edge provides certain affordances[9]—for cutting bread, but also for cutting other things—sound possesses particular attributes, and these attributes interact with human bodies in indeterminate but also nonrandom ways. Furthermore, as Cusick argues, the impact of aggressive acoustic tactics is complicated and intensified by the fact that auditors are not just unable to control their body's sympathetic vibrations when confronted by a sonic event; *they are incorporated into the sonic event itself*.

This, then, is the kernel of potential violence that exists within all sounds: the moment of forced resonance that precedes, and in extreme cases precludes, conscious recognition and interpretation. Of course, in healthy situations and at reasonable volumes, sound's ability to damage flesh and psyches is diminished or even removed. But it can be caused to return by simply increasing the volume or adjusting the auditory milieu. (As I have described elsewhere in this volume, when the auditory milieu is one of wartime vulnerability, even the quietest sounds can trigger acute anxiety and flashbacks to traumatic events.) In other words, sound's capacity to wound can be activated without changing the fundamental characteristics of sound qua sound. And it bears repeating: even when these acts of acoustic or psychoacoustic wounding are not taking place, even in the quietest and most pacific situations, sound coerces bodies into involuntary vibration and co-opts them into participation, through resonance, in the event that is sound itself. The co-vibration of resonance can be a deep-seated source of joy, and a visceral reminder of our fundamental interconnectedness, as choral singers the world over know in their bones. Formal and informal discourse on music has made this point emphatically for centuries. But far less attention has been paid to its corollary, that acoustic interconnectedness increases our ability to be affected by others and by our environment in negative ways as well. Because of this fact, a full or exhaustive consideration of sound cannot be undertaken without a consideration of the potential for violation and violence that sound constantly affords.

VIOLENCE (AND SOUND)

If the interconnectedness of resonance, with all that that entails, is at the heart of sound, what can we say about the nature of violence? Unlike sound, an understanding of which can be anchored in physics and in concrete experience (whatever questions we may have about its nature, we tend to recognize a sound when we hear one), the concept of violence has proven significantly more elusive and fluid. "Like power," Carolyn Nordstrom suggests, "violence is essentially contested: everyone knows it exists, but no one agrees on what actually constitutes the phenomenon."[10] Indeed, the term is at once ubiquitous and maddeningly opaque—so much so that, as philosopher Christopher Yates proclaims, "it is difficult to fully identify or comprehend the manifold subjects that play host to its careening course."[11] Sociologist Michel Wieviorka writes:

> The word 'violence' is in fact applied to countless phenomena, and used to describe all sorts of events and behaviours, both individual and collective: delinquency, crime, revolution, mass murder, riots, war, terrorism, harassment, and so on. Its spectrum of application can be extended almost to infinity, depending on whether or not we include its moral, and not simply physical, dimensions, and depending on whether or not we follow Pierre Bourdieu by introducing the notion of symbolic violence—the violence used, in this perspective, by a dominant system such as a state or actors that are so powerful as to prevent the dominated from producing for themselves the categories that would allow them to understand their own subordination.[12]

Given this exceedingly broad "spectrum of application," anyone who aspires to work with a degree of precision must first produce, or at the very least allude to, a provisional definition for the term. Philosopher James Dodd argues that this need, which is fundamental to the broader project of "articulating the problems of violence," is particularly acute when the subject is war, as "wars themselves, which normalize violence, seem to be premised on taking violence for granted."[13] What's more, the urgency of the questions generated whenever violence is defined—questions of intentionality, cultural specificity, teleology, individual versus collective responsibility, and the essence of harm—is only amplified when societal norms governing the legitimate use of violence are in a state of active contestation. War tends to bring about such states. We are living through one such historical moment now, in which conventional conceptions of violence have been complicated in the wake of 9/11 and the Iraq and Afghanistan wars. These events have spawned a series of troubling actions: from the Abu Ghraib photos to the hanging of burned corpses over a bridge in Fallujah, from the "music program" and harsh interrogation to the desecration of the Quran at Gitmo, from the purported use of human shields in the days leading up to the war's initial phase to the looting of museums in the days after the Hussein regime fell, from the 2006 bombing of the Al-Askari Mosque in Samarra to the prevalent use of suicide bombers over the course of Operation Iraqi Freedom. And these actions in turn put significant pressure on the definitions of violence and warfare that were embedded in the laws and mores of all the warring parties.

Historically, and particularly within legalistic frameworks, the purview of the term "violence" in the US and elsewhere has been restricted to situations in which physical damage is intended; hence the taut definition of sociologist Albert Reiss and criminologist Jeffrey Roth that delimits violence to "behavior by persons against persons that intentionally threatens, attempts, or actually inflicts physical harm."[14] Current US statutory law broadens the scope of "violence" to include damage to property but maintains the emphasis on "physical force."[15] By contrast, an increasing amount of social science work on violence favors a more expansive definition that does not require the specter of immediate physical harm to be present. Sociologist Mary Jackman presents violence as a phenomenon comprising "actions that inflict, threaten, or cause injury. Actions may be corporal, written, or verbal. Injuries may be corporal, psychological, material, or social."[16] These injuries may also be self-inflicted or willingly endured, as when workers "voluntarily" submit to dangerous conditions because they fear reprisals if they don't, or when parents suffer injuries in order to protect their children—or, more to the point here, when service members endure hearing loss generated by their own weapons out of a sense of duty or obligation or powerlessness.[17] Jackman sees such instances of self-inflicted violence as particularly illuminating:

> To comprehend the human propensity for violence, we need to analyze not only the factors that cause people to inflict injuries on others, but also the conditions and dispositions that lead people to tolerate—or even to seek—the infliction of injuries on themselves. . . . If injuries are sometimes endured willingly, inclusion of such instances may hold lessons about the myriad and sometimes turbid dynamics of violence in social life.[18]

This proposal significantly complicates any understanding of violence that is confined to a person (or set of persons) intentionally threatening harm to another (set of) person(s). The designations "perpetrator" and "victim" can, we must now admit, coexist within a single subject (as in the suicide bomber, or the self-immolating protester).[19] We must also acknowledge that injurious acts that are "endured willingly" may register as violence for one group but not for another. As controversial practices such as foot binding, breast augmentation, dogfights, first-person shooter video games, human sacrifice—and yes, the sonic dimension of warfare—demonstrate, the category of "violence" may be assigned not only by the victim at the moment of experience, but also after the fact by communities that react critically to those practices. The members of these communities may have nothing in common other than their overlapping ethical positions; but it is the instance of their disapprobation, their perception of unacceptable violation, that is a necessary condition for "violence," a phenomenon that we now understand to be culturally and historically contingent, to reach beyond the incommunicable private pain of the victim[20] and obtain its defining intersubjective dimension.

Strangely, this moment of public recognition both helps violence proliferate (e.g., when violent tactics create violent reprisals, or when violent tactics spawn copycats) and, in ideal conditions (when public outrage at acts labeled violent reaches a critical mass), leads to its attenuation. Complicating matters further, the potential for effective censure to follow an incident labeled "violent" is determined by the breadth, prestige, and collective audibility of these communities. In other words, if the victims of violence have been robbed of their collective voice—as many would argue is the case for millions of disenfranchised and displaced Iraqi civilians—their aggressors can easily define the violent act in other, more euphemistic terms: "collateral damage," "targeted attacks," "clean-up operations," "retribution," "noise." Violence is rendered broadly intelligible only when the experiences of victims are filtered through interpretive practices that acknowledge that their rights and their bodies have been violated. Its dynamics are turbid indeed.

And they grow more so. In tracing the lines of responsibility for violent acts, Jackman acknowledges that there are often vast assemblages of actors and actions that can be causally linked to public outbursts of violence. "Who is the responsible agent of violence," she asks:

> the lynch mob, the legal system and police who fail to prosecute the members of the mob, or the people who encourage lynchings by actively asserting white racial dominance or the heinousness of certain breaches of the moral order? Surely, it is a communal complicity made up of an accumulation of verbal and/or written actions that accomplishes the deed, even though only a small number of actors may be physically implicated.[21]

This observation draws some of the focus away from the spectacular "eventfulness" that is commonly associated with violence in favor of an examination of enabling acts that are by their nature unspectacular, mundane. In his 2008 treatise *Violence: Six Sideways Reflections,* Slavoj Žižek makes this case more emphatically, arguing that we "should resist the fascination of [the overt violent acts of] social agents, evil individuals, disciplined repressive apparatuses, fanatical crowds,"[22] focusing rather on the *longue durée* structural imbalances that predate, enable, and shape them. The "axiom" of his argument is that "subjective" (i.e., acute, overt) violence "is just the most visible portion of a triumvirate that also includes two objective kinds of violence":

> First, there is a "symbolic" violence embodied in language and its forms. . . . [This kind of violence] pertains to language as such, to its imposition of a certain universe of meaning. Second, there is what I call "systemic" violence, or the often catastrophic consequences of the smooth functioning of our economic and political systems.[23]

The argument here is straightforward: amid the spectacular acts of undeniable violence that obtain in wartime, it is all too easy to ignore the fundamental inequities that enable these acts to take place. From Žižek's vantage point, it is clear that the comprehensively violent environment of wartime is jointly constituted by (a) the sustained threat of these acts, (b) the acts themselves, and, most importantly (c) the structures that underlie both. But his call to forgo the examination of overt violent acts in favor of this kind of linguistic and ideological archaeology is designed to lead his readers to a predetermined end: a wholesale political critique of global capitalism and American hegemony. As a result, his proposal forecloses the possibility of gaining a nuanced understanding of the lived experience of wartime, which is my project here. *Pace* Žižek (and as I argued in the introduction), there are methods for studying subjective violence that don't lead to rapt uncritical "fascination" with violence's spectacle; ignoring the heartrending phenomenon of overt violence is not the only way of taking Žižek's call to "look . . . at the problem of violence awry" seriously.[24] What is needed is not a bracketing of violent acts that facilitates a "pure" examination of objective or structural violence, but models for thinking through the ontological overlap between violent acts and violent structures. I propose that—strangely, surprisingly—the case of belliphonic violence, combined with the above investigation of the dynamics of sound, provides us with the materials to build one such model.

Let us return to my depiction of sound as an inherently intersubjective (i.e., publicly perceptible) phenomenon, a perturbation that originates with a "disturbance event" (O'Callaghan) and results in an assemblage of forced resonances (Cusick). The deliberately provocative vocabulary of that last sentence ("perturbation," "disturbance," "forced") is a gesture toward the considerable conceptual overlap that exists between this characterization of sound and the emergent understanding of subjective violence that I've been cobbling together above.[25] Žižek himself defines subjective violence as "a perturbation of the 'normal,' peaceful state of things,"[26] and all of the theorists I have mentioned acknowledge the elements of coercion and intersubjectivity that are constitutive of the violent act.[27] The structural consonance between the two phenomena is indeed compelling: both sound and violence can be understood to involve *disturbance events introducing forced change to a system*. (In this sense, joining Steve Goodman, we could say that the ontologies of sound and violence are both essentially *vibrational*.)[28] Both are rendered intelligible through the judgment (or *audit*) of a community: "violence" requires the assessment of an ethical community that a violation has occurred, just as "sound" requires the assessment of an auditory community that an audible event has occurred.[29] Neither phenomenon can occur in a (literal or social) vacuum; both are shaped in large part according to the character of the medium (of particles) or milieu (of power imbalances and other structural inequities) in which they occur.

Having noted these similarities, I must acknowledge that there are some important distinctions separating (some) sounds from (some) acts of violence. The first has to do with the initial way in which sounds physically introduce "change to the system": by coercing bodies into the reverberative motion of resonance. It is true that resonance occurs forcefully, whether those bodies desire motion or not; but often they *do* desire it, and intensely. Often, no one objects to sound's resonant invasion—no community disapproves, no injury can be located, complacency reigns. By contrast, when violent acts introduce their "change to the system"—the system that is the body, the system that is the social group, the system that is the symbolic order—some more or less enfranchised community makes known its disapproval, and does so by pointing to a moment of injury, whether potential or performed. This recognition of violation and harm is one of the necessary conditions for violence to obtain.[30]

Second, and more obviously, sounds are by their nature audible, whereas violent acts are not necessarily so. Of course, in many instances, violent acts are memorably, painfully, searingly audible. If this book has proved anything, it is that some sounds in some circumstances can "inflict, threaten, or cause injury," and that the injuries sustained by these sounds can be, at a minimum, "psychological, corporal . . . and social" and therefore "violent" according to Jackman's definition of the term. But we can easily imagine instances of mute violence, in which the "disturbance event" is inaudible. (Inaudible, yes, but still vibrational, still disturbing the social or corporeal medium in a manner that allows it to spread throughout the system.) The distinct, albeit deeply imbricated, categories of sound and violence can thus be mapped out in a single Venn diagram (see figure 4.1):

Here, the largest circle represents forced change to a system. The smaller circle on the right represents violence, which is the subset of forced change that is linked to injury and that generates disapprobation among an auditing community. The oval in the center represents sound, or audible changes to the system, some of which meet the criterion for violence, others of which do not. In this sense, sound articulates with violence, but exceeds it; and violence overlaps with sound, but exceeds it. This characteristic of excess, of transgressing the structures that we may erect to contain them, is yet another commonality linking violence and sound.[31] But this is where that particular commonality ends. The excess of sound, its extension beyond harm, rescues it from the territory of violence, allowing it to attain its powerful life-affirming character in moments when its vibrations are welcomed. By contrast, the excess of violence, its extension beyond the auditory, renders it intersensorial, and thus all the more slippery and sinister.

THE OMNIDIRECTIONALITY OF SOUND AND VIOLENCE

A final characteristic that sound and violence share merits discussion here. Let us begin with sound, the simpler of the two categories. It is a matter of broad agreement that many if not most of the sounds we encounter are roughly locatable in space. The power to echolocate is dependent upon our physical "equipment"—two ears that pick up sound

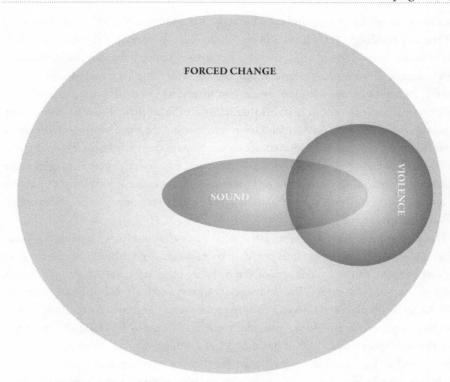

FIGURE 4.1 Overlapping Characteristics of Sound and Violence

waves at slightly different times as they pass through space and a brain that can translate those signals into a sense of the location of the waves' source—although this power can be expanded by practice and attentiveness, as the testimonies of wartime auditors indicate. At the same time, we can all agree that sounds are immersive: sound waves are not unilinear, but proceed outward in all directions, enveloping people and objects in front of, behind, and to the sides of the vibrating source.[32] As a result, when people make sounds, they also hear them—they are simultaneously senders and receivers of acoustic signals. Even when I am consciously directing my voice to a distant friend, cupping my mouth with my hands or yelling through a cone or megaphone, the omnidirectionality of sound means that there is always "sonic leakage," always sound moving in directions other than those I intend.[33]

But if the situatedness of a sound is always accompanied by some evidence of sound's omnidirectionality, the opposite is not universally true; some sounds refuse to yield to echolocation, appearing rather to come at us from all sides. Recently, while walking through my New York neighborhood on a cloudy day, I became aware of the sound of more than one helicopter hovering overhead. I spun around, searching the skies, but to no avail: the cloud cover made it impossible to see where the helicopters were located. Unable to fix the sound sources visually, I tried to pinpoint their approximate location through listening—and failed, utterly. The thump of the rotors was bouncing off the tall buildings on both sides of the street, leaving me with a disconcerting feeling of being surrounded by these invisible hovering machines. Acousmatic sounds like this—sounds whose sources cannot be pinpointed—have long been understood to "provoke . . . a degree of unsettledness, anxiety, or insecurity" in the listener.[34] Sounds like this, and particularly sounds like this that occur on the battlefield, can be disquieting, uncanny, overwhelming. As Mladen Dolar describes it, "the voice whose source cannot be seen, because it cannot be located, seems to emanate from anywhere, everywhere; it gains omnipotence."[35] During Shock and Awe, and to a lesser degree throughout the war, the pure omnidirectionality of belliphonic sounds occasionally attained this aspect of omnipotence, and with it, a particularly acute power to terrorize auditors who understood themselves to be targets.

If sound's mode of being is omnidirectional (though sometimes locatable in space), what is the mode of being of violence? Military tacticians and military historians have tended to think of the violent acts of war as being unidirectional, as moving cleanly from military asset to target. The language of military tactics (incoming and outgoing, attack and retreat, penetration and flanking maneuvers, targeted assaults and "smart" weapons) only reifies this idea. In modern warfare, weapons fly along thin trajectories through space, inflicting various degrees of harm on distant antagonists who are understood to be fundamentally separate from those who aim and release them. In such a case, it would be logical to assume that the phenomenon I call "violence," which the military tactician would call "engagement," if it is indeed locatable, travels along with the projectile, adhering to it, riding atop it unilinearly through space until it comes to rest, with the projectile, in the body it penetrates. Violence thus conceived is particular, in the sense of being like a particle that can be separated from the violent actor and then objectified along with the projectile (or fist, or piece of shrapnel) with which it is fused. From this vantage point, then, if the projectile was somehow intercepted in mid-flight, by a truck that drove into its path, for example, the delivery of violence to the intended victim would have been narrowly averted: the "target" was not "engaged."

And yet, as the systemic problem of shooter's ear (discussed briefly in chapter 3) and other types of belliphonic hearing loss demonstrates, even the most long-range and unidirectional of weapons (sniper rifles, rockets, cruise missiles) are capable of bringing some ancillary measure of physical harm to those who stand up-range, pulling the trigger or witnessing the act of shooting from nearby. Of course, it would be easy to dismiss the case of shooter's ear as anomalous, or at least epiphenomenal, to an investigation of the ontology of violence. Indeed, it seems almost perverse to compare something as devastating as a fatal gunshot wound to a little tinnitus or hearing loss. For me, though, this case, in which the execution of a violent act results in a subtle, often unperceived moment of widespread injurious "leakage," is emblematic of the general capacity of violence to degrade perpetrators and bystanders in subtle and unpredictable ways. In the introduction to this volume I argued that "in Iraq . . . civilians and military personnel found themselves in an ongoing process of enculturation into a common environment of extreme, and often extremely loud, armed violence," and that this violence blurred some of the distinctions that conventionally separate perpetrators from victims. The scenario of shooter's ear provides us with a structural analogue that will clarify the relationship between sound and violence, and their corporate effects on war's witnesses and auditors. My contention boils down to this: like sound, and in part through sound, *violent acts are immersive and omnidirectional*, enveloping perpetrators, bystanders, and targets into a single, expansive field of variegated and unpredictable effects.[36]

This is not to say that it makes no difference whether a violent act is aimed at you or away from you. Violence, like sound, can be directed or aimed. As with echolocation, and in part through echolocation, we can often pinpoint violent actors and assign them exclusive responsibility for violent acts directed toward discrete victims. But like the shooter or near bystander who suffers hearing loss or ringing in the ears while standing up-range from a weapon, perpetrators can be damaged, often imperceptibly at first, by their own violent acts. The damage that results from immersion in violence is not just physical but also psychological in character; it is therefore unpredictable and largely invisible until it is made manifest in subsequent acts. Just as the most directed sound produces "leakage" in all directions, it appears that even the most surgically precise attack produces its own kind of affective, psychosocial leakage, which flows over everyone within the field of the perceptible. In this sense, the directional-and-immersive ontology of violence is iconically related to the directional-and-immersive ontology of sound.

If the case for the omnidirectionality of violence makes you feel uncomfortable or even angry, I won't be surprised. One of my colleagues, who is from the Middle East and has Iraqi friends, objected to it vociferously. Even after I explained that I'm not claiming an equivalence between victims and perpetrators, she remained convinced that this argument ends up drawing attention and sympathy away from the "true" victims of violence and toward those who, according to her line of reasoning, deserve no sympathy. I must admit that part of me agrees with her, and I continue to feel somewhat ambivalent about my argument here. The urge to condemn violence is, for most of us, tightly bound together with the urge to demonize the perpetrators, and in so doing insert maximal distance between them and ourselves. But if we ignore the possibility that violent acts affect and injure the subjectivities of perpetrators as well as victims, we fail to grasp one of the mechanisms whereby the practice of violence renders the former group more likely to fall into repeated violent acts. The tendency of violence to be transmitted across spaces and generations, to re-erupt in the wake of reconciliation, and to "spiral out of control" despite incentives to curb it surely has something to do with the fact that perpetrators are also to some degree incapacitated by their own violent acts. Empirical evidence of this damage is abundant.[37]

In the previous chapter, I argued that some of the symptoms associated with PTSD can be understood to be the results of an inability to exit the auditory (and other sensory) regime(s) of wartime. We can now add to this claim the notion that prolonged immersion in the intersensorial onslaught of violence places everyone—victims, perpetrators, and bystanders—at increased risk of traumatic stress. This is another way to conceptualize combat PTSD: as the sustained aftereffects of the omnidirectional leakage of violent acts. In addition to the obvious damage inflicted upon the primary victim, there is a less visible secondary damage incurred by those who have committed armed violence or witnessed it at close quarters. Beyond its obvious destructive power, it carries hidden risks for all who are immersed in its sensory intensity—for all who are touched by it, disturbed by it, damaged by it, deafened by it.

SONIC CAMPAIGNS

The import of this argument is that the sonic materials of the Iraq war are something more urgent, powerful, and insidious than the simple audible residue of violent acts. Belliphonic sound is that residue, but it is also an instrument of violence in its own right. Sometimes that instrument is wielded consciously; at other times, its efficacy is unintentional. We can label the agglomeration of acts of belliphonic sounding over the course of Operation Iraqi Freedom the "sonic campaigns" of the war. Framing the belliphonic in this way forces a reorganization of the sounds that I catalogued in chapter 1. Now the core questions are no longer "what did the war sound like?" and "how did people learn to listen to those sounds?" but "who was responsible for the introduction and curtailment of sounds within the war zone?" and "what were the intentional and unintentional effects of those sounds?" These new questions mirror the questions that undergird descriptions of military campaigns throughout history: Who attacked? Who retreated? Who outflanked whom? And what were the results of these maneuvers?

A focus on the sonic campaigns of the war hence entails an investigation of agency. But where, or with whom, does (sonic) agency lie? The simplest, most obvious answer—that it lies with the individual who sounds, who shoots, who pushes the siren button—does not suffice. As Jackman argued above, this kind of mechanistic approach toward identifying responsible parties ignores the social networks that compel and enable acts of sonic (and other) violence. But it also occludes the technologies and sonic materialities that make a sonic act possible. A growing body of recent writing argues that agency is not the innate property of autonomous individuals, or even groups of them, but rather something that accrues within and among assemblages of human and nonhuman entities. Agency thus conceived is essentially elusive and "ungraspable": not an inborn quality of a human but the emergent capacity of a collective, be it big or small.[38] Political theorist

Jane Bennett writes that "it is a safe bet to begin with the presumption that the locus of political responsibility is a human-nonhuman assemblage":

> On close-enough inspection, the productive power that has engendered an effect will turn out to be a confederacy, and the human actants within it will themselves turn out to be confederations of tools, microbes, minerals, sounds, and other "foreign" materialities. Human intentionality can emerge as agentic only by way of such a distribution.[39]

Bennett's inclusion of sound as one element of the human "confederation" should make you think of Cusick's contention, discussed above, that people bombarded by sounds "become . . . the characteristic sounds of their captors." These two notions rub productively against one another, each problematizing the boundary between the human body and sensory stimuli. We will pick up this idea later, but for the present, the point I want to emphasize is simply that "agentic capacity" is distributed among humans (however complexly conceived) and the technologies and other "materialities" in which they are enmeshed. This is to say that sonic agency during the Iraq war was the emergent capacity of the humans who pulled triggers and drove Humvees and disguised IEDs and activated sirens and gave orders *and* the guns and vehicles and explosive devices and alarms systems and communication lines themselves. Following Bennett, we can expand the borders of agentic assemblages further, incorporating the industries that designed and produced these weapons as well as the characteristic sounds of the weapons themselves. The M4 was *made* to have a softer sound than the AK-47, and there is very little the shooter can do to alter this fact. The M4's sound, its sharp *pop-pop-pop,* is as inextricable a part of the firearm, and of the act of shooting, as is the round in the chamber or the finger on the trigger.

The sonic campaigns of the Iraq war were thus the corporate achievements of weapons, and rounds, and designers, and factories, and tacticians, and commanders-in-chief, and shooters, and drivers, and vehicles, and loudspeakers, and studios, and iPods, and the Internet, and musicians, and instruments, and military regulations, and child laborers, and mourners, and cassette tapes, and recorders, and the audible vibrations known as sounds. The vastness of this assemblage of things and people doesn't preclude us from assigning primary responsibility for a sonic act to the person who gave the order or pulled the trigger or drove the vehicle or screamed the epithet. Agency may be distributed, but choices are still made. And yet it pays to remember that the *pop-pop-pop* of the M4 and the louder *dadadadadadada* of the Kalashnikov—along with the lethal rounds that accompany them—are the products of more than lone actors. We can point to them, but let us not forget that there are chains of command, and political agendas, and cultural constraints, and technical affordances, and military-industrial complexes, and flows of capital and ideology that stand behind them. Thus, "who is responsible for that sound?" will remain a complex question even if we limit ourselves here to the simplest, most circumscribed answer possible.

Given that the clashing sonic campaigns of the Iraq war were waged with the sonic materials catalogued in chapter 1, I will refrain from describing them in detail again here. Rather, I want to concentrate on a few illustrative moments during the war when sound was being consciously deployed with the goal of achieving a coalition or insurgent objective. While the term "sonic campaign" can be stretched to cover all of the processes whereby sounds are introduced into a given environment, in instances like these it loses a great deal of its metaphoricity, revealing the aspect of sound that can be literally weaponized, drafted into service as part of a larger military operation.

Amplified sound

The US military's sonic campaign in Iraq began far in advance of the initial air sorties on March 19, 2003. US Central Command began conducting psychological operations (PSYOPS) over Iraqi airwaves as early as December 12, 2002. PSYOPS radio broadcasts, aimed largely at reducing confidence within the Iraqi military and general populace in the viability of Saddam Hussein's leadership, continued unabated in the months leading up to the invasion. The future area of operations was in this way being "prepared" through the deployment of a "nonlethal . . . weapons system" that consisted overwhelmingly of sound transduced from radio waves.[40]

Then, on March 17, 2003, two days before the first shot of the war was fired, in the middle of a televised address to the American public, then-president George W. Bush directed the following remarks to the Iraqi citizenry:

Many Iraqis can hear me tonight in a translated radio broadcast, and I have a message for them: If we must begin a military campaign, it will be directed against the lawless men who rule your country and not against you. As our coalition takes away their power, we will deliver the food and medicine you need. We will tear down the apparatus of terror and we will help you to build a new Iraq that is prosperous and free. In free Iraq there will be no more wars of aggression against your neighbors, no more poison factories, no more executions of dissidents, no more torture chambers and rape rooms. The tyrant will soon be gone. The day of your liberation is near.

It is too late for Saddam Hussein to remain in power. It is not too late for the Iraq military to act with honor and protect your country, by permitting the peaceful entry of coalition forces to eliminate weapons of mass destruction. Our forces will give Iraqi military units clear instructions on actions they can take to avoid being attacked and destroyed. I urge every member of the Iraqi military and intelligence services: if war comes, do not fight for a dying regime that is not worth your own life. And all Iraqi military and civilian personnel should listen carefully to this warning: In any conflict, your fate will depend on your actions. Do not destroy oil wells, a source of wealth that belongs to the Iraqi people. Do not obey any command to use weapons of mass destruction against anyone, including the Iraqi people. War crimes will be prosecuted, war criminals will be punished and it will be no defense to say, "I was just following orders."

This line of direct address to the Iraqi people was maintained throughout the war in the form of radio broadcasts and other short-range PSYOPS activities. From the very beginning through the exit of the last American combat troops in 2011, the territory of Iraq was constantly awash with radio waves containing music, news, instructions, warnings, and propaganda—all with the twin objectives of fighting the war more efficiently and "winning the hearts and minds" of the Iraqi people. This prolonged presence of broadcasts explicitly framed as weapons systems compels us to extend the timeline of military action in Iraq back from the initiation of the Shock and Awe campaign by several months. We can now see that "the Iraq War"—in the sense of a unified military campaign to overthrow the Hussein regime—began not with the first sorties of cruise missiles on March 19 but with the nonlethal sonic campaign initiated the previous December. President Bush's translated message to the Iraqi people was cast as a warning of possible future action ("If we must begin a military campaign . . ."), but it can be better understood as an escalation of a military campaign that was already in progress through sound.

The Hussein government recognized the threat posed by these broadcasts, and used its national radio and TV network to counter it. Led by the efforts of Information Minister Muhammad Sa'id al-Sahhaf,[41] Iraqi media put a strong propaganda spin on their accounts of the buildup to the US-led invasion and the coalition's actions once Operation Iraqi Freedom commenced. During the phase of major combat operations, from late March to mid-April 2003, the Hussein regime and the US-led forces fought the war in part over the airwaves, as Iraqi state radio competed with the increasing number of coalition-run stations that had been set up in the country. This competition took on even more of the formal elements of battle when, according to one account, "the Coalition attempted to electronically jam Iraqi radio stations to gain a monopoly on the information available to the Iraqi people through this medium."[42]

PSYOPS units used sound in a number of deception operations over the course of the war. The US Central Intelligence Agency is reported to have established "black PSYOP" radio stations that masqueraded as Iraqi stations:[43]

One such station, so-called "Radio Tikrit," tried to build up its credibility with a classic black PSYOP tactic by stating that it was managed by loyal Iraqis in the Tikrit area and by maintaining an editorial line slavishly supportive of Saddam Hussein. But within a few weeks, the tone changed and the station began to become more and more critical of Saddam.[44]

Beyond strategic efforts such as these, PSYOPS elements that were attached to army and marine units reportedly conducted tactical operations against Iraqi military elements. In April 2003, *Newsweek* reported that the PSYOPS loudspeaker was used to trick enemy troops into revealing their positions.

> Before plunging into Iraq, U.S. psychological-warfare operators studied certain cultural stereotypes. One was that young Arab toughs cannot tolerate insults to their manhood. So, as American armored columns pushed down the road to Baghdad, *400-watt loudspeakers mounted on Humvees would, from time to time, blare out in Arabic that Iraqi men are impotent.* The Fedayeen, the fierce but undisciplined and untrained Iraqi irregulars, could not bear to be taunted. Whether they took the bait or saw an opportunity to attack, many Iraqis stormed out of their concealed or dug-in positions—pushing aside their human shields in some cases—to be slaughtered by American tanks and Bradley fighting vehicles. *"What you say is many times more important than what you do in this part of the world,"* says a senior U.S. psy-warrior.[45]

By all indications, amplified sound was an important tactical weapon during the phase of major combat operations. In addition to taunting soldiers to reveal themselves, coalition troops launched "deception operations against Iraqi military elements by playing sound effects of tanks and helicopters through the loudspeakers."[46] Secretive tactics like these are poorly documented in official accounts of Operation Iraqi Freedom, but they are frequently the subject of stories passed around among Iraqi civilians. A young Iraqi man whom I'll call "Muhammad" once told me how a close friend and his family remained inside their house for days on end, listening to what they took to be the sounds of gunfire nearby. Based on these sounds,

> They felt that there were insurgents out in their neighborhood [engaged in heated battles]. So they stayed [in their home] for a week after the end of the war. After the week they couldn't [bear it any] longer—they wanted to see what's going on. And [the source of the noise turned out to be] a, what do we call it, a *sound system,* dropped by the air force. Like a barrel that keeps producing this sound. Yeah. Like a grenade, there are grenades that are totally just sound, there is no TNT or explosive in it. I didn't see it, but he described it to me as a barrel, that kept [up a stream of gunfire sounds], like fireworks.[47]

While Muhammad's secondhand story cannot be verified, it remains undeniable that sound played a pivotal role in PSYOPS activities throughout the war. Whether "battling for the hearts and minds" of the Iraqi citizenry or using deception to confuse the enemy, the PSYOPS loudspeaker was an important element in the assemblage of technologies, ideologies, personnel, sounds, and sensibilities that coalesced into the sonic campaigns of the US military.

US PSYOPS loudspeakers weren't the only loudspeakers being put to tactical use in the area of operations, however. Throughout the war, various local factions made use of loudspeakers attached to the minarets of mosques to broadcast a large variety of messages to all within earshot. The ubiquitous minaret loudspeaker, whose primary purpose is to transmit the call to prayer and other religious utterances to the Muslim faithful, acquired an additional purpose during the war, becoming a kind of local PSYOPS device for insurgents, sectarians, and unaffiliated Iraqis alike. Sometimes the messages were humanitarian in character. In October 2003, for example, after a large car bomb at a Sadr City police station killed ten people, a nearby mosque loudspeaker blared "warnings to the thousands of residents who had gathered at the station to leave the area for fear of a second booby-trapped car."[48] At other times, belligerent speakers bathed neighborhoods with the sound of speech acts designed to incite violence. In March 2004, Muqtada al-Sadr's forces reacted to a recent bombing of pilgrims by commandeering a mosque loudspeaker and shouting, "We blame the Americans, let's expel the Americans, let's unite to expel them from Iraq, let's unite as one religion." A videotape of this event was subsequently copied on to VCDs and distributed widely, giving the utterance a secondary audience that was exponentially larger than the first.[49]

The use of loudspeakers within the clashing sonic campaigns of the war was particularly prominent during the two Battles of Fallujah in 2004. Journalists reported that "mosque loudspeakers blared calls for jihad, or holy war" in the days before the first battle commenced.[50] During the second battle, several months later, the US forces launched a "harassment mission," blasting heavy metal music through Humvee-mounted PSYOPS loudspeakers for days on end in an attempt to annoy the insurgents and disrupt their sleep patterns.[51] The *Washington Post* reported that, as the battle wound down, with the US forces controlling the majority of the city, "loudspeakers mounted on Humvees urged that 'all fighters in Fallujah should surrender, and we guarantee they will not be killed or insulted.'" Insurgent fighters, speaking from a mosque loudspeaker, retorted with the gallows humor of wartime: "we ask the American soldiers to surrender and we guarantee that we will kill and torture them."[52] To think of these utterances as communication, as dialogue, is to mistake their form for their essence. The warring parties were indeed listening to one another—the insurgent response demonstrates this. But these utterances had no hope of convincing their target audiences of anything; they were rhetorically moot. Their nature, rather, was that of a volley—they were auditory mortars, lobbed over the front line to harass the enemy. During the war, with the use of heavy metal music, the hurling of amplified insults, and the exchange of utterances above, the inherent polysemy of language was often stripped away to reveal the affective power of words and music as imposed sounds. In situations like these, the capacity for uttered words and musical sounds to wound was purposefully intensified: their aesthetic value and semantic richness were radically attenuated, their damaging edge bared.

Weapon sounds as weapons

As the testimonies throughout this book make abundantly clear, experienced shooters of all stripes tended to have an intimate knowledge of the distinctive sounds their weapons make. They often accessed this archive of sonic knowledge when they were striving to make sense of incoming and ambient gunfire, taking pride in their ability to discern one weapon from another. At the same time, they cultivated a knowledge of the observable effects that different weapon sounds produce within different auditing populations. Armed with an understanding of the *acoustic* efficacy of their weapons, they sometimes fired them not to hit a target but to produce a sound, a weapon sound that was itself fully weaponized. An air force major on loan to the army who served in the early years of the war described the tactical value of the sound of his truck-mounted M2s:

> One of the neatest sounds, one of the most memorable sounds out there is a 50-cal [M2] machine gun, a very distinctive, commanding noise. And it's a very big gun, it's very intimidating, the noise is intimidating and the damage that the weapon can inflict is intimidating. We have those on our vehicles, and *I think it has more of a psychological value than a real physical value.* We always took them on our trucks, and we only had to fire the weapons once and you learn and the bad guys learn that *it makes a very loud distinctive sound that is something to be respected and feared.* And so, we took them with us more for the psychological value, and just hearing it would, bad guys would disappear quickly from hearing that noise. I didn't let the guys shoot it at, we wouldn't shoot it at targets because . . . it's such a big bullet that it has a tendency to travel *through* . . . through the vehicle, through the bad guy, out the other end, into the house in town, out through the mud-built houses, and through several houses so it was a lot of collateral damage that could happen so if we had to get into an engagement the guys shot their M16s or smaller weapons, but we always carried it because *it was loud, and it was commanding, and it garnered respect.*[53]

Here, the tactical value of the M2's sounds—its ability to cause "bad guys" to "disappear quickly"—doesn't just complement but overwhelms its value as a precision killing machine for the mission at hand. ("We wouldn't shoot it at targets because . . . it has a tendency to travel *through* . . .") The efficacy of the M2 as a sound weapon depended on the transparent indexical thrust of its sounds; in this case, a big sound was, logically, equated with big, lethal bullets. Without this, without the synchronous act of extreme violence to which it pointed, the weapon's loud report would have been merely annoying, not terrifying. The same indexical logic underwrote the Iraqi police (and US military contractor) practice of using gunfire to clear traffic jams. More broadly, the extremely common tactic of "suppression fire" relies upon this logic as well. The barrage of suppression fire isn't designed to kill the enemy so much as to force them to hide behind barriers while the shooters move around within range of the enemy's weapons. Upon hearing the telltale sounds of gunfire aimed at them, the targets of suppression fire take cover. Crouching down behind a wall or other barrier, they cannot visually surveil the battle area—and therefore, cannot be accurate shooters themselves. They are, at that moment, auditors who yearn to see but are unable to do so. They must wait until they hear the barrage stop before they can become intersensorial fighters again.

It is important to note that none of these "acoustic weapons" were shooting blanks. While they weren't aiming at targets, the airmen firing the M2, the Iraqi police firing their Kalashnikovs, fighters engaging in suppression fire—and, for that matter, many Iraqis who engaged in celebratory gunfire after soccer matches or Saddam Hussein's capture or the American withdrawal—were using live rounds. Bullets fired up into the air come down eventually, at speeds that allow them to seriously injure or potentially kill a bystander, or penetrate the thin metal roof of the standard military housing unit. (I spoke to several service members who returned to their housing units to find small holes in their ceilings and foreign rounds in their beds.) More to the point, a gun fired in the air can instantly be lowered and trained upon a fleshy target. All of this is to say that in Iraq, the sonic campaigns of both sides could never be fully separated from the campaigns of armed killing.

If the PSYOPS loudspeaker and the battle noise simulator are "pure" acoustic weapons, producing nothing other than weaponized sounds, the M2 and AK can be considered "hybrid" in these situations, to the extent that they create effects other than the auditory ones that their shooters intended. The much-documented—but sparsely deployed—LRAD, the "sonic gun" that can project an intelligible voice over a kilometer or shoot narrow bands of high-decibel sounds that can induce nausea, disorientation, and hearing loss, is similarly hybrid: it is a weapon that produces sensory effects across multiple registers, that can produce wounds as well as sounds. At the other end of the lethality spectrum, the IED, that most reliably destructive element in the insurgent and sectarian arsenals, was also at times used as a hybrid acoustic weapon. A common tactic involved a first step of detonating a relatively small IED, the sound and sight of which would draw the attention of military personnel in the area. Once they arrived at the scene to investigate and assist any wounded, a second, larger and more deadly, IED would be triggered.[54] When combined with the broader acoustic effect of the IED—as an indication to all within earshot that the insurgency was alive and active—the weapon's secondary value as a generator of loud belliphonic sound was formidable.

It is clear now that, within a discussion of the sonic campaigns of the Iraq war, the minimal unit of analysis cannot be the shooter-as-agent or the weapon-as-object; it must be the human-nonhuman assemblage comprising the weapon-in-use. From this standpoint, a Kalashnikov fired in the air by an Iraqi policeman to clear the street is a different entity than the same Kalashnikov fired with the intent of killing a human target; in use, the former is rendered a hybrid acoustic weapon, while the latter doesn't necessarily meet that threshold. A fine-grained examination of the culture of firing will demonstrate, however, that the instances in which the sonic dimension of weapon use is the object of conscious reflection are far more common than one might think. Service members routinely acknowledge the euphoric thrill that is triggered by the sound of their weapons-in-use. It is, in fact, impossible to fully disentangle the adrenalin-infused emotions that the sound and feel of firing create from the act itself. Firing is always an affectively heightened, sound-saturated act, and this fact complicates any argument that combat maneuvers can ever be the result of purely rational, dispassionate decisions. The jolt of a rifle's kick and the often deafening sound of its report destabilize any kind of Cartesian rationalism one might wish to bring to the battlefield. The sound of the weapon-in-use acts upon the body of the shooter and everyone else within close range; it complicates calculations. It demands to be taken into account.

What this means is that beyond the borders of the hybrid acoustic weapon—one that effects change in multiple registers but is used primarily to create sound—lies a far more expansive category of weapons and other wartime instruments that produce unintended or quasi-intended acoustic consequences. This is the general field of the belliphonic; in the end, it constitutes the long tail of the sonic campaign.

Belliphonic sounds are the substance of wartime acoustic ecology, and often the *sonic matériel* with which war is fought. And since sound and violence enter the world omni-directionally, the consequences of these acts—consequences that include but are not limited to hearing loss, traumatic stress, exhaustion, aggression, and depression—are distributed broadly. A full accounting of the war thus must include the acoustic violence and aggression produced by the sonic campaigns that emerged within it.

Given this chapter's focus on the deleterious effects of the sonic dimension of armed violence, one might conclude that the implicit solution to this problem is to build more and better silencers and stealthier bombs, and generally to make the prosecution of war less noisy, more efficient, "smarter." This is, to put it mildly, not the message I want to transmit. Belliphonic loudness has one obvious benefit: it renders violence a radically public phenomenon, one that announces itself loudly, and thus enables a large public to take measures to minimize its effects and keep an accounting, an audit, of its presence. The fact that an auditing public can take account of loud violent acts in this way is the sole benefit of the "amplitude of violence" in the narrow, auditory sense of the term. However, as the discussion of the audible inaudible in chapter 2 suggests, the testimonial capacity of armed violence is always degraded over time, to the point where the distant sound of gunfire is effectively "silenced" for most. How are we to understand the complex dialectic between sound and silencing in wartime? The following section takes up this question in detail.

Silencing

Whether in war or in peace, sonic campaigns always extend beyond the act of sounding. They are filled not just with sounds but with silences. Where sounds would normally be, one finds conspicuous absences, social or physical conditions having been imposed that render the act of sounding dangerous, subversive, or impossible. These conditions are abundant in peaceful situations, too, but in the midst of violent acts they are even more numerous and extreme. Violence itself resists representation,[55] and as such, manufactures silences of its own: over the course of the Iraq war, events transpired that remain "unspeakable" for participants and witnesses alike. Complicating the situation further, suppressed memories of traumatic events become literally "unthinkable," lost often to the only people who could testify that they occurred. And beyond these traumatic gaps lie other, institutionally encouraged, silences—silences that serve the interests of one or more of the warring parties.[56] These cultivated or enforced silences can serve as buffers preventing escalation of violence, framing devices for official narratives, screens obscuring culpability, or enabling conditions for future conflict. At times, they themselves become sources of secondary traumas, and in so doing strengthen the cloak of muteness that so often surrounds violent acts.

Given the many valences that silence takes in wartime, it should not be surprising that numerous forms of silencing were in play during Operation Iraqi Freedom. In neighborhoods where sectarian or insurgent activities were common, the imminent threat of violence produced a kind of civic silencing, as those who could tell an attack was forthcoming removed themselves from public spaces. As a result, an ebbing in urban noise that might have seemed like a moment of calm quietude to you and me could be recognized by residents and service members alike as the unbearable eerie stillness that precedes an ambush. As Shymaa, an Iraqi woman who lived in Baghdad during the war, explained:

> One of the [scariest things] is actually the silence. Because for us *the silence is always before the storm*. So yes, when you see a neighborhood, when you enter a neighborhood or a place where everything is so quiet and you cannot actually see anyone, that's a sign of danger.[57]

If silencing here is the indirect consequence of impending violence, in other moments, it was the explicit objective of tactical actions. Within the 400,000 classified documents released several years ago by wikileaks.org, one can find multiple documented cases of US military service members detaining Iraqi civilian drivers after routine checks revealed cassette tapes with music and chants praising the insurgency, effectively criminalizing the act of listening and attempting to remove an entire vocal genre from the public arena.[58] The fact that many of those who were found to have these tapes in their possession were subsequently detained (and therefore deprived of the ability to speak publicly) only complicates the chain of silencing that regularly occurred in wartime Iraq.

At the same time, enormous effort was put into the attempt to constrain the ability of al-Qaeda leaders to speak publicly or disseminate audio or videotapes of their pronouncements. In fact, one could say that part of the rationale of the US detention

program was not just to punish combatants or elicit information or remove active fighters from the combat zone but also to deny individuals who spoke out in favor of the
insurgency a platform to speak. This act of silencing may seem ancillary to the official
rationale for detaining prisoners, but it was in fact an unambiguous and strategic objective of the policy: when someone disappeared into one of the "black sites," their voice fell
out of discourse entirely.

In the post-9/11 era, the voice most thoroughly policed was surely that of al-Qaeda
leader Osama bin Laden. Unable to apprehend bin Laden himself, the Bush administration attempted to "capture" his voice by controlling media representations of the cassette
tapes he distributed to the Al Jazeera network. In an article provocatively titled "Enemy
Voice," Jonathan Sterne documents these attempts:

> Shortly after the 11 September 2001 attacks, the Bush administration implored
> networks not to broadcast bin Laden tapes, and if they did, to only broadcast little
> snippets and edit out any "flowery rhetoric urging violence against Americans."
> National security advisor Condoleezza Rice claimed that al-Qaeda could be
> using broadcasts of bin Laden speeches to "send coded messages to other terror-
> ists" and to "vent propaganda intended to incite hatred and potentially kill more
> Americans," especially because bin Laden was a "charismatic speaker."[59]

Sterne sees a "particular rhetorical significance" in this move. It is "as if restricting the
movement of al-Qaeda's discourse were the same thing as restricting the movement of
al-Qaeda."[60] Within the context of the Iraq war, this kind of conflation of voice, ideology, and combat was common. The sonic campaigns of the US-led forces policed the
movement of voices every bit as scrupulously as they did the movement of enemy bodies.
The prevailing logic, that enemy combatants don't just engage in violence themselves but
use their voices to call for more violence or even trigger secret planned attacks, provided
ample justification for US forces to prohibit interviews and tightly control other media
representations of detainees.

Killing as Silencing

Every death results in the permanent silencing of a unique voice, but some killings
emphasize this fact more than others. The videotaped beheading of American busi-
nessman Nick Berg in May 2004 is a case in point. Among the most disturbing media
products generated during the war, the low-fidelity video begins with Berg seated in
a chair, wearing an orange jumpsuit reminiscent of the uniform worn by detainees at
Guantanamo Bay. Speaking quietly, the young man states his name, the names of his
parents and siblings, and says he lives in a town near Philadelphia. After an abrupt cut of
the tape, Berg is seen sitting on the floor, wrists and ankles bound, with five men, their
faces obscured by kaffiyeh cloths, standing behind him. The man in the center, who will

subsequently be identified as al-Qaeda in Mesopotamia leader Abu Musab al-Zarqawi, reads a statement in Arabic. After urging Muslims to rise up and seek revenge for the prisoners who were tortured and humiliated at Abu Ghraib prison, the masked Zarqawi addresses President Bush, claiming that he and his soldiers "will regret the day you treaded on Iraqi land." At the conclusion of the address, Zarqawi claims that the insurgency is going to begin sending coffins filled with slaughtered Americans back to the mothers and wives of American soldiers. Brandishing a long knife, he then grabs Berg by the hair on his head, pulls him down to the ground, and, over the course of a long thirty seconds, laboriously decapitates him. The videotape captures Berg's terrified screams, which persist until the moment his windpipe is cut. The head of the man who seconds before was screaming is held aloft and then placed atop the body, a mute symbol of, among other things, the literal silencing that accompanies the cessation of a life.

Two years later, after prolonged surveillance by unmanned aerial vehicles, a US Air Force F-16 dropped two 500-pound guided bombs on a house known to hold Abu Musab al-Zarqawi, the man who decapitated Nick Berg. The bombs killed Zarqawi, his spiritual adviser Sheik Abd-al-Rahman, and four others. In a video widely distributed by news outlets around the world, President Bush, standing at a podium in the Rose Garden, announces the death of Zarqawi. His account blends details of Zarqawi's murderous activities with an acknowledgment of the danger Zarqawi posed as a speaker who could incite others to violence. He lists Zarqawi's terrorist activities: beheading American hostages, "masterminding the destruction of the United Nations headquarters in Baghdad," "bombing . . . a hotel in Amman." But in more than one place he gives particular emphasis to Zarqawi's activities as an ideologue and propagandist, mentioning that Osama bin Laden "called on the terrorists of the world to listen to [Zarqawi] and obey him." He saves this description for last:

> Through his every action, he sought to defeat America and our Coalition partners, and turn Iraq into a safe haven from which Al Qaeda could wage its war on free nations. To achieve these ends he worked to divide Iraqis, and incite civil war. *Only last week he released an audiotape attacking Iraq's elected leaders, and denouncing those advocating the end of sectarianism.*[61]

In addition to a pair of hands capable of killing, in other words, the insurgency lost a voice, one uniquely capable of fueling a violent sonic campaign directed against Iraqis and Americans alike.

Subsequent reports revealed that Zarqawi survived the attack but died an hour later of wounds sustained during the explosion. An autopsy revealed that the pressure of the blast wave had caused the blood vessels in his lungs and ears to burst.[62] But this is not what the public saw. Televised reports of the targeted killing feature video footage of the bombing taken from an aerial camera high above the scene. Filmed from a great distance, the house in the black-and-white video looks like a tiny cube. The silent detonation takes place precisely in the crosshairs on the screen, grey clouds of debris blooming noiselessly into the grove of palm trees that surrounded the house.

The complex affective territory of asymmetrical warfare is on full display in the videos showing the deaths of Berg and Zarqawi. The first portrays the war in all of its revolting and cacophonous intimacy; the act of killing here is low-tech, hands-on, and messy. By contrast, the press conference and drone footage present the antiseptic quietude of a "surgical strike," the product of sophisticated technologies, calm deliberations, and layers upon layers of mediation. We could use Michel Wieviorka's terminology to say that the parties behind Berg's beheading chose to depict the war as a "hot" phenomenon—retributive, impassioned, volatile, triumphant—while those behind the targeted killing of Zarqawi were invested in war as "cold"—rational, dispassionate, calculated, efficacious.[63] At the same time, these videos powerfully demonstrate the complicated symbolic terrain upon which wartime silencing takes place. It is a terrain that incorporates the literal and metaphorical, the vengeful and the banal, the tactical and the strategic, the hot and the cold.

Shots Heard Around the World

The US introduced the disruptive sounds of helicopters and Humvees and cruise missiles and M4s into wartime Iraq. The insurgency introduced the rattle of Kalashnikovs, the whine and crack of mortars, and the chilling boom of the IED. The Hussein regime maintained control of Baghdad's civil-defense sirens while it was in power. Elements of the local population made big noises at mass demonstrations. PSYOPS troops projected deceptive sounds into the timespace of the war. Voices were silenced by curfews, by detention, by emigration, by death. All of these events can be understood as contributing to local sonic campaigns (of the military, the civilian population, the insurgency, sectarian groups) that often found themselves in a zero-sum struggle for supremacy. These campaigns overlapped in urban areas, at times obscuring the more stable collection of "natural sounds" that we typically think of when we think of acoustic ecology: birds, dogs, foxes, rivers, wind.

While the campaigns of projectiles and shrapnel and PSYOPS speakers and sirens were intensely local and site-specific, insurgent videos and government news reports were designed to have a mediatic fluidity that allowed them to reach international audiences. The official narratives and counternarratives that they contained (in which the war was presented as the necessary liberation and democratization of oppressed peoples, or as hubristic imperialism and occupation by infidels) helped to naturalize some thoughts about the war and estrange others; the propagation of these narratives amounted to a joint operation of amplification and silencing that had implications for populations around the world. This should not be surprising, as the principal parties in the war—the United States and the transnational militant Islamist movement—both understood their purview, their "area of interest," in global terms. Without arguing for a moral equivalence between these entities, one can acknowledge the exceptionalist slant of their ideologies, the moralistic cast of the justifications for their actions, and, most germane here, the extent to which their audiovisual products were intended to convince a global audience of the righteousness of their cause. Traveling through the globalized networks of twenty-four-hour news and the internet, these mediatized narratives significantly increased the intensity and reach of the sonic campaigns of the Iraq war. They stretched the battle for hearts and minds far beyond the front lines, all the way out to the home front and the rest of the bystanding world.

Within the context of the sonic campaigns of the Iraq war, sound and silence were valued for their ability to wound, to communicate, and to move. Mediated by technologies and burrowed deep into memories, they continue to travel and persist in ways at best dimly foreseen by those who initiated the sounds and silences of the Iraq war's belliphonic ecology.

"Places come into us lastingly; once having been in a particular place for any considerable time—or even briefly, if our experience there has been intense—we are forever marked by that place, which lingers in us indefinitely and in a thousand ways, many too subtle for us to name."
—EDWARD CASEY[1]

"As place is sensed, senses are placed; as places make sense, senses make place."
—STEVEN FELD[2]

5

Acoustic Territories

HAVING FRAMED THE belliphonic sounds of the Iraq War as an aggregation of sonic campaigns advancing the objectives of the warring parties, and having examined the different assemblages of elements and experiences that lent structure to the listening practices of the war's auditors, we now need to investigate the ground on which these acts of sounding and listening occurred. What are the spatial consequences of sounding and listening? How do belliphonic sounds *take place*—in the simple sense of occurring, and the more complex sense of appropriating geographical areas and infusing them with affect and meaning? How do they help to bring places into being? How are belliphonic sounds, and sounds more generally, shaped by the places in which they resonate, and how does this site-specific resonance affect the listening bodies exposed to them?

EMPLACEMENT, DISPLACEMENT, TRANSPLACEMENT

The underlying assumption behind these questions is that we experience sound, like other sensory stimuli, *not* as an autonomous entity bound by its intrinsic qualities (e.g., not as it is represented in spectral analysis on a screen or musical notes on a staff) but always refracted through discrete bodies that are oriented in meaningful, feelingful environments. In other words, hearing, listening, and other more extreme modalities of exposure to sound are not merely *embodied* but *emplaced*. Anthropologist David Howes makes the following distinction between the two terms:

> While the paradigm of 'embodiment' implies an integration of mind and body, the emergent paradigm of emplacement suggests the sensuous interrelationship of body-mind-environment. This environment is both physical and social, as is well illustrated by the bundle of sensory and social values contained in the feeling of 'home.'[3]

Building on this formulation, we can assert that sound as phenomenon and listening as practice are both co-located in the environment, in the body, in individual consciousnesses, and in intersubjective understandings. The sounds we hear reverberate in and are shaped by the built environment, but they also permeate our bodies, setting parts of them into sympathetic vibration. These same sounds cause our synapses to fire and coalesce into thoughts, impressions, moods. These latter creations, along with the sounds themselves, constitute raw material for our conversations, relationships, and sense of self. Listening is an intentional act, involving the near-simultaneous activation of our skin, our ears, and our brains in reaction to sounds that vibrate through us and the surroundings we share with others; it is mental, physical, *and* social. Howes's "sensuous interrelationship" is one in which sounds, places, bodies, thoughts, affect, and discourse become tangled up in each other.[4]

The paradigm of emplacement suggests that the body as we experience it does not occupy a discrete coordinate in the "sheer extension" of Cartesian space but instead is always embedded in a *place* whose structure and character interacts with it.[5] Edward Casey, one of the most prominent theorists of place and space, calls the emplaced body *homo geographicus*, "the geographical self."[6] Throughout this chapter, we will follow the trajectories of geographical selves moving through the violent timespaces of the Iraq War, giving particular attention to aspects of the sonorous environment that bring harm to wartime auditors.

At the same time, I want to complicate Casey's formulation somewhat, folding *homo geographicus* in on itself to draw attention to internal geographies hidden *within* the body. In a very restricted sense, Casey does allow for the possibility that places can *come in* to the body.[7] As the epigraph to this chapter suggests, places can colonize the body and stay there, "linger[ing] in us indefinitely." Here, Casey treats place metaphorically, immaterially. His statement concerns not place itself but the aura of place that is manifest in memory: "What lingers most powerfully is the presence and, more particularly, *how it felt to be in this presence:* how it felt to be in the Crazy Mountains that summer, how I sensed the lower East Side during January."[8]

I would like to argue that, in addition to this psychical occupation of the body by the memory of a geographical place, the body itself harbors small places of its own that have many of the same characteristics as their geographical counterparts. Later in this chapter I will discuss how the internal territories of the inner ear, sinuses, meninges, and chest cavity are impacted by sounds originating in the external territories of the built landscape and broader environment. I will also argue that these internal cavities are distinct, both from more properly "geographical," external places and from the sentient body that encloses them, the body that maneuvers through the world. Understood in this way, emplacement is the condition in which bodies are simultaneously embedded within the macroterritories of the greater environment *and* permeated with discrete microterritories that react in their own ways to sensory stimuli. Sound is interesting here because unlike the visual, which doesn't penetrate the body, it is doubly emplaced, exerting physical changes on both types of territories at the same time.

At first glance, emplacement, even in this double sense, would appear to be a static aspect of the human condition: no matter where we move, we are always someplace, and we always carry our corporeal microterritories around with us. But what of the moments when our sensuous appreciation of our surroundings attenuates down to a state of crisis, when we feel like we've *lost our place* in the world? Howes calls this precarious state *displacement*: "the feeling that one is homeless, disconnected from one's physical and social environment." He identifies displacement as the frequent "plight of the socially marginal" or disenfranchised.[9] A radical, literal displacement takes place on a massive scale during armed conflicts, as entire populations are uprooted and forced into conditions that one could only describe as "desensualized." Foreign tongues, unfamiliar accents, curfews, the tight and unforgiving perimeter of the monochromatic refugee camp, the crippling problems of hunger and illness and fear, the overpowering presence of antebellum memories and the absences they trace—all of these factors bleed the sensory richness out of the lives of the displaced, creating instead an impoverished set of stimuli interacting weakly with sensoria that are compromised by the violent uprooting they endured.

For those who never leave the combat zone, displacement occurs within the body, through sound. Unlike other sensory evidence of armed conflict, belliphonic vibrations are uniquely invasive, comprising small-scale assaults that excite, perturb, and at times literally alter the body's corporeal microterritories, often with disastrous results. The blast waves that are a feature of the loudest belliphonic sounds violently displace air and tissues within the body, and these movements in turn can result in profound corporeal damage. From hearing loss to traumatic brain injury, the signature injury of the Iraq War, the cost of acoustic displacement can be lifelong and severe.

Severe, yes, but can the various displacements wrought by violence ever be absolute? Casey—who, we will recall, is concerned only with properly geographical macroterritories and not corporeal ones—argues that they cannot:

Places can never become utterly attenuated. They may become increasingly uni-form and unable to engage our concernful absorption, without, for all that, ceasing to exist altogether as places for us—places in which we orient ourselves and feel at home. In particular, places will not "merge with," much less *turn into,* space. To posit any such merger is to confuse two orders of being that are, in principle, separate.[10]

Here, once again, we encounter a moment in which the extreme edge of violence pushes existing categories to the point of failure. From the American cruise missile to the sui-cide bomber, the war was filled with explosive instruments that turned some of the rich-est, most sensually dynamic places, both internal and external, into raw space—a gaping emptiness in which no geographical self could make a home. The vehicle that turned into a crater, the body whose internal geographies were opened into the air—these have been absolutely and irrevocably *dis*-placed, turned into an "order of being" that refused to remain "separate" from the disembodied Cartesian coordinates that mark the loca-tion of a void.

We are now in a position to say that extreme violent acts can result in external *and* internal displacements of varying intensity. But what of the millions of people who do not flee the conflict zone, and whose bodily territories do not suffer injurious changes? Oral testimonies and written accounts of war frequently comment on the ways in which violent acts transform the affective environment of one's surroundings into something strange, *unheimlich* and foreboding.[11] In Iraq, these changes took place in many differ-ent registers: a complex of palaces in central Baghdad long associated with the Hussein regime is occupied by his enemies and renamed the Green Zone; a neighbor's house, viewed daily for decades, is turned by a bomb into a tangle of bricks and twisted metal, although the houses around it are untouched; a once-mixed neighborhood endures sec-tarian cleansing, and becomes a Shi'i or Sunni stronghold. Changes such as these take the familiar (e.g., a name, a street, a neighborhood), and render it unfamiliar through acts of violent recontextualization. Let us introduce the term *transplacement* to describe this kind of change, and the uncanny feelings it induces.[12] A figure of speech discussed in classical rhetoric, "transplacement" designates a repeated word or phrase whose mean-ing is altered the second time it appears. Take, for example, the line from Shakespeare's *Othello*, which the play's tragic protagonist mutters to himself before killing his wife Desdemona: "Put out the light, and then *put out the light*."[13] In the first instance, he refers to the candle in Desdemona's bedchamber he has just snuffed; in the second, to the life he is about to take. What changes between the two iterations of this phrase is not its phonetic makeup, but its referent and its context—in short, the denotative and connotative territory within which the repetition takes place.

The shifting acoustic territories of the war forced similar changes upon the sounds that reverberated within them. During the Hussein era, the sound of AK-47 fire in a neighborhood would have caused most people to assume that a wedding, sporting event, or other cause for celebration (and with it, celebratory gunfire) was taking place. It was only after the war began that these sounds became transplaced into the context of killing. Similarly, the relative quiet that marked many innocuous moments in a prewar day was thoroughly transplaced into a context in which silence drew widespread suspicion that an attack was imminent. In these and countless other incidents, bodies, sounds, and places remained more or less stationary, but their indexicality and their affective force were altered by the new wartime context and the state of sustained vulnerability that it engendered.

SOUND AND TERRITORIALITY

The aggressive acts that gave rise to belliphonic transplacements and displacements in Iraq contributed to a sense of acoustic territory as a place that one fights to establish and maintain. This sense is in line with much contemporary writing on territoriality more broadly, which emphasizes the ever-present element of force that accompanies its constitution.[14] Robert Sack, whose *Human Territoriality: Its Theory and History* (1986) is a classic in the field, defines territoriality as *"the attempt by an individual or group to affect, influence, or control people, phenomena, and relationships, by delimiting and asserting control over a geographical area."*[15] William Connolly goes even further, asserting that aggression and violence are built into the very etymology of the term. (While the etymological derivation Connolly cites has been debunked,[16] his definition of territory, for our purposes here, is apt.) He writes:

> *Terra* means land, earth, nourishment, sustenance; it conveys the sense of a sustaining medium, solid, fading off into indefiniteness. But the form of the word [according to the *Oxford English Dictionary*] suggests that it derives from *terrere*, meaning to frighten, to terrorize. And *Territorium* is a "place from which people are warned." Perhaps these two contending derivations continue to occupy territory today. To occupy a territory is to receive sustenance and to exercise violence. *Territory is land occupied by violence.*[17]

The violence that accompanies the establishment of geographical territories is often implied rather than enacted: many borders are never contested, which means that the threat of violence in reaction to their breach remains just that—a threat. Acoustic territories, by contrast, are in a constant state of active contestation.[18] Because sounds are ephemeral, a regular stream of sonic acts is necessary to maintain the spaces they occupy; this makes acoustic territories more volatile than territories that are held in place by hegemonic or legalistic forces. Of course, in wartime, when acoustic territories are carved out by virtue of repeated belliphonic acts, the constitutive element of violence is not metaphorical and implied, but concrete and ubiquitous.

Like Brandon LaBelle, who memorably theorized acoustic territories in a volume bearing the term as its title, I am here concerned with the acoustics of enclosed spaces, and the ways that the dimensions and composition of particular spaces "are conditioned and bring forward" particular acoustic effects—such as echo, sustain, and muffling.[19] But I also join LaBelle in probing the ways that "sound . . . carve[s] out a micro-geography of the moment," and in so doing "brings bodies together."[20] There are two conceptual schemata at work here, and for our purposes it will be helpful to separate them. On the one hand, we have the intersubjective places that are brought into existence through acts of sounding. The dimensions of these places, which I will call *radiant acoustic territories*, are largely determined by the amplitude and directionality of the sounds concerned. The defining characteristic of the radiant acoustic territory is not the nature of its interaction with the built environment but the number of auditors who are interpellated into the unified field of acoustic power it projects. On the other hand, we have the structured environments inside and outside the body that contain, shape, and in other ways mediate sound. The remarkable thing about these *resonant acoustic territories* is the effect of mediation—on the sound, on the auditor, and in extreme cases, on the territory itself. The archetypal space of the radiant acoustic territory is the urban agora, an open expanse dense with ears; the archetypal space of the resonant acoustic territory is the rotunda, an enclosed space thick with echoes.

If our earlier focus on auditory regimes drew attention to the factors that shaped the act of listening, and the discussion of sonic campaigns sketched out the lines of responsibility and intentionality through which acts of sounding occur, the present chapter shows how sounding and listening both affect and are affected by positionality and environmental design. The belliphonic narrative of wartime Iraq involves the emplacements, displacements, and transplacements that occurred when sounds animated the radiant and resonant acoustic territories, from the macro-level of the mediascape all the way down to the micro-level of the inner ear.

THE VIRTUAL ACOUSTIC TERRITORY OF RECORDED SOUND

Unless you were one of the civilians or service members or paramilitary fighters who lived through the Iraq War, your encounter with the belliphonic was staged at some distance, and subject to thorough mediation by an array of audiovisual and communication technologies. Belliphonic sounds were likely transmitted into your home or workplace via radio reports, televised news broadcasts, and, if you sought them out, professional and amateur war videos posted online. The acoustic territories that emerged as a result of these transmissions were global, rhizophonic,[21] and virtual. Reportage and amateur broadcasts from Iraq brought sporadic electronic representations of the belliphonic into millions of spaces throughout the world, affording disparate auditors the opportunity to "listen in" on highly mediated simulacra of combat. Most of the world encountered the belliphonic exclusively in this way.

Images were disseminated throughout the world's domestic and work spaces too, and many of them became powerful symbols of the conflict for various constituencies. Some of the best-trafficked among them ended up embodying radically conflicting narratives of the war. Think of the apparent finality of the shot of Saddam Hussein's statue being pulled down, or the celebratory aura of the "Mission Accomplished" photos; both of these outlived their initial utility as propaganda, acquiring over time a critical potency as symbols of the elusiveness of the victory they once commemorated. By contrast, the infamous photos from Abu Ghraib immediately took on a life of their own as metonyms for the injustice of the war, and admissible evidence of American mistreatment of detainees.[22]

Other widely disseminated, award-winning photos gave a human face to the massive armed conflict that was taking place. You would no doubt recognize the famous photo of the "Marlboro Marine," taken in November 2004 during the second battle of Fallujah. Standing against a wall, helmet on, a cigarette dangling from his lip, the lance corporal's eyes, set on a haggard white face speckled with a mixture of dirt, camouflage paint and dried blood, gaze wearily at—or, rather, through—the camera.[23] You are similarly likely to have seen the photo commonly called "Crying Soldier," a close-up of the face of an African-American staff sergeant as he participates in a memorial service for a fallen comrade. The jagged path of a single tear runs from the corner of his eye down to the chinstrap of his helmet; a second tear is captured midway down his cheek. Despite these signs of grief, the face is utterly composed, lips closed, eyes world-weary.[24] Or recall the heartrending "crying girl" photo, taken at dusk after a US army patrol shot at a car that failed to heed its command to stop in Tal Afar in 2005. The Iraqi girl in the photo looks to be about five years old.[25] Her body and face are illuminated by the flashlight attached to a soldier's rifle. She is looking up in the direction of the photographer, her mouth open in a terrified scream. Her parents' blood has trickled down her face, coated her hands and is spattered in front of her on the concrete. The color of the blood perfectly matches the bright red flowers that stand out on the grey cloth of her dress.

These images, among many others, have proliferated throughout the collective ecology of the global media, where they continue to participate in complex discourses regarding the Iraq War, patriotism, voyeurism, heroism, pain, and ethics. The global, fractal *scopic territory* that has been generated by their dissemination fluctuates with each viewing, but shows no sign of disappearing. As the Iraq War recedes into history, it is increasingly being understood through the prism of mute images like these, available at the touch of a keyboard.

What, in this vein, can be said about the acoustic territory that recordings of belliphonic sounds of the Iraq War created as they were distributed online and through the global media? What sounds escaped the combat zone and took up residence in the mediasphere? It would be hard to argue that any sound or collection of sounds ever attained the sustained salience that the aforementioned images did. This is not to say that they weren't plentiful; radio and television news reports regularly broadcast ambient sounds from the battlefield. But with very few exceptions, these sounds were subject to editing and other manipulations that reshaped and recontextualized them. Through established studio techniques (the voice-over, the soundtrack, the fade-out, sound layering, the cut, subtitles, noise reduction), belliphonic sounds were molded to fit the demands of a genre that values the magnetism of the visual and the communicative energy of talk over the ephemerality and abstractness of ambient sound.

This visualist bias is evident in the following transcription of a typical CNN news broadcast. The segment in question, on the Iraqi Awakening defying al-Qaeda, was aired on December 30, 2007. The audio layering techniques, and the exceedingly short amount of time that sounds recorded in the field are audible, are representative of the telejournalistic genre (see table 5.1):[26]

In a news segment of nearly two minutes, nearly all of which features video footage of outdoor activities, a mere eight seconds is devoted to the unobstructed presentation of the sounds of those activities. The rest of the time, the sounds of wartime Iraq are obscured by the reporter's narration or erased altogether.

In one prominent class of video recordings, sound from the battlefield was wholly absent. One of the distinctive communication technologies used throughout Operation Iraqi Freedom was the video feed from planes, helicopters, and unmanned aerial vehicles or "drones." For the service members who operated these airborne weapons systems, as for the viewers globally who watched them, the distant explosions they initiated were silent, blossoming far below in pixelated black-and-white while on-board or remote pilots engaged in dispassionate exchanges with command. The sonic dimension of such recordings, then, rather than providing sensory evidence, however mediated, of the destructive power of weapons, reinforced a narrative in which airborne attacks are understood to be "clean," rational, even therapeutic measures. The airborne combat films presented an image of war as surgery, a clinical exercise undertaken by calm professionals. The drones are the most recent instantiation of a long tendency within great-power warfare to remove whenever possible the soldier from the sensory field in which the violent act takes place. This practice, while overtly justified in terms of tactical safety and (in the case of unmanned drones flown from bases in the United States) economics, can also be read as a tacit recognition of the affective power the sonic and other sensory dimensions of violence possess. A bomb doesn't appear "smart" or an attack "surgical" if you can hear the victims screaming.

The silent videos of distanced warfare were distributed by mainstream news outlets, and at times by the military itself during its press briefings. At the same time, and to a degree unprecedented in past conflicts, individual actors on all sides of Operation Iraqi Freedom distributed media of their own to a global audience. The Iraq War coincided with the public release of YouTube (in 2005) and other platforms for online

TABLE 5.1

Timeline of a typical news broadcast

Time elapsed [min:sec]	Description of audio	Words spoken
0:00–0:02	**Ambient sound, including a single gunshot and a scream.**	
0:02–0:10	Unseen reporter narrates story. Ambient sound very low in the mix.	"A civilian militia practices tracking and detection techniques in an orchard, where just a day before a gun battle resulted in the arrest of two suspected al-Qaeda insurgents."
0:10–0:11	**Ambient sound, background noise, beginning of Iraqi conversation**	
0:11–0:32	Unseen reporter narrates. Ambient sound low in the mix.	"In nearby Taji a local sheikh tours checkpoints in his area, to supervise militia members on the job on a cold winter's night. These are the civilian groups known as Awakening Councils that have been widely credited with being a key factor in bringing levels of violence down in Iraq. And the subject of Osama bin Laden's latest internet message."
0:32–0:37	Osama bin Laden speaks in Arabic, untranslated.	
0:37–0:52	Unseen translator translates. Bin Laden's voice low in the mix.	"Our duty is to foil these dangerous conspiracies which seek to prevent the establishment of an Islamic state in the Land of the Two Rivers, to be an aid in victory for the people of Islam everywhere in thwarting America's mission in dividing Iraq."
0:52–0:57	Unseen reporter narrates. Ambient sound low in the mix.	"Attacks on the Councils were stepped up even before the latest bin Laden posting."
0:57–1:05	Unseen reporter narrates. Ambient crowd noise is slightly louder, but still largely masked by the reporter's voice. Three gunshots ring out softly amidst voices yelling.	"This funeral for the leader of a Council in Baqubah was targeted by a suicide bomber last week, resulting in the deaths of nine people."

Time elapsed [min:sec]	Description of audio	Words spoken
1:05–1:11	Unseen reporter narrates. No background sound.	"And attacks like this bombing of a Council member's house in Khod Rajab are becoming more frequent."
1:11–1:21	Reporter is now visible, talking to camera, standing on street.	"The U.S. says the Awakening Councils are continuing to grow. About 72,000 men have joined so far. And with each attack Council members are becoming more defiant."
1:21–1:24	**Off-camera Iraqi woman speaks (in Arabic, untranslated) as Iraqi man picks up a child.**	
1:24–1:30	Unseen reporter narrates. Ambient sound is faded out.	"This man was at the funeral for his son and five other militia members killed in that attack in Khod Rajab."
1:30–1:32	**Iraqi man speaks in Arabic, untranslated.**	
1:32–1:37	Unseen translator translates. Iraqi man's speech is low in the mix.	"We are ready to sacrifice our last drop of blood. We are defending our homes and our honor."
1:37–1:48	Unseen reporter narrates. Ambient sound is faded out.	"The U.S. says the attacks are a signal al Qaeda fears the Awakening Councils. Al-Qaeda's leader says they are traitors who must die. Harris Whitbeck, CNN, Baghdad."

video sharing. More broadly, it was the first major conflict to take place after the huge efflorescence, beginning in the 1990s, of low-cost, high-quality, consumer-grade digital video recorders. These devices were mounted on helmets, attached to rifles, and held in military, civilian, and insurgent hands as the fighting in Iraq unfolded. Many of the amateur recordings that resulted were posted online, where they were then eagerly consumed by curious parties globally.[27] A great number of military and insurgent videos posted online eschewed ambient sound altogether in favor of soundtracks: heavy metal being the genre of choice for amateur videos made by American troops; Iraqi nashids accompanying insurgent videos of successful IED attacks.[28] But others were posted unedited, with the ambient sound of gunfire and explosions available for all to hear. One might think that these raw, unexpurgated videos from the field would give the viewer a fairly accurate sense of the spectrum of belliphonic sounds that were generated during the war. I will allow the possibility that we can look and listen *through* the mediation of recording to give ourselves an imagined but significant sense of verisimilitude; indeed, we do this all the time when we experience voices or music or sporting events or news reports on television or online. But in the case of the loudest wartime sounds—gunfire, mortars detonating, IED explosions—the possibility to do this is foreclosed. The extreme nature of the loud end of the belliphonic spectrum stretches so far beyond the abilities of consumer technologies to record and reproduce them that even rough verisimilitude is impossible to achieve. When you listen to an IED explosion recorded by a soldier or an insurgent, what you hear is largely distortion and clipping. You hear, in other words, the sound of technology straining against an essentially *unrecordable* phenomenon. Even in the most pristine, high-tech conditions (such as a THX surround-sound theater during the much lauded scene in *Saving Private Ryan* where the beaches at Normandy are stormed), the sharp pain of the bullet's crack and the horrifying shock of its proximity are absent. Physiological pain and indexical terror, abundantly present when the violent acts of the Iraq war were recorded, cannot quite crawl through the technology and into our ears.

It is important to acknowledge this nonidentity between painful belliphonic sounds and the recorded sounds we hear in order to avoid the misimpression that one can use them unproblematically to access a visceral understanding of the experience of acoustic violence. And so, while there *is* a limited extent to which we can plausibly talk about the global mediascape as an acoustic territory in which the belliphonic was experienced by a vast and disparate audience, we need to admit that what the war's distant viewers and auditors witnessed was at best a faint refraction of the visual and acoustic event: a simulacrum of wartime "liveness" that was, in its artificiality, far removed from the presence of death.

Or perhaps we could say that the agglomeration of professional news recordings, radio reports, and choppy internet videos did create a full-blown acoustic territory, but one that was constituted by a distinct set of sonic campaigns waged by the warring parties in collaboration with propaganda producers, media outlets, and other online entities. The auditory regimes that intersected with this mediatized territory varied with the individuals watching and listening to reports from the war, but they were likely structured around thoroughly globalized notions of media consumption. The assemblage comprising the recordings, their consumers, and the sensory regimes (or "cultures of perception") that mediate them collaborated to produce a type of what Allen Feldman called "cultural anesthesia": a widely available but constrained perceptual field that paradoxically "render[s] the Other's pain inadmissible to public discourse and culture."[29] The constrained, compressed, clipped, garbled sounds of armed violence in the digitized representations of the war largely failed to transmit the violent affective force of the belliphonic to its distant auditors. And in general, the outrage that emerged from listening and looking at them was as highly perishable as the auditory fantasy—in which we choose to believe that we understand what it felt like to be there—was pernicious.

THE RADIANT ACOUSTIC TERRITORIES OF WARTIME

From the virtual global we move into the physical local: the densely populated topography of Baghdad, Iraq's capital and the site of the majority of war-related attacks during Operation Iraqi Freedom. Under normal circumstances, of course, these two territories would always be in a state of interpenetration and overlap. But wars, as a rule, do not engender normal circumstances, and Operation Iraqi Freedom proved no exception. With the persistent disruption of Baghdad's electric grid and communication lines, most residents were deprived of regular access to electronic media for long stretches of time. The presence of televised and radio news reports and online videos of the combat zone was therefore sporadic—indeed, continues to be sporadic for much of the country at the time of this writing. So we will need to understand the mediatized territory discussed above as only intermittently overlapping with the expanse of land called Baghdad, flickering in a pattern of articulation and disarticulation along with the lightbulbs in houses throughout the city.

The transition from the virtual acoustic territory of mediatized sounds to the radiant acoustic territory of ambient vibrations is most importantly a movement across the gaping chasm separating sounds that symbolize violence, on the one side, from sounds that either index or enact proximate violence on the other. In admitting this difference, we do not have to succumb to an anachronistic metaphysics of presence that uniformly privileges "live" ambient sounds over "schizophonic" recorded ones. As Jason Stanyek and Benjamin Piekut have trenchantly observed, "all sounds are severed from their sources—that's what makes sound sound."[30] But when the sounds in question are emplaced not within the aesthetic frame (the ground on which music scholars have tended to hold this debate), but instead within an etiological frame that foregrounds the corporeal and psychological damage that belliphonic sounds can cause, or within an ethical frame that highlights the choices for immediate action that an auditor might take, or even within an affective frame that points to the moments of adrenalin-infused exhilaration that survivors of the acoustic and haptic onslaught of a nearby explosion often felt, the distinction between the live and the recorded becomes obvious, and fundamental. The radiant acoustic territory of combat is marked by the unique dangers, obligations, and affective costs of exposure to belliphonic sounds that bespeak the synchronous presence of violence.

In wartime Baghdad, this territory was far from uniform. The belliphonic events that took place there over the course of the war were sporadic, if frequent, occurrences, subject to the circadian rhythms of combat and the exigencies of the warring parties' tactics. Moreover, each distinct event created its own unique penumbra of audibility, enveloping some fraction of the populace and never the entire city as a whole. Some events, like gun battles, often dragged on for hours, while others, like IED explosions, were over in seconds. So how can one take this jumble of local events and ephemeral intensities and talk about it as if it is a broad, citywide territory with relatively stable characteristics?

I would like to argue that the territorializing effect of belliphonic sounds (as opposed to most of their peacetime analogues) often persists long after the actual sound waves have died away. Wartime testimonies certainly buttress this notion. The vibratory dimension of a clattering exchange of bullets or an IED explosion decays within seconds, but how long does the acoustic territory—which we now understand to be the timespace over which an audible event reverberates, within ears *and* within habits, as an acoustic event *and* a traumatic memory—persist? And what social factors affect this persistence? When a violent event is singular and anomalous, the acoustic territory it carves out may prove to be relatively ephemeral. A random shooting in my downtown New York neighborhood may be remembered for years due to its rarity, but the area over which the shooting was audible reverts quickly to normal pedestrian use: the sound of gunfire, understood as an anomalous event, no longer territorializes the neighborhood. But when violent events occur with a certain frequency, the territorialization enacted by one bleeds into that of the next, and a neighborhood or a city or a country becomes trapped within a troubled acoustic territory with relatively stable characteristics. In Baghdad, as elsewhere in the country, belliphonic sound regularly disrupted normal human activities (unfettered movement through space, uninterrupted sleep or leisure or concentration) and provided immediate, widespread sensory evidence of the persistent state of vulnerability in which people lived.

Some of the sounds I have discussed in earlier chapters created territories that were deeply marked by the identities of the sounding parties. The far-reaching rumble of IEDs created a politically charged acoustic territory in which the power of the insurgency could not be denied; the Iraqi police and US military's use of loudspeakers and sirens, as well as the extremely frequent sound of US military helicopters overhead, asserted similar territorial rights throughout the country. Those caught within earshot of these events found themselves violently hailed—not by grand ideologies à la Althusser but by tactical sonic campaigns—into particular subject positions. Some belliphonic sounds interpellated auditors into the positions of residents of an explicitly sectarian neighborhood, citizens of an occupied state, or even subjects of an actual policeman's explicit "Hey, you there!" At the same time, belliphonic weapon sounds frequently, relentlessly interpellated auditors into the enforced position of witness—or, at times, victim—of proximate violence.

These territorial assertions and tactical interpellations very often overlapped in time and space: people in the combat zone were in a near constant state of being hailed by multiple belliphonic calls. Sometimes—not unlike sound waves—these calls coincided in patterns of resonance, amplifying one another. (To take a common example, not only did the tactic of triggering multiple IEDs simultaneously create more casualties, but the increased volume of the synchronized explosions expanded the area over which they were audible.) At other moments, when the calls came from multiple warring parties, they interfered with one another in a process of cancellation. When the single shots of American M4s coincided or alternated closely with the automatic stutter of Iraqi Kalashnikovs during a gun battle, one reached a situation where, as John Law has said, "interpellations wrestle themselves to a standstill."[31] When that happened, people were left in a territory that was not dominated by one party or another; the gun battle, and the silence that followed it, created the auditory equivalent of "no man's land." This was the always contested, culturally impoverished territory of exhaustion and vulnerability and fear that formed the frequent backdrop of wartime life in the combat zone. It was a territory of displacement—where bodies and the sounds that they made were removed through emigration, internal migration, and death, and where the sounds of generators and helicopters and loudspeakers and military vehicles and demonstrations and gun battles and IED explosions drowned out soft sounds of nature and civil existence. And it was a territory of transplacement, where the wartime context gave sinister new meanings to sounds and silences that once seemed normal.

THE RESONANT ACOUSTIC TERRITORIES OF BAGHDAD

The phenomenon of sound moving through space sets up a kind of dialectical tension. On the one hand, sound radiates outward, and as it does it performs an interpellative function, hailing all within earshot into one or more subject positions—minimally, the subject position of auditor. Sound, in this sense, *emplaces* auditors within a radiant acoustic territory that was, in wartime Iraq, always-already politically charged. On the other hand, when they enter a more or less contained environment, sound waves become hemmed in, folding back upon themselves in patterns of interference and amplification. In this sense, sound itself *is emplaced* within a pre-existing structure that, at the moment of sounding, becomes a resonant acoustic territory. Within this contained environment, sound commonly causes microscopic displacements of its boundaries, which are set into patterns of sympathetic vibration. If the radiant acoustic territory is a space of inclusion and intersubjectivity, the resonant acoustic territory is a space of exclusion and intensity. Here, sound waves become amplified, complicated, and co-implicated in a dynamic interaction with various types of architecture, topography, and anatomy. Along the way, they acquire different properties, properties that intensify the distinction between "inside" and "outside," while simultaneously blurring the distinction between "contents" and "vessel."

The most visible wartime alteration of resonant acoustic territory was surely the installation of thousands of semipermanent concrete blast walls throughout the Iraqi capital.[32] Beginning in 2003 and proliferating rapidly in concert with the escalation of sectarian violence in 2006 and 2007, the portable individual sections from which walls were built ranged in height from three feet (the "Jersey" barrier) to twenty feet (the "Alaska"). Most were made of relatively smooth steel-reinforced concrete, although one type, the stackable Hesco bastion, was made of block-shaped metal cages filled with dirt and rubble. The most common type was the 14,000-lb. twelve-foot Bremer (or "Texas") T-wall barrier. Installed in Baghdad ostensibly to protect neighborhoods from vehicular-borne IEDs (VBIEDS), sectarian attacks, and other threats, they lined streets and blocked off intersections throughout the city, transforming neighborhoods into policed areas that made Baghdad's residents feel, according to one commentator, "like caged animals."[33] Ad hoc attempts by graffiti artists to beautify them notwithstanding, residents weighed the increased safety that they arguably brought against the prison-like atmosphere they engendered. But the major source of frustration with the walls wasn't the grim grey aesthetic that they imposed on the capital; rather, it was the major alterations in pedestrian routes and traffic patterns that they created for Baghdad's residents. People who had once been neighbors found themselves separated into districts that had no easy access to one another. Similarly, a car trip to Baghdad University from the nearby Mansour neighborhood that once took fifteen minutes now took in excess of an hour.[34] Businesses that once had access to drive-by traffic were effectively ruined by the new isolation. Beginning in 2009, the blast walls began to be taken down and hauled away. But the task was so massive that when I visited Baghdad in early 2011, they were still a prominent presence in the city.

A blast wall is commonly defined as a structure that "reflects blast energy back towards the explosive source," rendering that energy "unavailable to damage the protected asset" on the other side.[35] While Baghdad's blast walls did periodically perform this function, the "energy" that they most regularly rendered "unavailable" was acoustic. The concrete T-walls reflected automobile noise back onto motorists, turning formerly open streets into loud sound corridors. Echolocation within these spaces became difficult, and thus complicated the already fraught encounters between military vehicles and civilian vehicles. On the other side of the walls, people living within the new divisions that they created found themselves isolated, visually *and* aurally, from adjoining neighborhoods. The changes that blast walls made to the acoustic territory of the city, while major, were invisible and hard to trace, and they seldom were the explicit targets of auditors' ire. But they subtly contributed to the general sense of displacement and uncanny transplacement that the war wrought (see figure 5.1, below). They amounted to one more alteration to the sensory environment of a population that was on every front besieged.

From the standpoint of service members, the majority of whom had not known Baghdad before the blast walls were installed, the acoustic territories that created the most perturbation were the loud enclosures inside the metal sheaths of the vehicles that they used to move around the city. As I mentioned in chapter 1, the engines of Humvees and MRAPs generated 95 decibels of engine noise, and their hulls prevented many environmental sounds from reaching the ears of passengers. To be inside these vehicles was to inhabit a vibrational box. Aside from tanks with their hatches closed in

FIGURE 5.1 Iraqi Pedestrian passing through the Circle 55 opening in the separation wall between the sectors of Sadr City controlled by the US and Iraqi armies, July 2008. (Photo by Benjamin Lowy/ Getty Images)

battle formation, most of these vehicles were not perfectly sealed, however. Humvees and MRAPs commonly featured an open hatch for a gunner operating an M2 or M240 machine gun. This hatch created the kind of "well-defined opening" that Stanyek and Piekut call, in a completely different context, *perforation*:

> A perforation controls and focuses flows between two spaces, but maintains separation between them. In the recording studio, sonically sealed spaces such as the control room or the vocal isolation booth depend on perforations that channel sound from one area to the next. . . . Isolation needs perforation. From the very beginning, recording studios have been perforated environments that favor a seemingly paradoxical co-process of connection and disconnection.[36]

Many military vehicles are similarly perforated, allowing the cabin to remain semi-isolated from but also semi-connected to the outside environment. While the reasons behind this design choice had more to do with the logistics of visual surveillance and tactical firing than with auditory considerations, gunners regularly reported on things they heard that were absolutely inaudible to their comrades. Standing half-exposed at the vehicle's perforation point, the gunner directed his attention to both environments. Recall the incident described earlier in this volume, where the marine gunner in a Humvee was temporarily deafened by the IED explosion. He was, more than his comrades sitting inside the cabin, a victim of a perforated acoustic territory.

From this standpoint, we can say that Iraqi civilians spent much of their time in perforated acoustic territories as well. In addition to their unarmored cars, which didn't provide anywhere near as much sound isolation as the military vehicles did, their houses were often opened to the environment for tactical reasons: the pressure created by a nearby IED or mortar blast could shatter a window if it was closed, and in a hot desert environment where access to electricity (and hence air conditioning) was unreliable, windows often needed to be open to create a cross breeze. But letting the air in and the pressure equalize also increased the number and intensity of sounds leaking in from the outside.

Iraqis living in Baghdad during the years of daily gun violence on the streets learned quickly how perforable their acoustic territories were; even windows that were closed proved no match for helicopter flybys and nearby gun battles. Once enclosed within their houses, these loud belliphonic sounds took on a vibrational life that set the immediate environment into motion: the low flyby of the Chinook helicopter made dishes fall off the table; the boom from a nearby explosion rattled the furniture and caused children to start crying. There were very few architectural spaces that could fully insulate civilians from the loudest sounds of the war.

In addition to resonating within enclosed spaces, explosive violence can drastically alter the physical—and hence acoustic—properties of a place. A large number of structures of great historical and religious significance were bombed by warring parties during the war, their roofs and walls opened up to the elements, their resonant properties diminished. The Al-Askari Mosque in the city of Samarra was among the most lamented architectural victims of the war. A holy shrine for Shi'i faithful, the mosque was built in the year 944 to commemorate two Shi'i imams, Ali al-Hadi and his son Hasan al-Askari, and house their remains. Work on the latest iteration of the mosque began in 1868, and culminated with the completion of a magnificent gilt dome in 1905. Roughly 68 meters high and 20 meters in diameter, the dome created a deeply resonant, marble-lined space in which the voices of the faithful reverberated. This acoustic territory, which coincided with a holy site of pilgrimage, was bombed in 2006 by the group al-Qaeda in Iraq. While no one was killed in the early-morning attack, the hushed, contemplative, reverberant space of the dome was violently opened to the air; the famously resonant acoustic territory was destroyed, subsumed into the radiant acoustic territory of the neighborhood.

Countless buildings were similarly gutted or destroyed over the course of the war, countless homes were opened up to the vicissitudes of outdoor ambience. In the face of the deaths that accompanied these territorial alterations, it may seem pointless to mention them. By acknowledging them I do not want to take away from the central story of human loss. But I do want to point to the fact that the removal of these resonant places represents yet another moment in the inexorable process of sensory impoverishment that accompanied the war. The violent partition of the sensible that the war produced affected all sensory modalities, including audition. Through the incursion of belliphonic sounds, the permanent removal of living voices, and the transformation of indoor places into outdoor places, the net effect was to homogenize and monotonize the acoustic environment (see figure 5.2). Through the war, this environment traded polyphony for monophony, echoic ("live") qualities for anechoic ("dead") ones. In this way, the acoustic environment becomes a metonym for all of the wartime losses whose magnitudes are too great to conceptualize.

As we move from the literal partitioning of Baghdad by blast walls to the architectural and vehicular spaces in which civilians and service members lived and worked, we are moving closer to the surface of the body. Closer still were technologies used by US forces to help shape the acoustic environment for two different populations. The

FIGURE 5.2 Former Baath Party Headquarters, Baghdad, 2011. During the Shock and Awe phase of the war, a US cruise missile destroyed the dome of this building, opening its resonant acoustic territory to the air. Years later, reconstruction is not yet complete. (Photo by the author)

Advanced Combat Helmet (ACH), developed by the US Army Soldier Systems Center in 2003 and subsequently fielded to troops throughout the army, was designed to "enable better situational awareness" by increasing the "field of vision and hearing" over the standard-issue helmet that preceded it.[37] The previous helmet extended down to the bottom of the wearer's ear, shielding it from shrapnel and bullets, but also from ambient sounds. The helmet's designers and the US army agreed that in this instance, the need for unencumbered hearing *was more important* than the need to provide soldiers with extra protection from physical injury. In our terminology, the small, perforated, resonant acoustic territory that the old helmet created near its wearer's ears was eliminated in order to expose them more directly to the information that the radiant acoustic territory of the battlefield contained.[38]

Situational awareness was precisely the affordance that the US military and intelligence services wanted to deny the large population of Iraqi men who were detained for questioning over the course of the war. The standard technology for achieving this purpose, the hood, was the ACH helmet's affective opposite: it was designed to close off the sensory world rather than open it up, disorient the wearer rather than orient him within his environment, and create an embodied state not of security but of vulnerability. The ostensible purpose of the hood was to remove the faculty of sight. But the hood served also as a small acoustic territory that muffled soft ambient sounds from outside and amplified the sounds of the wearer's own breathing and voice. In some instances, earmuffs were placed on the detainee's ears before he was hooded, muffling his hearing. While some leakage did occur, the overall effect was that of profound sensory deprivation.[39]

Throughout the war, hoods were used in the field to isolate detainees at the moment of capture and keep them from seeing "operational details" and from identifying one another as they were transported to detention facilities. Once they were confined within these facilities, "hooding" was conducted alongside other techniques to "soften up" detainees prior to interrogation. According to a report of the International Red Cross/ Red Crescent, common "methods of physical and psychological coercion" included:

> hooding, used to prevent people from seeing and to disorient them, and also to prevent them from breathing freely. One or sometimes two bags, sometimes with an elastic blindfold over the eyes which, when slipped down, further impeded proper breathing. Hooding was sometimes used in conjunction with beatings thus increasing anxiety as to when blows would come. The practice of hooding also allowed the interrogators to remain anonymous and thus to act with impunity. Hooding could last for periods from a few hours to up to two to four consecutive days.[40]

Those detainees who were hooded as part of the interrogation process regularly found themselves within the unseen but intensely felt acoustic territory of the interrogation chamber. Chained to painful stress positions, in rooms that were either cold or uncomfortably hot, some hooded detainees were bombarded with extremely loud music and/or other recorded sounds for periods long enough to cause extreme disorientation, fatigue, pain, and panic. This was a territory of absolute sensory control, where audition—along with the critical dimension I have assigned to that term—was replaced by brute acoustic exposure. Within the concentric confines of hood and cell, detainees fought to maintain their status as hermeneuts, as subjects capable of interpreting their surroundings. They frequently lost this battle, becoming instead abject acoustic victims, desubjectified subjects exposed to an unrelenting sensory onslaught, trapped in a resonant acoustic territory within which they were not and could never be citizens.

THE RESONANT ACOUSTIC TERRITORY OF THE BODY

A territory, as I have presented it here, is a place of contestation; a politically charged zone where power is exerted and endured; an open area where claims of sovereignty or control are asserted and contested; a "land occupied by violence." It can also be, I have argued, an enclosed space within which territorializing forces are amplified and transformed; a place that affects and is affected by these forces; a vessel in which claims to power are intensified, albeit one subject to perforation and leakage. If one frontier of the acoustic territory of war exists in the globalized mediascape, at a far remove from the sensate acts that constitute it, the other frontier can be found in the gas- and fluid-filled spaces inside the human body. Both of these frontiers, it should be mentioned, problematize conventional (Enlightenment) notions of the human. The first shows how the dominant way to be human in the twenty-first century is to be connected, partially dissolved into vast, fluctuating interactive networks of human and nonhuman actors. The second shows how the human body is shot through with microterritories that it does not fully own or control. Nowhere is this lack of control more palpable than in the human encounter with the belliphonic.

Theorists have been problematizing the Enlightenment view of the sovereign, autonomous body for some decades now. Since at least the 1980s, feminist theorists have been investigating the "specific contextual materiality of the body," and portraying it as a node in a dense network of biology, technology, and rhetoric.[41] Scholars following Julia Kristeva's work on the abject have drawn attention to boundary-blurring phenomena that "disturb[] identity" within and around the body and fail to "respect borders, positions, rules."[42] Running parallel to this argument, recent work in biology has underlined the extent to which the functioning body is a corporate achievement, the collective work of "foreign" microbes, parasites, technologies, environmental material, and host cells. In the context of this and other scholarship that presents the body as a porous assemblage open to colonization from within and without, a conception of the intracorporeal acoustic territories of the body finds its context and resonance.[43]

There are several passageways into the body, and loud belliphonic vibrations find all of them. A large IED or VBIED or cruise missile or bomb packed with high explosives creates a supersonic shock wave when it detonates. This wave of compressed air creates an abrupt change in pressure, which violently displaces the skin and outer tissues, jarring them, and the internal tissues connected to them, as if they had been hit with a solid object. The change in pressure occurs inside the body's cavities as well, transforming them into resonating chambers for a wave that will exit the body, speed away, slow down, regularize, and return to the victim as the thunderous sound of ambience. The wave's initial invasion can cause blood vessels to burst in the lungs, and the brain to concuss against the internal wall of the skull.[44] In the latter case, as I mentioned in chapter 2, the damage to the brain can result in the complex of pathologies commonly labeled Traumatic Brain Injury. Known as the signature injury of the war, its sufferers can experience prolonged "confusion, disorientation, slowed thinking, weakness, loss of balance, change in vision, praxis, paresis or plegia, sensory loss, and aphasia."[45] One study in 2008 estimated that 20 percent of service members who were wounded in bomb blasts suffer from TBI.[46]

Entering through the ear, the shock wave can perforate the tympanic membrane and wreak havoc in the cochlea.[47] The sound that the shock wave eventually becomes can penetrate and harm proximate bodies along with those that are farther away from the blast. The delicate stereocilia in the cochlea's basilar membrane are easily damaged by the high-amplitude boom of detonation (as well as by the loud crack of small arms). This damage can cause permanent cell death that manifests as tinnitus and hearing loss. Hundreds of thousands of auditors in Iraq, both civilians and service members, have had their hearing permanently altered, if not destroyed, when loud impulse sounds have territorialized their ears.[48] The fleshy territories of the body are, in other words, instantly conquered, and made to perform pathologically, against the interests of the human who had asserted control over them a moment before.

Tinnitus, hearing loss, and traumatic brain injury can all be understood as the result of waves (sonic and supersonic) that invade the body's fluid spaces and leave their mark upon them. Whereas the external acoustic territory is scarred by explosions and bullets, the delicate internal territories of the body bear the permanent inscriptions of "the sounds themselves."

If we acknowledge that even the most intimate internal territory of the inner ear is connected—literally, through the airways that link it to the auricle and the mouth and nose via the pharynx—to the external territories in which we operate, we then have an anatomically based conceptual mechanism for understanding how intersubjectivity works. As we have heard, some weapons-in-use create a kind of traumatic intersubjectivity by penetrating multiple individuals with projectiles or shrapnel. Similarly, sound waves territorialize, and in some cases scar, your body—and then move on, through flesh and passageway, to connect you with, and in some cases scar, your neighbor.

Complicating things further is the fact that all of the aforementioned acoustic territories do not merely shape sounds and move or inscribe themselves upon the walls of the vessels that contain them—they also shape the ways in which sounds are perceived. When the acoustic territory is part of what Steve Goodman calls "architectures of security," such as a detention cell or a combat vehicle, sounds and other sensory input that in other contexts would feel benign can feel bone-crushingly sinister.[49] The hoods and mufflers placed on detainees' heads removed all possibility of echo, creating a "dead" sound, but they also radically accentuated the atmosphere of terror within which the act of listening—or, more accurately, sonic exposure—occurred. The smooth concrete of the blast wall reflected sounds back on Iraqi auditors, but it also contextualized them as occurring against a backdrop of danger and occupation. The unseen territory of the middle and inner ear amplifies and translates sounds into electrical signals, but it is also one of the sites where sound gets assigned the affective label "pain." Sound design occurs within acoustic territories, and the position of the listening body—as exhilarated participant, dispassionate auditor, or unwilling victim of acoustic exposure—is in part determined by the particular affordances the territories themselves bring to the table.

What this means is that psychological territory—or even what Suzanne Cusick memorably called "the intrasubjective space that many religious traditions call the soul"—can be scarred by sound as well.[50] While sound alone seldom causes psychological trauma, it was frequently a prominent element of the intersensorial onslaught within which people in wartime Iraq witnessed traumatic and traumatizing events, and as such serves as a prominent trigger of the symptoms commonly gathered under the label of post-traumatic stress. In the aftermath of violent incidents, sound appears to serve as a Trojan horse of sorts; it carries within it the totality of traumatic memory, which can then be released upon the witness's consciousness with all the immediacy of the unmediated experience at the moment of audition. This is the power of the flashback: it is as if the traumatic experience, having territorialized the subject, leaves a secret occupying army inside her to link up with those that enter that space later, cloaked in sound or other stimuli. Noted trauma scholar Cathy Caruth describes this kind of occupation in similar terms: "The traumatized," she claims, "*carry an impossible history within them,* or they become themselves the symptom of a history that they cannot entirely possess." They cannot possess it because it possesses them, it territorializes them: "To be traumatized is precisely to be possessed by an image or event"[51]—or, we might add, the sonic residue of that event, the auditory component of that image. It is the confluence of sensory stimuli from the present with past stimuli, stored somewhere just out of reach of the witness's consciousness, that generates the traumatic thrust of the flashback.

Earlier, I used the terminology generated in this triptych of chapters to build two rough heuristics to help us think about the intractable problem of traumatic stress and the complex of symptoms associated with combat PTSD. First, in chapter 3, I suggested that hypervigilance and other symptoms seen as maladaptive to peacetime life were the result of an inability to exit the wartime auditory (and other sensory) regimes into which they are indoctrinated. Later, in chapter 4, I proposed that we think of post-traumatic stress as "the sustained aftereffects of the omnidirectional leakage of violent acts," the caustic penumbra that, like sound, radiates outward from the act, damaging all within the grasp of its sensory intensity and irrevocable facticity. To those two let us add a third: think of traumatic memory as an imprint of the acoustic (and other sensory) residue of violent acts that gets trapped in a territory to which the conscious mind has no access. And think of that imprint as being the footprint of forces that occupy this psychic territory independently of will or consciousness. In Jordan, I spoke with an Iraqi refugee who struggled to express the dreadful feeling of occupation that she experienced when she heard fireworks or backfiring engines or similar sounds whose envelopes approached those that had traumatized her in Iraq. "All of us," she said, "elders and children, when we moved to Jordan, every sound we hear we were terrified, because *the bombing was inside us, its voices were inside our heads.*"

LIFE AT THE INTERSECTION OF REGIME, CAMPAIGN, AND TERRITORY

This, then, is the roiling world that exists beneath the abstraction of the "soundscape" of the Iraq War: individuals, at various stages of indoctrination into one or more of the available *auditory regimes*, worked within—and sometimes outside—them as they both participated in and grappled with the aggregate effect of conflicting *sonic campaigns*, while simultaneously constructing, moving through, and encircling an unpredictable array of *acoustic territories* within and outside their bodies. In the process, they found themselves enlightened, exhilarated, exhausted, damaged, deafened, territorialized, traumatized, changed. The story of the belliphonic, like the story of sound more generally, could never be told in terms of sound alone. People, technologies, training, ideologies, time, agency, struggle, affordances, limitations, topographies, biologies—*and* sounds, in all their complex vibrational richness—are always present in one configuration or another, and all are moving targets, subject to interference, resonance, transformation, distortion, leakage, attack, and decay.

Indeed, we are now in a position to demonstrate the extent to which "the sounds themselves" is an empty ontological category. In Iraq, for example, "the sound of an IED" did not exist as a meaningful object of analysis. Rather, minimally, there was an insurgent sonic campaign within which the explosion was situated and cathected. There was also a localized military auditory regime that considered the belliphonic (1) a source of information, and so asked auditors to listen to it and decode it; (2) a contaminant, and so urged auditors to wear a technology (earplugs) to mitigate its force; and (3) a stimulant, and so encouraged auditors in the trauma zone to adopt a hypermasculine stance in response to it. There was simultaneously a looser, more inclusive set of regimes within which Iraqis of varying political persuasions interpreted the sound of the blast. And there was a radiant acoustic territory within which the residents of surrounding neighborhoods were interpellated, a set of resonant macroterritories comprising blast walls, vehicular enclosures, and other architectural surfaces that contained and shaped the explosion's compression waves, and a forest of resonant microterritories commonly called "ears" that funneled them into consciousness, and emerged either damaged or not.

In this hypothetical instance, the sonic campaign was the instrument through which a violent act was conceived and executed, the acoustic territory was the area over which the IED's acoustic violence was performed and shaped, and the auditory regimes were the mechanisms through which auditors contended with the effects of acoustic violence.

The relationship between these three interlocking structures was dynamic and, often, contestational. Belliphonic sounds interpellated auditors into violent acoustic territories, but auditors regularly pushed back, refusing to acknowledge that they were being hailed; recall the zone of the audible inaudible from chapter 2. This space of inaudition, which emerged and grew as the auditor's wartime experience deepened, formed an important point of overlap between the auditory regimes of Iraqi civilians and the US military; at the same time, it marked the shadowy fringe of the radiant acoustic territory, the distant band around each auditor within which sounds were coded as silence. As such, it comprised a front line of sorts—not the front line of the armed battle where warring parties fought, but the line of contestation along which belliphonic sounds and auditors clashed. This struggle, between the sonic campaigns that were constructing acoustic territories and the auditory regimes that were deconstructing them, amounted to a shadow war, the war between the subject and the stimuli. Given the far-reaching, immersive properties of sound, this war was fought within an expansive territory that began inside the body and reached far beyond the thin trajectories of bullets and the circumscribed ambit of shrapnel. It was less deadly, less bloody than the metallic war with which it was imbricated, but its impact has proven to be long-lasting and profound. Let us re-examine the story that Gavin told in chapter 1:

> Actually it was the Duck and Cover that kept me up at night during bad periods—and not the explosions. You know, the *"DEE-dee-DEE-dee-DEE-dee-DEE-dee:* Attention in the compound: duck and cover, duck and cover!" from our Peruvian guards. And you know that would keep you up all night, cause when they're shooting at you every 15 to 20 to 40 minutes, they'd hit the "Duck and Cover" and wake you up, and whether you responded or not you were awake. . . . In 2008 in April around Easter, I actually thought that Muqtada al Sadr's way of torturing us was to keep us up all night, keep us awake all night.

The insurgents' mortars, which in this particular instance were relatively ineffectual as killing devices, triggered a tactical reaction within the US military's sonic campaign, allowing the insurgents to use their enemy's own technologies against it. The result of the duck and cover drills was the creation of an acoustic territory of sleeplessness for residents of the Green Zone. With time, though, Gavin and his comrades became used to these interruptions, as well as to the other belliphonic sounds that once disturbed them. Their wartime auditory regime proved powerful enough to neutralize most of these disruptive sounds, shifting them from the neophyte's all-encompassing zone of trauma and fear into the seasoned auditor's more tactically useful spaces of hermeneutics (the narrational zone) and inaudition (the audible inaudible).

The auditory regime into which Gavin was indoctrinated was a significant resource over the course of his time spent in the war zone. This same regime became a liability, however, the moment he left Iraq. After flying out of Baghdad at the close of his contract, Gavin was held over in Jordan for several days before continuing home to the States. After a year in the constant noise of the International Zone, he found his quiet hotel room in Amman to be profoundly *disquieting*. This strange new acoustic territory—a territory devoid of the everyday sounds that had been, he only now realized, a source of comfort to him—triggered a sense of dread and hypervigilance in him that he could not shake. In response, Gavin initiated a small, self-directed, therapeutic sonic campaign of his own: he turned the TV to a station broadcasting static, and played a recording of the call to prayer on his cell phone until he was able to go to sleep. Altering the acoustic territory in this way was easier than exiting his wartime auditory regime, a task he only accomplished later, with time and effort.

In the first fragment, between the introduction and chapter 1, Ali's father's ears had been territorialized, and his hearing permanently damaged, by the loud belliphonic sounds of previous wars. His prior experience with these sounds formed a part of a remarkably durable auditory regime, which conditioned his quick reaction to the sound of an approaching cruise missile at the onset of Operation Iraqi Freedom. By removing his hearing aid, he altered his position within the regime to better contend with the sonic campaign of Shock and Awe that engulfed him and his son. As a result, the campaign failed to overwhelm him, failed to incorporate him into an expansive acoustic territory characterized by terror and helplessness. Throughout the war, people on all sides engaged in similar daily struggles, fighting to maintain their footing on the shifting sensory terrain.

To imagine human experience taking place at the intersection of auditory regimes, sonic campaigns, and acoustic territories is to confront the immensely complicated web of histories, actors, and influences that hides beneath the seemingly simple act of listening to the sounds that surround us. But the situation is significantly more complex than that. In the end, in order to move closer to an appreciation of the rich complexity of human sensory experience, we would have to imagine these three frameworks interacting in unpredictable ways with the scopic, tactile, olfactory, and other sensory regimes, campaigns and territories that are in a constant state of efflorescence around each one of us. We would have to make room for intersensorial hybridity, the merging of regimes of sight and smell and hearing and touch and thermoception and proprioception and the so-called "sixth sense."[52] And, to make matters even more confounding, we would have to acknowledge the myriad iconoclastic and sometimes downright subversive acts of listening, sounding, looking, moving, emitting, smelling, and in other ways interacting with the world that take place every day. The mind reels at the prospect of coming to terms with our essential experiential richness and constant state of sensory excess. In wartime, this sensory excess is amplified, sharpened, and directed onto vulnerable bodies, creating a cruel partition of the sensible within which violence flows freely.

Fragment #4

A Fatal Mishearing

WITHIN THE SO-CALLED Iraq War Logs, the large cache of US army field reports that were leaked to the public by the Wikileaks organization in 2010, one can find over 140 "escalation of force" entries that explicitly mention "noise" of one kind or another. Many of these reports involve service members hearing, and then acting upon, suspicious sounds. Hissing and soft popping overheard on a foot patrol sometimes turned out to be a misfiring IED. The sound of drilling or of people working after hours could indicate an insurgent hideout. Muffled bumps emanating from a car's trunk led to the discovery of more than one kidnapping-in-progress. But most of the reports involved service members hearing sounds that resembled gunfire ("popping"), rocket fire (a "whoosh," or whistling) or explosions ("boom").

In July of 2005, a number of military guards stationed at a remote base near the Syrian border opened fire on two individuals who had been driving a truck near the base's eastern guard tower. According to an escalation of force report filed on July 10 and subsequently released by Wikileaks, the incident began when the truck suffered a flat tire; the guards mistook the "loud noise" of the blown tire for "some form of close range enemy" attack, and opened fire on the truck. The truck's driver and passenger fled on foot, and were shot down by the guards. One of them was wounded, the other killed. The redacted report is reproduced in full below. (Redactions are represented by an underscore [___]. The bolded emphasis is mine, as are the bracketed italicized explanations of military abbreviations.)

ESCALATION OF FORCE BY/___ IN RAMADI: ___ CIV [*civilian*] KILLED, ___ CIV INJ [*injured*], ___ CF [*coalition forces*] INJ/___
2005-07-10 09:30:00:
AT 1530D,/___ ENGAGED (___) IZ [*Iraqis*] ___ ON ASR [*alternate service road*] ___ AT () ___ KM ___ OF AR RAMADI. THE (___) IZ ___ WERE IN A WHITE ___ TRUCK WITH A CONTAINER LOADED IN ITS TRAILER MOVING ___ ON MSR [*main service road*] ___. AS THE VEHICLE REACHED A DISTANCE OF ___ FROM THE CAMP TIGER'___ EASTERN GUARD TOWER, **THE VEHICLE BLEW A TIRE CAUSING A VERY LOUD NOISE. THE/___ GUARDS ENGAGED THE TRUCK, ___ THAT THE LOUD NOISE OF ONE OF THE BLOWN TIRE WAS SOME FORM OF CLOSE RANGE ENEMY ___, FOR EXAMPLE, AN IED BEING ___ OR POSSIBLE VBIED.** EARLIER IN THE DAY (AT 1022D) AN ADJACENT GUARD POST AT -___ OP ___ OBSERVED AN IED DETONATE IN FRONT OF THE OP'___ POSITION WHILE AN IED TM [*team member?*] ATTEMPTED TO ___ AN IED FROM A MOVING VEHICLE. AFTER /___ TOWER GUARDS ENGAGED THE ___ TRUCK, **THE DRIVER AND PASSENGER STOPPED THE VEHICLE AND FLED ON FOOT THROUGH THE PETROLEUM WAREHOUSE AREA TO THE SE [*southeast*] OF MSR./___ CONTINUED TO ENGAGE THE FLEEING IZ.** -___ IN SOLDIERS AT OP ___ JOINED THE ENGAGEMENT. **THEY ___ THAT THE TRUCK AND ITS OCCUPANTS HAD EXHIBITED ___ INTENT, BASED ON THE TRUCK PARKED NEAR THE EASTERN CAMP TIGER GUARD POST, HEARING THE //___ ENGAGEMENT, AND OBSERVING THE FLEEING ___. RESULTS OF THIS ENGAGEMENT WERE (___) CIV KILLED AND (___) CIV INJ.** THE CIV INJ WAS EVACUATED BY/___ TO THE RAMADI HOSPITAL WITH ROUTINE WOUNDS. THE (___) CIV KILLED WAS PICKED UP BY AN AMBULANCE FROM THE RAMADI HOSPITAL. THE TRUCK WAS SEARCHED WITH A MILITARY WORKING DOG AND CAME UP NEGATIVE. THE CIV KILLED WAS ADMINISTERED (___) GUN ___ RESIDUE TESTS AND CAME UP POSITIVE. AFTER SORTING THIS OUT AND SEARCHING THE ___, **WE ASSESS THAT THE IZ ___ WERE TRUCK DRIVERS AND NOT INSURGENT FIGHTERS.** THE -___ IN COMMANDER IS CONDUCTING A COMMANDER INQUIRY, AND IS CURRENTLY/___SOLDIERS AND MITT [*military intelligence training team*] MEMBERS TO BETTER UNDERSTAND THE ___

Despite the holes left by the redactions, this report clearly demonstrates the high stakes and existential challenges of belliphonic listening during Operation Iraqi Freedom. If we were to describe these challenges using the terminology laid out in the previous chapters, we could say that the attack took place when participants in the military's auditory regime, operating from within a tactical zone of audition, mistook a random sound for an element of a hostile sonic campaign. The exigencies of the tactical zone (i.e., the need to make fast decisions in the face of immediate threats) and the priorities and limitations of the auditory regime (i.e., the emphasis placed on hyperalertness, along with the fact that the regime failed to teach them the difference between the sound of a blown tire and the sound of a shot fired) tragically combined with the sound to create a radiant acoustic territory of indexical ambiguity. If an innocent sound such as this had taken place in an environment that was less frequently scarred by violent acts, or among a population that was less indoctrinated in the practices of wartime audition and reaction, it likely would have done nothing more than startle the auditors within earshot. As it was, the unforgiving conditions of wartime sensory regimes, combined with the irrevocable affordances provided by their weapons, made acts of fatal misprision such as this one a constant possibility.

Music, Mediation, and Survival

6

Mobile Music in the Military

THE IMPLICIT ARGUMENT of the previous three chapters is that there is much to gain by imagining human experience as unfolding within a continually efflorescing nexus of (1) the regimes that guide one's sensory practices, (2) the campaigns that bring sensory stimuli into being, and (3) the territories that shape and give spatial context to these stimuli. These are, I argue, the three interlocking dimensions of sensory experience, the dynamic processes that hide beneath the abstract terms "soundscape," "landscape," "the haptic," "the olfactory," etc. I hope also to have shown that, depending on their composition and context, each of these three dimensions can serve as a site of violence—or, it stands to reason, of reconciliation.

I would now like to follow some of the pathways that a particular technology carved through the auditory regimes, sonic campaigns, and acoustic territories of the Iraq War. My hope is that, by examining a single object (or, more accurately, class of objects) moving through the timespace of the war, we will be able to discern contours of these imagined fields that would otherwise go unnoticed. I could have picked any number of objects to track—earplugs, for instance, or comm systems, or even weapon systems. In the end, I settled on iPods, as they, more than many other pieces of equipment, have attained the status of "evocative objects," in Sherry Turkle's sense of the term: they are things that, independent of their utility, serve as "companions to our emotional lives" or "provocations to thought."[1] Increasing the logic behind my choice is the fact that the iPod's timeline coincides with that of the Iraq War to an uncanny degree. First appearing on the market in October 2001, less than six weeks after the 9/11 attacks, the iPod grew to dominate the digital music market during the early years of the war. By the time I began conducting interviews for this book in 2007, the iPod, in its iconic, click-wheeled iteration, was widely regarded as the signature auditory technology of Operation Iraqi Freedom. Seven years later, in the same month of 2014 that the Obama administration announced that it was initiating a new chapter in its military engagement in the region,[2] Apple quietly discontinued the last click-wheeled iPod. The war and Apple's MP3 player are thus phenomena of the same post-9/11 decade. Both, though formally defunct, have been swallowed up by new structures (the iPhone, Operations New Dawn and Inherent Resolve) whose creation they enabled; both, in other words, generated repercussions that persist into the present. Their interrelationship involves more than temporal coincidence, however; as this chapter will demonstrate, years of active use within the military rendered the iPod an icon, index, and, to a significant extent, militarized instrument of the war. After an introduction of the iPod in Iraq and a brief discussion of the history of recorded music in the military, we will examine the broad array of uses to which the wartime iPod was put, and the ways in which iPod use inflected the military's auditory regime, intensified its sonic campaigns, and expanded its acoustic territories.

INTRODUCING THE WARTIME IPOD

The iPod entered the Iraq War quietly. When US Army tanks rolled over the berms at the Kuwait border with the initiation of the ground campaign on March 20, 2003, most of the crews who were blasting "Highway to Hell" and the Ride of the Valkyries through their communication systems were using portable CD players and not the more rugged, compact, and capacious MP3 devices that would eventually replace them. Over the first two years of the war, however, the iPod grew into a near-ubiquitous mobile entertainment device, one that allowed military personnel to deploy music with great precision in service of multiple aims: smoothing and hastening the passage of time, tethering the troops to their civilian lives back home, memorializing the deaths of fallen comrades, and attaining and managing the mildly altered state of heightened aggression and awareness that characterizes the engaged and effective warrior.[3] By the time US forces pulled out of Iraq, the iPod had evolved into a fully militarized prosthetic technology—one that could be deployed in the service of media consumption, one-way translation, interrogation, crowd dispersal, intelligence gathering, and "winning hearts and minds."

Let us begin by attending to a small number of widely circulated images that power-fully draw iPods and the Iraq War, two seemingly disparate entities, into a single visual and conceptual field. If the "wartime iPod" trope is familiar to you (and provided that you haven't served or lived in Iraq yourself), it may well have been introduced into your consciousness not through lived experience or even news media coverage but through spectral, semi-anonymous, mute photos such as these.

Image #1 (Figure 6.1)

The Humvee's open window invites harsh white sunlight and the impression of heat into the photo's background. In the foreground, a soldier is buckled into the passenger seat, an M16 propped on his (or her) lap, muzzle pointing out the window. A standard-issue brown cloth neck gaiter keeps sand out of the soldier's face, just as the more colorful Iraqi kaffiyeh does for locals. The cloth obscures every facial detail, from below the soldier's chin all the way up to the ballistic sunglasses that reflect the glare from the road. The soldier wears a tan desert camouflaged ACH helmet,[4] with the standard-issue elastic band encircling it. Stuck into the band is a third-generation iPod, the one with a row of four round buttons between the clickwheel and the screen on the unit's iconic white face. The equally iconic white headphone cord snakes down the side of the helmet and disappears beneath the folds of brown cloth at the soldier's neck. With all visual markers of age, eth-nicity, and even gender erased, the two pieces of technology—firearm and iPod—stand out in high relief against the anonymous soldier. Both can be read as evidence of the

FIGURE 6.1 Soldier on Kuwait/Iraq border with iPod, ca. 2004. (Photo courtesy of iLounge.com)

technological sophistication of the US armed forces, attributes of a powerful and technologically integrated—one might be tempted to say "cyborg"[5]—fighting force.

At the same time, the iPod's position, strapped to the soldier's helmet, gestures backward in history by evoking well-known images from earlier conflicts. At first glance, in fact, the small white rectangle strapped to the soldier's helmet might be mistaken for the pack of cigarettes that soldiers since World War II have strapped to their helmets, so as to keep them both accessible and dry when fording streams. Should we compare the iPod to the M16 it accompanies or the Marlboros it replaced? Is the iPod—as an implement that, by all accounts, helped service members "pump themselves up" into a state of heightened acuity and aggression—a metaphorical extension of the weapon? Or, like a good smoke, is the iPod a technology for calming down, for creating a modicum of solace amid the chaos of combat? Is its presence humanizing or zombifying? Or is it simply decadent? Does the iPod point to the disparity in commitment between the American forces and their technologically inferior antagonists, who we imagine do not require such luxuries as music on the battlefield?

The image, which circulated widely on technophile websites such as *Ars Technica*, is clearly staged. (As one of my military interlocutors explained, "those helmet bands aren't particularly strong, and Humvees bounce like a ship in a storm unless they're on flat pavement.") As such, one might credibly dismiss it as one more example of the celebratory iPod photos that users around the world send to *ilounge.com*. Its symbolism, however, strikes me as deeply ambiguous. What exactly does it say about the relationship between the soldier, the mission, the iPod, and the music it brings into reach?

Image #2 (Figure 6.2)

The striking photos appeared on Flickr in early April 2007. The story was then picked up on iPodhacks.com, and eventually made it all the way to *Wired* magazine's website. While its provenance is unknown and some of the details strain credulity, the general thrust of the story is this: Kevin Garrad, a sergeant with the 3rd Infantry Division, was on a foot patrol in Tikrit when he rounded a corner and came face to face with an insurgent. A brief exchange of fire ensued, and the insurgent was killed. After concluding his patrol, Sgt. Garrad returned to base, put his earbuds in, and tapped his iPod through his breast pocket to activate it. When no music appeared he dug around in his pocket and pulled out the unit, which had been penetrated by what appeared to be an AK-47 round. It was only then, according to the story, that Garrad learned he had been shot in his encounter with the insurgent. (This last statement is pure fiction, as the impact from a close-range Kalashnikov is, I have been multiply assured, impossible to ignore.) In the photo, a close-up of the back of the iPod, one can see how the bullet cleanly drilled through the top-right corner of its face, and then separated the unit's two halves, bending the back side into a semi-concave shape, before exiting through an irregular opening it tore through the metal. A stray wire juts haphazardly out of the gap that has opened

FIGURE 6.2 Kevin Garrad's iPod

up between front and back; the iPod's circuitry is also visible. A second photo (for which I was unable to secure permission) shows Garrad in his uniform with what appears to be an Army nurse hanging on his arm. The nurse is laughing, it appears, at the remark of someone else in the room, while Garrad, stifling a laugh himself, looks into the camera. The white face of the iPod he holds in front of him is separated from the body, a crack runs down the length of the screen, and the bullet's entry hole is clearly visible. The initial version of the story asserted that the iPod stopped the bullet; bloggers who claim to have followed up with Garrad himself contend that it was Garrad's Interceptor Body Armor, and not the MP3 player, that played the pivotal role. Nonetheless, web accounts claim that the images circulated through the cubicles at Apple headquarters, and that Apple sent Garrad a replacement soon thereafter.

Apocryphal or not, the story and the images that accompany it point forcefully to the brutal asymmetry that defines the material relation between music and war. If any traces of romantic notions about music's transcendence continue to exist, the bullet piercing the iPod—the utter superiority of technologies of death over life-affirming technologies, of deathly practices over life-affirming practices—would seem to obliterate them.[6] Garrad was lucky to have survived, for the iPod is *not* mightier than the AK, and music, alas, is powerless against a hail of bullets. At the same time, Apple's reported replacement of Garrad's iPod, while a lovely gesture the soldier no doubt appreciated, can also serve to remind us of the strangely telescopic quality of the relation between the power of bullets and the power of capital. To wit: violent acts may indeed overwhelm musical technology at the level of the lived event, but at the level of global economics, the music and technology industries remain utterly unperturbed by local acts of violence. It is difficult, in other words, to imagine an armed conflict that would have a pronounced negative effect on global iPod or iTunes sales.[7]

Image #3 (Figure 6.3)

Two unrelated art collectives, Forkscrew Graphics and Copper Greene,[8] appear to have come up with the same general idea for a guerrilla art campaign at around the same time: their posters began to appear on the streets of Los Angeles and New York City in 2004. The posters' iconography duplicated that of the award-winning ad campaign designed by the firm TBWA\Chiat\Day for Apple in 2003: a brightly colored monochromatic background framing a black silhouette, with the telltale white lines of the iPod cord synecdochically evoking the advertised product. The most striking poster

FIGURE 6.3 iRaq [Abu Ghraib prisoner], Forkscrew Graphics, silkscreen, 2004, Los Angeles, California. (Photo courtesy of the Center for the Study of Political Graphics)

in the Copper Greene series featured a silhouette of the most infamous image of the war, the hooded detainee being submitted to mock electrocution in the US-run detention facility at Abu Ghraib. Against a bright yellow background, this most abject of figures stands on a box, arms outstretched, a white iPod cord hanging not from his ears but, like electrodes, from his fingers. In the upper right corner, in a font borrowed from the Apple campaign, is the word "iRaq." Running along the bottom, in a barbed allusion to the campaign's slogan ("10,000 songs in your pocket. Mac or PC"), runs the tag line: "10,000 volts in your pocket. Guilty or innocent."

Again, ambiguity reigns, and questions proliferate. Is this primarily a protest, primarily a joke, or equally both? Is the subject of this protest the war in Iraq in general, or US interrogation tactics specifically? Is the Apple ad campaign simply the neutral raw material from which this protest was fashioned, or is Copper Greene accusing Apple Inc. and the iPod of involvement in the war? The Forkscrew Graphics series was made up of four colored posters: three with a silhouetted figure representing an insurgent engaged in violent activities—throwing a Molotov cocktail, aiming a grenade launcher, and holding an AK-47 overhead (with the white iPod cord hanging provocatively from each silhouetted weapon)—and one of the Abu Ghraib figure that closely resembled (or perhaps anticipated) the Copper Greene poster. Beneath all four figures ran the tagline "10,000 Iraqis killed. 773 US soldiers dead." This more explicit indictment would seem to clarify the Forkscrew campaign as one that was protesting the war generally. But given the extent to which members of the Armed Forces had adopted the iPod as an essential piece of equipment, and given the role that iPods played in the very interrogations referenced by the Abu Ghraib silhouette, the symbolism of both groups' "iRaq" campaigns remains stubbornly open.[9]

These mute images frame the history of iPods in Iraq as one in which mobile audio technology is thoroughly imbricated with the daily exigencies of war and the symbolic and corporeal violence that surround them. In each image, the specter of music is set on a collision course with a contemporary manifestation of violence: firearm, bullet, detention facility. Taken together, they could easily serve as a discursive springboard for a general discussion of music, media, and violence.[10] The purpose of this chapter, however, is to better understand the dynamics of iPod within the regimes, campaigns, and territories of the war. To do so we will need to leave behind these anonymous pictures from the mediatized periphery and track instead the concrete ways the iPod was put to use on the ground in Iraq.

A CENTURY OF RECORDED MUSIC ON THE BATTLEFIELD

The iPod wasn't the first device to bring music to the front lines, of course. Throughout recorded history—and, we may safely speculate, much of human prehistory—music and violence have been locked in a tight dialectical embrace, with the former variously

mitigating, eliding, inciting, contradicting, facilitating, and at times embodying the latter.[11] For millennia, musical instruments have been used on the battlefield as technologies of communication (within and between military subdivisions), synchronization (of
time, of labor, of marching bodies), invigoration (of one's own troops), and intimidation
(of the enemy).[12] It seems safe to presume that music's utility as a means for both narrat-
ing violent events and healing the psychological wounds from combat has been recognized for a comparable period of time.

During the Revolutionary War, both the British and American armies used fife and
drum corps for "communicating orders during battle, regulating camp formations and
duties, and providing music for marching, ceremonies, and morale."[13] In addition to this
kind of "field music," the colonies had earlier adopted the model of the British "Band of
Musick," a group of "six to eight musicians performing on oboes, clarinets, horns, and
bassoons."[14] These groups played exclusively for ceremonies and other noncombat occasions, and served as the inspiration for the military bands that emerged in the United
States during the nineteenth century. In World War I, Allied commander General John
J. Pershing expanded the size and number of military bands and reduced the nonmusical duties of military band members.[15] Since then, military bands have accompanied US
troops on every major military action, up to and including Operation Iraqi Freedom.[16]

While live music in wartime may be as old as war itself, the history of recorded music
in wartime stretches back no further than the Spanish-American War of 1898, the first
major conflict to occur after the invention of the phonograph. In that year, several record
companies competed to bring the sonic campaigns of wartime to a distant civilian listenership. The Columbia Phonograph Company, for example, released "music of the war"
record lists that included the Columbia Orchestra's musical reenactment of the charge
of Roosevelt's Rough Riders.[17] Some recordings were even made in the field, including
ambient records of the sounds of guns in action. Civilian interest in the sounds of war
thus predates the practice of listening to recorded music during military deployment,
which would only flourish with the next generation of soldiers. Sixteen years later, during World War I, US military personnel began listening to recorded music in large numbers when rugged field phonographs (including one model invented by Thomas Edison)
were shipped to military "camps, ships, entrenchments and hospitals" in service of the
belief that "song makes a good soldier, a better soldier; a tired soldier, a rested soldier;
a depressed soldier, a cheery soldier."[18] From this point on, recorded music increasingly
supplemented live bands as a way to entertain the troops and alleviate the stress of
combat.[19]

As media theorists have long noted, many of the technologies that have been used
to disseminate music—from the radio to the reel-to-reel tape to the Internet—drew
upon or even originated as military technologies.[20] By World War II, music recorded on
and disseminated by these very technologies had become a central presence, with short-
wave and AM radio stations broadcasting to troops and civilians alike throughout the
European and Pacific theaters, and the Armed Forces Radio Service broadcasting from

London beginning in July 1943. In addition to Allied broadcasts, the Axis powers' propaganda programs, run by English-language DJs such as "Lord Haw-Haw" and the women collectively known as "Tokyo Rose," broadcast music and politically inflected news and propaganda into the theater with "the intent of instilling homesickness and weakening the American [and British] will to fight."[21] The Allies too used propaganda broadcasts, of course, and expanded them with the onset of the Cold War. The relative ease of radio operation, when compared to the ministrations required to maintain a record player and record collection in field conditions, made radio broadcasts the predominant music delivery device for combat troops in both World War II and the Korean War.

Radio continued to be popular among soldiers in the Vietnam War; many soldiers carried small transistor radios that picked up the American Forces Vietnam Network, which advertised itself as "serving the American fighting man twenty-four hours a day from the Delta to the DMZ."[22] But the advent of portable cassette players in the 1960s also made it easier for service members to bring their own music with them. The Vietnam War thus marked a pivotal moment in the history of mobile music and war, a moment in which a new technology facilitated a democratization of listening practices in theater. For the first time, combat troops could create their own acoustic environment, their own "soundtrack to war," and take it with them as they fought. These technological advances, combined with the ongoing aftereffects of the advent of rock and roll in the 1950s, led Vietnam vet William Broyles Jr. to dub Vietnam "our first rock and roll war."[23]

IPODS IN THE IRAQ WAR

With an intertextual nod to Vietnam, at least one journalist has referred to Operation Iraqi Freedom as our first "iPod war."[24] As I mentioned earlier, this wasn't always so; when George Gittoes shot *Soundtrack to War* in mid-2003, for example, the service members he interviewed were still plugging portable CD players, not iPods, into their vehicles. (This practice was also widespread during the NATO-led military intervention in Kosovo.) All the same, by 2007, when I began soliciting the testimonies of Iraq War veterans and active duty service members, the iPod had already overwhelmed all other mobile audio technologies to become the dominant music playback device for the troops; as more than one service member explained to me, anyone who didn't deploy with an iPod purchased one soon after arriving in Iraq.[25] Relatively rugged and skip-proof (as opposed to the finicky portable CD players they had used before), more capacious and easier to use than any of its predecessors, the device gave its users an unprecedented level of freedom to listen to their own music while deployed. In 2010, the Joint Readiness Training Center at Fort Polk, Louisiana included the iPod by name in its "packing list for plane ride down range," a list of recommended personal gear for making deployment more bearable.[26] On this list, the iPod is presented as every bit as essential as a sewing kit and foot powder.

Within the auditory regime of the military, where sound was presented as both a profound source of tactical information *and* a crippling source of trauma, the iPod could be
construed as a complex participant in a range of auditory acts, a technology that enabled
and encouraged some modes of listening while frustrating others. Within the military's
sonic campaigns, it introduced a host of new sounds into the lived environment while
obscuring other acts of sounding, facilitating some military activities while rendering
others less intuitive. At the same time, the iPod was used to create potent acoustic territories, ranging from the binaural virtual space of private listening to the expansive
radiant spaces in which publics were exposed to loud amplified voices. Most of these
acts were unregulated: they took place in an ad hoc manner, improvisationally, as the
situation demanded. The iPod in Iraq was, in other words, a fundamentally ambiguous
technology, one that interacted with soldiers, civilians (including both the Iraqis who
were subjected to it and the musicians whose recordings were stored on it) and other
technologies to produce a highly unpredictable, distributed agency, a set of strange new
possibilities for action, many of which were surely never envisioned by its inventors at
Apple or the military planners at the Pentagon.

AMPING UP, STAYING FOCUSED, COOLING DOWN: IPODS AS TECHNOLOGIES OF SELF-REGULATION IN COMBAT

iPod Use Outside of Combat

As I have discussed earlier, much of armed service, even in wartime Iraq, consisted of
sustained periods of downtime that were frequently accompanied by aching boredom.
In the stretches of time between missions, members of the armed forces stationed in Iraq
spent a lot of time listening to music, and they commonly presented their listening practices as being consonant with those of civilian life. Service members listened to music
on iPods while working out, while relaxing, while traveling from one place to another,
while daydreaming. Like the civilian users examined by sound studies scholar Michael
Bull, many American servicemen and women used their iPods to effect a turn "inward
from the world, living in an interiorised and pleasurable world of their own making,
away from the historical contingency of the world into the certainty of their own
past, real or imagined, enclosed safely within their very own auditory soundscape."[27]
Moreover, for many of the troops and military contractors who were engaged in support
activities—mechanics, food-service workers, administrators—the similarities between
their civilian and wartime lives could outweigh, or at least compete with, the differences
produced by their location in Iraq. When I interviewed civil servants and service members who were not involved in combat situations, they frequently told me that their iPod
use was "basically like it was back home." Their assertion of continuity between civilian/
peacetime and military/wartime iPod use complicates the conventional portrayal of war
as essentially foreign, and provides an important counterbalance to my description, in

previous chapters, of some of the more extreme situations civilians and combat troops encountered. At the same time, it points to the value that iPods (and other consumer technologies) had for these individuals as they strove to create a state, however fragile, of normalcy. Indeed, the iPod appears to have been a technology that was valued, in part at least, for the degree to which it could place auditors in a reasonable facsimile of the domestic acoustic territories they inhabited before deploying. Service members often strove to construct a semblance of normalcy by listening to music that made them feel as if they were "back home."

This fact notwithstanding, many of the troops who were part of Operation Iraqi Freedom contended with situations that were so violently distant from civilian life that evoking the territories of "back home" was an impossibility. For those who engaged in regular dangerous activities "outside the wire," the iPod's utility as a technology for connecting with civilian life was at times eclipsed by its value as a technology for tuning one's psychological state to the exigencies of combat.[28] As Jonathan Pieslak (2009), Lisa Gilman (2010), and others have documented, for the entire length of the US military engagement in Iraq, troops relied upon music—on iPods, on boom boxes, on PA systems, and, in violation of military regulations that were seldom enforced, plugged into headsets or speakers during missions—to attain the mildly altered state of heightened awareness and aggression that they deemed a necessary part of being an effective warrior.[29] It was extremely common for those who regularly engaged in combat and patrol missions to construct, in conversation with their comrades, one or more MP3 "battle playlists," which helped them "pump up" (or "amp up," or "get psyched up," or "get into the right mindset" or "get in the zone") before leaving base. In the words of an air force engineer tasked with repairing IED blast craters on the roads of Tikrit:

> Everybody in the military is type-A personality, and particularly in a combat situation you want them arrogant and confident and feeling that they're bulletproof, and so yeah ... we definitely used music to further solidify the idea that we're gonna go out there and kick butt and take names, and the bad guy's not gonna get us, we're bulletproof, you definitely needed everybody in the correct mindset and in the game. Much is true with sports as well ... you get the adrenalin fired up and everybody's highly motivated and highly focused.[30]

While listening to an iPod through earphones was a common ritual for combat service members attempting to get "in the correct mindset," iPods were often jacked into PA systems or boom boxes on base so that a group could listen to a common battle playlist while they were checking their weapons and loading up their vehicles. These group listening experiences ratified and sonically reified the group's sense of collective identity,[31] while synchronizing their moods and movements in a way not dissimilar to the Fordist ideal of musically coordinated factory workers.[32] At times, the boundaries between private and public listening become blurred in an auditory fog of earbuds and speakers. "Teflon Don," an Army engineer assigned the dangerous task of clearing Iraqi roads of live IEDs, related one such experience in a post on his award-winning milblog,[33] "Acute Politics" (2006):

> It's generally about 2 hours before a mission when the music starts. There's a lot of ways that guys here pump themselves up to get ready for a mission. Some get mad—mad at the Iraqis, mad at the Army for "screwing" them, mad at whatever makes them ready for whatever might be out there. Some guys become very quiet and focus on making sure that all of their gear is in exactly the right places. Some perform pre-mission rituals that they have established over the last few months in theater. Most of the guys, though, play music.
>
> There's a little bit of everything floating through the air. Some bands are favorites for their hardcore, often angry lyrics: Dope, Metallica, Drowning Pool, Rage Against the Machine (ironically enough), and so forth. There's country music going somewhere in the back. The LT [Lieutenant] is off listening to some classic rock—ACDC, or maybe Guns&Roses. Light rock forms a melodic counterpoint to the bass of the heavier music: Nickel Creek, Jack Johnson and Iron&Wine. In my own ears it's Project 86:
>
> *High noon cometh, not a moment too soon*
> *There's gonna be a firefight tonight*
> *A reckoning to confront the residents of this tomb*
> *A gunpowder party and it feels just right.*[34]

Some service members described the experience of listening to music during mission prep as being akin to ingesting amphetamines. But in addition to quickening the pulse, music was used to claim a measure of control in a terrifying situation. When they cranked the volume, they asserted control over noise in an environment where many noises were unpredictable and indexically related to death. When they chose the right beat for the moment, they asserted control over rhythm in an environment where coordination, dexterity, and timing were essential for survival. When they mouthed the lyrics, they asserted control over narrative to regularize their feelings about the immediate prospect of killing, and of being killed: in the words of Colby Buzzell, an author who served as an infantryman in a Stryker Brigade Combat Team in Iraq, "Sometimes . . . you're like, 'I don't want to play soldier today. . .' But then you hear 'The Good, the Bad and the Ugly' theme song and you're like 'Fuck yeah, hell yeah, I'll go out on a mission today'."[35]

In other words, Teflon Don picked the song, the song normalized an abnormal future, and the technology disappeared amid the illusion of pure, unmediated mimesis—or better, divination: *There's gonna be a firefight tonight.*

Building the Battle Playlist

The range of music on service members' battle playlists was surprisingly broad,[36] but the genres of metal, hard rock, and rap were, as one might predict given the demographics and stereotypical character profile of the US military, very well represented.[37] While I am not primarily concerned with musical tastes here but rather with the technological means of music delivery, examining one such playlist will be useful for understanding how the iPod deepened and broadened the discographies that service members drew upon. In June 2004, Buzzell, an early iPod user (he deployed in November 2003 with an iPod, and uploaded the CDs of many of his fellow soldiers onto it when he arrived in Iraq) published his personal iPod "Soundtrack to Violance" [*sic*] on his blog, "My War: Killing Time in Iraq":[38]

Kill The Poor/Dead Kennedys
You're Nobody Till Somebody Loves You/Dean Martin
Anything and everything by SLAYER
Stuck In The Middle With You/Stealers Wheel
What A Wonderful World/Louis Armstrong
Speak English Or Die/S.O.D.
Bombs Over Baghdad/Outcast
Theme Song from The Good The Bad And The Ugly
Imperial March from Star Wars
Kill Em All/Metallica
Lets Start A War, Army Life, and Blown To Bits/The Exploited
Stars and Stripes Forever
Welcome To The Jungle/Guns And Roses
Ride of the Valkyries/Wagner
Paint It Black/Rolling Stones
Die Die Die My Darling/Misfits
Give Peace A Chance/John Lennon
Shiny Happy People/REM
Show No Mercy/Cro-Mags
We Care A Lot/Faith No More
Danger Zone/Kenny Loggins (Top Gun song)
Countdown To Extinction/Megadeth
It's Clobberin' Time/Sick of it all
Iron Man/Black Sabbath
I Don't Care About You/FEAR
Bloody Sunday/U2
Orange Crush/REM
Never Gonna Stop/Rob Zombie
Won't Back Down/Johnny Cash Version
Seek and Destroy/Metallica

What stories might a playlist like this tell us? First, that ironic distanciation was likely one of Buzzell's tactics for staying sane during his tour of duty. (How else can one explain the inclusion of "You're Nobody Till Somebody Loves You," "Give Peace a Chance," or "Shiny Happy People" on a battle playlist?) Listening more closely, we can discern a fairly complex dialectical tension between the semantic field of the lyrics and performative elements such as prosody, timbre, instrumentation, and accent in many of the songs on this list. On the one hand, despite the arguably powerful antiwar theme of "Iron Man's" lyrics, its crushing power chords can be heard as a sonic icon of aggression, and therefore as appropriate for an environment in which "war *is* heavy metal." At the same time, Buzzell's playlist is remarkable for the degree to which song lyrics, independent of their musical delivery, reference experiences, emotions, and ideologies that are easily mapped onto the stereotyped and highly valorized mindset of the combat soldier serving in Iraq. (One assumes, for example, that it's the brutal resonance of the line "I won't . . . back . . . down," more than the languid strumming and placid voice of Johnny Cash's rendition, that propelled it onto this list.) More often, of course, musical and lyrical aggression were fused together, as in Megadeth's "Countdown to Extinction," Metallica's "Kill 'em All," or Outkast's "Bombs Over Baghdad."

Buzzell's playlist also invites questions about the importance of film as a mediator of service members' lived experience of combat. To take one of the more striking examples, many journalistic and firsthand accounts of the war have noted the prevalence on battle playlists of Wagner's "Ride of the Valkyries"—a clear reference to the scene in *Apocalypse Now* in which a squadron of helicopters projects a recording of the piece through loudspeakers as it attacks a Vietcong-held village.[39] Given that the average enlisted soldier wouldn't have been born in 1979 when *Apocalypse Now* was in theaters, the popularity of "Valkyries" is testament to the lasting power of the helicopter scene as a semi-ironic index of military daring and aggression.[40] The *Star Wars* theme and the theme from *The Good, the Bad, and the Ugly* are similarly ironic musical indices of violence (in one case on a galactic scale). For a generation that grew up with filmic depictions of battle and first-person-shooter video games, both of which tend toward music-heavy soundtracks, it is no surprise that the experience of live combat was at times interpreted through the prism of war movies or games.[41] The iPod gave added immediacy to this interpretation by allowing combat troops to enter into a simulacrum of a film, a film with a soundtrack, in which they become the ersatz viewers or even stars.[42] As Buzzell stated in his interview with Jonathan Pieslak:

It's kinda like . . . having your own soundtrack to your own movie, to your own war. If you watch a movie and they have a war scene . . . it's not the same without . . . some cool music dealt on top of it. When you're out there in real life, you know, hey, this is your movie. So [if] this is my movie then this is my soundtrack and this is what I'm listening to and it just gets you . . . pumped up for it.[43]

Lastly, Buzzell's "Soundtrack to Violence" is the kind of wild, genre-defying fever dream of a playlist that would have been exceedingly difficult to put together in a war zone without the help of an iPod or similar device. Buzzell did not compile his list by combing through the music he had available in his own CD collection prior to deployment, but rather by combing through his memory for songs that resonated with his unfolding experience. Some of these songs could be found among the 942 hours of music that he had uploaded onto his iPod from friends and acquaintances. Others, at least theoretically, could be acquired online. (It should be noted, however, that many Forward Operating Bases lack reliable broadband access, and military firewalls could make downloading difficult, though not impossible.) While Buzzell makes no mention of this, many service members told me they uploaded their personal music libraries onto a common server on the base to which everyone's device was synced. Service members could then download whatever songs they fancied from this massive master playlist.

The atomization of music consumption that digital music enables has been accused of killing the album, but it has produced an absolute renaissance of the mix tape. The playlists of OIF service members reflected the increased autonomy that they had to design their own musical microcampaigns, and this autonomy is in part the product of the synergy of technology and commerce that Apple and its competitors have engendered.

iPod Use During Combat

iPod use for military personnel in Iraq was subject to a bewildering number of occasionally contradictory regulations; some were created by base commanders and amount to in-house rules for a base, while others were more sweeping. Army Regulation 670-1, "Wear and Appearance of Uniforms and Insignia," was cited by some commanders as prohibiting the use of mobile music devices by omission: as there is no mention of iPods or other MP3 players within the prescriptions for the way dress, combat, or physical fitness uniforms should look, it would seem there is no place for a service member to carry an iPod, unless (as we shall see later in this chapter) "the commander issues and requires the use of . . . electronic devices in the performance of duties."[44]

Another regulation, published in a memorandum written for the Multi-National Force – Iraq (i.e., the coalition) in September 2008, mentions iPods specifically:

> Any entertainment device that requires earpieces or headphones will not be worn while conducting outdoor physical training or when walking, riding, bicycling or operating a motorized vehicle. Additionally, entertainment devices of any type will not be used at any time while serving as a crew member in any vehicle or aircraft. Earpieces/headphones/iPods/MP3 players will not be worn en route to or from the gym.

These injunctions notwithstanding, iPods were used during missions throughout the war, although never as frequently as they were used in the hours preceding and following them. I have spoken with several service members who said that, while they were aware of the practice of listening to music during missions, they had never witnessed it personally. An Iraqi civilian observer told me that in the first two and a half years of the war—that is, before the insurgents began targeting soldiers on patrol—the sight of a Humvee in her Baghdad neighborhood was regularly accompanied by the sound of loud rock music emanating from its speakers. (These may have been large PSYOPS loudspeakers, but more likely were smaller battery-powered speakers that the crew had installed—see below). One company commander mentioned that he tried to prohibit iPods in his Stryker armored personnel carrier, but admitted that his gunner would occasionally sneak a single earbud underneath his noise-canceling headphones as he scanned the streets for hostile actions on their route. By contrast, Richard Engel, an NBC correspondent who spent several years in Iraq, reported that the platoon in which he was embedded "had . . . rigged an iPod into the Stryker's comm system. They listened to the same ten songs every time they rolled out on a mission. The tenth song was 'My Humps' by the Black Eyed Peas. When it came on, they danced. 'It's kind of like a squad dance song,' one of the soldiers said. 'Even the driver dances in his hatch. Now everybody has got to dance because everyone is copying my squad, but it's all right.' "[45]

In correspondence with me, Teflon Don claimed that iPod use during missions was common in his company:

> We did most of our movement in mine-resistant trucks, with crew size ranging from 1 to 6 people, depending on the vehicle. Every vehicle we had played music while on mission. In my truck, we used a small set of portable speakers powered by 4 AAA batteries. . . . One truck in my platoon used intravehicle communication headsets to talk to each other while on mission; that squad wired an audio jack directly into the vehicle's communication system so that they could play their iPod over the headsets. In all cases, music was playing only when it didn't interfere with mission. We understood music to be a privilege—one that could be lost if we abused it. More than that—we hunted bombs, and we used music to stay awake and alert. When we were creeping up on a suspected bomb, we didn't need any help staying awake.[46]

By all accounts, disciplinary actions for using iPods in contravention of military regulations were relatively rare. Most of my interlocutors could not recall any punishments being levied for iPod use during their deployments. Teflon Don knew of one fellow soldier who regularly wore his iPod earbuds underneath his radio headset, and who listened to music so loudly that he was unable to hear the radio. "He never faced serious discipline," Don stated, "but he did do a lot of pushups on a few separate occasions."[47]

If the rules restricting the use of earphones for military personnel were not always rigorously enforced, the rules governing the behavior of civilians in the conflict zone were even more lax. Nonetheless, it would appear that some of the diplomats, civil servants, and contract employees who lived and worked in the Green Zone quickly internalized the logic behind military injunctions restricting iPod use. When the insurgency was at its peak, in 2006 and 2007, and mortar attacks occurred sporadically throughout the day and night, the residents of the International Zone felt as if they were always "on mission." This situation bred caution among some, and resignation among others.

Chris, a civil servant who worked in the International Zone between 2006 and 2008, listened to his iPod exclusively through a Bose Sounddock that he brought with him from the States. When asked if he ever used earphones, he answered: "no, because it seemed odd."

> I mean even though I would crank the Sounddock, I still wanted to be able to hear if anything was going on outside. There's something about putting on the headphones, I didn't want to be that distant, if that makes any sense. I still wanted that connection so I could hear if an emergency was happening or if someone was calling me or if my phone would go off. Putting the headphones on was just a little bit too closed for me.[48]

Here, the sensation of being closed off from the ambient world is presented as inherently dangerous, as something to be avoided. Given the frequency of mortar attacks visited upon the Green Zone in the period he was there, the need for aural acuity was very real.[49] Other individuals sought out that very sensation of removal from the world, in spite of the fact that to do so increased the risk that they might fail to hear the warning alarm that often precedes a mortar or rocket attack by a few seconds. Kelly, another civil servant who worked in the International Zone in 2006, tried to explain why listening to her iPod through headphones was valuable to her:

> When I would go work out in the gym I would always wear headphones because I couldn't stand . . . the music that they would play in the gym. . . . That was the one point when people would call me stupid, that I would drown everything else out. And it was like, if I get hit right now, at least I'm running. I don't know how to describe it, it was probably one of those—I needed that escape for some short period of time and if I didn't hear the explosion, so be it.[50]

The statements of Teflon Don, Chris, and Kelly embody three distinct attitudes toward the costs and benefits of iPod use in conflict zones. Kelly's argument—that her iPod earbuds "drown everything else out," fully closing out the ambient world in order to provide a needed sense of "escape"—resonates with Michael Bull's presentation of the iPod as a "privatized auditory bubble."[51] Bull contends that MP3 players allow their users to create an individualized "auditory world" that both exemplifies and feeds the desires of listening subjects to remove themselves from the cacophony of urban spaces and enter mediatized "non-spaces,"[52] closed acoustic territories that circumscribe what David Beer has called "a utopian zone of exclusion."[53] Kelly, along with a great number of military iPod users, used her iPod to create a small zone of sanity in a loud environment charged with the ever-present potential for violence. Chris's testimony similarly foregrounded the isolating nature of the iPod, but he framed it as a constricting, rather than liberating, phenomenon. For him, along with a great number of military and civilian personnel in Iraq, the potential costs of time spent in the non-space of the auditory bubble clearly outweighed the benefits. These two conflicting positions chart out the psychological terrain upon which belliphonic auditors in Iraq grappled with the fundamental philosophical question: what, in the end, is the value of music? The difference between their calculations and those a music scholar might make is that they were not calculating this value in a global or abstract sense, but on the ground, here and now, in the presence of the real threat of death. Was the solace music provided worth the reduction of one's odds of survival? The war presented its participants with myriad opportunities to calibrate and recalibrate their answers to this question.

In contrast, Teflon Don's earlier assertion—that the iPod can be used in certain situations to keep one focused on one's surroundings—refuses to place music and survival in an oppositional relation; rather than enveloping him in a mesmerizing sonic bubble, or helping him "tune out" the ambient world,[54] the iPod's music (with or without an earbud) helped Don and his fellow soldiers stay "tuned in" to the demands of the mission at hand. In situations where visual acuity was crucial—and "creeping up on suspected bombs" is one such situation—music could be used to keep the eye and the mind sharp. For soldiers like Teflon Don, the calculus of iPod use took the full sensorium into account, with the value of sustaining a heightened state of sensory awareness and mental alertness weighed against the cost of muffling the sounds of the ambient world.

In addition to the primary effects that iPod use had on service members' auditory perception, there were other, hidden costs to listening to music while on mission. According to one Iraqi source familiar with wartime life in Baghdad, homemade videos of American service members and, more often, Blackwater contractors engaging in gun battles with music blaring from their vehicle speakers, or with the unmistakable white cords dangling from their helmets, or simply with loud heavy metal soundtracks added after the fact, were widely available during the war, both on the Internet and in the form of DVDs or VCDs sold at local markets. While it is impossible to quantify their impact, my Iraqi interlocutor argued that they were marketed within Iraq and more broadly with the intent of portraying the US military as a group of callous, amoral killers who have aestheticized violence to the point where they equate their own violent acts with cinematic action: killing to a soundtrack. A complete tally of the costs and benefits of iPod use in combat would thus need to take the iPod's value within anti-US propaganda campaigns into account.

iPod Use After Combat

While the topic of iPod use during combat missions was, understandably, a source of ambivalence for many service members, there was much less equivocation about the iPod's value once the mission was completed or the attack had been weathered. Complementing the battle playlists discussed above, military iPod users regularly created another set of playlists designed to help them "cool down" after a stressful day spent outside the wire. Upon returning to their bases from their missions, it was extremely common for service members to listen to music on iPods, either individually with headphones or collectively over PA systems. These playlists featured an astonishingly wide variety of music, from Top 40 to the songs of Enya, from Bach's *Goldberg Variations* to smooth jazz compositions, from Billie Holiday to Christian contemporary music.[55] The therapeutic acoustic territories this music created were, like the aggressive territories of the battle playlist, in direct response to the physical and emotional needs of combat troops who found themselves intermittently in extreme situations of danger and exhaustion.

The air force major who commanded a construction crew that repaired roads damaged by IED explosions described the way that he and his men would listen to music after missions:

> I wanna say that a lot of times we'd come back and again it was the demobilization phase . . . and a lot of times the guys would turn on more of the top forty radio playlist, whatever was popular and common . . . it wasn't something to pump you up cause, by this point, everyone's coming down off the two-hour adrenalin rush, and we made it back safely, and nobody shot at us, or nobody hit us, or nobody got hurt, that was the big important part to it, when nobody got hurt, we'd play this music, and we predominantly chose the top-40, because, I don't want to say it was benign, but if you psychoanalyze it, it was because it was American music and it was what we were comfortable with and it just fit, it wasn't sad, it wasn't overly happy, it was *normal*. And, you know, "situation normal," we're all back safely.[56]

Not all missions ended this way, however. During his tour of duty, a number of the men serving under the major were killed. If a mission resulted in a casualty, the airmen turned the music off: "on those particular missions it was pretty much dead silence all the way home, and we would usually download the trucks in silence, and it was very quiet." Death and injury were marked by a lack of music. Similarly, the return of music to their routine signified death's absence, or at least its passage. Within a day or so after a death, while the complicated process of mourning continued, the music-infused routine of "situation normal" returned to the major's company.

Initially silenced to commemorate a death, the iPod often played a role at military funerals. A captain who also served as a bugler at funerals described how a fallen soldier's iPod could be mined for his favorite tunes that would play after the official service concluded:

> There's kind of the "each person can come up and give their respects" portion, and that . . . would range from an hour to five, sometimes the guys just had to get it all out right there. And they'd play background music, which was kind of strange. Sometimes it would be Eminem, because that was that guy's favorite music. Just playing in the background, but you know that's not very memorial type music. All the way to just R&B, Mary J. Blige just playing in the background. But all his buddies, they're all kneeling or just standing there in silence and that helps them I guess deal with it.[57]

As a technology of self-regulation in combat situations, the iPod helped service members convince themselves that they would be effective warriors. As a technology of mourning in funeral situations, it helped survivors remember the fallen and lament their passing. In this sense, military iPod use represents an extreme case of the phenomenon that Tia Denora explores in "everyday [i.e., civilian, peacetime] life," in which music is deployed "as a resource for creating and sustaining ontological security, and for entraining and modulating mood and levels of distress."[58] The iPod's versatility, its relevance to both the performance of state-sanctioned violent acts and the experience of grief in the wake of violent acts, was one of the defining characteristics of its use in the Iraq War.

MOVING BODIES, LOOSENING TONGUES, ADJUSTING CROSSHAIRS: IPODS AS TECHNOLOGIES FOR MANIPULATING OTHERS IN COMBAT

To recap the ground covered in this chapter thus far, over the course of the war the iPod emerged as a nearly ubiquitous mobile entertainment device for military and civilian personnel serving in Operation Iraqi Freedom. What should also be clear is that, in the extreme environment of combat, the iPod was being deployed for purposes that extend beyond conventional definitions of "entertainment." The device was used by troops to attain a heightened emotional, cognitive, and perceptual state of combat-readiness; it was used to maintain focus during missions; it was used to recover from the punishing ordeals of combat and patrols; it was used to memorialize fallen comrades; it was used to maintain a connection with civilian life. Now I want to move even further into the unconventional by briefly enumerating several of the other uses to which the iPod was put in Iraq.

In chapter 1, I discussed a number of the activities collected under the designation Psychological Operations, or "PSYOPS." These operations have been defined as "the planned use of communications to influence human attitudes and behavior . . . [They] consist of] political, military, and ideological actions conducted to induce in target groups behavior, emotions, and attitudes that support the attainment of national objectives."[59] In Iraq, PSYOPS units engaged in activities that ran the gamut from providing incentives designed to "win the hearts and minds" of the populace to deploying disincentives that blurred the boundary between psychological operations and punitive actions. The iPod and other MP3 players were utilized as both carrot and stick on these missions.

In December 2008, journalist Nathan Hodge reported on a humanitarian aid mission that took place in the troubled Baghdad neighborhood of Sadr City. As his fellow troops handed out halal food to the residents, Staff Sgt. Kent Crandall plugged an iPod that he had loaded with Iraqi pop music into an army PSYOPS loudspeaker; using local music to attract crowds, it turns out, was a common PSYOPS tactic (see figure 6.4). Separately, the United States Agency for International Development (USAID) distributed thousands of iPod clones (made by Zvox) that played "prepackaged civic messages" in Arabic.[60] Similarly, in a book documenting the full extent to which Apple Inc. is involved with the Department of Defense, historian Nick Turse reports that the military began "using iPods in its recruiting efforts—as a lure to get kids to hand over personal information. And the National Guard began offering free iTunes music downloads, in exchange for the same type of information, on its Web site."[61]

FIGURE 6.4 iPod connected to PSYOPS speakers, Sadr City, 2008. (Photo courtesy of Nathan Hodge)

More distressing, arguably, were reports from Iraq that detailed the use of recorded music as a tool for crowd dispersal and interrogation. In the early years of the war, for example, iPods, along with CD and minidisk players, were used in conjunction with the Long Range Acoustic Device (LRAD) to disperse large groups of hostile civilians.[62] Used as a battlefield communication tool, the latest version of the LRAD can broadcast an intelligible voice over two miles of open terrain. But the LRAD also serves as a tool for "behavior modification," in which an "attention-getting and highly irritating deterrent tone" can be aimed at a human target.[63] Projecting the tone at full strength over short distances can result in permanent hearing damage to the sound's "targets."[64] A Stryker commander familiar with the LRAD described this sound as capable of disorienting its targets, producing headaches and acute gastrointestinal distress—so acute that they dubbed it "the poo sound." He went on to explain that, in addition to using this preprogrammed sound, soldiers would jack their iPods into the LRAD and blast loud music at groups of Iraqis whom they wanted to disperse. This, the commander explained, provided the double benefit of invigorating the American troops while simultaneously frustrating the Iraqi crowds.[65] Suzanne Cusick has speculated that LRADs were deployed (albeit hooked up to CD and minidisk players rather than iPods) in November 2004 by the 361st PSYOPS Company, which blasted music including AC/DC's "Hell's Bells" and "Shoot to Thrill" in order to "prepare the battlefield" during the siege of Fallujah.[66]

Although it was used at times on the ground in Iraq to disperse crowds and frustrate the enemy, the LRAD continues to be classed as a signaling device rather than a nonlethal weapon. This classification renders the LRAD exempt from US export controls, as recent exports to China attest.[67] However, when attached to an iPod or other mobile playback device, the LRAD would appear to blur the distinction between weapon and nonweapon in a way that iPods attached to normal speakers (generally considered a nonweapon) or the unassisted use of the LRAD's "deterrent tone" (commonly understood as a kind of nonlethal weapon) would not. Some accounts of iPod-enhanced LRAD use in Iraq claim that the Iraqis subjected to heavy metal music may have actually been less disturbed than amused by the effort. Other accounts work from the assumption that the loud music blasting from LRADs is so painful and aggravating as to approach the threshold of torture.

Some of the ambiguity that lingers over the use of amplified music in the open spaces of the combat zone evaporates within the close confines of the interrogation chamber. As I have mentioned earlier, Suzanne Cusick has written a collection of powerful and disturbing articles about the use of music as a weapon on Iraqi battlefields and as a device for "softening up" detainees preceding their interrogation. The latter practice has generated a great deal of attention, both in the popular press and among music scholars.[68] A widely used tactic within interrogations conducted by the military and US intelligence services during the Bush presidency, the "music program" or "loud music" technique has been alleged in some instances to prescribe that detainees be "chained to walls, deprived of food and drinking water, and kept in total darkness with loud rap or heavy metal blaring for weeks at a time."[69]

While Cusick's work generally does not focus on the technological means by which music was delivered in these contexts, she does single out the iPod as being implicated in the military's appropriation of "private" musical experience in service of violent "public" musical projects.

> Mp3 players focus the radical privatisation of 'music' that we have come so to cherish right down to the ears, into the ears, inside the ears. . . . It is these very technologies of musical privatisation that have enabled our extremely flexible capacity to use the amplified sound of any soldier's mp3 player, wired through powerful speakers, against individual prisoners' whole bodies—not just their ears. Such amplified sounds project an invisible presence that irresistibly occupies a space—a threatening ship at sea, a city like Fallujah before the November 2004 assault, a prison's holding cells—before the invading troops roll in. The superstate uses amplified sound from any soldier's private iPod to occupy enemies' thoughts, or erase those thoughts, and thus to deny enemies the right to privacy. To silence the capacity for intelligible speech; to foreclose the possibility of either silent or spoken prayer, or of solidarity with others; and yet to make prisoners long for access to speech—for the ability to contribute to the acoustical environment over which they have had, for so long, no control, with the presumably truthful revelations of compulsive talk.[70]

The iPod was thus implicated in a sonic campaign that stripped the aesthetic dimension from music altogether, replacing it with the most brutal form of biopolitics, of compelling bodies to adopt certain positions and attitudes.[71] In the extreme acoustic territory that resulted from music-enhanced interrogation, the interrogee's agency was reduced down to its minimal binary: *talk, or suffer the music*—or, more commonly, removed altogether: *suffer the music, then talk.*

iPods as translation devices

As the war progressed, the iPod evolved, becoming smaller and more versatile with each generational release. And as it evolved, the military's relationship with it deepened. At the dawn of the era of twenty-first-century "network-centric warfare," the iPod emerged as the preferred multipurpose digital device for the US military. Relatively rugged, inexpensive, difficult to hack, and with an intuitive interface that the troops had already mastered, an increasing number of iPods were issued to service members for specific military purposes over the course of the war.[72]

The militarization of the iPod can be traced back to 2007, when Florida-based software company Vcom3D unveiled an iPod-based one-way translation platform specifically designed for Operation Iraqi Freedom. The program, called Vcommunicator

Mobile, used the iPod's "playlist" architecture to organize a large number of utterances that service members indicated they would like to be able to deliver to Iraqis in the field. This platform was designed to replace the Phraselator, an earlier, bulkier one-way translator built by VoxTec (a former division of Marine Acoustics). The Vcommunicator software could be loaded onto an off-the-shelf iPod, which could then be strapped to the wrist and attached to a small speaker Velcroed to the service member's arm. In the Vcommunicator platform, "conversations" are grouped by purpose: "winning hearts and minds," "cordon and search," "intel gathering," "detainee processing," "assessing needs of hospitals," "raid." By clicking on the playlist "vehicle checkpoint," for example, a soldier manning a checkpoint could scroll through a list of questions and statements designed to elicit short answers or mute compliance:

(01) Peace be upon you. (Greeting)
(02) We need to search your vehicle.
(03) Stop your vehicle.
(04) Turn off the car.
(05) Open the door.
(06) Stand over there.
(07) Please turn off the lights.
(08) Please get out of the car.
(09) Do you speak English?
(10) May I see your I.D.?
(11) Are you a police man?
(12) What is your name?
(13) Are you carrying weapons?
(14) Raise your hands.
(15) Please open the trunk.
(16) Open the hood.
(17) We are going to search your vehicle.
(18) You may get back in your car now.
(19) Entry is prohibited. Go back.

Clicking on a sentence triggered an audio recording of its translation into Iraqi Arabic or Kurdish, with a phonetic transliteration on the screen. Another click displayed an image of the sentence written in Arabic; a third click produced a uniformed animated avatar, who spoke the sentence while demonstrating "culturally appropriate hand gestures." In addition to the small speaker that came with the system, the Vcommunicator-loaded iPod could be connected to a megaphone, so that the Arabic voice could be broadcast at a distance. Unlike the larger and less versatile Phraselator, the iPod's small size allowed its users to keep one hand free while consulting the transliteration of the sentence they wished to utter (see figure 6.5).

FIGURE 6.5 Vcommunicator Mobile promotional photo. (Photo courtesy of Vcom3D)

By 2009, 600 iPods with Vcommunicator Mobile software had been distributed to soldiers in Iraq, with more orders filled for Afghanistan.[73] By 2011, soldiers with the 82nd
Airborne Division, 10th Mountain Division, and 4th and 3rd Infantry Divisions had
tested the device in the field.

Machine interpretation has been generating technophobic anxieties in peacetime contexts for decades now. But when "interpretation" is unidirectional and the stakes involve
human lives, some anxiety would appear to be justified. As Mary Louise Pratt wrote
in reaction to the earlier Phraselator device, the unidirectionality of these communication technologies renders them "instrument[s] of pure interpellation."[74] Literally hailed,
with extremely limited agency to recast their relations with their heavily armed military "interlocutors," Iraqi civilians who experienced Phraselator and Vcommunicator
through the questions and commands of a monolingual military user were constituted
as subjects who had hearing, but who are effectively mute. However, if these devices are
used not, or not only, as replacements for live translators but rather as training tools (as
their promotional materials suggest), then they carry the potential to expand the communicative possibilities between US forces and non-English-speaking civilian populations. Will Vcommunicator and similar technologies end up bleeding out the nuance
and reciprocity of interchanges that previously would have taken place with the aid of an
interpreter? Or will they ultimately reduce the odds of fatal misunderstandings between

parties and help them forge previously inconceivable relationships? As always, the outcome cannot be guaranteed by the companies' PR staffs or the technophobic naysayers; it will depend upon how they are used in the field.

The utility of the iPod for the US military increased significantly with the release of the Wi-Fi-enabled iPod Touch in the fall of 2007. This device, while incorporating the iPod's MP3 technology, was more intimately connected to the iPhone, sharing its touch-screen interface and capacity to support apps purchased through iTunes. In a piece written for *Newsweek* in 2009, Benjamin Sutherland claims that the Touch "fulfills the military's need to equip soldiers with a single device that can perform many different tasks." He continues:

> As the elegantly simple iPods—often controlled with a single thumb—acquire more functionality, soldiers can shed other gadgets. An iPod "may be all that they need," says Lt. Col. Jim Ross, director of the Army's intelligence, electronic warfare and sensors operations in Fort Monmouth, New Jersey. The iPod isn't the only multifunction handheld on the market, but among soldiers it's the most popular. Since most recruits have used one—and many already own one—it's that much easier to train them to prepare and upload new content. Users can add phrases to language software, annotate maps and link text or voice recordings to photos ("Have you seen this man?"). Apple devices make it easy to shoot, store and play video. Consider the impact of showing villagers a video message of a relaxed and respected local leader encouraging them to help root out insurgents.

A new stage in the development of the militarized iPod Touch was reached in 2008 with the release of BulletFlight M, a military-grade ballistics calculator application made by a company called Runaway Technology, Inc. After downloading the BulletFlight app (the military version can be purchased at the iTunes app store for $29.99; the basic version costs $3.99), shooters input variables such as the weapon being used, the angle to the target ("as measured by the built-in accelerometer"), and atmospheric conditions such as temperature, barometric pressure, humidity, wind speed, and wind direction. The app then instantaneously produces a readout that tells the shooter how many clicks he needs to change the scope for a true shot under those conditions. BulletFlight automatically figures in more subtle and esoteric variables such as "bullet spin drift" and the Coriolis effect (produced by the Earth's rotation). Clamped to an M110 sniper rifle or (more likely) held by a spotter, the iPod and the app work together to enable accurate shots from up to 3,000 meters (see figure 6.6). As of 2011, the BulletFlight website claimed that the app was "currently in combat use by military snipers in Iraq and Afghanistan."[75]

Clearly, promotional materials like the photo above were not destined to become part of Apple's iPod advertising campaign. The iPod's salience within the US military

FIGURE 6.6 BulletFlight promotional photo. Photo courtesy of Runaway Technology, Inc.

contradicted its image as a hip, even quasi-countercultural product. As a mobile music device, however, the iPod's popularity among service members during OIF simply mirrored its popularity among civilians in the same age bracket. And as for the one-way translator and ballistic calculator, it would appear that the logic of distributed competences that structures the iTunes app store—in which third-party developers create and market apps (within some constraints) to potential iPhone and iPod Touch users—enabled the iPod to be reimagined as a robust instrument for military use without the active initiative of Apple *or* the military. (Vcom3D and Runaway Technologies are independent companies; they were not given a contract by either party to develop their applications.) The relationship of the iPod to the military, then, represented one moment in a long-term shift from military planning and production to military consumption. As Geoffrey Winthrop-Young has noted, after decades of actively funding the development of media technologies, from radio to the Internet to virtual reality, "the [military] . . . is now more into shopping than handing out exclusive contracts. To be sure, this does not mean that the military is out of the picture, but on the whole it appears that military technology, which once took the lead, now tends to lag behind what is available in games, rides, and movie special effects."[76] It is worth noting, though, that a collaborative relationship between Apple and the military does exist: iPods have been sold in military PXs around the world, Apple computers are currently being used to plan military operations in the field, and Apple appears to enjoy a robust relationship with the Department of Defense, servicing contracts in numbers and for sums it chooses not to publicize.[77]

iPods as technologies for regulating emotions in wartime; iPods as technologies for frustrating the enemy; iPods as technologies for reaching out to the civilian population, or compelling confessions from detainees—these applications set the parameters within which we may begin to assess the impact of mobile music technology within the US military's evolving auditory regime and the sonic campaigns that accompany each of its operations. It is clear that the advent of the iPod helped the participants of Operation Iraqi Freedom deploy music, in all its mercurial intensity, toward an astonishingly wide range of aims. Alternately carrot and stick, incentive and weapon, iPod-enabled music resounded in many contexts, from the barracks to the battlefield to the interrogation room.

Most fundamentally, the service members who have spoken to me (and to Lisa Gilman, Jonathan Pieslak, and a number of journalists) about their music listening practices regarded the iPod as a cherished instrument that helped them get through a tough deployment. By alleviating tedium, soothing nerves, steeling one for the trials of combat, and lessening the distance between the theater of war and the home front, the iPod amounted, for many, to a kind of aural armor, a protection against the taxing onus of war. As we take stock of the iPod in Iraq, it is important to take seriously the value that individual service members placed upon this technology, and the solace they derived from the music it delivered.

This solace was dearly purchased. If service members used their iPods (along with their video games, DVDs, laptops, and Skype sessions) to render war less psychologically taxing, they also exposed themselves to the risk of disengagement from the ambient world. Service members with iPods enjoyed unprecedented access to music during their deployments, which means that their experience of wartime was necessarily more mediated, more virtualized, than ever before. In creating their own "soundtracks" and listening to music on missions, service members had to grapple with the temptation of aestheticizing violence, and hence trivializing it, as well as desensitizing themselves to it. Beyond the purely tactical issue of mobile music masking potentially important ambient sounds lie open questions about the real-world costs of musicalizing and cinematizing combat.

It is also important to acknowledge that by the conclusion of Operation Iraqi Freedom, the iPod was no longer exclusively an audio device. Over the course of the war, the iPod evolved into a full-spectrum interface for a number of the tasks associated with military action. American military action is currently taking place in an environment in which bodies have partially merged with media technologies, media technologies have partially merged with weapons, and weapons-in-use mark the boundaries of a topography of sensory violence. The iPod, more than any previous technology, introduced mobile music *and* interactivity into the theater of war, and with them, new tactics, and new potential stabilities and instabilities.

This inherently ambiguous technological agency—for the agency of all technologies is ambiguous—has altered, in ways both subtle and profound, how warfare is conducted and experienced. The auditory regime of the military during the war was composed of the new and curtailed possibilities for listening that the iPod—along with other technologies, regulations, practices, and discourses—introduced for the service members who served there. The sonic campaigns of Operation Iraqi Freedom were influenced by the iPod and similar devices that allowed individual service members to walk around with large libraries of music, voices speaking Arabic, and other sounds in their pockets. And the acoustic territories of the Iraq War were stretched by these devices, providing "privatized auditory bubbles" for individual service members, small social circles for troops in barracks and vehicles, and, for Iraqi civilians, large radiant zones of unidirectional intelligibility and weaponized sound. Whatever the fate of the state of Iraq, it seems clear that the US military's future operations will involve ever more sophisticated and immersive interactive technologies. The iPod, a highly evocative object now largely consigned to history, was neither the beginning nor the end of this trend.

Fragment #5

From "Hell's Bells" to "Silent Night"

A CONVERSATION ABOUT MUSIC IN THE MILITARY

THIS IS AN extended excerpt from a group interview I conducted at an American military post in 2009. Six army officers, ranging in rank from captain to major, participated. One of the officers was a woman, all were under forty-five years of age, and all had recently returned from active duty in Iraq. Over the course of the roughly thirty minutes excerpted here, many of the themes relating to music and listening that can be found throughout the book are discussed.

> *J. Martin Daughtry [JMD]:OK, let's talk about music in the minutes that we have left. Did any of you own iPods or other MP3 devices when you were over there? Did any of you not?*
>
> OFFICER #1: I didn't have an iPod, I had a Sony player for MP3s.
>
> OFFICER #2: I owned one and then it died and I remember I was pretty upset about that. Because I had spent hours at home, in the weeks before the deployment,

putting all of my music on my iPod. And then when I got to Iraq I plugged it in to the wrong computer to charge and it had a setting to download that computer's library and that computer had no music, so then it erased my entire iPod.

Multiple officers: Ooh! [laughter]

JMD: So what did you do?

OFFICER #2: I got mad. [laughter] I wrote home to my wife and had her mail me another one. But, I mean, realistically there was nothing I could do because all of my music was back home, so I ended up listening to my soldiers' music.

OFFICER #1: When was this in?

OFFICER #2: This was in '05.

OFFICER #1: '05. Cause see, '03, when I was there . . .

OFFICER #2: This is not record players, you understand . . . [laughter]

OFFICER #1: It's funny you say that, because in Desert Storm it was cassette tapes and a few CDs. But '03, when I went in, I looked at getting an iPod and didn't because I didn't know if I was going to have reliable access to power. So I bought an MP3 CD player that used double-A batteries that I knew I could always get because our MVGs ran on double-A batteries, so they would be available in the supply system. So, same concept.

JMD: So you had a collection of songs on it, MP3s burned onto discs?

OFFICER #1: Yeah, I took my entire CD collection with me on about fifteen MP3 CDs.

JMD: Now, for those of you who did have iPods, did you construct playlists specifically for your life there, or did you just use the same playlists that you had or randomly put it on shuffle or, you know, how did you design your music choices?

OFFICER #4: I'll tell you a cheesy story, this is cheesy . . .

OFFICER #3: Tell us what's on your playlist, man, come on! [laughter]

OFFICER #4: One of the things my company did . . .

OFFICER #5: Barbra Streisand . . . [laughter]

OFFICER #4: Yeah, a lot of Barbra Streisand and Frank Sinatra. One of the things we did was these TST raids, time sensitive target raids to capture bad guys. So, it's like, it's sort of like that scene from *Black Hawk Down* where they're going to get the bad guys and they're all rolling out, so we would do, we had a short alert to launch, so we would get alerted and we would need to be out the door in forty-five minutes or less. So the time sequence roughly is we'd get alerted and we'd do a FRAGO [*fragmentary order, introducing changes to an existing order*] and the FRAGO would be done by alert plus twenty minutes, and then we have about ten minutes to get our stuff on and head out the door and roll out. So from twenty to thirty was about ten minutes of "get your stuff on" and "get ready to go," so we had total stereotypical music, like Godsmack and Slipknot and Metallica, stuff like that. So we'd blare that in our little warehouse thing that we were getting ready in.

JMD: What would you blare it on?

OFFICER #4: Well, at first it was my laptop, which didn't work so well, and then finally we got some external speakers, we'd do that.

JMD: *Hooked up to a laptop?*

OFFICER #4: Right.

JMD: *So was that almost like a ritual for you?*

OFFICER #4: Yeah.

JMD: *Same songs every time?*

OFFICER #4: No, different, flavor of the day. Something that would get everyone fired up, or try to get everyone fired up.

OFFICER #3: We had, I guess it was a ritual within our Stryker vehicle, with our crew we would have music going out the gate and then coming back in we could play a different set of music. If we were going on an actual mission we would play a different music.

JMD: *Do you remember any of the songs or artists that were on these sort of things?*

OFFICER #3: Yes. Def Leppard, Ozzy Osbourne, "Crazy Train" and a little bit of KISS and, uh, yeah, so we would play those musics. But I want to make it clear, I don't know if it's going on, but outside of the gate there's no music, so everything is just a prep and within the FOB as we're rolling out towards the gate. As soon as you go out the gate and you lock and load it's, it's silence.

OFFICER #5: Pre- and postgame.

OFFICER #3: Right.

OFFICER #4: Yeah, for this reason we didn't have any iPods or any MP3 players, at risk of an ass chewing. None of that stuff in the vehicles, period, because I . . . felt like it was too, you know, too much temptation, we didn't want any of that stuff. It's like smoking; we don't smoke outside the wire. We don't listen to music. So it was strictly in our little warehouse.

JMD: *Did you ever hear of other people being reprimanded for violating regulations about listening to music?*

OFFICER #4: I would reprimand people for listening to music on missions, cause if you're a machine gunner and you're rocking out to whatever on your machine gun, it's not appropriate, you need to focus on whatever you're doing. In my mind you need to focus on whatever you're doing.

OFFICER #6: I reprimanded people. I'm logistics, so we deliver supplies and they get bored. You'll send them from one FOB to another, for ten hours they're out, so it's always a challenge to make sure they're paying attention, that they're with it, and especially when you're working with Iraqis or training Iraqi truck drivers and they just leave, or go home, or take our stuff. But, something that's interesting is you do end up sharing. Like, I would never listen to gangster rap, but I kind of started listening to it cause you're around people for fourteen hours a day and you're sitting in your truck with your driver and, "Do you like this band?" "No," but by the end of the deployment you're like, "Can I borrow Jay-Z again?" You share a lot of different things, tastes, it's good I guess.

OFFICER #2: And soldiers have probably some of the more eclectic playlists around.

OFFICER #6: Absolutely! [Laughter]

JMD: That has been one of my great, joyous discoveries in this project, is how broad actually the listening is.

OFFICER #1: Yeah, I didn't know who the White Stripes were until I deployed. But, the same kid that listened to that was also listening to the Pogues, so um . . .

OFFICER #5: I do have Frank Sinatra on mine though [laughter]. And AC/DC, so I mean, that tells you sort of the spectrum.

JMD: Now, you said that, you used the analogy "pregame/postgame." Did your postgame music, kind of, at the end of the day either—as you were rolling back or when you were alone, getting ready for bed—did that music differ from the sort of music you would listen to before you went out? [Heads nod affirmatively.] How so?

OFFICER #1: Well, for me, at night, that was the way for me to drown out the generators and all the crap. So I was listening to a lot of classical, a lot of jazz, mellow things in the evening, just trying to go to sleep.

OFFICER #6: I'd listen to Norah Jones and I'd hear the fork lifts in the background, "beep beep beep beep." It kind of lulls you to sleep actually, the sound of, you know, containers moving.

OFFICER #1: The one thing that I will say about that is at night, the one sound—absence of sound—that pissed me off greater than any other was when the air conditioner quit working. I mean I was awake like that [he snaps his fingers] when the air conditioner quit working cause I knew it was about to be 190 degrees in there.

OFFICER #2: I had a white noise file that was about ten minutes long and so I'd loop it on my computer.

JMD: For nighttime?

OFFICER #2: Yeah.

JMD: And have it going all the way through?

OFFICER #2: Yeah.

JMD: OK, when you were listening to music at night, was it through your laptop speakers or did you have headphones on? How did that work?

OFFICER #2: Mine was through the computer and the speakers on the computer.

OFFICER #1: Cause you still need to be able to hear if somebody is actually . . .

JMD: Could you ever hear people next door to you, could you hear their music as well? Was there bleed-through . . . between living quarters?

OFFICER #3: We were in a big warehouse, so we were all together. First Arm in fact had to lay down the law and say "hey, no music unless you have some kind of [headphones], just can't have it."

OFFICER #5: I hate when people know that I was listening to Frank Sinatra! [laughter]

JMD: Well I appreciate your candor. [laughter]

OFFICER #5: For me, the premission stuff was to get you amped up, you know, so all the things you're talking about: Metallica, Slipknot, for me it was AC/DC, Styx, that kind of stuff. But you try to get amped up and alert, motivated and ready to go, and then when I would come back in it was, do your debrief and time to chill out and try to unwind and mellow out, so the music kind of went with that ebb and flow.

JMD: When you were in urban area on patrol would you ever hear Iraqi music coming from storefronts or just in public spaces?

OFFICER #5: I mean I don't consciously remember, but it seems like we would.

OFFICER #1: What I remember are the taxicabs, it's like getting in a taxi in New York, with the crazy music going.

JMD: Were you regularly taking cabs?

OFFICER #1: No, but I was regularly out on the streets.

JMD: OK, so you would hear the music from taxicabs while you're in your vehicle.

OFFICER #1: Well, and two because of what I was doing I remember spending a lot of time with the different ethnic groups in Kirkuk. So, if I would go into an office that was primarily Kurd, you would hear Kurdish music sometimes playing. Or, if they were Arab, you know, vice versa. And we did a project with a museum in the city of Kirkuk, and they had specific ethnic music and dance and costume and art and things like this, so, you know, I was exposed to it that way as well.

JMD: So could you, by the end, discern Kurdish music from Arabic music?

OFFICER #1: Yeah, probably. I would say with about 80 percent certainty.

JMD: Is it safe to say that was something you didn't know how to do before you were deployed?

OFFICER #1: Oh yeah.

JMD: Last question, because I think, how are we doing on time? Yeah, we're past [the agreed-upon time limit]. So, you spent a fair amount of time listening to music while you were deployed and you still have that music, right? You still have your iPods. Do you find yourself—is there any change in your music listening practices, having been there? Like is there any music you listened to there that you no longer listen to? Like has your taste for gangster rap extended into . . .

OFFICER #6: I still listen to some gangster rap. It reminds me of my soldiers. When you hear a certain song you're like, "Oh! Sergeant Ortiz!! This is his song." So I think it kind of stayed with me.

OFFICER #2: "Hells Bells" is probably a song that I have no interest in hearing cause it got played over and over and over and over and over again.

OFFICER #5: I listen to that all the time. It's a good song.

OFFICER #4: One thing I think is interesting is sort of based on what you said is that I've always listened to rock music but I didn't listen to as much of the really hard stuff until I deployed and I think it's part deployment and part being around young soldiers, but you're just introduced to new types of music and I definitely listened to more hard metal than I would have listened to beforehand. And I still do. So that's change and I haven't changed back or anything.

JMD: Did you or any of your soldiers play music while you were there? Did any of your soldiers have guitars?

OFFICER #3: Yeah, I did, several, actually, soldiers had guitars.

OFFICER #6: I had a harmonica, it's kind of sad.

OFFICER #1: We had bagpipes. We had a lieutenant that played bagpipes.

JMD: Did you really?

OFFICER #1: And he used to play them around call to prayer time in the evening. But the thing that struck me is that he played them for all of the memorial services.

JMD: Did he play "Amazing Grace"? [Officer #1 nods affirmatively.]

OFFICER #1: And that's somewhat unsettling.

OFFICER #4: We had the exact same thing.

JMD: Unsettling how?

OFFICER #1: Well, just to be in that situation and hear that then, when it's being played for somebody you know . . . And then to hear that same kind of haunting sound now, I guess one thing that we haven't really talked to now is the importance of sound in context and out of context. Like, that big bang when we first started this [he is referring to a loud bang that emanated from a nearby construction site at the beginning of our interview]. In Iraq, you know, it means one thing. Here, it means something else and it took me a long time to get used to hearing sounds out of that context.

OFFICER #4: Yeah, like fireworks. When you first redeploy and you hear fireworks, your heart rate escalates, you move away from the windows and you can't, at least with me, if I wanted to stop I could not stop, like my neighbor would shoot off some bottle rockets and they were popping out back and I'd move away from the windows but I'd be like, "It's just fireworks." And so I'd stop and my heart rate was getting up and I moved back and then it sets off again and I move away from the windows and I know not to move away from the windows, but I can't help but move away from the windows and get anxious about these fireworks and stuff, but of course that goes away after a little bit.

OFFICER #5: On my R and R I come back to Fort Lewis, and the brigade that's training to go is doing artillery and in the middle of the night all of a sudden [makes explosive sounds] it's like, "oh my gosh!" You just wake up thinking "what IED went off?" and all that kind of stuff. So sounds are associated with events, they're sort of the physically, emotional responses to it. You know, the bagpipes and "Amazing Grace," every time I hear that I get shot back [in time] because I associate it with memorial ceremonies. There are certain songs that remind me of my family and the songs I would play that would comfort me with home and when I hear them now I get kinda choked up. "Silent Night": that's associated with a particular memory about being away at Christmas time and it always gets me. Those sorts of songs continue in my listening repertoire because they're associated with something more than just the music itself.

Fragment #6

Keeping the music turned down low

SHYMAA'S STORY

Shymaa is an intensely thoughtful young woman, described by her friends as loyal and quietly humorous.[1] She grew up in Baghdad, going to college there and later working, along with her husband, for the department in the Iraqi government that implemented the UN Oil-for-Food program. Before the war started, no one in her family or social circles spent much time thinking about their sectarian heritage. Back then, the fact that she, a Sunni, chose to marry a Shi'i man was not considered remarkable in any way, or even worthy of comment. It was only after the post-invasion fighting began that their sectarian affiliations became conspicuous, and even dangerous. This, along with the fact that both Shymaa and her husband risked their lives by spending five of the wartime years working for a US government agency, provided ample rationale for their decision, in 2008, to emigrate to the United States.

In 2009, as we sat in their sparsely furnished living room in suburban Northern Virginia, Shymaa described the considerable challenges she and her family had faced during their years in wartime Baghdad. On the day the war began, she was in her third month of pregnancy. She recalled the discomfort she endured during the Shock and Awe campaign: "I do remember with all the nausea of pregnancy and stuff like that I would want to go to the bathroom—sorry to tell you about that—but my husband would say, 'Well, you can't. You can't. We have to hide [i.e., seek shelter from the bombing].'" Their house was in the Saydiya neighborhood, just around a bend in the Tigris from Saddam Hussein's principal palaces, which meant they were within earshot of some of the most intense bombing of the campaign. Like many others in the neighborhood, Shymaa's family was worried that Hussein would order the use of chemical weapons, so they had designated a small room in their house as the place where they would take refuge if the bombs got too close or clouds of gas rolled up the streets. The windows were taped shut and covered with sandbags, and almost all of the furniture had been removed so that nothing would fall on them if the house shook from a blast. "It was like a lab," she recalled, with "all the room . . . wrapped, like surrounded with covering so that nothing will get in." Aside from gas masks and boxes of cotton balls and a few other supplies, the room was bare. When the bombing started, they retreated to that room, isolated and insulated from everything—except, of course, the sound of the explosions, which easily penetrated the walls, rattling the family within.

WORKING FOR THE US GOVERNMENT

They were shaken, but they survived. They survived the bombing, the invasion, and the fall of the Hussein regime a few weeks later. In early 2004, when her daughter Rania was five months old, Shymaa applied to work with a US government agency in the Green Zone. Soon after, her husband got a job with the same agency as a driver. Their jobs were rewarding, their colleagues interesting, and it was a relief to have money coming in to the household again. But like all Iraqis who worked for the US-led forces, they were in a state of near-constant risk. For one thing, in the Green Zone, mortars were lobbed around them so frequently that they soon learned to ignore them. (One of her cowork- ers said that after a while, when Shymaa and her fellow FSNs [foreign service nation- als] heard the "duck and cover" alarm, "they'd just pat their helmets and keep typing.") More nerve-wracking was the journey to and from work; if they were recognized upon entering or leaving the Green Zone, insurgent forces would target them for kidnapping, torture, or execution.

I would totally feel safer in the Green Zone. Because what I'm mostly afraid of is when I come into and I go out of the Green Zone. We were afraid of the check- points. Because the thing that happened is people started to target FSNs, locally engaged staff who have been working with the US government and with the [new] Iraqi government as well.

As the insurgency gained strength and sectarian violence also increased, the residents of Saydiya, like many others documented in this book, regularly heard Kalashnikov battles on their streets. The violence got so bad that the military, in conjunction with the local government, surrounded their neighborhood with blast walls and closed off all roads except for a single, heavily guarded entrance and exit point. This arrangement extended their commute into and out of the Green Zone considerably, as it would often take over ninety minutes of waiting in line at the checkpoint before they would be allowed to return home. According to Shymaa, crossing through the checkpoints into their neighborhood and into the Green Zone was the most dangerous activity they regularly performed.

SOCIAL LIFE, MUSICAL PRACTICES

As I have discussed earlier, this constriction and complication of physical movement, when combined with the temporal restrictions of the citywide curfew, effectively obliterated many of the social practices of Iraqis in the capital. Shymaa wistfully described Baghdad's nightlife before the war:

> It was normal, it was like anywhere else in the world. We used to go to parties, we used to celebrate the New Year's Eve, I do remember that . . . Even [during] Eid and [days that] people would describe as a religious holiday . . . we would go to parties, we'd go to clubs. We used to come back home, my husband and I, at 2:00 or 3:00 in the morning if it's a party, because it was safe, it was normal. People did that the whole time, just like anything else, life was normal, just like driving, just like [going to] the swimming pool . . . all of these habits or things we used to do normally before the war, but then after the war [they were] prohibited.

In this atmosphere of constrained possibilities, musical expression came under increasing attack. Before the war, Shymaa and her friends were strikingly ecumenical consumers of music: in public and in private, in nightclubs and in their houses, they listened to a broad array of Iraqi and western popular music, from Kazem al-Saher to the Irish boy band Westlife. But, she explained, after the Sunni-led al-Qaeda in Iraq (also called the Islamic State of Iraq or ISI) and a number of conservative Shi'i clerics began denouncing music—particularly western and Arabic popular music—labeling it *haram*, or forbidden, it became dangerous to play music publicly.[2] She described incidents where fighters targeted weddings, killing the band and even the bride and groom simply because music was being played. These killings were often videotaped, she said, and then sold on VCDs on the street or posted on the Internet. The warning was clear: secular musical expression would not be tolerated.

Shymaa took this warning to heart. While she didn't stop listening to music at home, she did develop a hypersensitivity to music played at high (read: dangerous) volume:

> Ah, one thing probably worth saying is that before the war, I used to like hearing music loud, but after the war, no. I would get really nervous when my husband would turn the volume on and we'd hear something very loud. I can't just bear it so I always hear stuff really with a low volume. I cannot stand very high—although before I used to hear it loud.

Under these circumstances, the safest music was privatized music, listened to on a portable device, through headphones. Shymaa didn't know of anyone who had an Apple-produced iPod, but inexpensive Chinese MP3 players were widely available throughout the country. These machines afforded her, her family, and her friends the ability to listen to music privately, without putting herself at risk. When I asked her if she still had the MP3 player she had used during the war, she said, "I do have one of them—it's one of my old friends." It took her a few minutes to find, but she eventually came back into the living room and placed a small, generic, purple unit in my hand. Her daughter Rania, now five years old, approached me and peered at it with curiosity. I turned it on. The tiny black-and-white screen of the generic device flashed a single word, pirated from the west: "IPOD." Shymaa beamed and said, "That's an old friend of mine!"

It's a black picture. . . . It's a black picture.
—*RAED GEORGE*

7

A Time of Troubles for Iraqi Music

THE PAST DECADE has witnessed a significant wave of scholarship on music and violence, with conferences, edited volumes, and professional organizations all taking up the theme.[1] Much of this activity has been clustered around two general questions: how music composition and performance can be deployed in service of reconciliation and memorialization; and, conversely, how music can incite, exacerbate, symbolize, and even embody violence. These questions share an epistemological frame that foregrounds music's agential dimension, its ability to either "promot[e] peace or perpetuat[e] discord."[2] One could write voluminously about recent attempts to exploit the agential dimension of Iraqi music within projects of conflict and/or reconciliation; one could also spend comparable space conducting close readings of pieces composed and performed by Iraqi musicians during the war to uncover their richness as symbols of, and heuristic models for, these processes. But to do these topics justice, one would have to have more experience with Iraqi music and Arabic language than I do, and so I will leave that important work to specialists in music traditions of the region.[3] My goal here is much simpler: I want to create a small space for a provisional accounting of the range of violent and aggressive acts that were directed toward musicians, music listeners, music venues, musical instruments, musical repertoires, and sounds coded as "music" during Operation Iraqi Freedom.[4] In doing so, I am not arguing that Iraqi music was devoid of efficacy in all instances—quite the contrary: the survival of music practices within the crucible of the war is ample testament to the value they have for practitioners and listeners alike. I merely submit that in a shocking number of cases, musicians and musical practices ended up performing the role not of *agent* but of *victim*: they were recipients of acts of violence, aggression, and silencing that were directed specifically toward music qua music. The frequency and intensity of these violent acts, I argue, severely degraded music's capacity to serve as a force for reconciliation during the war. As a member of an academic field (music studies) that generally understands music to possess a special affective power in the world, I recognize that a chapter devoted entirely to music's *powerlessness* or inefficacy is something of an anomaly. But this is precisely what the situation on the ground demands.

One thing bears repeating: the following is an anecdotal account of the *range* of violent acts toward music, not their number. While I do mention some provisional figures that have appeared in public forums, I must stress that there are no reliable statistics for the types of violent incidents that concern me here. What follows is a partial record of incidents that were documented in the English-language press, both professional and amateur (i.e., newspapers, TV news accounts, and well-known blogs); and classified US military reports that were subsequently leaked to the public. The documentation for even these incidents is exceedingly sparse—hence the brevity of the descriptions below. I include this chapter despite the paucity of available information because the import of these incidents strikes me as profound, and profoundly troubling. The story of sound and listening in the Iraq War cannot be told without them.

IRAQ'S MUSICAL LEGACY

In order to understand the site-specific resonance of the acts that follow, it is important to note the prominent role that music has played throughout Iraq's history. Beginning in the Abbasid period (750–1258 C.E.), Baghdad enjoyed a reputation as one of the central locations for the study and practice of art music in the Arab world. For more than a millennium, the area now known as Iraq was a center for makers and players of the oud and an important site for Muslim, Christian, and Jewish music. In the early twentieth century, the collaborative influence of all three religions (but especially of Jewish instrumentalists) could be discerned in the efflorescence of the *Baghdadi maqam*, a vibrant music tradition that made a powerful contribution to the art musics of the Arab world. Later, numerous cultural institutions supported a range of musical activities, from *maqam* to western classical music; the Iraqi National Symphony Orchestra, Baghdad Institute of Music, Baghdad Music Academy, and Baghdad Music and Ballet School attracted professional musicians from every corner of the country and the region more broadly. Contemporary musicians and other observers have frequently noted the bitter irony that one of the principal historical centers of music in the Arab world has become a place where Arab musicians are regularly killed for playing music.[5]

To acknowledge this irony is not to say that attacks against musicians and musical practices never occurred prior to Operation Iraqi Freedom. Without dwelling on violent acts that have been lost to antiquity or even those that Iraqi musicians may have endured during the Ottoman period or the Hashemite monarchy, it is incontestable that the Hussein regime visited many cruelties upon Sufi singers and Kurdish musicians, from low-grade disruption of music events to imprisonment and torture, and in so doing established itself as a regime that was hostile to musicians of marginalized populations. The UN-imposed sanctions that followed the first Gulf War added extreme privation to the list of challenges musicians faced, compelling even more musicians, along with ordinary citizens, to flee Iraq for Jordan, Syria, Egypt, the United Arab Emirates, and other places where an Arab musician might stand a greater chance of making a living.

A particularly surreal chapter in Iraq's musical history was initiated around 1993, when Saddam Hussein's son Uday emerged as the head of a media empire that included the country's most popular television station and Voice of Iraq FM, a youth-oriented radio station that broadcast western pop music and featured English-speaking DJs—in flagrant contradiction of a Baath Party edict prohibiting American cultural products.[6] In order for Iraqi musicians to get airtime on his stations or even perform in public, the "Music Czar," as he was popularly known, had to give them his personal stamp of approval, confirming that they had the requisite amount of "patriotic" (i.e., pro-Hussein) songs in their repertoires and that their music conformed to his personal tastes. In a state that jammed foreign radio broadcasts, outlawed satellite dishes, and controlled all Internet servers, Uday enjoyed a virtual monopoly on the TV and radio dissemination of popular culture.[7] He was known to harass and torture musicians whom he didn't like, but he was terrifying even to those whom he patronized. In an interview with the *New York Times* conducted in early April 2003, musician Ismail Hussain described his harrowing interactions with Uday:

> The security people picked me up at the Rashid Hotel. They always picked me up at a hotel. And it was always at night. The car had curtained windows because they didn't want us to know where we were going. I was scared for my life. At Uday's house the security was all around—men with guns in green uniforms. The guards took us in, and an hour later Uday came. This was in 1993. He said, "I want to hear this song and that song," and I played them.
>
> . . . Uday didn't need an occasion to have a party. While many people in Iraq were starving, he'd bring out tables and tables of food and drink. Uday liked barbecues and Hennessy and rum; Hennessy was his favorite drink. . . . He'd get drunk and dance—he was a good dancer too. Later, he'd bring out the machine guns and

start shooting them off. He'd point the guns right over my head, and the bullets would spray all over the place. . . . I would sing right through the flying bullets. I couldn't hear the music anymore. I'd just keep going, because I couldn't stop. You just can't. I'd sing until dawn or later. It ended when Uday was ready for it to end."[8]

In the face of such abuse, many Iraqi musicians emigrated. Kazem al-Saher, Iraq's most famous living musician, angered Uday by refusing to perform at Hussein family gatherings. Uday subsequently banned al-Saher's songs from TV and radio, and, according to al-Saher, threatened his life, compelling him to flee the country.[9] Other respected musicians such as Raed George, Hussam al-Rassam, and Naseer Shamma emigrated during this period as well.

POST-INVASION CHALLENGES

When the Hussein regime began to crumble in April 2003, two major fluctuations in the country's musical life occurred—one immediately, the other more gradually. First, patriotic songs praising Hussein and the regime, songs which had been a ubiquitous presence on Iraqi airwaves for decades, vanished, seemingly overnight, as the regime's radio and TV employees fled their posts. The regime change, in the political sense, was in this way preceded by the end of the mass-mediated wing of Saddam Hussein's decades-long sonic campaign. This development in turn enabled a regime change in the auditory sense of the term: no longer was the consumption of Iraqi media filtered through the knowledge that it was coming from the Hussein government. Suddenly, coalition forces controlled a large portion of the airwaves, and with this control, local ideas about the nature of media, and about how to interpret radio broadcasts, were recalibrated according to the political sensibilities of the listenership.

Later, in the ensuing weeks, as exiled musicians began returning to the country and domestic musicians who had been suppressed by the Hussein regime began testing the waters, music in numerous registers began to fill the airwaves and public spaces in the capital and major cities. Now the music one heard was no longer that which Uday Hussein had vetted. The Hussein government could no longer jam the coalition broadcasts, and its control over live music performance in the capital was broken. In the new, ostensibly democratic, post-Hussein era, American officials predicted, a cultural renaissance would soon blossom.

As it happened, both of these developments proved ephemeral: over time, as anti-occupation sentiment and nostalgia for the Hussein era grew, some of the paeans praising Saddam returned, circulated this time on CDs sold at markets and on the internet. And political instability, along with sectarian campaigns directed against music, ended up creating a strikingly inhospitable environment for musicians, dashing the hopes for a revival of a vibrant culture of public music in post-Hussein Iraq.

Raed George was one of the musicians who attempted to return. A beloved figure throughout Iraq and laureate of numerous international festivals, George was a model of musical ecumenicalism. In his compositions and arrangements, many for film soundtracks, his knowledge of *maqam* and traditional instrumentation complemented his fluency with the idioms and instrumentarium of the western orchestra. He had served in the army band throughout the Iran-Iraq War in the 1980s, where he traveled up and down the front line singing patriotic songs and entertaining the troops. In the 1990s, he gravitated toward popular music, composing a number of successful pop songs before he emigrated to the United States in 1997. In the States, he began composing sacred music for the Chaldean Christian community, of which he was a member.

In 2003, as soon as the Hussein regime fell, George returned to Iraq. His plan was to relocate there permanently, but after a year, he realized it was impossible:

After the war it was chaos. After the war, when the country fails, everything fails, including the arts. The songs [in postwar Iraq] are not deep [i.e., not profound]. And there are many religious styles now in Iraq that [are clashing]. So it's different, and it's a black picture. Not only the songs, everything is not deep in Iraq, all of the art. . . . It's a black picture.[10]

By early 2004, it was clear to George that the atmosphere in Baghdad was far too unstable and chaotic for him to stay. He returned, reluctantly, to his adopted home in Dearborn, Michigan. In the ensuing months and years, as the insurgency gained strength, sectarian violence mounted, and the situation for musicians grew immeasurably worse, he became increasingly convinced that he had made the right choice. And he wasn't alone: according to the Iraqi Ministry of Culture, by 2008, roughly 80 percent of singers who were performing during the Hussein era had left the country.[11] The challenges faced by those who stayed were immense. In addition to the threat of violence, something as pedestrian as the absence of reliable electricity played havoc with musical practices. (Those who needed amplifiers had to fuel them, transport them to their engagements, and then compete with the sound of their gas generators to be heard by their audiences, for example.) More fundamentally, though, the war created a pervasive atmosphere of vulnerability, in which many people began to regard music as an unattainable luxury, or as an anachronistic cultural product at odds with the radical pragmatics of the moment. As an Iraqi woman who, like her idol Raed George, emigrated to Dearborn, told me:

We weren't really paying attention to music, because we were worried about staying safe. During bombing we only listened to news. *The situation was too serious for music.* . . . How can I listen to the music when I'm worrying about sirens and bombing and having no gas or electricity?[12]

Utterances like these give shade and contour to the "black picture" for Iraqi music that Raed George painted. While a wide range of music practices indisputably survived throughout the war, musicians and listeners faced political, logistical, and psychological obstacles that increased the risk and labor involved in performance and public listening.

POLITICAL VIOLENCE

Physical violence toward Iraqi music and musicians took place in two waves and came from multiple sources. The first wave was political, retributive, and swift. After decades of uncontested authority, the musicians who were patronized by the Hussein regime found themselves the objects of criticism, scorn, and physical attacks as soon as the regime crumbled in the spring of 2003. The first well-known musician to fall victim to this political shift was named Daoud Qais. Qais was a member of the Baath party, and a personal favorite of Saddam Hussein. Once described as "the voice of public adoration for Saddam Hussein," his songs praising the leader were a ubiquitous presence on radio and television in the years before Operation Iraqi Freedom. According to an employee of the artists' union, which Qais chaired, "If there was a symbol of the regime, it was Daoud. . . . He stood for everything Saddam did, and we hated him as much as Saddam. To kill him would be an honor." On May 21, 2003, less than a month after President Bush declared "major combat operations" to be over, Qais was shot dead. Assassins called out his name and shot him "at the gate of the house Hussein had given him."[13] Qais may have been killed for his political affiliation, but it was his *music* that made this affiliation public and active; it was through his music that he contributed to the authoritarian government's propaganda campaign. In the weeks to follow, other cultural figures who had been allied with the Hussein regime were similarly killed.

SECTARIAN VIOLENCE

The second, more sustained wave of aggressive acts toward music and musicians had little to do with the musicians' political affiliations. Rather, it represented a spectacularly violent episode within—or, some would call it, *distortion of*—an intrafaith debate on the status of music that has persisted, in various registers and locales, through the entire history of Islam. The culturally inflected dynamics and historically contingent details of this debate have been extensively discussed elsewhere.[14] Here, I will limit myself to describing its general contours so as to contextualize the contemporary situation in Iraq.

A scholarly ambivalence toward the large subset of sounds and practices that are commonly called "music" can be traced back at least as far as the ninth century C.E. with an enormous range of discrete positions articulated over the centuries. The key Islamic texts possess enough polysemy to buttress the arguments of all parties in this debate. The

Quran, the ultimate authority upon which matters of Islamic law are based, makes no explicit mention of music; hence exegetes have chosen to interpret some of its passages as giving implicit approval or disapproval to music. Further justification of contrasting positions has been found in the Hadith, collections of sayings that have been attributed to the Prophet Muhammad. Examples of these positions can be found throughout the literature on music and Islam. In an influential volume on the subject, Amnon Shiloah describes the position of Ibn al-Jawzi (d. 1200), a prominent medieval theologian, as "claim[ing] that music is basically a temptation of the devil who dominates the soul and makes it a slave to passion." Music, according to this line of reasoning, is an intoxicant, "provoking worldly passions and sensual pleasures usually associated with other indulgences such as drinking to excess and fornication."[15] Shiloah follows this description with a counterexample from another scholar, this time from the late fourteenth century. Ibn Rajab (d. 1392) "speaks of two categories of music: one discusses it as an amusing pastime, the other as a means for consolidating faith in God and purifying the heart."[16] Intermediate positions between these two extremes are plentiful.

Within the spectrum of attitudes toward music, some are more widespread than others. The majority of the faithful in both camps consider some sounds that non-Muslims might hear as "musical" to be wholly outside this debate; for example, Quranic cantillation and some kinds of devotional vocal practice—the very vocalizations that American service members defined in musical terms in chapter 1. Conversely, many devout Muslims who consider much music to be either pious and enlightening or simply innocuous would agree that some music—such as that with explicitly erotic lyrics—should be labeled *haram*.

While music may have generated some ambivalence among a considerable plurality of the world's Muslim faithful, it does not follow that this attitude leads ineluctably to violence against music and musicians. Aggressive intolerance toward music is the product of a volatile complex of theological arguments, influential voices, local histories, emplaced sentiments, and other sociopolitical factors.[17] The situation that obtained in wartime Iraq, while hardly singular, was deeply inflected by local dynamics. In particular, the presence of two radicalized, heavily armed, and deeply antagonistic sectarian groups was a distinctive element in the Iraqi case. The ethos of these groups contrasted sharply with that of the secular Hussein regime, which had suppressed religious intolerance of music for decades.[18] For the Sunni warriors of al-Qaeda in Iraq and the Shi'i soldiers of the Mahdi Army, two groups that clashed violently in the years following the fall of Hussein, music provided an exceedingly rare point of convergence. Both groups, when they weren't targeting one another, were involved in attacks on musicians in Iraq. As Muhammad Rashid, the owner of a music shop in Baghdad, memorably remarked to journalist Sammy Ketz in 2008, "The Mehdi Army and Al-Qaeda only ever agreed on one point—that we are servants of the devil."[19]

Ketz's article documents a number of violent acts directed at Iraqi musicians. (Figure 7.1 depicts a minor music store bombing similar to the ones he discusses.) One

FIGURE 7.1 An Iraqi boy walks out from a music CD shop that fundamentalists had bombed the night before in Baghdad's Saydiya neighborhood, 2004. (Photo by Ali al-Saadi/AFP/Getty Images)

involved saxophonist Ayad Hair, who, in 2006, "was killed at his home in Sadr City by militiamen—in front of his children." His corpse was subsequently burned. Later that day, Ali Mohammad, a tambourine player and acquaintance of Hair, was also killed. "The militiamen explained to the musicians' families that this will be the fate of all those 'who transgress holy law.'"[20] The article lists a number of other incidents, including the bombing of Mohammad Rashid's music shop, and describes the practice whereby elements of the Mahdi Army and the Sunni al-Qaeda affiliate each independently assaulted musicians on the street and destroyed their instruments. One particularly chilling practice was described by Ali Kassem, a Baghdad-based trumpet player. "We have had some really rough times!" he exclaimed. "I have friends who were killed when they showed up to play for fake weddings set up as ambushes. . . . And yet I am sure that nothing in the Koran forbids our art."[21]

A Reuters report from 2008 describes another bombing of a music shop, this time in the southern port city of Basra. Members of the Mahdi Army bombed Haider Lefta's music shop three times. He closed the shop for three years, opening up again in 2008 when it looked like the violence had subsided somewhat. On his first day back at work, someone threw a grenade into the shop.[22] This practice was lamentably common.[23] US military reports that were leaked to the public by the Wikileaks organization document an epidemic of bombings and armed attacks on music shops in 2007 and 2008.

FREEMUSE, the World Forum on Music and Censorship, is a nongovernmental organization based in Denmark. In 2007, the group's website published the story of Seif Yehia, a twenty-three-year-old singer. That year, Yehia was beheaded "for singing western songs at weddings." The article cited sobering figures released by the Iraqi Artists' Association: by their count, at least 115 singers were killed in the first five years of the war. Concert halls in Baghdad and Basra had been damaged by grenade and mortar attacks, attacks which left an unspecified number of victims in their wake.[24]

In 2006, the news service of the UN Office for the Coordination of Humanitarian Affairs published a story about Youssef Jabry. Jabry, thirty-nine, was a well-known singer from Baghdad. He and his brother sang western music at weddings and other events. In 2006, his brother was killed. "They broke into our house shouting his name loudly. They carried him off and a week later we found his decapitated body with a note saying that this was the destiny of those who sing American words." His brother was twenty years old; Jabry, weeping, remembered him as "a happy boy whose life was ended by those who twist Islamic law according to their own ideology and change it according to what suits them." Ten months earlier, a group of extremists had approached him while he was singing at a wedding. "[They] told me that I cannot sing the music of the devil and if I continued I was going to be killed. Since then, I only sing Arabic songs. People still insist that I sing western songs but I cannot put my life at risk."[25]

In 2008, Selcan Hacaoglu, a journalist who worked for Bloomberg and the Associated Press, reported a suicide bombing in Balad Ruz, a majority Shi'i town northeast of Baghdad. A woman who was attending a wedding "blew herself up as people were dancing and clapping while members of the passing wedding party played music." Minutes later, once first responders had arrived at the scene, a male bomber triggered a second detonation. In all, thirty-five people were killed, with another sixty-five, including the bride and groom, wounded.

The pace of attacks on musicians and their audiences has slowed since its peak in 2008, but music-related violence continues to occur as of this writing. As recently as the spring of 2012, news began to spread of a large-scale attack on Iraqi youths who participated in a local iteration of the American-derived musical subculture known as "emo." Extremist forces in Iraq have branded the "emos"—whom they identify through their hairstyles, manner of dress, and musical choices—as devil worshippers. With the possible participation of local police and in the face of a number of contradictory pronouncements by the government (including one by the Interior Ministry that supported efforts to "eliminate" the "Satanists"), unidentified killers have murdered somewhere between a few dozen and over a hundred young people, often by crushing their heads with concrete blocks. In an article for the *Guardian,* Scott Long reported that two of the killed were members of an emo metal band; they were murdered shortly after one of the band members uploaded their music video onto YouTube, along with their names.[26]

US FORCES TARGETING MUSIC

In stark contrast to the sectarian groups who launched the attacks above, the US forces in Iraq had no philosophical or religious qualms with music. They did not equate musical sounds with devil worship, or regard them as an affront to God. As a group, they did, however, regard some modes of religious vocality (which they invariably labeled "music") with considerable suspicion, hearing in them the potential for the transmission of enemy messages, insurgent instructions, and a general ethos of violent rebellion. Within the classified military reports labeled "the War Logs" by the Wikileaks organization, one can find evidence of great apprehension when "music" was projected from mosque minarets to the belligerent crowds below. A typical report describes an engagement between US forces and a large contingent of insurgents on April 21, 2004, in Fallujah. After taking fire from a grove of palm trees, the patrol called in for air support. In the ensuing ground/air battle, thirty-six people labeled "enemy" were killed. Other than these numbers, the sole detail given in the report concerns the ominous presence of "music" and speech coming from the mosque:

> [One of the] commanding officers reported music coming from the mosque to the [southeast]. The lyrics said "God is good, God is great" and "holy warriors come out to fight." The mosque was also telling the people to rise up and fight and appeared to be giv[ing] orders.[27]

At times "music" triggered military action even when it was not being played. Numerous reports document incidents in which the possession of "music" recordings was presented as cause for suspicion. The following report is typical. On March 9, 2006, a Marine detachment detained two Iraqi males in central Fallujah, "while conducting intelligence driven cordon and searches." The report continues:

> Abed Deiaa Fallah and Massod Abed Fallah were detained for possessing insurgent newsletters and music relating to the insurgency. The music on their cell

phone matched the music used in numerous insurgent propaganda sniper videos. Both [men] are currently en route to 2/6 BDF to undergo further questioning.[28]

Similarly, on May 25, 2006, a report details how the Iraqi army (IA), in a "partnered patrol" with the US army, detained six Iraqis near Tikrit. The patrol "noticed a speeding vehicle with plates from Ramadi," stopped it, and searched the driver and passengers. After labeling them "suspicious," the report details how:

> the interpreter listened to their audio cassettes that were in the vehicle. The tapes included AIF[29] propaganda. The IA confiscated the vehicle and moved the detainees to their home in Tikrit . . . to check for more propaganda with nothing found. All [passengers] were detained and vehicle was towed by the IA because of AIF audio tapes and a cell phone with a ring tone of music that praises AIF. The IA has started the questioning and will report results to the [task force] . . .[30]

On September 28 of the same year, an Army group in Ulwan al Khalf detained four alleged AIF members after searching their house and finding a small cache of arms and a cell phone that had "jihad music" on it. The "music" in question in all three reports was almost certainly the nashid, a genre of praise song that predates, but has come to be tightly associated with, the insurgency and militant Islam more generally.[31] Iraqi nashids run the gamut from austere unaccompanied monophony (and therefore unlikely to cross the conservative threshold that regards music as *haram*) to much more slickly produced, multitrack pieces with drums and, often, other instrumental accompaniment.

It is impossible to know how many Iraqi men were detained for possessing nashids or other "suspicious" recordings. Questions regarding this practice proliferate: Were these detentions anomalies? Or were they part of a broader effort to effectively criminalize the militant nashid, along with the act of listening to it, or even of possessing it? How reliably could service members—who were radically dependent upon the expertise of interpreters or Iraqi army elements attached to their units—identify a recording as one praising "anti-Iraq forces?" How many Iraqi men were detained and interrogated because of a cassette tape found in a car's glove box?

What is striking here is the degree to which "music," in the form of recorded sound, acquired the status of irrefutable evidence of affiliation. It appears that, in some instances at least, possession of a suspicious ringtone served as sufficient grounds for the prolonged detention and interrogation of Iraqi subjects. The extreme challenges detainees endured, and the difficulty of proving one's innocence once one entered the detention system, have been well documented.[32] The crushing role that music has played within the US-controlled detention system has been intensively explored.[33] But the extent to which recorded sound, in the form of "music" or speech, participated in the processes whereby Iraqi auditors were inducted into that system is only now beginning to be uncovered.

THE ATTENUATED ACOUSTIC TERRITORY OF IRAQI MUSICAL PRACTICE

Eleven years after Operation Iraqi Freedom was launched and over two years after the last US combat troops left the country, Iraq has emerged as a place of fragile possibility for musical practices. The country finds itself at the intersection of opposing trends. On the one hand, Iraqis have far freer access to music than they ever did under Hussein, when the music industry was controlled by his psychopathic son, the internet was tightly regulated, and the digital manifestation of globalization was in its infancy. Today, music in Iraq is sold and consumed throughout the country in an unregulated free market of (largely pirated) recordings, and downloaded by anyone wealthy enough to have access to a networked computer. On the other hand, aggressive opponents of western music, and secular music more broadly, continue to pose a threat to Iraq's musicians, harassing music store owners, killing emos, and disrupting secular musical life. Through these activities (as well as through a more organic attenuation of interest on the part of the younger generation), Iraq's rich musical heritage—as a crucible for Arab music and a cosmopolitan haven for western classical forms—has been compromised. The old music institutions, the conservatories and other schools where Arab and western music were taught, have eroded, and no new state-run institutions have grown up to take their place.

The tripartite model found in chapters 3 through 5 can be used to clarify the complicated impact the war had on musical practices in Iraq. According to its terms, one could say that during the war, Shi'i and Sunni sectarian forces fought sonic campaigns in parallel; theirs were campaigns of erasure, silencing secular musical expression and any music that could be tied to the west. At the same time, they worked to adjust the auditory regimes of the Iraqi citizenry, criminalizing a genre of audition (aesthetic secular listening) that they claimed fueled decadent secularism and western-oriented modernity. Through violence, they attempted to conquer the acoustic territory, transforming it into a zone of audible fundamentalist Muslim devotion.

On the surface, the US-led coalition fought these moves, working instead to establish an expansive auditory regime of tolerant, one might say "neoliberal," audition that would exist within a socioeconomic framework of representative democracy and free markets. But the exigencies of the conflict demanded that the US forces attempt to exert regimental control over some sounds and modes of audition, and so they launched a sonic campaign against the militant nashid, a campaign that turned some locally-resonant modes of devout audition into suspicious activities, or even detainable offenses.

In the end, neither group fully succeeded in accomplishing its aims. The overlapping acoustic territories that they fought to establish are currently so deeply perforated as to be in tatters. According to the new Iraqi government's policies, Iraqi auditors can listen to whatever they want—but it is only safe to do so in private. Conservative critics of music have intimidated many musicians and convinced people like Raed George that it's better to remain in self-imposed exile—but in an era of internet and satellite TV, anti-music forces will always be fighting an uphill battle.

Regardless of their successes or failures, one thing appears clear: in an environment that remains only semi-electrified, where exhaustion and fear and privation and vulnerability are widespread, where the anti-musical forces of ISIS are ascendent, and where some choose to address theological disputes with guns drawn, the question of listening to music will always be posed as a problem. How can we listen to music without a reliable electric grid? How can we listen to music when the news is so troubling? How can we listen to music when life is so difficult? How can we listen to music if we are in mourning? How could one possibly listen to music if to do so is to offend God? How could one possibly listen to music if to do so is to risk being shot? On any given day, some people will eagerly expend the energy necessary to address these problems for themselves, and others will elect to leave them untouched. This is a roundabout way of saying that life in Iraq continues to be complicated, that complex persons (à la Gordon) are living complex lives in which the wartime distribution of the sensible continues to sow violence and instability. Coming to terms with that complexity has been one of the underlying objectives of this book.

Conclusion

Sound wounds.

This was the first working title of the book you are reading. It was the name I gave to my first lecture on the sounds of Operation Iraqi Freedom, back in 2008, when the war was in full swing, the troop surge at its peak. I liked it at the time because it could be taken in two ways: subject–predicate (i.e., what does belliphonic sound do? It *wounds*, it damages the ears and psyches of those who are exposed to it); but also adjective–noun (i.e., what kind of wounds are we talking about? *Sound* wounds, the invisible and omni-directional sensory and psychological damage incurred by those within the ambit of loud violent acts). I liked the economy of the phrase: two monosyllabic words, sharing almost all of their letters. The first word felt like the cruise missile passing Ali's third-story window, the second like the explosion echoing in the distance.[1]

I return to it here, at the end of this project, because the phrase encapsulates many of my thoughts regarding the role sound plays in wartime. Belliphonic sound is indexically rich and therefore a great source of information about proximate violent acts, yes . . . until it isn't: until through its intensity, proximity, tactility, or traumatic circularity it becomes a manifestation of violence in its own right. From the brute facticity of deafness and TBI to the echoic haunting of traumatic memory, the pain caused by the belliphonic can be insidious, debilitating, and lasting.

Sound wounds. The argument is simple, the implications profound.

Another working title of this book, and one that I frequently used while presenting this research in public, was *The Amplitude of Violence*. This phrase doesn't single out sound as an ontologically distinct phenomenon; rather, it draws attention to the sensory

272 Listening to War

intensity of the myriad violent acts that took place over the course of the war. For acousticians and other people who work with sound, the word *amplitude*, "the distance which an individual particle [in a medium such as air] moves from side to side in performing a complete vibration,"[2] describes the variable intensity of acoustic waves, an intensity that humans perceive as "loudness" or "volume": the greater the amplitude, the louder the sound. "Amplitude" thus points to the sonic dimension of armed violence, a crucial and complex parameter that has often been ignored by scholarly studies of war. At the same time, "amplitude" is commonly used among artillery specialists to describe "the range of a projectile," the circle of its potential reach. It is in this sense of range that a number of political scientists have employed the metaphorical phrase "amplitude of violence" to describe the area over which the repercussions of a violent act can be discerned.[3] Within the context of my work, I hear the phrase as addressing the fusion of the sensory and the geographical—the vast territories over which sonic violence exerts its complicated and often long-lasting effects.

In writing this book, I sought a deeper understanding of the dynamics of sound and listening in wartime, in the hopes that such an understanding would create new, productively estranged vantage points from which to bear witness to the violent acts that occurred during the Iraq war. I began by dealing with the specific characteristics of belliphonic sounds and the challenges they presented to military and civilian auditors (chapter 1). Thinking through these challenges, in turn, led to an explication of the different modes of audition that emerged and evolved as auditors confronted the belliphonic (chapter 2). A curiosity about the processes whereby service members and civilians learned to listen to the belliphonic resulted in an analysis of wartime auditory regimes (chapter 3). Attending to the causes and effects of sounds in the combat zone fueled my argument that the ontology of violence, like that of sound, is omnidirectional and vibrational. That argument in turn necessitated an expansion of the discursive category of victim to incorporate all parties who fall within the sensory field of a violent act (chapter 4). Tracing the lines of sound's emplacement, displacement, and transplacement in wartime Iraq highlighted the interpenetration of body and environment: sound's radiant properties territorialize spaces in and outside of bodies, while the resonant properties of body and environment both shape and are shaped by sounds (chapter 5). In these middle chapters, I pointed to the co-constitutive nature of auditory regimes, sonic campaigns, and acoustic territories, and argued that human experience unfolds at the nexus of these structures and those of their intersensorial analogues.

In the final section of the book I gave special attention to the subcategory of sounds called "music," the people who create and consume them, the technologies that deliver them, and the violent acts both enabled by and directed toward them. I dwelled on the ways that music served as a technology of the self that facilitates war fighting, and I showed how thoroughly mobile music technology was incorporated into the US military's activities in Iraq (chapter 6). Last, I bore witness to acts of violence and aggression that targeted Iraqi musicians, music listeners, musical instruments—even music itself (chapter 7).

One of my mantra-like arguments throughout this book has been that in wartime sound *matters*, that it is an important part of the sensory field through which violence, survival, and traumatic memory are enacted. But is it the only thing that matters? Obviously, tragically, not. Wartime violence creates vast numbers of auditory victims, and many of those sound wounds are grave—but acknowledging these invisible wounds doesn't erase the death and other more visible types of damage war produces. The expansive field of victimhood created by the omnidirectionality of sound and violence doesn't remove the distinction between the culpable and the innocent or the living and the dead. Nor does it obviate the need to acknowledge the networks of loss created by death, temporal networks that extend far beyond the reach of sensory stimuli, across generations. Over the course of Operation Iraqi Freedom the coalition lost 4,804 military service members, at least 468 contractors, and 10,125 Iraqi soldiers. A well-sourced conservative estimate puts the number of Iraqi civilians killed at 125,052 and rising as of 2013, although some estimates are significantly higher. Tragically, the number of Iraqi war casualties, which declined throughout the final years of Operation Iraqi Freedom, has risen over the past year to its previously high wartime levels as the population continues to suffer from the violent campaign of the "Islamic State" (aka IS, ISIS, ISIL, Daesh). We will never know how many civilians, let alone how many Iraqi insurgents and sectarian fighters, have been lost in the war and its complex aftermath. Collectively these losses vastly exceed the realm of sound. All the same, the mind reels and the ear rings at the number of unique voices that have been permanently silenced.

Ultimately, a study of the structures undergirding wartime sound and listening reveals some of the hidden complexities of wartime experience, and gives those in positions of power one more set of costs to consider before deciding whether or not to go to war. We all know war is terrible, but a focus on the sonic dimension of armed violence demonstrates that the ranks of victims are even larger, the costs of war even greater, the amplitude of violence even more intense and extensive than we have been conditioned to think.

At the same time, by focusing intermittently on the fine-grained experiences of individuals, I have attempted to get underneath these structures to gesture at the complex persons who populate the abstractions of regime, campaign, and territory. People may experience the world at the intersection of these macro forces, but they are not, or at least not always, immobilized within them. Outside the zone of extreme sensory assault (the trauma zone) that I document in chapter 2, iconoclastic auditory acts are possible, listening or sensing or thinking against the grain is possible—although extricating oneself from the homogenizing forces of radical sensory pragmatism sometimes requires more labor and energy than war-exhausted auditors possess. Still, in the utter absence of a solution to the problem of armed violence in general, or belliphonic violence more specifically, perhaps pointing out

such brazen acts of audition is the best one can do. Allen Feldman has argued that it
is not the mission of ethnographers of violent timespaces to "uncover conclusive exits
from the world-historical labyrinth of political terror." Instead, their best contribution may lie in "explor[ing] the 'middle passage' of oppression" and in "assembl[ing]
counterlabyrinths and countermemories against the forgetting of terror."[4] With this
in mind, I want to end with one last account of acoustic oppression and resistance,
one countermemory to place up against the terror of the Iraq war's sensory onslaught.
As soon as I heard this story, in 2008, I knew I wanted to end the book with it. Amid
all the accounts of pain and loss and defiance and survival that were told to me, the
small moment of auditory brilliance described in the final fragment was one of the
most inspiring and life-affirming that I encountered.

Fragment #7

Listening as Poiesis

TAREQ'S STORY

TAREQ IS A tall, lanky dentist from Baghdad.[1] His wavy hair and mustache offset a ready smile and almost perpetual state of bemusement. When I met him in Amman shortly after he sought refuge there in 2007, Tareq's horsy, infectious laugh struck me as simultaneously goofy and heroic. It was evidence that, despite having endured some horrifying experiences, he had not been completely beaten down.

From childhood until the moment he left the country, Tareq had lived with his mother in the al-Binouq neighborhood, the gateway to the Shi'i stronghold of Sadr City and a location of extraordinary violence during the hot years of the war. In 2006, he and his mother witnessed dozens of battles between members of the Shi'i Mahdi Army down the street and the Sunni militia across the river. Both groups would routinely lob mortars at each other directly over his house. Occasionally, the US army would deploy tanks in his neighborhood from a nearby FOB to control the conflict. In 2006, he and his mother would spend hours each day, with irregular electricity, pinned down in their hot dark house while fighters shot Kalashnikovs up and down their street.

With much time on their hands and few options, Tareq and his mother became connoisseurs of the belliphonic sounds in their neighborhood:

> We can recognize if it's an AK-14 or RPK or PKC or it's a sniper shot . . . and if it's an American bullet or an Iraqi bullet. Iraqi bullets make a lot of loud [noise]. [I] like American [bullets]—it's more silence. [laughter]

Like other wartime auditors, Tareq learned how to listen to these sounds and mine them for information about the unseen battles going on in his neighborhood. This, as I have argued earlier, is something most people who spend time in war zones learn to do. But at some point, Tareq and his mother began doing something a little different.

> The Kalashnikov there has become like a symphony of firing. . . . So, staying and hearing the Kalashnikov—and so we tried to do something, so we tried to make this sound like a symphony.

"We tried to make this sound like a symphony . . ." What was he talking about? I asked for clarification, and Tareq explained how he and his mother transformed the sounds of gunfire into music. The music that Tareq had in mind relied upon a broad acoustic similarity between the sectarian gunfights that were taking place outside his house and a Bedouin drum, the *zanbur*. With a venerable history in Iraq that predates the invention of the Kalashnikov by centuries, the zanbur's resemblance to the AK was a matter of pure coincidence:

> We have a musical device called zanbur, and zanbur makes a sound like Kalashnikov fire. . . . And it has a speedy sound: drrrrrrrrrrrr. [laughter]
> *Me: So you would imagine that the Kalashnikov fire was a zanbur?*
> Yes, because they have the same sound! [laughter]

Confined to their house, Tareq and his mother would while away the hours by intentionally "mishearing" the Kalashnikov fire, imagining that this sound, whose indexical power was all too clear to them, was actually emanating from a different source, the zanbur. They then went on to imagine the music that would logically accompany this percussive track. In other words, through listening, they transformed the insistent *dadadadadadadadadada* of the AKs into the energetic *pabadapabadapabadapabada* of an imaginary drummer doing finger-rolls on the zanbur. Then, they augmented this ambient "percussion" coming from the street with their own imagined violins, qanuns, and ouds.

I would like to position this act of listening-as-composition, of listening-as-poiesis, as evidence of the resilience of wartime auditors, and of their ability to cobble together some measure of agency within an extreme environment of violence. A truly iconoclastic act of listening such as this enabled Tareq and his mother to escape, if only temporarily, the wartime auditory regime in which they were enmeshed. This life-affirming act of acoustic transplacement confounded the sonic campaign of the street, creating a fragile acoustic territory of aesthetics within the cacophonous politics of the combat zone. In that moment, the austere and hyperrational "war culture" into which they had been indoctrinated was temporarily eclipsed by the older, richer, more nourishing cultural matrices of Iraqi musical tradition.

Small listening games, silent mashups, imaginary compositions-in-miniature: humble acts such as these are wholly unable to stop bullets or stanch bleeding. The fighters in al-Binouq continued their battle, absolutely unaware of the radical listening act taking place inside the house. But for Tareq and his mother, this game, this tactic of the weak, mattered. In those rare stretches when the half-heard composition gelled, when the imagination could stretch to make the battle sound, for an elusive moment, "like a symphony," they accomplished something quite remarkable. Through listening, they did not aestheticize belliphonic violence—quite the opposite:

They pacified it.

Acknowledgments

If one takes my argument about the omnidirectionality of sound and violence seriously, the number of people who were wounded within the acoustic territories of wartime Iraq runs to the millions; these besieged auditors have occupied the center of my attention in this book. At the same time, as I have stated periodically throughout, the penumbra of armed violence extends farther and persists longer than do its immediate sensory effects, disfiguring families, towns, nations, regions, economies, and cultural practices, often for generations. In this space of acknowledgment, I want first to acknowledge those who lost their lives in the war, and then to recognize those vast numbers of the living who must contend with the war's long half-life.

The individuals whose testimonies populate this book continue to face challenges borne in wartime. Many of them remain in positions of profound vulnerability and risk. I offer them my deepest gratitude for entrusting me with their stories and their identities. I would like to particularly thank Ammar, Tareq, Saif, Noor, Ali S., Ali A., Bassma, and Arakel for their friendship, help, and inspiration throughout the years that I researched and wrote this book. I am also grateful to the Iraqi blogger Riverbend, and to the mil-bloggers who allowed me to reproduce their blog entries, especially Teflon Don, Colby Buzzell, and the authors of "One Marine's View" and "A Day in Iraq." Jason Sagebiel deserves special thanks for being my interlocutor, sounding board, bullshit detector, copyeditor, and steady pal for the past several years.

My work on sound and violence over the past several years has involved a lot of thorny logistics, including a string of over 400 e-mail exchanges with military officials that preceded my trip to Iraq to record sounds for the *Virtual Iraq* project. Bill Gallagher helped me get that particular ball rolling, for which I am grateful. The hospitality I received in Iraq from the members of the USF-I Surgeon's Office was extraordinary and unforgettable. First and foremost, Major Aric Bowman's role in my trip and my work extended far beyond logistics and deep into substance and friendship. I thank him, along with Colonel Stephens, Lt. Col. Sassano, Sergeant Guy, Sergeant Major Bond, and the amazing group of Army majors, all members of the 82nd Airborne Division, who hosted my stay at Camp Victory. I would also like to thank Captain Defede and the intrepid Iraqi interpreters who went by the handles Samir, Carlos, and Daniel for their help with my recording activities in Baghdad, particularly those that took place on the roof of the former Baath Party Headquarters building.

Stateside, Clay Moltz was instrumental in helping me find my first set of interlocutors for this project. I am grateful to Clay's students at the Naval Postgraduate School in Monterey, CA, and to the officers who worked with me at the United States Military Academy at West Point. Gavin Helf and Theresa Sabonis-Helf were immensely helpful during my time spent in Washington, DC. And Skip Rizzo and his colleagues at USC's Institute for Creative Technologies have earned my special thanks for involving me in their work on post-traumatic stress. I have been honored to play a small role in their activities by supplying them with recordings of ambient sound from Iraq, and I look forward to future collaborations with them.

I feel immensely lucky to be a member of the vibrant intellectual community that is New York University, and I would like to thank my friends and colleagues throughout NYU's "global network" for their aid and encouragement. Institutionally, I have been the recipient of research support from the NYU Humanities Initiative, the NYU Faculty of Arts and Science, and NYU Abu Dhabi. Personally, I have benefited greatly from the unflagging advocacy of Michael Beckerman, Suzanne Cusick, Patrick Deer, Allen Feldman, and Deborah Kapchan, all of whom I consider friends and mentors in this business. I have also been the grateful recipient of questions, thoughts, critique, and support from Sinan Antoon, Hilary Ballon, Stanley Boorman, Brigid Cohen, Elizabeth Hoffman, Lou Karchin, Clara Latham, Anne Lounsbery, Maureen Mahon, John Melillo, Rena Mueller, Jaime Oliver, Crystal Parikh, Arvind Rajagopal, David Samuels, Martin Scherzinger, Jessica Schwartz, Lytle Shaw, Matty Silverstein, Sharon Street, Ben Tausig, Helga Tawil-Souri, Jane Tylus, John Waters, Lawren Young, María José Zubieta, and a wonderfully congenial cadre of graduate and undergraduate students both in and outside the Department of Music. Among these, I would like to acknowledge Ghazi al-Mulaifi for organizing my research trip to Kuwait; Friedrich Kern, Siv Lie, Alysse Padilla, Catherine Provenzano, and Anna Reidy for helping with technical aspects of the book; Sonia Gaind Krishnan for reading early drafts of several chapters; and Amir Moosavi and Siv Lie for reading and critiquing the whole thing.

Beyond the walls of NYU, my work has benefited greatly from conversations with a large number of colleagues and friends. In particular, the ideas in this book have been honed through interactions with Jonathan Sterne, Jonathan Ritter, Tim

Rice, and Maria Cizmic, and with the inspirational work that they have produced. I am grateful for the feedback and camaraderie I received from Jon Pieslak and Lisa Gilman, and for the generous and critical reception that my colleagues at Amherst College, Brown University, Carleton University, CUNY Graduate Center, Cornell University, SUNY Binghamton, Syracuse University, the University of Pennsylvania, and Wesleyan University have given my work. Jason Stanyek, Sumanth Gopinath, Eric Weisbard, and the editing collective at *Social Text* gave critical input and support to my earlier published work on sound, listening, and violence: chapter 6 of this book is a revised version of my chapter in Jason and Sumanth's *Oxford Handbook of Mobile Music Studies*, chapter 1 is a major expansion and rethinking of my contribution to Eric's edited volume *Pop When the World Falls Apart: Music in the Shadow of Doubt*, and my thoughts on the omnidirectionality of sound and violence first appeared in article form in the journal *Social Text*. I give particular thanks to Suzanne Ryan, my steadfast editor at Oxford University Press, whose intellectual generosity and belief in this project helped shape the book into its present form. Pete Mavrikis and the extremely professional production team at OUP deserve my praise as well, as does Andrew Maillet, who produced all of the figures. I would also like to thank my friends the Goldbergs, Lehrner-Sartoris, Michelena-Zubietas, and Perrettes for the sustained interest they took in the book and its progress.

An author's debts to family always make up a special section of a book's acknowledgments, and for good reason: this is where the mutual webs of influence, love, and responsibility are at their most dense. My in-laws, my sister, and the rest of my extended family all buoyed me as the years of my engagement with this project stretched on. My parents, Donald and Kathleen Daughtry, spent their entire adult lives involved in the struggle for social justice, and I have felt their steady hands on my moral tiller as I have written this book, and charted my course as an academic more broadly. My father—civil rights advocate, maverick clergyman, nuclear-weapons-freeze activist, altruistic cab driver, poet, mensch—is deep in my head when I write. It is my great sorrow that my mother did not live to see this book in print, and my great joy that my father is still around to tell me what I got right, what I got wrong, and what I might do next.

At the end of this page and the end of this project is the real bottom line—those for whom, with whom, and through whom I live and, it follows, write. I don't have adequate words to express my love for them, so let their names here suffice:

Benjamin
Joseph
Nora
Emily

Notes

INTRODUCTION

1. Harlan K. Ullman and James P. Wade introduced the strategy in a 1996 paper titled "Shock and Awe: Achieving Rapid Dominance" (Washington, DC: National Defense University Press). The strategy called for a show of overwhelming military force that would "dominate an adversary's will both physically and psychologically," in part through producing a combination of noise and lights that disorients the adversary and renders him "impotent and vulnerable." While a number of military strategists have claimed that Rapid Dominance was imperfectly implemented in Iraq, there is compelling, albeit anecdotal, evidence to suggest that the sonic dimension of the attack was consciously designed. Also, I have gathered ample commentary from Iraqi civilians about the overwhelming and debilitating effect of the attack, which was experienced by most Baghdad residents, gathered together in their homes, in auditory/tactile rather than visual terms.

2. "Service member" is a widely accepted inclusive term for military personnel from all branches of the Armed Forces. The more common "soldier" technically refers only to enlisted personnel in the army. In order to acknowledge my interlocutors who serve in the marines and air force, and in order to avoid the cumbersome "soldiers, sailors, airmen, and marines," I have settled on "service member," or occasionally "military personnel," here. Any mention of "soldiers" in this text, outside of quotations, refers to army enlisted personnel. Also, for convenience's sake, I have tended to gloss over the so-called Coalition of the Willing when referring to the US-led military presence in Iraq. While technically a multinational force, the coalition consisted over-whelmingly of American troops, and American service members constituted the vast major-ity of coalition casualties. According to the Iraq Coalition Casualty Count (http://icasualties. org), of the 4,804 coalition troops killed in Iraq, 4,486 were members of the American armed

forces. The next two nations, the United Kingdom and Italy, lost 179 and 33 troops respectively. Given these statistics, and in order to reflect the fact that all of my military interlocutors were American, I generally refer to the "US military" rather than to the "coalition."

3. These epigraphs were gleaned from military blogs ("milblogs"), Iraqi civilian internet posts, and other published accounts of Operation Iraqi Freedom. Two of the largest clearinghouses of military blogs can be found at http://www.milblogging.com and http://www.mudvillegazette. com/milblogs. For a review of the history of milblogs and attempts by the military to censor them, see Noah Shachtman, "Army Squeezes Soldier Blogs, Maybe to Death," *Wired*, May 2, 2007, last accessed June 10, 2012, http://www.wired.com/politics/onlinerights/news/2007/05/army_bloggers.

4. Durham, NC: Duke University Press, 2003.

5. Emily Thompson, *The Soundscape of Modernity: Architectural Acoustics and the Culture of Listening in America, 1900–1933* (Cambridge, MA: MIT Press, 2004).

6. Bruce Smith, *The Acoustic World of Early Modern England: Attending to the O-Factor* (Chicago: University of Chicago Press, 1999).

7. John M. Picker, *Victorian Soundscapes* (New York: Oxford University Press, 2003).

8. Karin Bijsterveld, *Mechanical Sound: Technology, Culture, and Public Problems of Noise in the Twentieth Century* (Cambridge, MA: MIT Press, 2008).

9. Brandon Labelle, *Acoustic Territories: Sound Culture and Everyday Life* (New York: Continuum, 2010).

10. New York: Oxford University Press, 2011.

11. See, for example, *Dumbstruck: A Cultural History of Ventriloquism* (New York: Oxford University Press, 2001) and "Edison's Teeth: Touching Hearing," in *Hearing Cultures: Essays on Sound, Listening, and Modernity,* ed. Veit Erlmann (Oxford and New York: Berg, 2004), 153–72.

12. Bruce Johnson and Martin Cloonan, *Dark Side of the Tune: Popular Music and Violence* (London: Ashgate, 2008).

13. John O'Connell and Salwa Castelo-Branco (eds.), *Music and Conflict* (Urbana: University of Illinois Press, 2010).

14. Eric Weisbard (ed.), *Pop When the World Falls Apart: Music in the Shadow of Doubt* (Durham: Duke University Press, 2012).

15. Kip Pegley and Susan Fast (eds.), *Music, Politics, and Violence* (Middletown, CT: Wesleyan University Press, 2013).

16. Zagreb, Croatia: Institut za etnologiju, 1998.

17. Cambridge, MA: MIT Press, 2009.

18. Bloomington: University of Indiana Press, 2009.

19. E.g., "'You Are In a Place That Is Out of the World . . . ': Music in the Detention Camps of the 'Global War on Terror'," *Journal of the Society for American Music* 2, no. 1 (2008): 1–26; "Towards an Acoustemology of Detention in the 'Global War on Terror'," in *Music, Sound and Space: Transformations of Public and Private Experience,* ed. Georgina Born (Cambridge, UK: Cambridge University Press, 2013), 275–91.

20. See David Howes, *The Varieties of Sensory Experience: A Sourcebook in the Anthropology of the Senses* (Toronto: University of Toronto Press, 1991); Constance Classen, *Worlds of Sense: Exploring the Senses in History and Across Cultures* (London and New York: Routledge, 1993); Paul Stoller, "Sound in Songhay Cultural Experience," *American Ethnologist* 11

(1984): 559–70; Steven Feld, "Waterfalls of Song: An Acoustemology of Place Resounding in Bosavi, Papua New Guinea," in *Senses of Place*, ed. Steven Feld and Keith Basso (Santa Fe: School of American Research Press, 1996), 91–135; Anthony Seeger, *Nature and Society in Central Brazil: The Suya Indians of Mato Grosso* (Cambridge, MA: Harvard University Press, 1981).

21. See Shoshana Felman, *The Juridical Unconscious: Trials and Traumas in the Twentieth Century* (Cambridge, MA: Harvard University Press, 2002); Ruth Leys, *Trauma: A Genealogy* (Chicago: University of Chicago Press, 2013); Cathy Caruth, *Unclaimed Experience: Trauma, Narrative and History* (Baltimore: Johns Hopkins Press, 1996); Elaine Scarry, *The Body in Pain: The Making and Unmaking of the World* (New York: Oxford University Press, 1985).

22. Cathy Caruth, *Listening to Trauma: Conversations with Leaders in the Theory and Treatment of Catastrophic Experience* (Baltimore: Johns Hopkins Press, 2014), xiii–xiv.

23. It is exceedingly common for scholars of violence to argue that they did not set out to write about violence, but rather found themselves pulled into the topic by the gravitational force of violent acts. Allen Feldman has claimed (orally, in conversation with me and my students) that "all good writers on violence stumble upon their projects." E. Valentine Daniel begins his "anthropography of violence" in Sri Lanka with an explanation that he initially embarked upon fieldwork in the 1980s in order to record folk songs of Tamil women. Upon arriving in the field, he discovered that "none of my singers were in a mood to sing, and . . . my best singer [was] rummaging for what she might salvage from the shell of her fire-gorged home" (Daniel, *Charred Lullabies*, 3). Carolyn Nordstrom explains that she too was caught up unexpectedly in the violence in early-1980s Sri Lanka; one of her friends there urged her to "tell this story. Write about it. Tell the truth of war and what happens to people . . . who stand on the thin edge of survival" (Nordstrom, *Shadows of War,* 9). While I sympathize with, and even share, the instincts of these writers, I must also acknowledge that such a rhetorical move serves also to absolve them (us) of the charge of voyeurism and capitalizing on others' suffering. (See my discussion of this charge below.) *We didn't want to write about violence,* we seem to be saying, *we found ourselves obligated to do so.*

24. J. Martin Daughtry, "The Intonation of Intimacy: Ethics, Emotion, and Metaphor among Contemporary Russian Bards" (PhD diss., University of California, Los Angeles, 2006).

25. Abraham Maslow, *The Psychology of Science: A Reconnaissance* (New York: Harper and Row, 1966), 15.

26. My specific curiosity about iPods in Iraq was triggered by an incisive two-page article in an issue of *Rolling Stone* magazine. Evan Serpick's "Soundtrack to War" (August 24, 2006) raised a number of probing questions that I subsequently brought up in interviews with service members.

27. Dana Priest and Anne Hull, "Soldiers Face Neglect, Frustration at Army's Top Medical Facility," *Washington Post,* February 18, 2007, A1.

28. As of January 2014, the *Virtual Iraq* platform was being used in fifty-five Veterans Administration hospitals throughout the United States. Part of a broad program of exposure therapy, the platform is designed to help veterans access and talk through traumatic memories of combat. For more details on how the platform works, and how sound figures within it, see A. A. Rizzo, J. Difede, B. Rothbaum, J. M. Daughtry, and G. Reger, "Update and Expansion of the Virtual Iraq/Afghanistan PTSD Exposure Therapy System" in *Future Directions in Post-Traumatic Stress Disorder,* ed. M. Safir, H. Wallach, and A. A. Rizzo (New York: Springer, 2015), 303–328.

29. This quote was widely reported in the press. See for example Eric Schmitt, "Iraq-Bound Troops Confront Rumsfeld Over Lack of Armor," *New York Times,* December 8, 2004, last accessed June 10, 2012, http://www.nytimes.com/2004/12/08/international/ middleeast/08cnd-rumsfeld.html.

30. Jo Boyden, "Anthropology Under Fire: Ethics, Researchers and Children in War," in *Children and Youth on the Front Line: Ethnography, Armed Conflict, and Displacement,* ed. Jo Boyden and Joanna DeBerry (Oxford: Berghahn, 2004), 238.

31. Ibid.

32. Ibid.

33. Nancy Scheper-Hughes, *Death without Weeping: The Violence of Everyday Life in Brazil* (Berkeley: University of California Press, 1992), xii. Scheper-Hughes' work deals with domestic and societal violence rather than warfare, but her assertion here reflects a common opinion among anthropologists of violence. See, for example, Danny Hoffman, "Frontline Anthropology: Research in a Time of War," *Anthropology Today* 19, no. 3 (2003): 9–12.

34. See, for example, E. Valentine Daniel's *Charred Lullabies* and Allen Feldman's *Formations of Violence.*

35. I was not alone in being unable to conduct traditional fieldwork in wartime Iraq. In *Iraq at a Distance: What Anthropologists Can Teach Us About the War* (Philadelphia: University of Pennsylvania Press, 2009), editor Antonius C. G. M. Robben explains that "the physical danger to foreign civilians in Iraq has been so great that even experienced war correspondents have for years been able to leave Baghdad's Green Zone only on day trips surrounded by private security contractors or embedded in military units" (vii).

36. Renauld Dulong, *Le témoin oculaire: Les conditions sociales de l'attestation personnelle* (Paris: EHESS, 1988). Quoted in Paul Ricoeur, *Memory, History, Forgetting,* trans. Kathleen Blamey and David Pellauer (Chicago: University of Chicago Press, 2004), 163.

37. Paul Ricoeur, *Memory, History, Forgetting,* 161–6.

38. Veena Das, "Commentary: Trauma and Testimony: Between Law and Discipline." *Ethos* 35, no.3 (2007): 330. The issue of testimony versus direct observation takes on a particular acuteness here, in a work that deals with sound and, more specifically, music. Within my discipline of ethnomusicology, being present and participating is commonly regarded as the sine qua non of research. With the exception of the relatively few works that take up historical themes or online communities, I can't think of a single ethnomusicological monograph that is not based upon fieldwork experiences lasting months or years. In the recent second edition of *Shadows in the Field,* an edited collection of reflections on ethnomusicological fieldwork, the editors confirm fieldwork as a sine qua non for the discipline, claiming that "ethnomusicologists derive from fieldwork their most significant contributions to scholarship in general" (Barz and Cooley, *Shadows in the Field,* 4).

39. Ricoeur, *Memory, History, Forgetting,* 166.

40. Nordstrom, *Shadows of War,* 80.

41. Ibid., 81.

42. Veena Das, "Anthropological Knowledge and Collective Violence," *Anthropology Today* 1, no.3 (1985): 5, quoted in Carolyn Nordstrom, *A Different Kind of War Story* (Philadelphia: University of Pennsylvania Press, 1997), 79.

43. Robert Neimeyer, "Narrative Strategies in Grief Therapy," *Journal of Constructivist Psychology* 12 (1999): 67.

44. See, for example, David Howes, ed., *The Varieties of Sensory Experience* (Toronto: University of Toronto Press, 1991); Michael Jackson, ed., *Things as They Are: New Directions in Phenomenological Anthropology* (Bloomington: Indiana University Press, 1996); and C. Jason Throop, *Suffering and Sentiment: Exploring the Vicissitudes of Experience and Pain in Yap* (Berkeley: University of California Press, 2010). Notable phenomenological studies in ethnomusicology include Harris Berger, *Metal, Rock, and Jazz: Perception and Phenomenology of Musical Experience* (Hanover, NH: Wesleyan University Press, 1999), and Stephen Friedson, *Dancing Prophets: Musical Experience in Tumbuka Healing* (Chicago: University of Chicago Press, 1996).

45. Robert Desjarlais and C. Jason Throop, "Phenomenological Approaches in Anthropology," *Annual Review of Anthropology* 40 (2011): 87–102.

46. Ivana Macek, *Sarajevo Under Siege: Anthropology in Wartime* (Philadelphia: University of Pennsylvania Press, 2009).

47. Ted Swedenburg, "Prisoners of Love: With Genet in the Palestinian Field," in *Fieldwork Under Fire: Contemporary Studies of Violence and Culture*, ed. Antonius C. G. M. Robben and Carolyn Nordstrom (Berkeley: University of California Press, 1995), 25–41.

48. Liisa H. Malkki, *Purity and Exile: Violence, Memory, and National Cosmology among Hutu Refugees in Tanzania* (Chicago: University of Chicago Press, 1995).

49. Frank N. Pieke, "Accidental Anthropology: Witnessing the 1989 Chinese People's Movement," in *Fieldwork Under Fire*, ed. Robben and Nordstrom, 62–80.

50. Antonius C. G. M. Robben and Carolyn Nordstrom, "The Anthropology and Ethnography of Violence and Sociopolitical Conflict," in *Fieldwork Under Fire*, ed. Robben and Nordstrom, 14.

51. Mary Louise Pratt, "Violence and Language," *Social Text: Periscope* (2011), ed. Elena Bellina, J. Martin Daughtry, Crystal Parikh, and Arvind Rajagopal, http://www.socialtext-journal.org/blog/2011/05/new-periscope-dossier-on-violence.php. See also Keith Brown and Katherine Lutz, "Grunt Lit: The Participant-Observers of Empire," *American Ethnologist* 34, no.2 (2007): 322–28.

52. Steven Feld's groundbreaking work among the Kaluli people of Papua New Guinea explains how the Kaluli have applied a coherent system of action and interpretation to structure their relations with the rich sonorous world of the rainforest. This system—comprising locally inflected notions of "flow," culturally specific notions such as "lift-up-over sounding," and distinct cultural attitudes toward birdsong and weeping—is comprehensive enough to constitute a culturally situated "acoustemology," a new auditory mode of being-in-the-world. Rooted in a radically non-Western tradition and solidified in real-community practice, one can argue that Kaluli attitudes toward sound and listening are (or were) fundamentally different than dominant attitudes in the postindustrial world. The case for a culturally distinct Iraqi acoustemology would be difficult to advance in the cosmopolitan environment of contemporary Baghdad; however, I do use this term in a more restricted sense in chapter 2. See Feld's classic text *Sound and Sentiment: Birds, Weeping, Poetics, and Song in Kaluli Expression* (Philadelphia: University of Pennsylvania Press, 2nd ed., 1990).

53. Nordstrom, *A Different Kind of War Story*, 6.

54. Clifford Geertz, *The Interpretation of Cultures* (New York: Basic Books, 1973), 89.

55. Nordstrom, *Shadows of War*, 4.

56. I attempt to do just this in chapter 2.

57. Writing, after all, is a methodology, although it is rarely recognized as such.

58. Avery Gordon, *Ghostly Matters: Haunting and the Sociological Imagination* (Minneapolis: University of Minnesota Press, 2008), 4–5.

59. E. Valentine Daniel, *Charred Lullabies: Chapters in an Anthropography of Violence* (Princeton: Princeton University Press, 1996), 106.

60. E. Valentine Daniel, "The Limits of Culture," in *In Near Ruins: Cultural Theory at the End of the Century*, ed. Nicholas B. Dirks (U of Minnesota Press, 1998), 67–91, quote p. 75. George Bataille, *Inner Experience,* trans. Leslie Ann Boldt (Albany: State University of New York Press, 1988), 208.

61. Tim O'Brien, *The Things They Carried* (New York: Houghton Mifflin Harcourt, 1990), 68.

62. The orientation of Hayden White, the best-known investigator of history's fictive dimension, is most pithily expressed in his collection of essays *The Content of the Form* (Baltimore: The Johns Hopkins University Press, 1987). His statement that rather than "revealing the true essence of past reality, historical narrative imposes a mythic structure on the events it purports to describe" (113) calls into question the ability of history to accurately represent the reality of the past.

63. In Clifford and Marcus's groundbreaking edited collection *Writing Culture: The Poetics and Politics of Ethnography* (Berkeley: University of California Press, 1986), the authors argue that ethnographic writing is not so much a reflection of lived subaltern realities but is rather constitutive of a tropological "reality."

64. Feldman's formal presentation at the roundtable can be found at http://socialtextjournal. org/periscope_article/the_state-become-nonstate_-_allen_feldman/.

FRAGMENT #1

1. Based on an interview with the author in Amman, Jordan, 2008.

2. Neeraj N. Mathur, "Noise-Induced Hearing Loss Clinical Presentation," Medscape Reference, last updated April 16, 2012, http://emedicine.medscape.com/article/857813-clinical.

CHAPTER 1

1. For a history of medical auscultation, "the activity of listening to the sound of the movements of organs, air and fluid in the chest" (*Oxford English Dictionary*, s.v. "auscultation"), see Jonathan Sterne, *The Audible Past: Cultural Origins of Sound Reproduction* (Durham: Duke University Press, 2003), 87–136.

2. A similar injunction "to be especially watchful" in the hours immediately before and after dusk and dawn is part of US Marine Corps General Order #11.

3. Oliver Poole, *Red Zone: Five Bloody Years in Baghdad* (London: Reportage Press, 2008), 61–2.

4. Andrew Exum, "For Some Soldiers the War Never Ends," *New York Times,* June 2, 2004, http://www.nytimes.com/2004/06/02/opinion/02EXUM.html?smid=pl-share. See also Ann Scott Tyson and Josh White, "Strained Army Extends Tours to 15 Months," *Washington Post,* April 12, 2007, http://www.washingtonpost.com/wp-dyn/content/article/2007/04/11/AR2007041100615.html.

5. Paul Virilio, *War and Cinema: The Logistics of Perception* (London and New York: Verso, 2000 [1989]), 48.

6. Of course, for Iraqis, who have endured three major wars in as many decades, "normalcy" is a tenuous concept. Elsewhere in this chapter, I discuss the ways in which Iraqi experiences of these wars inform their listening practices. For now, however, it is important to note that for residents of Zayouna, daily life in 2002 was generally peaceful, and the onset of the war did bring about major changes that were not just heard on the news but were apprehended directly by the senses.

7. Not the same Ali as in the first fragment. Ali A.'s account is pieced together from a string of interviews with the author in Abu Dhabi, UAE, 2010–11.

8. For a broad overview of recent theories on the physiology of auditory memory, see Bob Snyder, *Music and Memory: An Introduction* (Cambridge, MA: MIT Press, 2000). A more detailed discussion of the way the auditory system participates in the production of memory can be found in Norman M. Weinberger, "The Cognitive Auditory Cortex," in *The Oxford Handbook of Auditory Science: The Auditory Brain,* edited by Adrian Rees and Alan R. Palmer (Oxford and New York: Oxford University Press, 2010), 440–77. For more on the complicated relationship between sound, listening, and memory, see Ron Emoff, *Recollecting from the Past: Musical Practice and Spirit Possession on the East Coast of Madagascar* (Middletown, CT: Wesleyan University Press, 2002).

9. The one arguable exception to this statement is of course September 11, 2001, a day on which, according to the repeated proclamations of politicians and news organizations, foreigners waged war on the American mainland for the first time since the War of 1812. The sonic consequences of the 9/11 attacks are examined in *Music in the Post-9/11 World,* edited by Jonathan Ritter and J. Martin Daughtry (New York: Routledge, 2007). In the end, though, it is impossible to compare one violent day with a decade of ongoing war that produced exponentially more casualties.

10. This topic is treated in depth in chapter 7, "A Time of Troubles for Iraqi Music."

11. That number reflects documented killings. The true number may be exponentially larger.

12. See http://www.iraqbodycount.org/ for detailed statistics on Iraq War casualties.

13. According to military regulations, each Iraqi household was allowed one small arms firearm for domestic defense.

14. This phrase is a rather noisy and dystopian appropriation of Michael Bull's discussion of the "auditory bubble" effect created by listening to music on headphones. See Michael Bull, *Sound Moves: iPod Culture and Urban Experience* (New York: Routledge, 2007, 3–5).

15. Interview with the author. Baghdad, Iraq, 2011.

16. John J. McGrath, "The Other End of the Spear: The Tooth-to-Tail Ratio (T3R) in Modern Military Operations," The Long War Series, Occasional Paper 23 (Fort Leavenworth, KS: Combat Studies Institute Press, 2007), 52–5.

17. Testimonies indicate that the practice of listening to music while driving through the Iraqi streets was widespread in the beginning of the war, but dropped off significantly once guerrilla attacks on service members became common. See chapter 6 for a more detailed discussion of music listening practices within the US military.

18. Riverbend, *Baghdad Burning: Girl Blog From Iraq* (New York: Feminist Press at CUNY, 2005), 72–3.

19. Interview with the author. Amman, Jordan, 2008.

20. Interview with the author. Abu Dhabi, UAE, 2010.

21. A full transcript of this interview can be found at: http://www.defense.gov/transcripts/ transcript.aspx?transcriptid=2522. The interview was also mentioned in Poole, *Red Zone*, 52. My emphasis.

22. "Truck commander" is an army term. In the Marine Corps this person is called a "vehicle commander."

23. Interview with the author. West Point, NY, 2010.

24. A 2004 military study classified as "Secret" and released on WikiLeaks concluded that, for the majority of comm systems in use at the time, "no communications across the 2-km convoy radio link were possible when either the WARLOCK-Red or the SSVJ [IED jamming systems] was operating within the same vehicle." James Smith and James Billingsley, "Abbreviated Test Report for Blue Force Communications Electromagnetic Compatibility (EMC) with WARLOCK-Green, WARLOCK-Red, and Self-screening Vehicle Jammer Systems, (FOUO)" (Aberdeen Proving Ground, MD: U.S. Army Developmental Test Command, May 2004), 2–3, 2–4, http://wikileaks-press.org:81/file/blue-force-comms-emc-warlock-test-results-2-2004.pdf.

25. The sirens on military bases in Iraq were the latest instantiation of a long history of siren use within the US military and domestic civil defense programs. One of the earliest academic studies of the psychological effects of air-raid sirens was published at the beginning of World War II. See P. E. Vernon, "Psychological Effects of Air-Raids," *Journal of Abnormal and Social Psychology* 36, no. 4 (1941): 457–76. The previous fall, three contributors to the *Musical Times* wrote descriptions of the air-raid sirens of London. See, for example, E. H. Walker, "Air Raid Sirens," *Musical Times* 81, no. 1173 (1940): 458. For a more recent historical reflection on air-raid sirens during the Blitz, see Peter Adey, "Holding Still: The Private Life of an Air Raid," *M/C Journal: A Journal of Media and Culture* 12, no. 1 (2009), http://journal.media-culture.org.au/ index.php/mcjournal/article/viewArticle/112.

26. Interview with the author. Washington, DC, 2010.

27. See chapters 4 and 6 for a discussion of the LRAD.

28. "Psychological Operations Tactics, Techniques and Procedures" (Washington, DC: Headquarters, Department of the Army, December 2003), FM 10–12, www.fas.org/irp/ doddir/army/fm3-05-301.pdf; my emphasis.

29. Christopher J. Lamb, "Review of Psychological Operations Lessons Learned from Recent Operational Experience" (Washington, DC: National Defense University Press, 2005), http:// ics-www.leeds.ac.uk/papers/pmt/exhibits/2736/Lamb_OP_092005_Psyops.pdf; my emphasis.

30. "Special Forces Foreign Internal Defense Operations" (Washington, DC: Headquarters, Department of the Army, February 2007), FM 3–05.202, http://wlstorage.net/file/ fm3-05x202.pdf.

31. "Loudspeaker teams and radio broadcasts helped to discourage looting as well as reduce tolerance of looters. Emerging leaders joined in the call for looting to cease." Anthony H. Cordesman, *The Iraq War: Strategy, Tactics, and Military Lessons* (Westport, CT and London: Praeger, 2003), 136.

32. Anthony Shadid, "Sadr's Disciples Rise Again to Play Pivotal Role in Iraq," *Washington Post*, August 30, 2005, http://www.washingtonpost.com/wp-dyn/content/article/2005/08/29/ AR2005082901795.html.

33. The *New York Times* reported in 2008 that "while there is no detailed tracking of the total number of Iraqis who have worked as interpreters, their advocates estimate that more than 20,000 people have filled such roles since 2003. In the last quarter of 2007 alone, 5,490 Iraqis were

employed by the multinational force as interpreters, according to the Department of Defense."
Conrad Mulcahy, "Iraqi Interpreters," *New York Times*, May 10, 2008, http://topics.nytimes.
com/top/news/international/countriesandterritories/iraq/interpreters/index.html?8qa.

34. Conrad Mulcahy, "Officers Battle Visa Hurdles for Iraq Aides," *New York Times,* May
14, 2008, A1.

35. In September 2008, the US military instituted a regulation forbidding interpreters from
wearing face masks. Several months later, in response to criticism that the new policy put interpreters' lives at risk, it was largely reversed. See Ernesto Londoño, "Iraqi Interpreters May Wear
Masks," *Washington Post,* February 13, 2009, for a full account of these events.

36. From a series of interviews with the author. Amman, Jordan, 2008.

37. The small units were called "Tigers" by locals, as this was a popular brand name, but also
perhaps due to the growling noise they emitted.

38. Interview with the author. Washington, DC, 2010.

39. Tong Soon Lee, "Technology and the Production of Islamic Space: The Call to Prayer in
Singapore," *Ethnomusicology* 43, no. 1 (1999): 86–100. Cf. Alain Corbin, *Village Bells: Sound and
Meaning in the 19th-Century French Countryside,* trans. Martin Thom (New York: Columbia
University Press, 1998).

40. This is not to say that the adhan is always cherished as beautiful. As my colleague Amir
Moosavi notes, in everyday experience, "the terrible speaker equipment, and bad voices also
create a cacophony that can be really trying to listen to," regardless of your level of devotion.
(Personal correspondence with the author, October 2014.)

41. As of 2008, and despite an effort on the part of the US armed forces to recruit more
Muslims, a *Wall Street Journal* article reported that the total Muslim population in the
active-duty military numbered a mere 3,409. (Yochi J. Dreazen, "Muslim Population in
the Military Raises Difficult Issues," *Wall Street Journal,* November 9, 2009, http://online.
wsj.com/article/SB125755853525335343.html.) I have not encountered any Muslim service
members, but one can imagine the difficulties they would face when confronting some of
the attitudes toward the adhan documented below. In 2013, an Army publication featured
a story of an Islamic Center that had recently opened on Kandahar Airbase in Afghanistan.
It appeared this was one of the first such centers made available for US troops; one soldier mentioned never finding such a place during his tour of duty in Iraq. (Mark Albright,
"Soldiers Find Place to Worship, Observe Ramadan on Kandahar Airfield." *www.army.
mil: The Official Homepage of the United States Army*, http://www.army.mil/article/109184/
Soldiers_find_place_to_worship__observe_Ramadan_on_Kandahar_Airfield/.)

42. Phone interview with the author, 2007.

43. Phone interview with the author, 2007.

44. "American Call To Prayer," YouTube video, 1:50, posted by SUNDROPisGOOD01, June
16, 2009, http://www.youtube.com/watch?v=snymjGFYN8Q.

45. Debra Merskin, "The Construction of Arabs as Enemies: Post-September 11 Discourse
of George W. Bush," *Mass Communication and Society* 7, no. 2 (2004): 157–75; Erin Steuter
and Deborah Wills, "'The Vermin Have Struck Again': Dehumanizing the Enemy in Post 9/11
Media Representations," *Media, War & Conflict* 3, no. 2 (2010): 152–67.

46. R. Murray Schafer, *Soundscape: The Tuning of the World* (Rochester, VT: Destiny Books,
1994), 10. Tong Soon Lee uses this terminology in his article "Technology and the Production
of Islamic Space."

47. A small number of differences separate the Shi'i and Sunni calls to prayer. Most notably, the Shi'i version is longer, as it includes two repeated lines dedicated to the Imam Ali. After the common lines "I bear witness that there is no Allah but Allah" and "I bear witness that Muhammad is the messenger of Allah," the Shi'i version continues: "I bear witness that Ali is the friend of Allah" and "I bear witness that Ali is the proof of Allah."

48. A 2010 article in *Time* magazine placed the number of Christians in Iraq at 400,000, down significantly from the size of the prewar population. Nizar Latif and Charles McDermid, "Iraq's Christians Vow to Survive, with Muslim Help," *Time,* November 11, 2010, http://www.time.com/time/world/article/0,8599,2030747,00.html. A large number of deadly church bombings that year sparked an increase in Christian emigration. The Jewish population, which numbered 130,000 before World War II, had dwindled down to seven or eight individuals by 2006: Stephen Farrell, "Baghdad Jews Have Become a Fearful Few," *New York Times,* June 1, 2008, http://www.nytimes.com/2008/06/01/world/middleeast/01babylon.html. While no precise figures exist for the number of secular Iraqis, secularism was widespread during the Hussein period and surely persists in the post-Hussein era. It should also be noted that the figures above predate the emergence of the so-called Islamic State (also known as ISIS) and the wave of violence directed toward Christians and other groups that is ongoing as this book goes to press.

49. Beginning in the early 1980s, the Hussein government initiated a multifaceted program designed to regulate, contain, and disenfranchise the activist wing of the Shi'i population. This included banning mourning ceremonies "so as to forestall possible sedition." Ofra Bengio, "Shi'is and Politics in Ba'thi Iraq," *Middle Eastern Studies* 21, no. 1 (1985): 11.

50. David Zucchino, "In Baghdad Area, Shiite Festival is Held without Incident," *Los Angeles Times,* December 9, 2011, http://articles.latimes.com/2011/dec/09/world/la-fg-iraq-ashura-20111209-22; Reuters "Shi'a in Iraq Mark Ashura as a Show of Strength," *Radio Free Europe Radio Liberty,* January 7, 2009, http://www.rferl.org/content/Shiites_In_Iraq_Mark_Ashura_In_Show_Of_Strength/1367483.html; CHN, "Ashura Commemorated Throughout the World," *Payvand Iran News,* February 11, 2006, http://www.rferl.org/content/Shiites_In_Iraq_Mark_Ashura_In_Show_Of_Strength/1367483.html.

51. Interview with the author. New York, 2012.

52. In 2004, during the first post-Hussein Ashura ceremonies, suicide bombers killed over 160 Shi'i pilgrims in Karbala and Baghdad. These killings in turn helped to spark the wave of sectarian violence that resulted in the deaths of untold tens of thousands of civilians in 2006 and 2007. In 2009, three days before the Ashura procession, thirty-five pilgrims were killed by a suicide bomb outside a Baghdad shrine. In 2011, two dozen pilgrims were killed in Baghdad and other cities in the days leading up to Ashura. See "Shi'a in Iraq Mark Ashura as a Show of Strength," *Radio Free Europe Radio Liberty,* January 7, 2009, http://www.rferl.org/content/Shiites_In_Iraq_Mark_Ashura_In_Show_Of_Strength/1367483.html.

53. The only activities that appear to cause near-trajectory weapon sounds to fade into the background are those that involve the immediate taking or saving of a life. Service members who engaged in returning fire or worked to keep a wounded comrade alive speak of a kind of sensory tunnel effect in which sounds appeared to fade as they concentrated on the tasks at hand. Nevertheless, for most instances in which the sounds of weapons overlapped in space with the projectiles that produced them, they were assigned paramount importance.

54. Phone interview with the author, 2007.

55. Interview with the author. West Point, NY, 2010.

56. Kate Hillis and Ziad Turkey, dir., *Hometown Baghdad*, "Symphony of Bullets," New York: Chat the Planet Productions, 2007.

57. "Mortar Attack on Camp Echo, Iraq" YouTube video, 8:41, posted by mento666, June 24, 2008, http://youtu.be/dMeIcUfvPUU.

58. Phone interview with the author, 2007.

59. G. Richard Price, "Weapon Noise Exposure of the Human Ear Analyzed with the AHAAH Model," US Army Research Laboratory online site www.arl.army.mil, September 2010, http://www.arl.army.mil/www/default.cfm?page=351.

60. Interview with the author. West Point, NY, 2010.

61. Interview with the author. Washington, DC, 2010.

62. Clay Wilson, "Improvised Explosive Devices (IEDs) in Iraq and Afghanistan: Effects and Countermeasures" (Washington, DC: Congressional Research Service, 2007); quoted in Catherine Lutz, "US and Coalition Casualties in Iraq and Afghanistan," Brown University: Watson Institute, June 6, 2011. In 2009, the *New York Times* reported that "I.E.D.'s cause the highest raw numbers of injuries in both [the Afghanistan and Iraq] wars. From Oct. 7, 2001, through Aug. 1, 2009, explosive devices caused 25,353 casualties in the American ranks. Gunshot injuries caused 4,102 casualties."

C. J. Chivers, "Why Do Bullets Kill More Soldiers in Iraq," *New York Times*, August 19, 2009, http://atwar.blogs.nytimes.com/2009/08/19/why-do-bullets-kill-more-soldiers-in-iraq/.

63. Interview with the author. Washington, DC, 2010.

64. Interview with the author. Washington, DC, 2010.

65. Interview with the author. West Point, NY, 2010.

66. "I get blown up!" YouTube video, 2:51, posted by stevenhelton, March 27, 2006, http://www.youtube.com/watch?v=CrdcddNx29c.

67. Interview with the author. New York, 2010.

CHAPTER 2

1. Phone interview with the author, 2007.

2. Jacques Rancière, *The Politics of Aesthetics* (London: Continuum, 2005).

3. Interview with the author. Washington, DC, 2010.

4. This position resonates with philosophical arguments for the essential relationality of existence, such as those found within Martin Buber's *I and Thou* (1970) and Kwame Appiah's *Cosmopolitanism* (2006, esp. 155–176). For both thinkers, recognition of the Other as a subject (or, in Avery Gordon's terminology, as a "complex person") is the first step of the process of entering into an ethical relation of respect and caring.

5. I would like to thank Jason Sagebiel for articulating this position in an oral critique of this section.

6. The zone of the audible inaudible shares some characteristics with Georg Simmel's description of the desensitization of the sensorium in response to the overstimulating nature of modernity. See Georg Simmel, "The Metropolis and Mental Life," in *Social Sciences III: Selections and Selected Readings,* Vol. 2, 14th ed. (Chicago: University of Chicago Press, 1948). See also R. Murray Schafer's discussion of techniques for tuning out the noise of urban life in *The Soundscape* (1994). While the processes of tuning out or armoring the sensorium bear a surface

resemblance to the audible inaudible, the ethical charge of these operations differs markedly from my discussion here.

7. Phone interview with the author, 2007.

8. The standard M4 carbine is issued to regular army troops. The M4A1, a variant with a fully automatic setting, is issued to US special operation units.

9. Interview with the author. West Point, NY, 2010.

10. "YOU BETTER PRAY I hit," blogpost for *One Marine's View* posted by Maj Pain on December 12, 2005, http://www.onemarinesview.com/one_marines_view/2005/12/you_better_pray.html.

11. In their book *Spaces Speak, Are You Listening,* Barry Blesser and Linda-Ruth Salter discuss a related phenomenon: how hearing furnishes access to multiple overlapping "acoustic arenas." They analyze the "multiple auditory channels" that compete with each other. Two conversations across the same dinner table, each with its own arena, compete with each other. Arenas collide and intersect with each other, opening and closing channels, including and excluding listeners. For example, the sudden ringing of the telephone shrinks the acoustic arena for television sound, and a cessation of traffic noise enlarges the acoustic arena of chirping crickets." Barry Blesser and Linda Ruth-Salter, *Spaces Speak, Are You Listening?: Experiencing Aural Architecture* (Cambridge, MA: MIT Press, 2006), 22.

12. "Crump!," blogpost for *One Marine's View,* posted by Maj Pain, November 30, 2005, http://www.onemarinesview.com/one_marines_view/2005/11/.

13. "Brief Uncertainty," blogpost for *A Day in Iraq: A Former Soldier's Daily Experiences while Living and Fighting in Iraq,* posted by MICHAEL, August 05, 2005, http://adayiniraq.blogspot.com/2005/08/brief-uncertainty.html.

14. Phone interview with the author, 2007.

15. "Roadside Bomb," post by SGT "Roy Batty," posted on *Slate,* "The Sandbox," October 24, 2006, http://gocomics.typepad.com/the_sandbox/2006/10/index.html.

16. Interview with the author. West Point, NY, 2010.

17. "TacSat" are remote radio transmissions relayed by a Department of Defense satellite.

18. Interview with the author. West Point, NY, 2010.

19. James Meek, "Iraq War Logs: How Friendly Fire from US Troops Became Routine," *The Guardian,* October 22, 2010, http://www.guardian.co.uk/world/2010/oct/22/american-troops-friendly-fire-iraq.

20. See Thomas Helfer, Nikki N. Jordan, and Robyn B. Lee, "Postdeployment Hearing Loss in U.S. Army Soldiers Seen at Audiology Clinics from April 1, 2003, through March 31, 2004," *American Journal of Audiology* 14 (2005): 161–8.

21. A new electronically modulated set of earphones was introduced into the combat zone in 2008, and promises to change this landscape somewhat. The earphones, which are connected to a small device slightly bigger than an iPod, electronically cancel out sounds above a certain decibel threshold, while actually amplifying softer sounds.

22. Interviews with the author. Washington, DC, 2007.

23. An IED explosion can generate over 180 decibels near the point of impact. Earplugs cannot reduce a sound that loud to a decibel level that is safe for human ears. A military study published in the *American Journal of Audiology* concluded, "It is important to note that some NIHLI [noise-induced hearing loss injury] is unavoidable despite the availability/use of hearing

protection and other preventive measures. This is because some exposures, particularly those experienced in the operational setting, are so extreme that they will exceed the protective capability of hearing protective devices. In addition, skull transmission of intense noise, the element of surprise, and the coeffects of inhaled toxins such as carbon monoxide in conjunction with noise can affect hearing loss outcomes." Helfer et al., "Postdeployment Hearing Loss," 166.

24. Helfer et al, "Postdeployment Hearing Loss," 161–8.

25. Thomas M. Helfer, Nikki N. Jordan, Robyn B. Lee, Paul Pietrusiak, Kara Cave, and Kim Schairer, "Noise-Induced Hearing Injury and Comorbidities Among Postdeployment U.S. Army Soldiers: April 2003–June 2009," *American Journal of Audiology* 20 (June 2011): 33–41.

26. Tom Philpot, "Vets Face Hearing Loss Epidemic," military.com, September 9, 2011, http://www.military.com/features/0,15240,235886,00.html.

27. In 2008, I spoke to an Iraqi otologist who reported that his Baghdad clinic witnessed a marked increase in trauma-induced hearing loss among civilians of all age groups following the invasion. While this evidence is anecdotal and in need of verification, it seems logical to assume that the civilian population would be affected by the same sounds that have deafened thousands of troops.

28. Chelsea J. Carter, "US Troops Losing Hearing," *Associated Press,* March 7, 2005. Reproduced on the website of the Better Hearing Institute, http://www.betterhearing.org/press/hearingnews/US_troops_losing_hearing_prtroops.cfm.

29. For more information on the effect of primary blast waves on the human brain, see Katherine H. Taber, Deborah L. Warden, and Robin A. Hurley, "Blast-related Traumatic Brain Injury: What Is Known?" *Journal of Neuropsychiatry and Clinical Neurosciences* 18, no. 2 (2006): 141–5.

30. See Jenny Johnson, "The Luminous Noise of Broken Experience: Synaesthesia, Acoustic Memory, and Childhood Sexual Abuse in the Late 20th Century United States" (PhD diss., New York University, 2009); Suzanne G. Cusick, "Music as Torture/Music as Weapon," *Revista Transcultural de Música* 10 (2006), http://www.sibetrans.com/trans/trans10/cusick_eng.htm; and Suzanne G. Cusick, "'You Are In a Place That Is Out of the World . . . ': Music in the Detention Camps of the 'Global War on Terror,'" *Journal of the Society for American Music* 2, no. 1 (2008): 1–26.

31. Interview with the author. Detroit, MI, 2012.

32. Interview with the author. New York, 2012.

33. Interview with the author. Amman, Jordan, 2008.

34. Steven Feld, "Waterfalls of Song: An Acoustemology of Place Resounding in Bosavi, Papua New Guinea," in *Senses of Place,* ed. Steven Feld and Keith Basso (Santa Fe, NM: School of American Research Press, 1996), 97.

35. Patrick Deer's important discussion of the concept of "war culture" within the context of WWII-era Britain provides a discursive complement to the battlefield dynamics I describe here. While he frames the term in a more expansive way than I do, his notion of an overarching, nationally inflected war culture shares with mine an emphasis on its ruthless pragmatism and recursive structure: ". . . modern war culture is self-perpetuating and self-replicating; it normalizes and naturalizes a state of war. Peace is not the end of war culture. . . . It struggles to control history and freeze time. At its core, war culture seeks a postponement of peacetime 'for the duration'; it seeks an adjustment to a state of permanent war." Patrick Deer, *Culture in Camouflage: War, Empire, and Modern British Literature* (Oxford: Oxford University Press, 2009), 242.

36. Cited in Elise Forbes Tripp, *Surviving Iraq: Soldiers' Stories* (Northampton, MA: Olive Branch Press, 2009), 138.

37. Terri Tanielian and Lisa H. Jaycox, eds., *Invisible Wounds of War: Psychological and Cognitive Injuries, Their Consequences, and Services to Assist Recovery* (Santa Monica: RAND, 2008), 332.

38. Andy Grimm, "Fireworks Trigger Stress in War Vets," *Chicago Tribune*, July 2, 2011, http://articles.chicagotribune.com/2011-07-02/news/ct-met-fireworks-ptsd-0702-20110702_1_war-vets-ptsd-fireworks-laws.

39. Erin P. Finley, *Fields of Combat: Understanding PTSD among Veterans of Iraq and Afghanistan* (Ithaca, NY and London: Cornell University Press, 2011), 38.

40. Clinical literature unanimously presents sound as a trigger for PTSD. See, for example, Albert Rizzo et al., "A Virtual Reality Exposure Therapy Application for Iraq War Military Personnel with Post Traumatic Stress Disorder: From Training to Toy to Treatment," in *NATO Advanced Research Workshop on Novel Approaches to the Diagnosis and Treatment of Posttraumatic Stress Disorder*, ed. M. Roy (Washington, DC: IOS Press, 2006), 235–50; and Carol S. Fullerton and Robert J. Ursano, eds., *Posttraumatic Stress Disorder: Acute and Long-Term Responses to Trauma and Disaster* (Washington, DC: American Psychiatric Press, 2009). Studies of shell-shock immediately after World War I speculated on the importance of sound as an instigator of anxiety (Fullerton and Ursano, *Posttraumatic Stress Disorder*, 243). But the exact nature of this relationship—and why some people are affected by sounds and others aren't—is more of an open question. Statistics for PTSD among Iraq War veterans are almost certainly lower than the actual number of veterans who experience acute anxiety and stress upon their return to civilian life.

41. Thomas J. Csordas, "Embodiment and Cultural Phenomenology," in *Perspectives on Embodiment: The Intersection of Nature and Culture*, ed. Gail Weiss and Honi Fern Haber (New York: Routledge, 1999), 143.

42. For a detailed discussion of this end of the auditory spectrum, see J. Martin Daughtry, "Thanatosonics: Ontologies of Acoustic Violence," *Social Text* 32, no. 2 (2014).

FRAGMENT #2

1. Based on interviews with the author. New York, 2009–14.

FRAGMENT #3

1. John Sutherland, Rick Baillergeon, and Tim McKane, "Cordon and Search Operations: A Deadly Game of Hide-and-Seek," *Air Land Sea Bulletin* 3 (2010): 5, http://www.alsa.mil/library/alsb/ALSB%202010-3.pdf (originally published in *Armchair General Magazine*, April 23, 2008).

2. Col. James K. Greer, "Operation Knockout: COIN in Iraq," *Military Review*, November–December 2005, reprinted in *The U.S. Army Professional Writing Collection*, http://www.army.mil/professionalWriting/volumes/volume4/february_2006/2_06_3.html.

3. Laila Al-Arian and Chris Hedges, "The Other War: Iraq Vets Bear Witness," *The Nation*, July 30, 2007, http://www.thenation.com/article/other-war-iraq-vets-bear-witness-0 (accessed September 3, 2012). Sergeant John Bruhns, one of the primary sources, claimed that "he uncovered illegal material about 10 percent of the time, an estimate echoed by other veterans. 'We

did find small materials for IEDs, like maybe a small piece of the wire, the detonating cord,' said Sergeant Cannon," another interviewee, but "'we never found real bombs in the houses.'" A third interviewee testified that, "in the thousand or so raids he conducted during his time in Iraq . . . he came into contact with only four 'hard-core insurgents.'"

4. Ibid.

5. The practice of hooding prisoners for prolonged periods was officially banned in the wake of the 2004 Abu Ghraib scandal, but five soldiers in Al-Arian and Hedges' "The Other War: Iraq Vets Bear Witness" claim that it continued after that date.

6. "Night Raid," 3:06, posted by MontanaWildExtreme on September 26, 2011, http://www.youtube.com/watch?v=pjzsioo9JyI&feature=channel&list=UL.

7. One of the few Arabic words that all service members know, "yalla" roughly translates as "hurry up!" or "come on!" Here it is being yelled by a member of the raid team.

INTRODUCTION TO SECTION II

1. Composer Pauline Oliveros memorably defined "soundscape" as "all of the waveforms faithfully transmitted to our audio cortex by the ear and its mechanisms." Pauline Oliveros, *Deep Listening: A Composer's Sound Practice* (Lincoln, NE: iUniverse, 2005), 18. For a close reading of Schafer and examination of the use of the term within recent sound studies scholarship, see Ari Y. Kelman, "Rethinking the Soundscape: A Critical Genealogy of a Key Term in Sound Studies," *Senses & Society* 5, no. 2: 212–34.

2. David W. Samuels, Louise Meintjes, Ana Maria Ochoa, and Thomas Porcello, "Soundscapes: Toward a Sounded Anthropology," *Annual Review of Anthropology* 39 (2010): 329–45.

3. Schafer, *The Soundscape*, 71.

4. In his major opus on soundscapes (1994), Schafer devotes a scant two pages to "the aberrational noises of war" throughout history (49–51).

5. See, for example, John M. Picker, *Victorian Soundscapes* (New York: Oxford University Press, 2003).

6. Samuels et al., "Soundscapes," 330. Schafer (154) does point to the variability of listening in a discussion of "sonological competence," but his conclusions generally remain speculative and broad (such as arguing that "the Eskimo's space awareness is acoustic" in contrast to the visually constituted space of the West).

7. Samuels et al., "Soundscapes," 335.

8. Here and below, etymology and definitions are taken from the *Oxford English Dictionary*, 2nd ed., 1989, and 3rd ed., 2000– (online edition).

9. Hence, the use of "auditory" in the anatomy of the human hearing apparatus: "auditory canal," "auditory nerve," etc.

10. See Michele Friedner and Stefan Helmreich, "Sound Studies Meets Deaf Studies," *The Senses and Society* 7, no. 1 (2012): 72–86, for an overview of the two fields and a discussion of noncochlear modalities of experiencing sound.

11. My use of "auditory regime" follows Kate Lacey's call for an investigation of the "hierarchically differentiated and competing auditory regimes analogous to [French film theorist Christian] Metz's scopic regimes (scientifically and technologically generated 'techniques of observation')," as part of her study of American radio listening practices. Lacey's work was

inspired by scholars of visual studies who "draw attention to the ruptures, discontinuities and multiplicity of viewing positions within and across historical moments and in relation to different techniques and technologies of spectatorship." Kate Lacey, "Towards a Periodization of Listening: Radio and Modern Life," *International Journal of Cultural Studies* 3 (2000): 280–1. A dozen years earlier, Kaja Silverman employed the term, without explicitly defining it, to point to the structured sensibilities embedded in the sounds of films within a given period. Kaja Silverman, *The Acoustic Mirror: The Female Voice in Psychoanalysis and Cinema* (Bloomington: Indiana University Press.1988), ix, 31, 38, and 177. The notion of historically contingent, technologically enabled listening practices has been circulating for some time. See most prominently Peter Manuel, *Cassette Culture: Popular Music and Technology in Northern India* (Chicago: University of Chicago Press, 1993). See also the discussions of "structures of listening" in John Mowitt, "The Sound of Music in the Era of Its Electronic Reproducibility," in *Music and Society: The Politics of Composition, Performance and Reception*, ed. Richard Leppert and Susan McClary, 173–97 (Cambridge, UK: Cambridge University Press, 1987); "regimes of aural sensibility" in Charles Hirschkind, *The Ethical Soundscape: Cassette Sermons and Islamic Counterpublics* (New York: University of Columbia Press, 2006); and "audile techniques" in Jonathan Sterne, *The Audible Past: Cultural Origins of Sound Reproduction* (Durham, NC: Duke University Press, 2003). In describing what I would call the general foundation of all auditory regimes of musical listening, Richard Leppert wrote, "listening, to belabour the obvious, demands a listener. But listen*ing* is not properly understood as a biological phenomenon, rather a historico-sociocultural one: the listener is framed by history, society, and culture": "The Social Discipline of Listening," in *Aural Cultures*, ed. Jim Drobnick (Toronto: YYZ Books, 2004), 27. It is with a similar awareness of the multiple domains that surround, frame, and partially structure any act of auditory perception that I deploy the term here.

12. See Robert C. Schank and Robert P. Abelson, *Scripts, Plans, Goals, and Understanding: An Inquiry into Human Knowledge Structures* (Hillsdale, NJ: L. Erlbaum Associates, 1977).

13. For a discussion of the ways in which listening can be made public, see Peter Szendy, *Listen: A History of Our Ears*, trans. Charlotte Mandell (New York: Fordham University Press, 2008).

14. The assumption that sound is public and intersubjective has been treated as self-evident throughout the entire history of acoustics, music studies, and more recently sound studies. Works focusing on the coordination of sounding outside of musical contexts are numerous, ranging from Alain Corbin's *Village Bells: Sound and Meaning in the 19th-Century French Countryside* (New York: Columbia University Press, 1998) to Jonathan Sterne's "Enemy Voice," *Social Text 96* 26, no. 3 (2008): 79–100. Among the works that investigate sounding within a context of violence, see Steve Goodman, *Sonic Warfare: Sound, Affect, and the Ecology of Fear* (Cambridge, MA: MIT Press, 2010). Suzanne Cusick's work, cited throughout this volume, is similarly premised upon the alarmingly public nature of sound.

15. This term is the title of a recent book by Brandon LaBelle, *Acoustic Territories: Sound Culture and Everyday Life* (New York: Continuum, 2010).

16. Steven Feld and Keith H. Basso, "Introduction," in *Senses of Place*, ed. Steven Feld and Keith H. Basso (Santa Fe, NM: School of American Research Press, 1996), 7.

17. The history of thinking about sound's relationship with architectural spaces is almost as long as written history itself. Conservatively, one can point to ancient Greek discussions of amphitheaters as an example of an explicit theory of sound interacting with architecture. The

past two centuries of scientific literature on room acoustics represent the modern iteration of a very old conversation. Among sound studies scholars and anthropologists of sound, in addition to Feld and Basso's landmark work *Senses of Place*, Labelle's *Acoustic Territories* adopts a somewhat looser and more flexible definition of acoustic territory. See also Emily Thompson's discussion of the ways in which sonic preferences in the early twentieth century led to the development of new architectural forms, *The Soundscape of Modernity: Architectural Acoustics and the Culture of Listening in America, 1900–1933* (Cambridge, MA: MIT Press, 2002).

18. See Bruno Latour, *Reassembling the Social: An Introduction to Actor-Network-Theory* (New York: Oxford University Press, 2007).

CHAPTER 3

1. Raviv Ganchrow, "Perspectives on Sound-Space: The Story of Acoustic Defense," *Leonardo Music Journal* 19 (2009): 71.

2. Pierre Bourdieu, *The Logic of Practice* (Stanford, CA: Stanford University Press, 1990 [1980]).

3. Ibid., 57.

4. Craig Calhoun, "Pierre Bourdieu," in *The Blackwell Companion to Major Contemporary Social Theorists,* ed. George Ritzer (Malden, MA: Blackwell, 2000), 293.

5. A recent (2012) Navy commercial bears the title "Feel the Rush." http://www.defensenews.com/VideoNetwork/57432191001/New-Navy-Commercial-Feel-the-Rush.

6. Donald Mosher, "Hypermasculinity Inventory," in *Handbook of Sexuality-Related Measures,* ed. Clive M. Davis et al. (Thousand Oaks, CA: Sage, 1998), 472. Cf. Leora N. Rosen et al., "Cohesion and the Culture of Hypermasculinity in U.S. Army Units," *Armed Forces and Society* 29, no. 3 (2003): 325–51.

7. "I am an American Soldier./I am a warrior and a member of a team./I serve the people of the United States, and live the Army Values./I will always place the mission first./I will never accept defeat./I will never quit./I will never leave a fallen comrade./I am disciplined, physically and mentally tough, trained and proficient in my warrior tasks and drills./I always maintain my arms, my equipment and myself./I am an expert and I am a professional./I stand ready to deploy, engage, and destroy, the enemies of the United States of America in close combat./I am a guardian of freedom and the American way of life./I am an American Soldier."

8. Throughout the whole scene, while kissing Ilsa, listening to the guns, and drinking up the champagne so the Germans won't get it, Rick never lets go of the lit cigarette that burns in his steady hand.

9. Even though she is about to perform an act of selfless bravery—leaving Rick, the man she loves, to risk her life by accompanying Victor Laszlo on his campaign of anti-Nazi activism—Bogie is the one who exhibits the kind of stoic unflappability that is one of the central conventions of masculinity.

10. Pinch and Bijsterveld delineate four "modes of listening" that are distinctive practices within multiple professions: "Diagnostic listening" describes "the mode of listening that physicians apply to identify pathologies when using a stethoscope . . . and that engineers use to detect the origin of calculation mistakes in computers by amplifying their sound. . . . Diagnostic listening reveals what is wrong." Trevor Pinch and Karin Bijsterveld, "Introduction," in *The Oxford Handbook of Sound Studies,* ed. Trevor Pinch and Karin Bijsterveld (New York: Oxford

University Press, 2012), 14. In the AK-47 scene from *Heartbreak Ridge,* the "pathology" is the violent act indexed by the sound of the rifle firing.

11. Murphy was the most decorated combat veteran in the history of the United States Armed Forces. After retiring from active duty, he became an outspoken advocate for veterans' affairs, opening up a national conversation on the "battle fatigue"—later redefined as post-traumatic stress disorder—from which he suffered.

12. Luigi Russolo, *The Art of Noise,* trans. Robert Filliou (New York: Something Else Press, 1967 [1913]).

13. Interview with the author. Washington, DC, 2010.

14. See chapter 7, "Mobile Music in the Military," and Jonathan Pieslak, *Sound Targets: American Soldiers and Music in the Iraq War* (Bloomington: Indiana University Press, 2009), for an extended discussion of the prevalence of metal and other musics on service members' "battle playlists."

15. For a discussion of metal's transgressive dimension, see Keith Kahn-Harris, *Extreme Metal: Music and Culture on the Edge* (Oxford: Berg, 2006), 27–50. For an analysis of the implication of timbre for transgression, see Harris M. Berger and Cornelia Fales, "'Heaviness' in the Perception of Heavy Metal Guitar Timbres: The Match of Perceptual and Acoustic Features over Time," in *Wired for Sound: Engineering and Technologies in Sonic Cultures,* ed. Paul D. Greene and Thomas Porcello (Middletown, CT: Wesleyan University Press, 2005), 181–97.

16. "Iraq incoming bomb missile morter drill not a funny joke [sic]," YouTube video, 1:17, posted by aaahandyman4u, September 20, 2011, http://www.youtube.com/watch?v=umAPUYkmydQ.

17. John Mowitt, "The Sound of Music in the Era of Its Electronic Reproducibility," in *Music and Society: The Politics of Composition, Performance and Reception*, ed. Richard Leppert and Susan McClary, 173–97 (Cambridge, UK: Cambridge University Press, 1987).

18. Jonathan Sterne, *The Audible Past: Cultural Origins of Sound Reproduction* (Durham, NC: Duke University Press, 2003).

19. Field Manual No. 3–21.75 (21–75), *The Warrior Ethos and Soldier Combat Skills* (Washington, DC: Headquarters, Department of the Army, 2008).

20. Ibid., chap. 9, Introduction.

21. Ibid., Section 7.21.

22. Scott D. McIlwain, "The Army Hearing Program: Expanding Audiology's Military Reach," *ASHA Leader,* Jan. 20, 2009, http://www.asha.org/Publications/leader/2009/090120/090120g.htm.

23. "Army Hearing Program," ST 4–02.501, February 1, 2008, 1–1, Headquarters, Department of the Army.

24. "'The numbers are staggering,' says Theresa Schulz, PhD, CCC–A, PS/A, Lt Col (ret) USAF, past president of the National Hearing Conservation Association and a 21-year veteran Army and Air Force audiologist. Schulz penned an article in 2004 for *Hearing Health* magazine titled 'Troops Returning with Alarming Rates of Hearing Loss,' confirming the epidemic proportions of the problem. Since then, she affirms, the military has substantially intensified its efforts to reduce the frequency and severity of the problem." http://www.hearingreview.com/products/16720-armed-forces-battle-invisible-disability.

25. D. Scott McIlwain, Kathy Gates, and Donald Ciliax, "Heritage of Army Audiology and the Road Ahead: The Army Hearing Program," *American Journal of Public Health* 98, no. 12 (2008): 2167–72, http://www.ncbi.nlm.nih.gov/pmc/articles/PMC2636536/

26. Interview with the author. New York, 2010.

27. "Boomerang III Shooter Detection System—State-of-the-Art Shooter Detection," LiveLeak.com, posted by bravo61, March 2, 2009, http://www.liveleak.com/view?i=9cf_1235900066.

28. Kris Osborn, "Army Deploying Individual Gunshot Detector," *Army News Service,* March 14, 2011, http://www.army.mil/article/53292/army-deploying-individual-gunshot-detector/.

29. Samuel Soza, "Shooter-Detection 'Boomerangs' Helping in Iraq," *Official Homepage of the US Army,* December 17, 2009, http://www.army.mil/-news/2009/12/17/32029-shooter-detectio n-boomerangs-helping-in-iraq/index.html.

30. Amy Belasco, "Troop Levels in the Afghan and Iraq Wars, FY2001–FY2012: Cost and Other Potential Issues," *CRS Report for Congress* (Washington, DC: Congressional Research Service, 2009), 35.

31. Steven Carney, *Allied Participation in Operation Iraqi Freedom* (Washington, DC: Center for Military History, U.S. Army, 2011), 27.

32. Haider al-Abadi succeeded al-Maliki as Prime Minister in 2014.

33. This is not to say that global media stereotypes are not present. Many of my Iraqi interlocutors—particularly the younger ones—are familiar with a broad array of American cinematic representations of war, from *Rambo* to *Black Hawk Down*. What I mean to emphasize here is the element of overdetermination that is often ignored in scholarly treatments of media influence. In other words, the similarity of practices of masculine audition cannot be linked causally to the ubiquity of American pop culture.

34. Robin Bernstein, "Dances with Things: Material Culture and the Performance of Race," *Social Text* 27, no. 4 (2009): 75.

35. Interview with the author. Detroit, MI, 2012.

36. By comparison, this number of casualties would be "the equivalent of 5.6 million for a population the size of the United States." "Iran-Iraq War (1980–1988)," GlobalSecurity.org, last updated November 7, 2011, http://www.globalsecurity.org/military/world/war/iran-iraq.htm.

37. Interview with the author. Amman, Jordan, 2008.

38. Interview with the author. Detroit, MI, 2012.

39. Noor's story and my analysis of it were published in J. Martin Daughtry, "Thanatosonics: Ontologies of Acoustic Violence," *Social Text* 32, no. 2 (2014): 34.

40. Saddam Hussein was a relatively fluent English speaker, many Iraqi children were exposed to English in high school, and some university programs were conducted in English, for example.

41. See chapter 6 for a description of one-way translation devices used during Operation Iraqi Freedom.

42. Jacques Rancière, "Ten Theses on Politics," *Theory and Event* 5, no. 3 (2001).

43. To take one example, if a combat soldier gathered his comrades into a sincere hug in order to render the sound of sirens less scary, the social costs of this act would likely be real and immediate. In the final fragment of this volume, I examine one such idiosyncratic listening act, which was absolutely the result of massive labor.

CHAPTER 4

1. See, for example, Matthew Nudds and Casey O'Callaghan's essay, "Introduction: The Philosophy of Sounds and Auditory Perception," in *Sounds and Perception: New Philosophical Essays*, ed. Matthew Nudds and Casey O'Callaghan (New York: Oxford, 2009), 2–24.

2. The quote is from Connor's essay, "Edison's Teeth: Touching Hearing." In *Hearing Cultures: Essays on Sound, Listening, and Modernity*, edited by Veit Erlmann, 153–72. Oxford and New York: Berg, 2004.

3. Casey O'Callaghan, *Sounds: A Philosophical Theory* (Oxford and New York: Oxford University Press, 2007), 29–43. For O'Callaghan, acoustic waves, as distinct from sounds, carry information about sounds and their locations to the auditor.

4. Steve Goodman, *Sonic Warfare* (Cambridge, MA: MIT Press, 2010), 10.

5. Curtis Roads, *Microsound* (Cambridge, MA: MIT Press, 2001), 7–8.

6. Kevin Powers, *Yellow Birds: A Novel* (New York: Little, Brown, 2012), 117, Ibid., 124–5.

7. János Maróthy, "Rite and Rhythm: From Behaviour Patterns to Musical Structures," *Studia Musicologica Academiae Scientiarum Hungaricae* 35, fasc. 4 (1993–4): 426. See also Don Ihde, *Listening and Voice: Phenomenologies of Sound* (Albany: State University of New York Press, 2007), 98.

8. Suzanne Cusick, "Towards an Acoustemology of Detention in the 'Global War on Terror,'" in *Music, Sound and Space: Transformations of Public and Private Experience,* ed. Georgina Born (Cambridge, UK: Cambridge University Press, 2013), 276; my emphasis.

9. James J. Gibson, "The Theory of Affordances," in *Perceiving, Acting, and Knowing: Toward an Ecological Psychology,* ed. R. Shaw and J. Bransford (Hillsdale, NJ: Lawrence Erlbaum, 1977), 67–82.

10. Carolyn Nordstrom, *A Different Kind of War Story* (Philadelphia: University of Pennsylvania Press, 1997), 6.

11. Christopher Yates, "Introduction," *Philosophy and the Return to Violence: Studies from this Widening Gyre,* ed. Nathan Eckstrand and Christopher S. Yates (New York: Continuum, 2011), 1.

12. Michel Wieviorka, *Violence: A New Approach,* trans. David Macey (London: Sage, 2009), 3.

13. James Dodd, *Violence and Phenomenology* (New York: Routledge, 2009), 1.

14. A. J. Reiss Jr. and J. A. Roth, eds., *Understanding and Preventing Violence,* Vol. 1 (Washington, DC: National Academy Press, 1993), 35, cited in Mary Jackman, "Violence in Social Life," *Annual Review of Sociology* 28 (2002): 389.

15. "The term 'crime of violence' means (a) an offense that has as an element the use, attempted use, or threatened use of physical force against the person or property of another, or (b) any other offense that is a felony and that, by its nature, involves a substantial risk that physical force against the person or property of another may be used in the course of committing the offense." 18 U.S.C. § 16—Crime of violence defined.

16. Jackman, "Violence in Social Life," 405.

17. Ibid., 398.

18. Ibid.

19. See Talal Asad, *On Suicide Bombing* (New York: Columbia University Press, 2007); Banu Bargu, "The Weaponization of Life," *Constellations* 16, no. 4 (2009): 634–43; Banu Bargu, "Forging Life into a Weapon," *Social Text*/Periscope (2011), http://www.socialtextjournal.org/periscope/2011/05/the-weaponization-of-life---banu-bargu.php.

20. See Elaine Scarry, *The Body in Pain: The Making and Unmaking of the World* (New York: Oxford University Press, 1985).

21. Jackman, "Violence in Social Life," 396.

22. Slavoj Žižek, *Violence: Six Sideways Reflections* (New York: Macmillan, 2008), 11. See also Susan Fast and Kip Pegley, "Introduction," in *Music, Politics, and Violence,* ed. Susan Fast and Kip Pegley (Middletown, CT: Wesleyan University Press, 2012), 1–33.

23. Žižek, *Violence*, 1–2. Žižek's discussion of "subjective" (acute) and "objective" (structural) violence is echoed in Wieviorka's analysis of "hot" ("expressive") and "cold" ("instrumental") violence. See Wieviorka, *Violence: A New Approach,* 89–90.

24. Žižek, *Violence,* 3.

25. In his oft-cited essay on intersensoriality, Steven Connor points to the "stubborn association" of sound "with violence and suffering." "Unlike the other senses," he argues, "which have been conceived in terms of the neutral or contingent commingling of traces, sound can come about only as a result of some more or less violent disturbance: the collision of objects with each other . . . and the transmission of this agitation through the air to the ears or skin of another. Sound beats, stretches, compresses, contorts." Steven Connor, "Edison's Teeth: Touching Hearing," in *Hearing Cultures: Essays on Sound, Listening, and Modernity,* ed. Veit Erlmann (Oxford and New York: Berg, 2004), 161–2.

26. Ibid, 2. Connor goes on to state that "objective violence is precisely the violence inherent to this 'normal' state of things."

27. On the intersubjectivity of violence, see also Michael Jackson, *The Politics of Storytelling: Violence, Transgression, and Intersubjectivity* (Copenhagen: Museum Tusculanum Press, 2002), 44.

28. See Goodman's "ontology of vibrational force" in *Sonic Warfare,* xix.

29. Two or more auditors are needed to confirm that a sound is physically present in the world and not an imagined event occurring in a single person's head.

30. This element of coercion is singled out in Krohn-Hansen's contention that "violence is a way to social advancement characterized by the fact that the others—victims and witnesses—are by definition *unwilling* others." Christian Krohn-Hansen, "The Anthropology of Violent Interaction," *Journal of Anthropological Research* 50, no. 4 (1994): 370. Jackman's discussion of voluntary victimhood problematizes this distinction.

31. The similarity between these quotes is indicative: (1) "Anything worthy of the name 'violence' inevitably signals a certain transgression of what a body of actors regards as legitimate means, no matter whether we are talking about individuals, groups, or wider ensembles that function on an international scale. Violence is a resource that is different to any other, to the extent that it implies the idea of non-legitimacy and marks a break from what is acceptable within a given social or political space." Wieviorka, *Violence: A New Approach,* 93–4. (2) "Noise is widely considered to be situated within excess, as a transgressive act that exceeds managed data. Noise is 'out of control,' and as such its theorists are pulled into its chaos with ringing ears." Caleb Kelly, *Cracked Media: The Sound of Malfunction* (Cambridge, MA: MIT Press, 2009), 63.

32. One exception: the LRAD and other advanced technologies that create narrowly directional sound.

33. For more on acoustic leakages, and technocultural responses to them, see Jason Stanyek and Benjamin Piekut, "Deadness: Technologies of the Intermundane," *TDR* 54, no. 1 (2010): 14–38, esp. 25–6.

34. Brian Kane, "Acousmatic Fabrications: Les Paul and the 'Les Paulverizer,'" *Journal of Visual Culture* 10, no. 212 (2011): 215. See also Michel Chion *Audio-Vision: Sound on Screen*, ed. and trans. Claudia Gorbman (New York: Columbia, 1994), esp. 129–31; Mladen Dolar, *A Voice and Nothing More* (Cambridge, MA: MIT Press, 2006), 60–71.

35. Dolar, *A Voice and Nothing More*, 62.

36. In a move that complements my argument here, over the past decade a focus on the "bidirectionality of violence" has emerged in clinical literature on trauma. Here bidirectionality is usually understood in a diachronic context in which children who are the recipients of domestic violence become violent themselves. See Izaskun Ibabe, Joana Jaureguizar, and Oscar Diaz, "Adolescent Violence Against Parents: Is It a Consequence of Gender Inequality?" *The European Journal of Psychology Applied to Legal Context* 1, no. 1 (2009): 3–24. See also S. Barkin, S. Keriter, and R. H. DuRant, "Exposure to Violence and Intentions to Engage in Moralistic Violence During Early Adolescence," *Journal of Adolescence* 24, no. 6 (2001): 777–89; K. J. Mitchell and D. Finkelhor, "Risk of Crime Victimization Among Youth Exposed to Domestic Violence," *Journal of Interpersonal Violence* 16, no. 9 (2001): 944–64.

37. Sociologist Robert Agnew's work on "general strain theory" has recently been applied to an empirical analysis of criminal aggression among OIF/OEF veterans who have been diagnosed with PTSD. See Robert Agnew, "Foundation for a General Strain Theory of Crime and Delinquency," *Criminology* 30, no. 1 (1992): 47–87. In a 2012 study, researchers found that veterans who were traumatized by violent acts during their tours of duty appeared to be significantly more likely to engage in aggressive acts once they returned home. The study notes that, according to the U.S. Bureau of Justice, "over 200,000 veterans [of all US wars] are in U.S. jails and prisons, and more than half have been incarcerated for violent offenses." This figure, which is likely low, as data on veterans in prison have not been systematically collected, accounts for roughly 10 percent of all inmates: Eric B. Elbogen, Sally C. Johnson, Virginia M. Newton, Kristy Straits-Troster, Jennifer J. Vasterling, H. Ryan Wagner, and Jean C. Beckham, "Criminal Justice Involvement, Trauma, and Negative Affect in Iraq and Afghanistan War Era Veterans," *Journal of Consulting and Clinical Psychology* 80, no. 6 (2012): 1097–102. A study based on interviews with 676 veterans concluded that "veterans who said they had difficulty controlling violent behavior were more likely to report witnessing pre-military family violence, firing a weapon during deployment, being deployed more than 1 year, and experiencing current hyperarousal symptoms" that mirrored those they felt when exposed to violence during the war: University of North Carolina School of Medicine, "Specific PTSD Symptoms Related to Anger and Aggressiveness Among Iraq/Afghanistan Veterans, Study Finds," *Science Daily,* June 15, 2010, http://www.sciencedaily.com/releases/2010/06/100615093234.htm. Another recent study of 2,797 active-duty soldiers returning from Operation Iraqi Freedom found a statistically significant elevation in the level of self-reported hostility and anger among the 40 percent of those surveyed who reported killing someone in combat. See Shira Maguen, Barbara A. Lucenko, Mark A. Reger, Gregory A. Gahm, Brett T. Litz, Karen H. Seal, Sara J. Knight, and Charles R. Marmar, "The Impact of Reported Direct and Indirect Killing on Mental Health Symptoms in Iraq War Veterans," *Journal of Traumatic Stress* 23, no. 1 (2010): 86–90. See also Chris Lawrence and Jennifer Rizzo, "Under Fire: Wartime Stress as a Defense for Murder," *CNN,* May 11, 2012, http://www.cnn.com/2012/05/05/justice/ptsd-murder-defense/index.html.

38. Noortje Marres, "Issues Spark a Public into Being: A Key but Often Forgotten Point of the Lippmann-Dewey Debate," In *Making Things Public,* ed. Bruno Latour and Peter Weibel,

216 (Cambridge, MA: MIT Press, 2005), quoted in Jane Bennett, *Vibrant Matter: A Political Ecology of Things* (Durham, NC: Duke University Press, 2010), 36.

39. Bennett, *Vibrant Matter,* 36.

40. FM 3–05.30/MCRP 3–40.6, "Psychological Operations" [a manual], April 2005, Headquarters, Department of the Army.

41. Al-Sahhaf was nicknamed "Baghdad Bob" in the United States, a name that linked him to other wartime propagandists such as "Tokyo Rose" and "Hannoi Hannah." A recent article in *The Atlantic* described him as "everybody's favorite inadvertent comedian. Sporting a kicky black beret and delightfully bombastic lexicon, [he] appeared on TV daily to predict American failure and deny the Baghdad invasion—sometimes even as U.S. tanks appeared behind him. 'He's great,' President George W. Bush said of Sahaf, admitting that he occasionally interrupted meetings to watch Sahaf's briefings. 'Someone accused us of hiring him and putting him there. He was a classic." The same article went on to argue that, surprisingly, many of Sahhaf's pronouncements—about the lack of weapons of mass destruction, the widespread rejection of the American-led invasion, the threat posed by insurgents—turned out to be presciently true. Emily Deprang, "'Baghdad Bob' and His Ridiculous, True Predictions," *The Atlantic,* March 21, 2013, http://www.theatlantic.com/international/archive/2013/03/baghdad-bob-and-his-ridiculous-true-predictions/274241/.

42. Steven Collins, "Psychological Operations in Combat, Peacekeeping, and Fighting Terrorism," in *Military Life: The Psychology of Serving in Peace and Combat,* ed. Thomas W. Britt, Amy B. Adler, and Carl Andrew Castro, Vol. 1 (Westport, CT: Praeger Security International, 2006), 73.

43. Nick Grace, "Bush Address Underscores Importance of Radio PSYOP," http://www.clandestineradio.com/crw/news.php?id=176&stn=75&news=529, quoted in Collins, "Psychological Operations in Combat," 74.

44. Collins, "Psychological Operations in Combat," 74.

45. Evan Thomas, "The Secret War," *Newsweek,* April 20, 2003, http://www.thedailybeast.com/newsweek/2003/04/20/the-secret-war.html; my emphasis.

46. Collins, "Psychological Operations in Combat," 74.

47. Interview with the author. Amman, Jordan, 2008.

48. "Explosion Rocks Northeast Baghdad Police Station, 10 Dead," *Associated Press,* October 9, 2003. Reprinted in *Haaretz,* October 9, 2003, http://www.haaretz.com/news/explosion-rocks-northeast-baghdad-police-station-10-dead-1.102209.

49. Nir Rosen, "Muqtada al-Sadr and the Army of the Mahdi," *The Progressive,* June 2004, http://progressive.org/mag_rosen0604.

50. "U.S. Hits Mosque Compound in Fallujah," Foxnews.com, April 7, 2004, http://www.foxnews.com/story/2004/04/07/us-hits-mosque-compound-in-fallujah/#ixzz2VAIwgwLc.

51. Lane DeGregory, "Iraq 'n' Roll," *St. Petersburg Times [Tampa Bay Times],* November 21, 2004, http://www.sptimes.com/2004/11/21/Floridian/Iraq__n__roll.shtml.

52. Jackie Spinner and Karl Vick, "Troops Battle for Last Parts of Fallujah," *Washington Post,* November 14, 2004, A1.

53. Phone interview with the author, 2007; my emphasis.

54. See, for example, the following description, an action report filed by a member of the US Army 10th Cavalry Regiment in 2008, subsequently distributed on wikileaks.org. (Bracketed text replaces abbreviations with full words and phrases): "[Iraqi Army] conduct a show of

force patrol on [Route] Poison. They come upon a suspicious black bag in the street and set a cordon. While the cordon is set, a small IED detonated with 1 [Iraqi Army soldier] receiving minor wounds. When the other soldiers went to give aid, a second, larger IED detonated on the [Iraqi Army troops] resulting in 4 additional [wounded-in-action]." In the same report, another similar incident is described: "IED detonates on . . . [Iraqi Army] patrol killing the [Iraqi Army] platoon leader (Lt. Latif) and wounding 4 others. . . . [Second] IED detonate on [Iraqi Army] patrol resulting in 1 [Iraqi Army killed-in-action] and 2 [wounded-in-action]. . . . Assessment: this attack is likely perpetrated by the same [Al-Qaeda in Iraq] cell that is responsible for the 24 April and 26 April bombings on [Route] Cinderella and [Route] Cardinals respectively as they have used a very similar [tactic, technique, and procedure] in all three attacks." See http://wikileaks.org/irq/report/2008/04/IRQ20080427n11220.html for the full text of the anonymous and untitled report.

55. E. Valentine Daniel, *Charred Lullabies,* 120–3. See also Dodd, *Violence and Phenomenology,* 53. In *The Human Condition* (Chicago: University of Chicago Press, 1958), Hannah Arendt famously wrote that "violence is mute" (26).

56. In his 2009 monograph on British war literature, Patrick Deer examines discursive silences for the ideological genealogies they contain. His operative assumption is that, in wartime especially, "silence is actively produced." Patrick Deer, *Culture in Camouflage: War, Empire, and Modern British Literature* (Oxford and New York: Oxford University Press, 2009), 184. See also Brandon Labelle's discussion of silence and violence in *Acoustic Territories: Sound Culture and Everyday Life* (New York: Continuum, 2010), 66–83.

57. Interview with the author. Washington, DC, 2010.

58. I return to this topic in chapter 7, "A Time of Troubles for Iraqi Music."

59. Jonathan Sterne, "Enemy Voice," 84.

60. Ibid.

61. "Zarqawi was the operational commander of the terrorist movement in Iraq. He led a campaign of car bombings, assassinations and suicide attacks that has taken the lives of many American forces and thousands of innocent Iraqis. Osama bin Laden called this Jordanian terrorist 'the prince of Al Qaeda in Iraq.' He [bin Laden] called on the terrorists of the world to listen to him [Zarqawi], and obey him. Zarqawi personally beheaded American hostages and other civilians in Iraq. He masterminded the destruction of the United Nations headquarters in Baghdad. He was responsible for the assassination of an American diplomat in Jordan, and the bombing of a hotel in Amman. Through his every action, he sought to defeat America and our Coalition partners, and turn Iraq into a safe haven from which Al Qaeda could wage its war on free nations. To achieve these ends he worked to divide Iraqis, and incite civil war. Only last week he released an audiotape attacking Iraq's elected leaders, and denouncing those advocating the end of sectarianism. Now Zarqawi has met his end, and this violent man will never murder again. . . . The ideology of terror has lost one of its most visible and aggressive leaders." Video of the full press conference may be found at: "Bush's Full Speech On Zarqawi," CBSNews.com, June 8, 2006, http://www.cbsnews.com/video/watch/?id=1693089n.

62. Joshua Partlow and Michael Abramowitz, "Officials Detail Zarqawi's Last Hour," *Washington Post,* June 13, 2006.

63. See Michel Wieviorka, *Violence: A New Approach,* 98; and "Violence and the Subject," *Thesis Eleven* 73 (2003): 44–5. Both depictions hide elements of their opposites, however. The beheading was premeditated, composed, performed, and captured for an international audience,

and the technocratic language of Bush and other public figures only partially concealed their glee at having destroyed one of their most prominent adversaries.

CHAPTER 5

1. Edward S. Casey, "Between Geography and Philosophy: What Does It Mean to Be in the Place-World?" *Annals of the Association of American Geographers* 91, no. 4 (2001), 688; my emphasis.

2. Steven Feld, "Places Sensed, Senses Placed: Toward a Sensuous Epistemology of Environments," in *Empire of the Senses: The Sensual Culture Reader*, ed. David Howes (Oxford and New York: Berg, 2005), 179.

3. David Howes, "Introduction: Empires of the Senses," in Howes, *Empire of the Senses*, 7.

4. As we have seen elsewhere, the unstated assumption is that this tangling up is either a good thing, adding richness to human experience, or at worst a neutral thing, a knot of registers (body-mind-environment) that scholars may dispassionately loosen.

5. Edward S. Casey, "Smooth Spaces and Rough-Edged Places: The Hidden History of Place," *Review of Metaphysics* 5, no. 2 (1997): 270

6. Edward S. Casey, "Between Geography and Philosophy," 683. Elsewhere, Casey describes the way in which emplacement persists in the body: "Moving in or through a given place, the body imports its own emplaced past into its present experience: its 'local history' is literally a history of locales. This very importation of past places occurs simultaneously with the body's ongoing establishment of directionality, level, and distance—and indeed influences these latter in myriad ways. Orientation in place (which is what is established by these three factors) cannot be continually effected *de novo* but arises within the ever-lengthening shadow of our bodily past." Edward Casey, *Remembering: A Phenomenological Study* (Bloomington: Indiana University Press, 1987), 194.

7. Ibid., 688.

8. Ibid.

9. Howes, *Empire of the Senses*, 7.

10. Casey, *Remembering*, 685.

11. Yael Navaro-Yashin. *The Make-Believe Space: Affective Geography in a Postwar Polity* (Durham, NC: Duke University Press, 2012).

12. Also called *antistasis* or *antanaclasis*, transplacement (Caplan's English rendering of the Latin *traductio*) is discussed in Cicero's *Ad Herennium*, trans. Harry Caplan, Loeb Classical Library (Cambridge, MA: Harvard University Press, 1964), 299. See also J. Bunselmeyer, "Appearances and Verbal Paradox, Sonnets 129 and 138," *Shakespeare Quarterly* 25, no. 1 (1974): 103–08. Another well-known vernacular example of transplacement came from a speech Vince Lombardi is said to have given to his players before they took the field: "If you are not fired with enthusiasm," he shouted, "you will be *fired with enthusiasm*."

13. William Shakespeare, *Othello*, act 5, scene 2, line 7.

14. The most prominent theorists of sound and territoriality are Deleuze and Guattari, whose chapter, "Of the Refrain," in their co-authored book *A Thousand Plateaus* is a sustained meditation on, among other themes, the ways that sound can create or disrupt a sense of home. While too allusive and complex to fit my purposes here, their treatment of "the refrain" has been very influential throughout the humanities, and could prove valuable for further investigations of

belliphonic territoriality. Gilles Deleuze and Félix Guattari, *A Thousand Plateaus: Capitalism and Schizophrenia*, trans. Brian Massumi (Minneapolis: University of Minnesota Press, 1987), 310-350.

15. Robert Sack, *Human Territoriality: Its Theory and History* (Cambridge, UK: Cambridge University Press, 1986), 19; emphasis in the original.

16. The current edition of the *Oxford English Dictionary* has eliminated all language suggesting a link between "territory" and "terror." My thanks to Steve Dodson for pointing this out to me, and for his impeccable copyedits throughout this book.

17. William Connolly, "Tocqueville, Territory, and Violence," in *Challenging Boundaries: Global Flows, Territorial Identities*, ed. M. Shapiro and H. Alker (Minneapolis: University of Minnesota Press, 1996), 144; my emphasis.

18. See Tong Soon Lee, "Technology and the Production of Islamic Space: The Call to Prayer in Singapore," *Ethnomusicology* 43, no. 1 (1999): 86–100.

19. Brandon LaBelle, *Acoustic Territories: Sound Culture and Everyday Life* (New York: Continuum, 2010), xxv.

20. Ibid., xvii and xxiv.

21. "*Rhizophonia* describes the fundamentally fragmented yet proliferative condition of sound reproduction and recording, where sounds and bodies are constantly dislocated, relocated, and co-located in temporary aural configurations. We don't offer up rhizophonia as schizophonia's other, to use R. Murray Schafer's well-trodden term (1977). It's not the missing twin. Rather, we suggest it as a *replacement* for schizophonia, itself a problematic, tautological term that seems to describe an exception (sound severed from source) to some impossible, full presence (sound as identical with its source; see Sterne 2000, 20–21). Indeed, schizophonia describes sound itself. All sounds are severed from their sources—that's what makes sound sound. Rhizophonia is our term for taking account both of sound's extensity and the impossibility of a perfect identity between sound and source." Jason Stanyek and Ben Piekut, "Deadness: Technologies of the Intermundane," *TDR* 54, no. 1 (2010): 19.

22. Recall the "mock electrocution" photo that depicts a hooded detainee, clothed in a dirty tasseled cloth, standing barefoot atop a box. His arms are outstretched in a pose of supplication. Electrodes attached to his fingers and neck lead to wires that snake up the cinderblock wall behind him. We cannot see his face to read his emotions, but the terrifying situation and his body language combine to create a sense of absolute, existential vulnerability.

23. James Blake Miller, the Marine in question, was photographed by *Los Angeles Times* photographer Luis Sinco. Three years later, Sinco reflected on the experience in an article for his newspaper. In the interim, Lance Corporal Miller had been diagnosed with PTSD and given a medical discharge from the military. The auditory event that triggered his discharge is described later in this chapter. See Luis Sinco, "Two Lives Blurred Together by a Photo," *Los Angeles Times*, November 11, 2007, http://www.latimes.com/news/nationworld/nation/la-na-marlboro11nov11,0,4380908.story?page=1 See also the continuation of that article: Luis Sinco, "Rescue Operation Aims to Save a Wounded Soldier," *Los Angeles Times*, November 12, 2007, http://www.latimes.com/news/nationworld/nation/la-na-marlboro12nov12,0,4839662.story.

24. The photo, taken by David Leeson for the *Dallas Morning News,* can be found at: http://www.dallasnews.com/photos/20130317-10-year-anniversary-of-the-iraqi-war.ece?ssimg=927692.

25. Indeed, she was five at the time the photo was shot. In a story for the *New York Times,* Tim Arango documents the moment in 2011 when the girl, Samar Hasan, then twelve years old, first saw the photo from 2005. The photographer, Chris Hondrow, worked for Getty Images until he was killed in combat in Misurata, Libya. See Tim Arango, "Face that Screamed War's Pain Looks Back, 6 Hard Years Later," *New York Times,* May 7, 2011, http://www.nytimes.com/2011/05/07/world/middleeast/07photo.html?pagewanted=all&_r=0.

26. See "Iraq Militias Defy al-Qaeda," CNN, December 30, 2007, http://www.cnn.com/video/?/video/world/2007/12/30/whitbeck.iraq.awakening.cnn.

27. Military videos and insurgent videos were clearly aimed at two distinct populations, and as such were elements of two separate political projects. But beyond this core dissimilarity, they resembled one another in terms of their recording techniques, production values, and valorization of violent acts.

28. See Jonathan Pieslak, *Sound Targets: American Soldiers and Music in the Iraq War* (Bloomington: Indiana University Press, 2009), 46–77.

29. Allen Feldman, "On Cultural Anesthesia: From Desert Storm to Rodney King," *American Ethnologist* 21, no. 2 (1994): 406. In the case of the video recordings that emerged from the Iraq War, the mediatized frame increased the salience of the visual while radically attenuating the importance of the auditory. If the urge to survive in the combat zone turned seeing into a sporadic phenomenon while embracing the ubiquity of hearing, the recordings of the war tended to invert that relationship.

30. Stanyek and Piekut, "Deadness," 19.

31. John Law, "On the Subject of the Object: Narrative, Technology, and Interpellation," *Configurations* 8, no. 1 (2000): 28. Drawing on Donna Haraway's use of optical metaphors such as diffraction, Law discusses the effect of overlapping interpellations in optical terms, comparing them to light waves coinciding with or interfering with each other (24–5). Given Althusser's reliance on "the call" to explain interpellation, the wave metaphor works even better when transposed to a discussion of sound.

32. The Iraqi capital is a low-rise city, built largely from locally produced monochromatic tan bricks. Over the course of his reign, Saddam Hussein ordered millions of the date palms that surrounded the city to be cut down, which allowed the desert to encroach on the former oasis. These factors, along with traffic patterns and weather, shaped the acoustic territory of the city.

33. "They're trying to isolate us from other parts of Baghdad," claimed a doctor from the Adhamiya neighborhood. "The native Americans were treated better than us." Edward Wong and David S. Cloud, "U.S. Erects Baghdad Wall to Keep Sects Apart," *New York Times,* April 21, 2007, http://www.nytimes.com/2007/04/21/world/middleeast/21iraq.html.

34. Michael Rubin, "Less Is More in Iraq," *Washington Post,* August 9, 2005.

35. P. D. Smith, "Blast Walls for Structural Protection Against High Explosive Threats: A Review," *International Journal of Protective Structures* 1, no. 1 (2010): 67.

36. Stanyek and Piekut, "Deadness," 20, 22.

37. ACH helmet operator's manual, *Specialty Defense,* Aug. 2007, 10.

38. Similarly, the visor on the old helmet was removed to afford a greater field of vision for the wearer.

39. See Cusick's description of Donald Vance's incarceration in "'You Are in a Place that Is Out of the World . . .,'" 19–23.

40. "Report of the International Committee of the Red Cross (ICRC) on the Treatment by the Coalition Forces of Prisoners of War and Other Protected Persons by the Geneva Conventions in Iraq During Arrest, Internment and Interrogation, [February 2004], in *The Torture Papers: The Road to Abu Ghraib*, ed. Karen J. Greenberg and Joshua L. Dratel (Cambridge and New York: Cambridge University Press, 2005), 392.

41. Margrit Shildrick with Janet Price, "Openings on the Body: A Critical Introduction," in *Feminist Theory and the Body: A Reader*, ed. Janet Price and Margrit Shildrick (Edinburgh: Edinburgh University Press, 1999), 5. See also Donna Haraway, *Simians, Cyborgs, and Women: The Reinvention of Nature* (New York: Routledge, 1991).

42. Julia Kristeva, *Powers of Horror: An Essay in Abjection* (New York: Columbia University Press, 1982), 4.

43. The notion that the ear, along with other spaces in the body, can be territorialized bears a debt to Elizabeth Grosz, who, in interpreting Deleuze and Guattari's famous aphorism about the ear ("the ear is itself a refrain, it is shaped like one"), asks "is it not the case that the voice and the ear in human subjects are contrapuntally tied to each other? *Is not the ear itself a refrain that is continually deterritorialized by the voice?*" Elizabeth Grosz, *Chaos, Territory, Art: Deleuze and the Framing of the Earth* (New York: Columbia University Press, 2008), 40. (Emphasis added.) In Grosz's treatment, the ear is a metonym for the listening body, the voice is generally a musical voice, the deterritorialization is less physical than psychical, and the result is generally not disastrous. In the more literal, militaristic sense that I intend here, the act of territorialization takes place independently of the act of listening. At issue here is the physical invasion of waves into the physical space of the inner ear.

44. "The most vulnerable parts of the body to primary blast injury are considered to be those with air–fluid interfaces, particularly the lungs, bowel, and middle ear. Rupture of the tympanic membrane is the most frequent injury." Robin A. Hurley and Katherine H. Taber, eds., *Windows to the Brain: Insights from Neuroimaging* (Arlington, VA: American Psychiatric Publishing, 2008), 77.

45. Thomas M. Helfer et al., "Noise-Induced Hearing Injury and Comorbidities Among Postdeployment U.S. Army Soldiers: April 2003–June 2009," *American Journal of Audiology* 20, nos. 33–41 (2011): 33–41.

46. T. Tanielian and L. H. Jaycox, eds., *Invisible Wounds of War: Psychological and Cognitive Injuries, Their Consequences, and Services to Assist Recovery* (Santa Monica, CA: Rand, 2008). Also see Helfer et al., "Noise-Induced Hearing Injury and Comorbidities."

47. "Tympanic membrane perforation is the most common primary blast injury in the current conflicts and occurs in approximately one tenth of service members wounded by combat explosions." Amber E. Ritenour, Aaron Wickley, Joshua S. Ritenour, Brian R. Kriete, Lorne H. Blackbourne, John B. Holcomb, and Charles E. Wade, "Tympanic Membrane Perforation and Hearing Loss From Blast Overpressure in Operation Enduring Freedom and Operation Iraqi Freedom Wounded," *Journal of Trauma* 64(2 Suppl):S174–8, abstract.

48. See Peter M. Rabinowitz, "Noise-Induced Hearing Loss," *American Family Physician* 61, no. 9 (2000): 2749–56.

49. Steve Goodman, *Sonic Warfare*, 189.

50. Cusick, "'You Are In a Place that is Out of the World . . .,'" 17.

51. Cathy Caruth, "Introduction," in *Trauma: Explorations in Memory*, ed. Cathy Caruth (Baltimore: Johns Hopkins Press, 1995), 4–5; emphasis added.

52. See David Howes, ed., *The Sixth Sense Reader* (London: Berg, 2009).

CHAPTER 6

1. Sherry Turkle, "Introduction: The Things that Matter," in *Evocative Objects: Things We Think With,"* edited by Sherry Turkle (Cambridge, MA: MIT Press, 2007), 5.

2. Mark Landler, "Obama, in Speech on ISIS, Promises Sustained Effort to Rout Militants," *New York Times,* September 10, 2014, http://nyti.ms/1lUDSFs.

3. Important new works that deal with mobile music in the Iraq War include Pieslak, *Sound Targets: American Soldiers and Music in the Iraq War* (Bloomington: Indiana University Press, 2009), and Lisa Gilman, "An American Soldier's Ipod: Layers of Identity and Situated Listening in Iraq," *Music and Politics* 4, no. 2 (2010), http://www.music.ucsb.edu/projects/musicandpolitics/archive/2010-2/gilman.pdf.

4. The camouflage pattern marks the helmet as part of the US army's Desert Camouflage Uniform (DCU), which began to be phased out in 2005.

5. Donna Haraway's oft-cited "Cyborg Manifesto" (*Simians, Cyborgs, and Women: The Reinvention of Nature* [New York: Routledge, 1991]) presents the cyborg as a powerful trope for theorizing modern humans as biotechnological hybrids who are always already bound to technologies. Haraway uses the cyborg to "suggest a way out of the maze of dualisms in which we have explained our bodies and our tools to ourselves" (181). Thus framed, "modern war is a cyborg orgy, coded by C3I, command-control-communication-intelligence" (151). See also Bruno Latour's influential discussion of hybrids in *We Have Never Been Modern* (Cambridge, MA: Harvard University Press, 1993).

6. Photos, along with an account of Garrad's experience and a robust discussion of the images, can be found at http://www.flickr.com/photos/tiki/445621299/[http://www.flickr.com/photos/tiki/445621299/]. The *Wired* story carries the same photos: http://www.wired.com/gadgetlab/2007/04/ipod_vs_ak47_ip/. This image has circulated more than the first, showing up on well over a dozen websites and often including extensive commentaries on the physics of the incident or the possibility that the whole thing was a stunt pulled by Apple. In addition to English-language sites, Japanese, German, Russian, Czech, and Spanish sites covered the images.

7. One exception would be the local act of violence commonly referred to as 9/11. The 2001 attacks on the Pentagon and World Trade Center triggered a number of changes (most of them temporary) to the music industry in the United States and elsewhere. See Ritter and Daughtry, eds., *Music in the Post-9/11 World* (New York: Routledge, 2007), for a discussion of these events.

8. Copper Greene appears to have taken their name from the notorious Operation Copper Green, the black-ops interrogation program that Seymour Hersh had exposed in the *New Yorker* some months earlier.

9. The iRaq posters have received by far the most coverage of the three images I treat here. They have been discussed, in varying levels of detail, in Peter Howard Selz and Susan Landauer, *Art of Engagement: Visual Politics in California and Beyond* (Berkeley: University of California Press, 2006), 71–2; Steven Heller and Mirko Ilic, *The Anatomy of Design: Uncovering the Influences and Inspirations in Modern Graphic Design* (Gloucester, MA: Rockport, 2007); and Jasbir K. Puar, *Terrorist Assemblages: Homonationalism in Queer Times* (Durham, NC: Duke University Press, 2007), 102.

10. Bruce Johnson and Martin Cloonan engage in a sustained investigation of music and violence. See their volume *The Dark Side of the Tune: Popular Music and Violence* (London: Ashgate, 2008).

11. I argue a related point using similar language in J. Martin Daughtry, "Charting Courses through Terror's Wake: An Introduction," in Ritter and Daughtry, *Music in the Post-9/11 World*, xxi.

12. The Bible gives ample mention to music in martial contexts; earlier, Ancient Egyptian artists frequently depicted soldiers holding trumpets. Curt Sachs has argued that the military was the principal milieu for the trumpet in ancient Rome (Curt Sachs, *The History of Musical Instruments* [New York: W.W. Norton, 1940, 145–8]). See also Henry George Farmer, "Crusading Martial Music," *Music & Letters* 30, no. 3 (1949): 243–49.

13. Warren P. Howe, "Early American Military Music," *American Music* 17, no. 1 (1999): 87.

14. "A History of U.S. Army Bands," Teaching materials from the United States Army School of Music, Norfolk, VA (2005).

15. Ibid.

16. Military bands have adjusted in recent years to meet the exigencies of twenty-first-century combat. In July 2010, the US army released an updated field manual to formalize a number of these changes that had been made to reflect on-the-ground needs in Iraq. The current army band structure is modular; it consists of a large number of "music performance teams" (MPTs), which can be combined into larger ensembles, or conduct "musical missions" on their own ("U.S. Army Bands" 2010: 2–1). MPTs range from brass and woodwind ensembles to pop bands to a heavy metal quartet called "The Four Horsemen of the Arockalypse": Daniel J. Wakine, "US Military Bands: Lighter, Faster," *New York Times*, September 3, 2010, http://www.nytimes.com/2010/09/04/arts/music/04army.html?_r=0.

17. Columbia Phonograph Company, cylinder #15195. An excerpt of this cylinder, from the collection of Bruce Stinchcomb, can be found on www.tinfoil.com/cm-9807.htm. See also Frank W. Hoffmann and Howard Ferstler, *Encyclopedia of Recorded Sound*, Vol. 1, 2nd ed. (New York: Routledge, 2004), 210.

18. Quoted in William H. Kenney, *Recorded Music in American Life: The Phonograph and Popular Memory, 1890–1945* (New York: Oxford University Press, 1999), 194.

19. The increasing salience of recorded music during and after World War II provoked negative reactions from some cultural critics, with Theodor Adorno most prominent among them. While they were concerned with music in civilian rather than military life, at least one critique, from Marshall Bartholomew, was leveled explicitly against the increase of recorded music in the combat zone. Writing in 1942, Bartholomew's position amounted to a rejection of mobile music in the technologized sense found in the present volume. I quote him here at length: "We must realize not only that we are living in an age of steel, but in an age when the very machines which should have made life smoother and less laborious are in a fair way to destroy us. Take, for example, the field of transportation. The steamship, the automobile, and the airplane, which should have drawn the world closer together, instead have been turned into battleships, tanks, and heavy bombers designed to create hell on earth and to blast in a few seconds that which it has taken a thousand years to build. The radio, hailed as a unifier of the nations, is made into an instrument of destructive propaganda. . . . Watching what has seemed to be in many cases a losing battle of man against the machine, we must regard with suspicion and with mixed feelings the gradual mechanization of music. . . . And to make music play its full part in winning this present war we must put much greater pressure upon the War Department to encourage and emphasize *active* participation in music in both the Army and the Navy. . . . [o]ur Army is a mechanized army, in music as in everything else. In the realm of entertainment, millions of

dollars have been spent on mechanized music—radios, phonographs, juke boxes—and moving picture theatres, but practically no intelligent effort has been made and little money has been spent to encourage and organize musical talent among themselves. Bartholomew, Marshall, "Music in a World at War," *Music Educators Journal* 28, no. 6 (1942): 15 and 52. Bartholomew went on to advocate singing lessons and "song-leader training" for servicemen throughout the military, arguing that "almost the only music a soldier or sailor can take with him into active service is the music he makes himself" (53). Singing is presented here as the ultimate "mobile music," more portable, durable, and healthy than a music playback device could ever be. While it is beyond the scope of this chapter, one could easily argue that the widespread practice of live singing (often with acoustic guitar accompaniment) and active composing (with the aid of laptops) that has characterized the American military presence in Iraq shows that "passive" listening and "active" *poiesis* are not necessarily in a zero-sum relation with one another, on the battlefield or elsewhere. See Jonathan Pieslak, *Sound Targets: American Soldiers and Music in the Iraq War* (Bloomington: Indiana University Press, 2009), for a discussion of a group of active duty soldiers who composed, recorded, produced, and released an album of rap music, all while deployed in Iraq.

20. Friedrich Kittler's widely discussed *Gramophone, Film, Typewriter*, trans. Geoffrey Winthrop-Young (Stanford: Stanford University Press, 1999 [1986]), makes perhaps the strongest argument in favor of the military's role in determining civilian media practices: at the close of World War II, he argues, "captured [German military] magnetic tapes aroused sleepy U.S. electric and music giants who had, naturally, taken on duties other than commercial ones between 1942 and 1945. Inserted into the signal path, audiotapes modernized sound production; by replacing gramophones they modernized sound distribution. Tape decks made music consumers mobile, indeed automobile, as did the radio producers in the Magnetophone-equipped German lead tanks of old" (108). Geoffrey Winthrop-Young and Steve Goodman undertake productive critical readings of Kittler's media theory, focusing on the totalizing ambiguity of the Kittlerian conception of war and situating his insights within less rigid networks that allow for some human agency. See Geoffrey Winthrop-Young, "Drill and Distraction in the Yellow Submarine: On the Dominance of War in Friedrich Kittler's Media Theory," *Critical Inquiry* 28, no. 4 (2002): 825–54; and Steve Goodman, *Sonic Warfare: Sound, Affect, and the Ecology of Fear* (Cambridge, MA: MIT Press, 2010). Goodman, influenced by Winthrop-Young, attempts "to submerge [Kittler's] theory of media into a more general affective ecology in which technical machines become just another entry in the inventory of actual entities in a nexus of vibrational experience" (34). The present chapter, in situating iPod use within the concrete practices of a military engagement and refusing to regard the military as a monolithic institution but rather a (highly but not totalizingly structured) collection of individual agents, attempts a similar move: to present mobile music media as a floating resource that opens some possibilities and forecloses others for individual users within the US military.

21. W. Anthony Sheppard, "An Exotic Enemy: Anti-Japanese Musical Propaganda in World War II Hollywood," *Journal of the American Musicological Society* 54, no. 2 (2001): 304.

22. Former AVFN announcer Billy Williams has created a website with a history of the network, along with a link to an audio archive of Vietnam-era broadcasts at http://home.earthlink.net/~bfwillia/index.html. The archive includes a recording of the "Dawn Buster" show, which was the subject of the 1987 film "Good Morning Vietnam," at http://www.afvn.org/audio/index.html.

23. William Broyles Jr., *Brothers in Arms: A Journey from War to Peace* (Austin: University of Texas Press, 1996), 11.

24. Leslie Albrecht, "Soldier Loses Good Friend, Finds his Father in Iraq War," *Merced Sun-Star*, November 17, 2007, http://www.mercedsunstar. com/2007/11/17/77423_p2_soldier-loses-good-friend-finds.html. Press articles exploring the use of iPods in the war include Benjamin Sutherland, "Apple's New Weapon," *Newsweek*, April 27, 2009; Evan Serpick, "Soundtrack to the War, *Rolling Stone*, August 24, 2006, 20 and 22; and Robert Mackey, "The Pentagon Adds iPods to Its Arsenal," The Lede: The New York Times News Blog, May 6, 2009, http://thelede.blogs.nytimes.com/2009/05/06/.

25. iPods were readily available at base PXs in Iraq; according to one source, bulk purchases by the Pentagon keep the prices relatively low (*Asian News International* 2009).

26. "Personal Items for Deployment," Joint Readiness Task Force, Fork Polk, Louisiana website, http://www.jrtc-polk.army.mil/115th_BDE/personalitems.pdf (accessed September 7, 2010).

27. Michael Bull, *Sound Moves: iPod Culture and Urban Experience* (New York: Routledge, 2007), 134–5.

28. My discussion of iPod-enabled music listening as a technology of self-regulation owes much to Tia Denora's work on music "in everyday life," *Music in Everyday Life* (Cambridge, UK: Cambridge University Press, 2000). Just as Denora's research subjects often used "self-administered music" as "a catalyst, a device that enabled [them] to move from one set of feelings to another over a relatively short time span" (16), so have soldiers "self-administered" music to achieve this goal throughout their deployments. But while Denora focuses on music as a technology in Heidegger's sense, as a world-revealing instrument, I here focus on the literal, mechanical technology that makes mobile music listening possible in wartime. We are really dealing with multiple, nested technologies here, as playback devices, music recordings, and bodies work (or fail to work) in concert to produce affective embodied experiences in the fraught timespace of combat.

29. See also George Gittoes, *Soundtrack to War*, a documentary film (Visual Entertainment, 2003), and Nate Anderson, "iPods at War," *Ars Technica*, August 2006, http://arstechnica.com/apple/2006/08/ipods-war/.

30. Interview with the author. Washington, DC, 2007.

31. Gilman, "An American Soldier's Ipod."

32. Ibid.

33. "Milblogs," the online journals of active-duty troops, have proliferated rapidly since the beginning of the Iraq War. A May 2005 *USA Today* story estimated the number of milblogs as growing from 50 to 200 over the previous twelve months. See Mark Memmott, "'Milbloggers' are Typing Their Place in History," *USA Today*, May 11, 2005, http://usatoday30.usatoday.com/news/world/iraq/2005-05-11-milblogs-main_x.htm. As of September 2010, *milblogging.com*, one of the primary milblog sites, contained 2,823 milblogs written in forty-five different countries.

34. The song Teflon Don quotes here, from the Christian rock band Project 86, is called "My Will Be a Dead Man." I am listening to it now, on my own iPod, as I sit typing at my desk at NYU. It's a well-crafted, idiomatic piece: a double hit of the bass drum on beats one and two, a hard snare hit on beat three, a rest on beat four, with power chords following this rhythm in

a minor progression. The singer's gravelly voice belts out an evocative line, continuing where Teflon Don left off:

> *There comes a time, there comes a day, there comes an hour when*
> *In every man's life, in every man's life*
> *Brandish your steel, mount up your steed,*
> *In every man's life, in every man's life,*
> *My will, my will be a dead man.*

35. Jonathan Pieslak, *Sound Targets*, 51.

36. Gilman, "An American Soldier's Ipod."

37. Jonathan Pieslak argues that the intersecting ideologies of power, lyrical references to death and violence, and other musical indexes of aggression that pervade metal and gangsta rap may account for their popularity among soldiers. Pieslak, *Sound Targets*, 135–67.

38. A nearly identical list, which Buzzell called "my 'Stryker Soundtrack' playlist," was published in the 2006 book adaptation of his blog: Colby Buzzell, *My War: Killing Time in Iraq* (New York: Berkley Trade, 2006), 146–7. Jonathan Pieslak interviewed Buzzell in 2006, and an audio recording of their discussion of the Stryker Soundtrack can be found on Pieslak's website, http://www.soundtargets.com.

39. Lt. Col. Kilgore, the commanding officer played by Robert Duvall, explains to a gunner's mate who has never flown with him: "We'll come in low out of the rising sun, and about a mile out we'll put on the music." "Music?" asks the gunner's mate. "Yeah, I use Wagner. It scares the hell out of the slopes. My boys love it!"

40. Pieslak relates an incident in which the Ride of the Valkyries was used in combat, during a "thunder run" into Baghdad. See Pieslak, *Sound Targets*, 85–6.

41. See also Michael Bull, *Sounding Out the City: Personal Stereos and the Management of Everyday Life* (Oxford and New York: Oxford University Press, 2000), 85–96.

42. Michael Bull dwells at length on the cinematizing power of the iPod in *Sound Moves*. As Berklee, one of Bull's interviewees, states, "The world looks friendlier, happier, and sunnier when I walk down the street with my iPod on. It feels as if I'm in a movie at times. Like my life has a soundtrack now. It also takes away some of the noise of the streets, so that everything around me becomes calmer somewhat. It detaches me from my environment, like I'm an invisible, floating observer" (43).

43. http://jon.pieslak.com/asom/ColbyBuzzell.htm

44. The relevant section of the regulation reads: "At the discretion of the commander, and when required in the performance of duties listed above, soldiers may wear an electronic device on the belt, belt loops, or waistband of the uniform. Only one electronic device may be worn; it may be either a pager or a cell phone. The body of the device may not exceed 4×2×1 inches, and the device and carrying case must be black; no other colors are authorized. If security cords or chains are attached to the device, soldiers will conceal the cord or chain from view. Other types of electronic devices are not authorized for wear on the uniform. If the commander issues and requires the use of other electronic devices in the performance of duties, the soldier will carry them in the hand, pocket, briefcase, purse, bag, or in some other carrying container." Army Regulation 670–1, "Wear and Appearance of Uniforms and Insignia."

45. Richard Engel, *War Journal: My Five Years in Iraq* (New York: Simon and Schuster, 2008), 297–8.

46. "Teflon Don," correspondence with author, 2009.

47. Ibid.

48. Interview with author. Washington, DC, 2009.

49. For an account of the increase in mortar attacks on the Green Zone, see Karin Brulliard and Robin Wright, "Blast Kills 8 at Iraqi Parliament Building," *Washington Post*, April 13, 2007, http://www.washingtonpost.com/wp-dyn/content/article/2007/04/12/AR2007041200265.html.

50. Interview with author, 2009.

51. Michael Bull, "No Dead Air! The iPod and the Culture of Mobile Listening," *Leisure Studies* 24, no. 4 (2005): 344.

52. Bull, *Sound Moves,* 5; cf. Mark Auge, *Non-Places: Introduction to an Anthropology of Supermodernity*, trans. John Howe (London and New York: Verso, 1995).

53. David Beer, "Tune Out: Music, Soundscapes and the Urban Mise-en-scène," *Information, Communication & Society* 10, no. 6 (2007): 846–66.

54. Ibid.

55. Gilman ("An American Soldier's iPod," 2010) and Pieslak (*Sound Targets*, 2009) have documented the breadth of musical tastes represented by these and other military playlists.

56. Interview with the author. Washington, DC, 2007.

57. Interview with the author. Washington, DC, 2007.

58. Tia Denora, *Music in Everyday Life* (Cambridge, UK: Cambridge University Press, 2000), 16.

59. Alfred Paddock Jr., "Military Psychological Operations," in *Political Warfare and Psychological Operations*, ed. Carnes Lord and Frank R. Barnett (Washington, DC: National Defense University Press, 1989), 45. See also Jerrold M. Post, "Psychological Operations and Counterterrorism," *Joint Force Quarterly* 37 (2005): 105–11.

60. Jeff Gerth, "Military's Information War Is Vast and Often Secretive," *New York Times*, December 11, 2005.

61. Nick Turse, *The Complex: How the Military Invades Our Everyday Lives* (New York: Metropolitan Books, 2008), 65.

62. As of this writing, it is unclear whether this practice continues.

63. The American Technology Corporation website contains detailed information on the LRAD at http://www.atcsd.com/site/content/view/15/32/.

64. Robert M. McNab and Richard L. Scott, "Non-lethal Weapons and the Long Tail of Warfare" *Small Wars and Insurgencies* 20, no. 1 (2009): 147.

65. Such instances lend a powerfully visceral edge to the "double-edged" quality of all "musical transactions" that Bruce Johnson and Martin Cloonan put forward in their recent volume on music and violence: "Every time music is used to demarcate the territory of self or community, it is incipiently being used to invade, marginalize or obliterate that of other individuals or groups." Johnson and Cloonan, *Dark Side of the Tune*, 4.

66. Suzanne G. Cusick, "Music as Torture/Music as Weapon." See also Lane DeGregory, "Iraq 'n' Roll," *St. Petersburg Times* [*Tampa Bay Times*], November 21, 2004, http://www.sptimes.com/2004/11/21/Floridian/Iraq__n__roll.shtml.

67. McNab and Scott, "Non-lethal Weapons and the Long Tail of Warfare," 147.

68. See for example Johnson and Cloonan, *Dark Side of the Tune* (2008); Goodman, *Sonic Warfare*, 2010; and Lara Pellegrinelli, "Scholarly Discord: The Politics of Music in the War on Terrorism," *Chronicle of Higher Education* 55, no. 35 (2009): B6.

69. Carlotta Gall, "The Reach of War: Detainees' Rights Group Reports Afghanistan Torture," *New York Times*, December 19, 2005 (quoted in Suzanne Cusick, "You Are in a Place," 2). Other accounts, such as Pieslak's, stress the claim that "interrogators could not be reckless with their choice of sounds because they were required by law to listen along with the detainee" (2009:88).

70. Suzanne Cusick, "Musicology, Torture, Repair."

71. I have described this replacement elsewhere as an instance of "thanatosonics." Drawing on Achille Mbembe's (2003) definition of "necropolitics," thanatosonics is a form of the "subjugation of life to the power of death" that takes place through sound: J. Martin Daughtry, "Thanatosonics: Ontologies of Acoustic Violence," *Social Text* 32, no. 2 (2014): 25–51; Achille Mbembe, "Necropolitics," trans. Libby Meintjes, *Public Culture* 15, no. 1 (2003): 9.

72. As this book goes to press, the fate of the militarized iPod is unclear. The enthusiasm for the iPod that was so palpable when I began drafting this chapter in 2009 has been replaced with a more circumspect stance, as new technologies, by Apple and other companies, compete for the military's attention.

73. In order to cater to troops serving in Afghanistan, the program was also designed to translate into Pashto and Dari, and Vcommunicator designers are readying new versions that provide translations into other languages of strategic significance. Also, when purchased with authoring software, new sentences could be added in the field, increasing the flexibility of the one-way translation program.

74. Mary Louise Pratt, "Harm's Way: Language and the Contemporary Arts of War," *PMLA* 124, no. 5 (2009): 1519.

75. http://www.knightarmco.com/bulletflight/.

76. Geoffrey Winthrop-Young, "Drill and Distraction in the Yellow Submarine: On the Dominance of War in Friedrich Kittler's Media Theory," *Critical Inquiry* 28, no. 4 (2002): 834.

77. Historian Nick Turse writes: "By the time of the Iraq War in 2003, Apple had . . . penetrated [the military and government] marketplace—a fact that was likely unknown to the many bloggers who saw no connection between the U.S. occupation and the iPod maker. The targeting tool of choice for Major Shawn Weed, an intelligence planner with the Army's Third Infantry Division as it readied for the invasion, was Apple's Titanium G4 PowerBook." Turse also claims that in 2004, Apple had "no fewer than twenty separate contracts with the Department of Defense." When contacted in 2010 for this chapter, a representative of Apple said that since 1998 it has been company policy "not to participate in any kind of research" or divulge information about contracts. However, the Federal Procurement Data System lists hundreds of "contract actions" between Apple and the Department of Defense during the years of the Iraq War, ranging from extremely small sums (e.g., $1) to well over $1 million per action. Turse, *The Complex*, 65.

FRAGMENT #6

1. Based on an interview with the author. Washington, DC, 2010.

2. The Islamic State of Iraq was the predecessor organization of the current group known as ISIS (the Islamic State of Iraq and Syria) or ISIL (the Islamic State of Iraq and the Levant), or

by its Arabic acronym Da'esh. Events of the kind depicted here have increased significantly in Iraq since 2013.

CHAPTER 7

1. Within the past decade, the International Council For Traditional Music (ICTM), the Society for Ethnomusicology, and the American Musicological Society all convened sessions dealing with music and violence, conflict, and/or war. The Society for Ethnomusicology has a standing special interest group dedicated to the study of music and violence. Recent book-length treatments of the broad subject include Svanibor Pettan, ed., *Music, Politics, and War: Views from Croatia* (Zagreb: Institute of Ethnology and Folklore Research, 1998); Jonathan Ritter and J. Martin Daughtry, eds., *Music in the Post-9/11 World* (New York: Routledge, 2007); Bruce Johnson and Martin Cloonan, *Dark Side of the Tune: Popular Music and Violence* (Surrey: Ashgate, 2009); Steve Goodman, *Sonic Warfare: Sound, Affect, and the Ecology of Fear* (Cambridge, MA: MIT Press, 2010); John Morgan O'Connell and Salwa el-Shawan Castelo-Branco, eds., *Music and Conflict* (Urbana: University of Illinois Press, 2010); and Susan Fast and Kip Pegley, eds., *Music, Politics and Violence* (Middletown, CT: Wesleyan University Press, 2012).

2. John Morgan O'Connell, "Introduction: An Ethnomusicological Approach to Music and Conflict," in O'Connell and Castelo-Branco, *Music and Conflict*, 12.

3. In this chapter I am less interested in tracking the fate of "Iraqi music" as it is conventionally understood—i.e., the traditional, classical, and popular genres that are historically associated with Iraq—and more interested in documenting the ways in which the war affected the practice of making and listening to music in Iraq, regardless of that music's provenance. In this sense, the "Iraqi music" of this chapter's title refers not to the music that is unique to Iraq but to the musics that Iraqis listen to—including, notably, the western popular music that so incited the ire of sectarian forces.

4. A number of scholars have undertaken similar projects. I draw particular inspiration here from Veronica Doubleday's detailed account of the troubled recent history of music in Afghanistan: Veronica Doubleday, "9/11 and the Politics of Music-Making in Afghanistan," in Ritter and Daughtry, *Music in the Post-9/11 World*, 277–314.

5. As a result of violence toward musicians, along with the more common problems of inadequate state support and the proliferation of heavily mediated popular music, Taha Gharib, the leader of one of five *maqam* troupes that remained in Iraq as of 2010, stated that "Iraqi maqam risks disappearing with our generation." Jacques Clement, "Iraqi Maqam Emerges as Casualty of Modernity and War," *AFP*, December 7, 2010, http://www.google.com/hostednews/afp/article/ALeqM5ixbs8SktIW4TsyF-H3i1nUNvkc_A?docId=CNG.1a0489b5796eb5cb11ee2ade1f8ffb1a.d1.

6. John F. Burns, "O Iraqi Youth, Dig It, the Time Has Come to Rock," *New York Times*, April 9, 2001, http://www.nytimes.com/2001/04/09/world/baghdad-journal-o-iraqi-youth-dig-it-the-time-has-come-to-rock.html.

7. Topaz Amoore, "Saddam's Son Builds His Powerbase on Western Rock," *Telegraph*, May 26, 2002, http://www.telegraph.co.uk/news/worldnews/middleeast/iraq/1395413/Saddams-son-builds-his-powerbase-on-Western-rock.html.

8. Christopher Stewart, "Uday's Music Man," *New York Times Magazine*, April 6, 2003, http://www.nytimes.com/2003/04/06/magazine/06QUESTIONS.html.

9. "Kathem al Saher: 'I Sang for Saddam Only After Receiving Death Threats,'" *Albawaba Entertainment,* February 22, 2004, http://www.albawaba.com/entertainment/kathem-el-saher-i-sang-saddam-hussein-only-after-receiving-death-threats.

10. Interview with the author. Detroit, MI, 2012.

11. Afif Sarhan and Caroline Davies, "Iraqi Artists and Singers Flee Amid Crackdown on Forbidden Culture," *Guardian,* May 10, 2008, http://www.theguardian.com/world/2008/may/11/iraq.

12. Interview with the author. Detroit, MI 2012.

13. E. A. Torriero and Tom Hundley, "Once Powerful Iraqis Fear for their Lives," May 21, 2003, *Chicago Tribune,* http://articles.chicagotribune.com/2003-05-21/news/0305210234_1_baathists-baath-party-iraqis.

14. See, for example, Fadlou Shehadi, *Philosophies of Music in Medieval Islam* (Leiden and New York: Brill, 1995).

15. Amnon Shiloah, *Music in the World of Islam: A Socio-Cultural Study* (Detroit: Wayne State University Press, 1995), 35.

16. Ibid.

17. As Jonas Otterbeck and Anders Ackfeldt recently stated in the pages of *Contemporary Islam*: "A couple of trends are discernable in newer Islamic discourse on music. There is a dominance of a moderate, fairly tolerant, but still in part restrictive interpretation. A reactionary, hard-line attitude is prominent in areas where Wahhabi discourse dominates and in areas where Islamist political groups gain power through military means and where the rule of national law break[s] down, as in Somalia, southern Iraq, Algeria during civil war, the rule of Hamas, Afghanistan during the Taliban, and Iran. In fact, it needs to be stressed that while, as most know, the issue of female dress and behavior in public is a predictable issue on the agenda upon any given Islamist takeover (local, regional, or national), so is the issue of regulating and censuring music." Jonas Otterbeck and Anders Ackfeldt, "Music and Islam," *Contemporary Islam* 6 (2012): 227–33, quote on 232.

18. The post-9/11 situation in Afghanistan provides a fruitful instance of comparison and contrast. In Afghanistan, US-led forces overthrew the Taliban, a conservative religious regime notorious for its extreme antipathy toward music. The Iraqi situation was the inverse, involving the overthrow of a secular regime that, despite the pathological behavior of Uday Hussein, was quite permissive toward music qua music, so long as music was available to serve the needs of the regime. For more on the Afghan case, see Doubleday, "9/11 and the Politics of Music-Making in Afghanistan."

19. Sammy Ketz, "Music Returns to Streets of Baghdad as Both Sunni and Shiite Fundamentalists Recede," *Agence France-Presse,* November 17, 2008, reprinted in *The Daily Star* (Lebanon), http://www.dailystar.com.lb/Culture/Art/2008/Nov-17/116918-music-returns-to-streets-of-baghdad-as-both-sunni-and-shiite-fundamentalists-recede.ashx#axzz3GjoTwOoo.

20. Ibid.

21. Ibid.

22. Aref Mohammed, "Iraq: Feature—Music and Weddings in Basra, for Now," *Reuters—AlertNet,* reproduced at reliefweb: http://reliefweb.int/report/iraq/iraq-feature-music-and-weddings-basra-now.

23. One such attack on a music store killed Ahmed, one of Jason Sagebiel's friends, who happened to be browsing in the store when the explosion occurred.

24. "Musician Shot Dead in 2007, Remembered on Day to End Impunity," FreeMuse, http://freemuse.org/archives/5175. See also Afif Sarhan and Caroline Davies, "Iraqi Artists and Singers Flee amid Crackdown on Forbidden Culture," *Guardian/ Observer*, May 10, 2008, http://www.theguardian.com/world/2008/may/11/iraq.

25. "Iraq: Singing 'the Devil's Music' Will Get You Killed," IRIN, November 23, 2006, http://irinnews.org/report/61962/iraq-singing-the-devil-s-music-will-get-you-killed.

26. Scott Long, "Massacre of Emos in Iraq Goes to Core of a Damaged Society," *Guardian*, March 18, 2012, http://www.theguardian.com/commentisfree/2012/mar/18/iraq-massacre-e mos-killing-gay.

27. "Small Arms Fire Attack on 2/1 MAR in NW Fallujah: 3 CF WIA; 36 EN KIA," WarDiaries, April 21, 2004, http://wardiaries.wikileaks.org/id/B41A1E5E-3C46-449D-9 B24-CD054E762034/

28. "AIF Detained by F 2/6 in Fallujah: 0 Inj/damage," WikiLeaks, March 9, 2006, http://warlogs.wikileaks.org/id/F25BD7C4-F05C-43A3-80B5-19DD60FA5A18/.

29. "Anti-Iraq Forces"—this was one of the military's euphemistic terms for insurgents.

30. "AIF Detained by 1-1/4 IA IVO Tikrit: 6 Det, 0 CF Inj/Damage," WarDiaries, May 25, 2006, http://warlogs.wikileaks.org/id/12ABF94C-3D7B-4C51-A032-DB92480D6AC9/.

31. See Behnam Said, "Hymns (Nasheeds): A Contribution to the Study of the Jihadist Culture," *Studies in Conflict and Terrorism* 35, no. 12 (2011): 863–79, and Pieslak, *Sound Targets*, 59–77.

32. See Karen Greenberg and Joshua L. Dratel, eds., *The Torture Papers: The Road to Abu Ghraib* (Cambridge, UK: Cambridge University Press, 2005).

33. See Cusick, "Music as Torture/Music as Weapon," *Revista Transcultural de Música* 10 (2006); "'You Are in a Place That Is Out of the World . . . ': Music in the Detention Camps of the 'Global War on Terror,'" *Journal of the Society for American Music* 2 no. 1 (2008): 1–26; and "Musicology, Torture, Repair," *Radical Musicology* 3 (2008), http://www.radical-musicology.org.uk/2008/Cusick.htm.

CONCLUSION

1. It was only after my intrepid editor, Suzanne Ryan, delicately pointed out that the perfect repetition of vowels in the phrase leads the reader to the nonsensical and confusing conclusion that the two words rhyme—"sound *wounds?*"—that I let the title go.

2. Here and below, etymology and definitions are taken from the *Oxford English Dictionary*, 3rd ed., 2000–(online edition).

3. See for example Ted Robert Gurr and Charles Ruttenberg, *The Conditions of Civil Violence: First Tests of a Causal Model* (Princeton: Center of International Studies, Woodrow Wilson School of Public and International Affairs, Princeton University, 1967).

4. Allen Feldman, "Epilogue," in *Fieldwork Under Fire: Contemporary Studies of Violence and Culture*, ed. Carolyn Nordstrom and Antonius Robben (Berkeley: University of California Press, 1995), 227. See also Doug Henry, "Trauma and Vulnerability During War," in *Cultures of Fear: A Critical Reader*, ed. Uli Linke and Danielle Taana Smith (London and New York: Pluto Press, 2009), 129.

FRAGMENT #7

1. Based on a series of interviews with the author. Amman, Jordan, 2008.

Glossary

ACOUSTIC TERRITORY: The shifting environments, structures, and other absorptive and resonating elements that enclose, modify, and otherwise mediate the sounds in a given timespace; also, the distinct places whose boundaries and characters are constituted by sound and listening. (See also *auditory regime, sonic campaign, radiant acoustic territory, resonant acoustic territory*.)

AMPLITUDE OF VIOLENCE: The area over which a violent act is discernable. Also, the sensory (esp. auditory) intensity of violent acts. (See *belliphonic*.)

AUDIBLE INAUDIBLE: The outermost zone of wartime audition. The zone within which audible sounds are intentionally ignored or do not rise to the level of consciousness.

AUDIONARRATIVE: A description of an unseen event based solely on an interpretation of its sounds. A typical *belliphonic audionarrative* is a detailed description of an unseen but clearly heard exchange of gunfire.

AUDITOR: Someone who is within earshot of a sound; also, someone who has the right to hold others accountable for their actions, and for the sensory consequences of those actions.

AUDITORY REGIME: The technologies, regulations, formal and informal training exercises, casual conversations, and shared life histories that help to shape audition for a given population. An auditory habitus. (See also *sonic campaign, acoustic territory*.)

AUSCULTATION: Diagnostic listening within an etiological frame. Listening to discern the cause of an entity's ill health, whether that entity is a person, a machine, or a neighborhood.

BELLIPHONIC: The spectrum of sounds produced by armed conflict. The imagined total of sounds that would not have occurred had the conflict not taken place.

DISPLACEMENT: "The feeling that one is homeless, disconnected from one's physical and social environment" (David Howes). The undesired movement of people, sounds, or other entities away from the place they label "home." (See also *emplacement, transplacement*.)

EMPATHIC MATERNAL AUDITION: A mode of listening to belliphonic sounds as if through the ears of another, in order to lessen the other's fear. This mode of listening is commonly coded feminine. (See also *euphoric auditory hypermasculinity, expert masculine auscultation, hypermasculine inaudition.*)

EMPLACEMENT: "The sensuous interrelationship of body-mind-environment" (David Howes). The embodied state of being integrated into a particular social matrix. (See also *displacement, transplacement.*)

EUPHORIC AUDITORY HYPERMASCULINITY: A mode of listening to belliphonic sounds as if they were thrilling and cathartic. This mode of listening treats the sonic residue of violence as aesthetic spectacle. It is commonly coded masculine. (See also *empathic maternal audition, expert masculine auscultation, hypermasculine inaudition.*)

EXPERT MASCULINE AUSCULTATION: A mode of listening to belliphonic sounds in order to calmly decode their indexical significance. Listening in order to identify. This mode of listening is commonly coded masculine. (See also *euphoric auditory hypermasculinity, empathic maternal audition, hypermasculine inaudition.*)

EXPOSURE: Being in the presence of a sound that one cannot interpret. This commonly happens in situations of extreme stress, or in situations where the sound is so loud as to be debilitating. Exposure is the area that lies beyond listening.

HYBRID ACOUSTIC WEAPON: An instrument that produces weaponizable sounds in addition to other effects.

HYPERMASCULINE INAUDITION: A mode of listening as if one is not affected by, or even cognizant of, a loud, proximate belliphonic sound. This mode of listening is commonly coded masculine. (See also *euphoric auditory hypermasculinity, empathic maternal audition, expert masculine auscultation.*)

INAUDITION: An intentional decision or unconscious ability to not recognize or acknowledge a sound that is physically audible. The process of *unhearing*. A deadening or "armoring the sensorium" (Georg Simmel) that is the result of auditory experience.

NARRATIONAL ZONE: The middle zone of wartime audition. The zone in which sounds are mined for their narrative significance. The space of auditory hermeneutics, where stories of unseen but heard events are created.

PURE ACOUSTIC WEAPON: An instrument whose sole purpose is to produce weaponizable sounds.

RADIANT ACOUSTIC TERRITORY: An intersubjective place that is brought into existence by an act of sounding. The area over which a sonorous event is audible and attracting the attention of a public.

RESONANT ACOUSTIC TERRITORY: A structured environment inside or outside the body that contains, shapes, and in other ways mediates sound.

SONIC CAMPAIGN: The processes and entities that introduce sounds into a particular acoustic territory. The semi-structured field of technologies, regulations, objectives, procedures, training, and informal conversations that shape the way sounds are created in a given timespace. (See also *acoustic territory, auditory regime.*)

TACTICAL ZONE: The inner reaches of the narrational zone of wartime audition. The zone where the sounds of projectiles overlap in space with the projectiles themselves. In this zone, the audionarrative gets flattened out into a quick tactical assessment.

TESTIMONY: The "autobiographically certified narrative of a past event" (Renauld Dulong). A statement of an ordeal witnessed or injustice endured.

TRANSPLACEMENT: When the familiar is rendered unfamiliar through acts of recontextualization. When a sound stays the same but the connotative field around it changes. The process that produces uncanny sounds. (See also *emplacement, displacement.*)

TRAUMA ZONE: The innermost zone of wartime audition. The zone where sounds produce physiological damage.

WEAPON-IN-USE: The minimal unit of analysis for examining belliphonic weapon sounds. The weapon-in-use comprises the instrument (the weapon), its user (the shooter), and its intended purpose. For example, a gun becomes a hybrid acoustic weapon at the moment it is shot in the air to clear an intersection rather than aimed at a target.

Bibliography

"A History of U.S. Army Bands." Teaching materials from the United States Army School of Music, Norfolk, VA (2005). https://fas.org/irp/doddir/army/armybands.pdf .

Adey, Peter. "Holding Still: The Private Life of an Air Raid." *M/C Journal: A Journal of Media and Culture* 12, no. 1 (2009). http://journal.mediaculture.org.au/index.php/mcjournal/article/viewArticle/112.

Agnew, Robert. "Foundation for a General Strain Theory of Crime and Delinquency." *Criminology* 30, no. 1 (1992): 47–87.

Appiah, Kwame Anthony. *Cosmopolitanism: Ethics in a World of Strangers.* New York and London: W. W. Norton, 2006.

Arendt, Hannah. *The Human Condition.* Chicago: University of Chicago Press, 1958.

Asad, Talal. *On Suicide Bombing.* New York: Columbia University Press, 2007.

Auge, Mark. *Non-Places: Introduction to an Anthropology of Supermodernity.* Translated by John Howe. London and New York: Verso, 1995.

Bakht, Nikolaus. "Introduction." *Journal of the Royal Musical Association* 135, no. 1 (2010): 1–3.

Bargu, Banu. "Forging Life into a Weapon." *Social Text/Periscope* (2011). http://www.socialtext-journal.org/periscope/2011/05/the-weaponization-of-life—banu-bargu.php.

Barkin, S., S. Keriter, and R. H. DuRant. "Exposure to Violence and Intentions to Engage in Moralistic Violence During Early Adolescence." *Journal of Adolescence* 24, no. 6 (2001): 777–89.

Bartholomew, Marshall. "Music in a World at War." *Music Educators Journal* 28, no. 6 (1942): 15 and 52–55.

Barz, Gregory, and Timothy J. Cooley. *Shadows in the Field: New Perspectives for Fieldwork in Ethnomusicology.* 2nd ed. New York: Oxford University Press, 2008.

Bataille, George. *Inner Experience*. Translated by Leslie Ann Boldt. Albany: State University of New York Press, 1988.

Batchen, Geoffrey, Mick Gidley, Nancy K. Miller, and Jay Prosser, eds. *Picturing Atrocity: Photography in Crisis*. London: Reaktion Books, 2012.

Beer, David. "Tune Out: Music, Soundscapes and the Urban Mise-en-scène." *Information, Communication & Society* 10, no. 6 (2007): 846–66.

Belasco, Amy. "Troop Levels in the Afghan and Iraq Wars, FY2001–FY2012: Cost and Other Potential Issues." *CRS Report for Congress*. Washington, DC: Congressional Research Service, 2009.

Bengio, Ofra. "Shi'is and Politics in Ba'thi Iraq." *Middle Eastern Studies* 21, no. 1 (1985): 1–14.

Bennett, Jane. *Vibrant Matter: A Political Ecology of Things*. Durham, NC: Duke University Press, 2010.

Berger, Harris. *Metal, Rock, and Jazz: Perception and Phenomenology of Musical Experience*. Hanover, NH: Wesleyan University Press, 1999.

Berger, Harris, and Cornelia Fales. "'Heaviness' in the Perception of Heavy Metal Guitar Timbres: The Match of Perceptual and Acoustic Features over Time." In *Wired for Sound: Engineering and Technologies in Sonic Cultures*, edited by Paul D. Greene and Thomas Porcello, 181–97. Middletown, CT: Wesleyan University Press, 2005.

Bernstein, Robin. "Dances with Things: Material Culture and the Performance of Race." *Social Text* 27, no. 4 (2009): 67–94.

Bijsterveld, Karin. *Mechanical Sound: Technology, Culture, and Public Problems of Noise in the Twentieth Century*. Cambridge, MA: MIT Press, 2008.

Blesser, Barry, and Linda Ruth-Salter. *Spaces Speak, Are You Listening?: Experiencing Aural Architecture*. Cambridge, MA: MIT Press, 2006.

Bourke, Joanna. *An Intimate History of Killing: Face-to-Face Killing in Twentieth-Century Warfare*. New York: Basic Books, 1999.

Bowden, Mark. *Black Hawk Down: A Story of Modern War*. New York: Grove Press, 1999.

Boyden, Jo. "Anthropology Under Fire: Ethics, Researchers and Children in War." In *Children and Youth on the Front Line: Ethnography, Armed Conflict, and Displacement*, edited by Jo Boyden and Joanna DeBerry, 237–60. Oxford: Berghahn Books, 2004.

Brown, Keith, and Catherine Lutz. "Grunt Lit: The Participant-Observers of Empire." *American Ethnologist* 34, no. 2 (2007): 322–8.

Broyles, William, Jr.. *Brothers in Arms: A Journey from War to Peace*. Austin: University of Texas Press, 1996.

Buber, Martin. *I and Thou*. Translated by Walter Kaufmann. New York: Touchstone, 1971 [1923].

Bull, Michael. *Sounding Out the City: Personal Stereos and the Management of Everyday Life*. Oxford and New York: Oxford University Press, 2000.

———."No Dead Air! The iPod and the Culture of Mobile Listening," *Leisure Studies* 24, no. 4 (2005): 343–55.

———. *Sound Moves: iPod Culture and Urban Experience*. New York: Routledge, 2007.

Bunselmeyer, J. "Appearances and Verbal Paradox, Sonnets 129 and 138." *Shakespeare Quarterly* 25, no. 1 (1974): 103–8.

Buzzell, Colby. *My War: Killing Time in Iraq*. New York: Berkley Trade, 2006.

Calhoun, Craig. "Pierre Bourdieu." In *The Blackwell Companion to Major Contemporary Social Theorists*, edited by George Ritzer, 274–309. Malden, MA: Blackwell, 2000.

Carney, Steven. *Allied Participation in Operation Iraqi Freedom*. Washington, DC: Center for Military History, U.S. Army, 2011.

Caruth, Cathy. "Introduction." In *Trauma: Explorations in Memory*, edited by Cathy Caruth, 3–12. Baltimore: Johns Hopkins Press, 1995.

———. *Unclaimed Experience: Trauma, Narrative and History*. Baltimore: Johns Hopkins Press, 1996.

———. *Listening to Trauma: Conversations with Leaders in the Theory and Treatment of Catastrophic Experience*. Baltimore: Johns Hopkins Press, 2014.

Casey, Edward. *Remembering: A Phenomenological Study*. Bloomington: Indiana University Press, 1987.

———. "Smooth Spaces and Rough-Edged Places: The Hidden History of Place." *Review of Metaphysics* 51, no. 2 (1997): 267–96.

———. "Between Geography and Philosophy: What Does It Mean to Be in the Place-World?" *Annals of the Association of American Geographers* 91, no. 4 (2001): 683–93.

Chion, Michel. *Audio-Vision: Sound on Screen*. Edited and translated by Claudia Gorbman. New York: Columbia, 1994.

Cicero. *Ad Herennium*. Translated by Harry Caplan. Loeb Classical Library. Cambridge, MA: Harvard University Press, 1964.

Cizmic, Maria. *Performing Pain: Music and Trauma in Eastern Europe*. New York: Oxford University Press, 2011.

Clifford, James, and George E. Marcus. *Writing Culture: The Poetics and Politics of Ethnography*. Berkeley: University of California Press, 1986.

Collins, Steven. "Psychological Operations in Combat, Peacekeeping, and Fighting Terrorism." In *Military Life: The Psychology of Serving in Peace and Combat*, Vol. 1, edited by Thomas W. Britt, Amy B. Adler, and Carl Andrew Castro, 61–78. Westport, CT: Praeger Security International, 2006.

Connolly, William. "Tocqueville, Territory, and Violence." In *Challenging Boundaries: Global Flows, Territorial Identities*, edited by M. Shapiro and H. Alker, 141–64. Minneapolis: University of Minnesota Press, 1996.

Connor, Steven. "The Modern Auditory I." In *Rewriting the Self: Histories from the Middle Ages to the Present*, edited by Roy Porter, 203–23. London: Routledge, 1997.

———. *Dumbstruck: A Cultural History of Ventriloquism*. New York: Oxford University Press, 2001.

———. "Edison's Teeth: Touching Hearing." In *Hearing Cultures: Essays on Sound, Listening, and Modernity*, edited by Veit Erlmann, 153–72. Oxford and New York: Berg, 2004.

Corbin, Alain. *Village Bells: Sound and Meaning in the 19th-Century French Countryside*. New York: Columbia University Press, 1998.

Cordesman, Anthony H. *The Iraq War: Strategy, Tactics, and Military Lessons*. Westport, CT and London: Praeger, 2003.

Csordas, Thomas J. "Embodiment and Cultural Phenomenology." In *Perspectives on Embodiment: The Intersection of Nature and Culture*, edited by Gail Weiss and Honi Fern Haber, 143–62. New York: Routledge, 1999.

Cusick, Suzanne G. "Music as Torture/Music as Weapon." *Revista Transcultural de Música* 10 (2006). http://www.sibetrans.com/trans/a152/music-as-torture-music-as-weapon.

———. "'You Are In a Place That Is Out of the World . . . ': Music in the Detention Camps of the 'Global War on Terror.'" *Journal of the Society for American Music* 2, no. 1 (2008): 1–26.

———. "Musicology, Torture, Repair." *Radical Musicology* 3 (2008). http://www.radical-musicology.org.uk/2008/Cusick.htm.

———. "Towards an Acoustemology of Detention in the 'Global War on Terror.'" In *Music, Sound and Space: Transformations of Public and Private Experience*, edited by Georgina Born, 275–91. Cambridge, UK: Cambridge University Press, 2013.

Daniel, E. Valentine. *Charred Lullabies: Chapters in an Anthropography of Violence*. Princeton, NJ: Princeton University Press, 1996.

Das, Veena. "Anthropological Knowledge and Collective Violence." *Anthropology Today* 1, no. 3 (1985): 4–6.

———. "Commentary: Trauma and Testimony: Between Law and Discipline." *Ethos* 35, no. 3 (2007): 330–5.

Daughtry, J. Martin. "The Intonation of Intimacy: Ethics, Emotion, and Metaphor among Contemporary Russian Bards," PhD diss., University of California, Los Angeles, 2006.

———. "Charting Courses through Terror's Wake: An Introduction." In *Music in the Post-9/11 World*, edited by Jonathan Ritter and J. Martin Daughtry, xix–xxxi. New York: Routledge, 2007.

———. "Thanatosonics: Ontologies of Acoustic Violence." *Social Text* 32, no. 2 (2014): 25–51.

Dean, Carolyn. "Empathy, Pornography, and Suffering." *differences* 14, no. 1 (2003): 88–124.

Deaville, James. "The Sounds of American and Canadian Television News after 9/11: Entoning Horror and Grief, Fear and Anger." In *Music in the Post-9/11 World*, edited by Jonathan Ritter and J. Martin Daughtry, 43–70. New York: Routledge, 2007.

Deer, Patrick. *Culture in Camouflage: War, Empire, and Modern British Literature*. Oxford and New York: Oxford University Press, 2009.

Deleuze, Gilles and Félix Guattari. *A Thousand Plateaus: Capitalism and Schizophrenia*. Translated by Brian Massumi. Minneapolis: University of Minnesota Press, 1987.

Denora, Tia. *Music in Everyday Life*. Cambridge, UK: Cambridge University Press, 2000.

Desjarlais, Robert, and C. Jason Throop. "Phenomenological Approaches in Anthropology." *Annual Review of Anthropology* 40 (2011): 87–102.

Dodd, James. *Violence and Phenomenology*. New York: Routledge, 2009.

Dolar, Mladen. *A Voice and Nothing More*. Cambridge, MA: MIT Press, 2006.

Doubleday, Veronica. "9/11 and the Politics of Music-Making in Afghanistan." In *Music in the Post-9/11 World*, edited by Jonathan Ritter and J. Martin Daughtry, 277–314. New York: Routledge, 2007.

Dulong, Renauld. *Le Témoin oculaire: Les conditions sociales de l'attestation personnelle*. Paris: EHESS, 1988.

Elbogen, Eric B., Sally C. Johnson, Virginia M. Newton, Kristy Straits-Troster, Jennifer J. Vasterling, H. Ryan Wagner, and Jean C. Beckham. "Criminal Justice Involvement, Trauma, and Negative Affect in Iraq and Afghanistan War Era Veterans." *Journal of Consulting and Clinical Psychology* 80, no. 6 (2012): 1097–102.

Emery, Frank. *The Red Soldier: Letters from the Zulu Wars, 1879*. London: Hodder and Stoughton, 1977.

Emoff, Ron. *Recollecting from the Past: Musical Practice and Spirit Possession on the East Coast of Madagascar.* Middletown, CT: Wesleyan University Press, 2002.

Engel, Richard. *War Journal: My Five Years in Iraq.* New York: Simon and Schuster, 2008.

Farmer, Henry George. "Crusading Martial Music." *Music & Letters* 30, no. 3 (1949): 243–49.

Fast, Susan, and Kip Pegley, eds. *Music, Politics and Violence.* Middletown, CT: Wesleyan University Press, 2012.

———. "Introduction." In *Music, Politics, and Violence,* edited by Susan Fast and Kip Pegley, 1–33. Middletown, CT: Wesleyan University Press, 2012.

Feld, Steven. *Sound and Sentiment: Birds, Weeping, Poetics, and Song in Kaluli Expression.* 2nd ed. Philadelphia: University of Pennsylvania Press, 1990.

———. "Waterfalls of Song: An Acoustemology of Place Resounding in Bosavi, Papua New Guinea." In *Senses of Place,* edited by Steven Feld and Keith Basso, 91–135. Santa Fe, NM: School of American Research Press, 1996.

———. "Places Sensed, Senses Placed: Toward a Sensuous Epistemology of Environments." In *Empire of the Senses: The Sensual Culture Reader,* edited by David Howes, 179–91. Oxford and New York: Berg, 2005.

Feld, Steven, and Keith H. Basso. "Introduction." In *Senses of Place,* edited by Steven Feld and Keith H. Basso, 3–12. Santa Fe, NM: School of American Research Press, 1996.

Feldman, Allen. *Formations of Violence: The Narrative of the Body and Political Terror in Northern Ireland.* Chicago: University of Chicago Press, 1991.

———. "On Cultural Anesthesia: From Desert Storm to Rodney King." *American Ethnologist* 21, no. 2 (1994): 404–18.

———. "Epilogue." In *Fieldwork Under Fire: Contemporary Studies of Violence and Culture,* edited by Carolyn Nordstrom and Antonius Robben, 224–252. Berkeley: University of California Press, 1995.

Felman, Shoshana. *The Juridical Unconscious: Trials and Traumas in the Twentieth Century.* Cambridge, MA: Harvard University Press, 2002.

Field Manual No. 3-21.75 (21–75). *The Warrior Ethos and Soldier Combat Skills.* Washington, DC: Headquarters, Department of the Army, 2008.

Finley, Erin P. *Fields of Combat: Understanding PTSD among Veterans of Iraq and Afghanistan.* Ithaca, NY and London: Cornell University Press, 2011.

FM 3-05.30/MCRP 3-40.6, "Psychological Operations" [a manual], April 2005. Washington, DC: Headquarters, Department of the Army.

Forbes Tripp, Elise. *Surviving Iraq: Soldiers' Stories.* Northampton, MA: Olive Branch Press, 2009.

Fremantle, James Arthur Lyon. *The Fremantle Diary.* Edited by Walter Lord. New York: Little, Brown, 1954.

Friedner, Michele, and Stefan Helmreich. "Sound Studies Meets Deaf Studies." *The Senses and Society* 7, no. 1 (2012): 72–86.

Friedson, Stephen. *Dancing Prophets: Musical Experience in Tumbuka Healing.* Chicago: University of Chicago Press, 1996.

Fullerton, Carol S., and Robert J. Ursano, eds. *Posttraumatic Stress Disorder: Acute and Long-Term Responses to Trauma and Disaster.* Washington, DC: American Psychiatric Press, 2009.

Ganchrow, Raviv. "Perspectives on Sound-Space: The Story of Acoustic Defense." *Leonardo Music Journal* 19 (2009): 71–5.

Geertz, Clifford. "Religion as a Cultural System." In *The Interpretation of Cultures*, 87–125. New York: Basic Books, 1973.

Gibson, James J. "The Theory of Affordances." In *Perceiving, Acting, and Knowing: Toward an Ecological Psychology*, edited by R. Shaw and J. Bransford, 67–82. Hillsdale, NJ: Lawrence Erlbaum, 1977.

Gilman, Lisa. "An American Soldier's Ipod: Layers of Identity and Situated Listening in Iraq." *Music and Politics* 4, no. 2 (2010). http://www.music.ucsb.edu/projects/musicandpolitics/archive/2010-2/gilman.pdf.

Gittoes, George, dir. *Soundtrack to War* [documentary film]. Distributed by Visual Entertainment, 2003.

Goodman, Steve. *Sonic Warfare: Sound, Affect, and the Ecology of Fear*. Cambridge, MA: MIT Press, 2010.

Gordon, Avery. *Ghostly Matters: Haunting and the Sociological Imagination*. Minneapolis: University of Minnesota Press, 2008.

Greenberg, Karen, and Joshua L. Dratel, eds. *The Torture Papers: The Road to Abu Ghraib*. Cambridge, UK: Cambridge University Press, 2005.

Grosz, Elizabeth. *Chaos, Territory, Art: Deleuze and the Framing of the Earth*. New York: Columbia University Press, 2008.

Gurr, Ted Robert, and Charles Ruttenberg. *The Conditions of Civil Violence: First Tests of a Causal Model*. Princeton: Center of International Studies, Woodrow Wilson School of Public and International Affairs, Princeton University, 1967.

Hakobian, Levon. "The Reception of Soviet Music in the West: A History of Sympathy and Misunderstandings." *Muzikologija* 13 (2012): 125–37. http://www.doiserbia.nb.rs/img/doi/1450-9814/2012/1450-98141200015H.pdf.

Handel, Stephen. *Listening: An Introduction to the Perception of Auditory Events*. Cambridge, MA: MIT Press, 1989.

Haraway, Donna. *Simians, Cyborgs, and Women: The Reinvention of Nature*. New York: Routledge, 1991.

Helfer, Thomas, Nikki N. Jordan, and Robyn B. Lee. "Postdeployment Hearing Loss in U.S. Army Soldiers Seen at Audiology Clinics from April 1, 2003, through March 31, 2004." *American Journal of Audiology* 14 (2005): 161–8.

Helfer, Thomas M., Nikki N. Jordan, Robyn B. Lee, Paul Pietrusiak, Kara Cave, and Kim Schairer. "Noise-Induced Hearing Injury and Comorbidities Among Postdeployment U.S. Army Soldiers: April 2003–June 2009." *American Journal of Audiology* 20, no. 1 (2011): 33–41.

Heller, Steven, and Mirko Ilic. *The Anatomy of Design: Uncovering the Influences and Inspirations in Modern Graphic Design*. Gloucester, MA: Rockport, 2007.

Hemingway, Ernest. *Selected Letters 1913–1961*. Edited by Carlos Baker. London: Granada Publishing, 1981.

Henry, Doug. "Trauma and Vulnerability During War." In *Cultures of Fear: A Critical Reader*, edited by Uli Linke and Danielle Taana Smith, 117–131. London and New York: Pluto Press, 2009.

Herr, Michael. *Dispatches*. New York: Knopf, 2009 [1977].

Hirschkind, Charles. *The Ethical Soundscape: Cassette Sermons and Islamic Counterpublics*. New York: Columbia University Press, 2006.

Hoffman, Danny. "Frontline Anthropology: Research in a Time of War." *Anthropology Today* 19, no. 3 (2003): 9–12.

Hoffmann, Frank W., and Howard Ferstler. *Encyclopedia of Recorded Sound.* Vol. 1. 2nd ed. New York: Routledge, 2004.

Homer. *The Iliad.* Translated by Samuel Butler. Seattle: Pacific Publishing Studio, 2010.

Howe, Warren P. "Early American Military Music." *American Music* 17, no. 1 (1999): 87–116.

Howes, David, ed. *The Varieties of Sensory Experience.* Toronto: University of Toronto Press, 1991.

Howes, David. "Introduction: Empires of the Senses." In *Empire of the Senses: The Sensual Culture Reader,* edited by David Howes, 1–20. Oxford and New York: Berg, 2005.

———, ed. *The Sixth Sense Reader.* Oxford and New York: Berg, 2009.

Hurley, Robin A., and Katherine H. Taber, eds. *Windows to the Brain: Insights from Neuroimaging.* Arlington, VA: American Psychiatric Publishing, 2008.

Ibabe, Izaskun, Joana Jaureguizar, and Oscar Diaz. "Adolescent Violence Against Parents: Is It a Consequence of Gender Inequality?" *European Journal of Psychology Applied to Legal Context* 1, no. 1 (2009): 3–24.

Ihde, Don. *Listening and Voice: Phenomenologies of Sound.* Albany: State University of New York Press, 2007.

Jackman, Mary. "Violence in Social Life." *Annual Review of Sociology* 28 (2002): 387–415.

Jackson, Michael, ed. *Things as They Are: New Directions in Phenomenological Anthropology.* Bloomington: Indiana University Press, 1996.

———. *The Politics of Storytelling: Violence, Transgression, and Intersubjectivity.* Copenhagen: Museum Tusculanum Press, 2002.

Johnson, Bruce, and Martin Cloonan. *The Dark Side of the Tune: Popular Music and Violence.* London: Ashgate, 2008.

Johnson, Jenny. "The Luminous Noise of Broken Experience: Synaesthesia, Acoustic Memory, and Childhood Sexual Abuse in the Late 20th Century United States." PhD diss., New York University, 2009.

Jones, Dylan. *iPod, therefore I Am: Thinking Inside the White Box.* New York: Bloomsbury, 2005.

Kahney, Leander. *Cult of iPod.* San Francisco: No Starch Press, 2005.

Kane, Brian. "Acousmatic Fabrications: Les Paul and the 'Les Paulverizer.'" *Journal of Visual Culture* 10, no. 212 (2011): 212–31.

Keith Kahn-Harris, *Extreme Metal: Music and Culture on the Edge.* Oxford: Berg, 2006.

Kelly, Caleb. *Cracked Media: The Sound of Malfunction.* Cambridge, MA: MIT Press, 2009.

Kelman, Ari Y. "Rethinking the Soundscape: A Critical Genealogy of a Key Term in Sound Studies." *Senses & Society* 5, no. 2: 212–34.

Kennard, George. *Loopy: The Autobiography of George Kennard.* London: Leo Cooper, 1990.

Kenney, William H. *Recorded Music in American Life: The Phonograph and Popular Memory, 1890–1945.* New York: Oxford University Press, 1999.

Kittler, Friedrich. *Gramophone, Film, Typewriter.* Translated by Geoffrey Winthrop-Young. Stanford: Stanford University Press, 1999 [1986].

Kristeva, Julia. *Powers of Horror: An Essay in Abjection.* Translated by Leon S. Roudiez. New York: Columbia University Press, 1982.

Krohn-Hansen, Christian. "The Anthropology of Violent Interaction." *Journal of Anthropological Research* 50, no. 4 (1994): 367–81.

LaBelle, Brandon. *Acoustic Territories: Sound Culture and Everyday Life.* New York: Continuum, 2010.

Lacey, Kate. "Towards a Periodization of Listening: Radio and Modern Life." *International Journal of Cultural Studies* 3 (2000): 279–88.

Lamb, Christopher J. "Review of Psychological Operations Lessons Learned from Recent Operational Experience." Washington, DC: National Defense University Press, 2005. http://ics-www.leeds.ac.uk/papers/pmt/exhibits/2736/Lamb_OP_092005_Psyops.pdf.

Latour, Bruno. *We Have Never Been Modern*. Translated by Catherine Porter. Cambridge, MA: Harvard University Press, 1993.

———. *Reassembling the Social: An Introduction to Actor-Network-Theory*, New York: Oxford University Press, 2005.

Law, John. "On the Subject of the Object: Narrative, Technology, and Interpellation." *Configurations* 8, no. 1 (2000): 1–29,

Lecourt, Edith. "The Musical Envelope." In *Psychic Envelopes*, edited by Didier Anzeiu and translated by Daphne Briggs, 211–235. London: Karnac Books, 1990.

Lee, Tong Soon. "Technology and the Production of Islamic Space: The Call to Prayer in Singapore." *Ethnomusicology* 43, no. 1 (1999): 86–100.

Leppert, Richard. "The Social Discipline of Listening." In *Aural Cultures*, edited by Jim Drobnick, 19–36. Toronto: YYZ Books, 2004.

Levy, Steven. *The Perfect Thing: How the iPod Shuffles Commerce, Culture, and Coolness*. New York: Simon & Schuster, 2007.

Leys, Ruth. *Trauma: A Genealogy*. Chicago: University of Chicago Press, 2013.

Lomax, Eric. *The Railway Man: A POW's Searing Account of War, Brutality and Forgiveness*. London: Jonathan Cape, 1995.

Lutz, Catherine. "US and Coalition Casualties in Iraq and Afghanistan." 2013. http://costsofwar.org/sites/default/files/articles/10/attachments/USandCoalition.pdf.

Macek, Ivana. *Sarajevo Under Siege: Anthropology in Wartime*. Philadelphia: University of Pennsylvania Press, 2009.

MacLeod, Arlene Elowe. "Hegemonic Relations and Gender Resistance: The New Veiling as Accommodating Protest in Cairo." *Signs* 17, no. 3 (1992): 533–57.

Maguen, Shira, Barbara A. Lucenko, Mark A. Reger, Gregory A. Gahm, Brett T. Litz, Karen H. Seal, Sara J. Knight, and Charles R. Marmar. "The Impact of Reported Direct and Indirect Killing on Mental Health Symptoms in Iraq War Veterans." *Journal of Traumatic Stress* 23, no. 1 (2010): 86–90.

Malkki, Liisa H. *Purity and Exile: Violence, Memory, and National Cosmology among Hutu Refugees in Tanzania*. Chicago: University of Chicago Press, 1995.

Manuel, Peter. *Cassette Culture: Popular Music and Technology in Northern India*. Chicago: University of Chicago Press, 1993.

Maróthy, János. "Rite and Rhythm: From Behaviour Patterns to Musical Structures." *Studia Musicologica Academiae Scientiarum Hungaricae* 35, fasc. 4 (1993–4): 421–33.

Marres, Noortje. "Issues Spark a Public into Being: A Key But Often Forgotten Point of the Lippmann-Dewey Debate." In *Making Things Public*, edited by Bruno Latour and Peter Weibel, 208–17. Cambridge, MA: MIT Press, 2005.

Maslow, Abraham. *The Psychology of Science: A Reconnaissance*. New York: Harper and Row, 1966.

McGrath, John J. "The Other End of the Spear: The Tooth-to-Tail Ratio (T3R) in Modern Military Operations." The Long War Series, Occasional Paper 23. Fort Leavenworth,

KS: Combat Studies Institute Press, 2007. http://usacac.army.mil/cac2/cgsc/carl/download/csipubs/mcgrath_op23.pdf.

McIlwain, D. Scott, Kathy Gates, and Donald Ciliax. "Heritage of Army Audiology and the Road Ahead: The Army Hearing Program." *American Journal of Public Health* 98, no. 12 (2008): 2167–72. http://www.ncbi.nlm.nih.gov/pmc/articles/PMC2636536/

McNab, Robert M., and Richard L. Scott. "Non-lethal Weapons and the Long Tail of Warfare." *Small Wars and Insurgencies* 20, no. 1 (2009):141–59.

Merskin, Debra. "The Construction of Arabs as Enemies: Post-September 11 Discourse of George W. Bush." *Mass Communication and Society* 7, no. 2 (2004): 157–75.

Metz, Christian. *The Imaginary Signifier: Psychoanalysis and the Cinema.* Translated by Celia Britton et al. Bloomington: Indiana University Press, 1986.

Mitchell, K. J., and D. Finkelhor. "Risk of Crime Victimization Among Youth Exposed to Domestic Violence." *Journal of Interpersonal Violence* 16, no. 9 (2001): 944–64.

Mosher, Donald. "Hypermasculinity Inventory." In *Handbook of Sexuality-Related Measures,* edited by Clive M. Davis, William L. Yarber, Robert Bauserman, George Schreer, and Sandra L. Davis, 55–6. Thousand Oaks, CA: Sage Publications, 1998.

Mowitt, John. "The Sound of Music in the Era of Its Electronic Reproducibility." In *Music and Society: The Politics of Composition, Performance and Reception,* edited by Richard Leppert and Susan McClary, 173–97. Cambridge, UK: Cambridge University Press, 1987.

Navaro-Yashin, Yael. *The Make-Believe Space: Affective Geography in a Postwar Polity.* Durham, NC: Duke University Press, 2012.

Neimeyer, Robert. "Narrative Strategies in Grief Therapy." *Journal of Constructivist Psychology* 12, no. 1 (1999): 65–85.

Nordstrom, Carolyn. *A Different Kind of War Story.* Philadelphia: University of Pennsylvania Press, 1997.

———. *Shadows of War: Violence, Power, and International Profiteering in the Twenty-First Century.* Berkeley: University of California Press, 2004.

Nudds, Matthew, and Casey O'Callaghan. "Introduction: The Philosophy of Sounds and Auditory Perception." In *Sounds and Perception: New Philosophical Essays,* edited by Matthew Nudds and Casey O'Callaghan, 2–24. New York and Oxford, 2009.

O'Brien, Tim. *The Things They Carried.* New York: Houghton Mifflin Harcourt, 1990.

O'Callaghan, Casey. *Sounds: A Philosophical Theory.* Oxford and New York: Oxford University Press, 2007.

O'Connell, John Morgan, and Salwa el-Shawan Castelo-Branco, eds. *Music and Conflict.* Urbana: University of Illinois Press, 2010.

Oliveros, Pauline. *Deep Listening: A Composer's Sound Practice.* New York: iUniverse, 2005.

Osmont, Marie-Louise. *The Normandy Diary of Marie-Louise Osmont: 1940–1944.* New York: Random House, 1994.

Otterbeck, Jonas, and Anders Ackfeldt. "Music and Islam." *Contemporary Islam* 6 (2012): 227–33.

Owen, Wilfred. *The Complete Poems of Wilfred Owen.* Edited by Jon Stallworthy. London: Chatto & Windus, 1983.

Paddock, Alfred. Jr. "Military Psychological Operations." In *Political Warfare and Psychological Operations,* edited Carnes Lord and Frank R. Barnett, 45–65. Washington, DC: National Defense University Press, 1989.

Pellegrinelli, Lara. "Scholarly Discord: The Politics of Music in the War on Terrorism." *Chronicle of Higher Education* 55, no. 35 (2009): B6.

Pettan, Svanibor, ed. *Music, Politics, and War: Views from Croatia.* Zagreb: Institute of Ethnology and Folklore Research, 1998.

Picker, John M. *Victorian Soundscapes.* New York: Oxford University Press, 2003.

Picton, Sir Thomas. *Memoirs of Lieutenant-General Sir Thomas Picton.* 2 vols. London: R. Bentley, 1836.

Pieke, Frank N. "Accidental Anthropology: Witnessing the 1989 Chinese People's Movement." In *Fieldwork Under Fire: Contemporary Studies of Violence and Culture,* edited by Antonius C. G. M. Robben and Carolyn Nordstrom, 62–80. Berkeley: University of California Press, 1995.

Pieslak, Jonathan. *Sound Targets: American Soldiers and Music in the Iraq War.* Bloomington: Indiana University Press, 2009.

Pinch, Trevor, and Karin Bijsterveld. "Introduction." In *The Oxford Handbook of Sound Studies,* edited by Trevor Pinch and Karin Bijsterveld, 3–38. New York: Oxford University Press, 2012.

Poole, Oliver. *Red Zone: Five Bloody Years in Baghdad.* London: Reportage Press, 2008.

Post, Jerrold M. "Psychological Operations and Counterterrorism." *Joint Force Quarterly* 37 (2005): 105–111.

Powers, Kevin. *Yellow Birds: A Novel.* New York: Little, Brown, 2012.

Pratt, Mary Louise. "Harm's Way: Language and the Contemporary Arts of War." *PMLA* 124, no. 5 (2009): 1515–31.

———. "Violence and Language." *Social Text: Periscope* (online journal), May 21, 2011. http://socialtextjournal.org/periscope_article/violence_and_language_-_mary_louise_pratt/.

Price, G. Richard. "Weapon Noise Exposure of the Human Ear Analyzed with the AHAAH Model." US Army Research Laboratory online site www.arl.army.mil, September 2010. http://www.arl.army.mil/www/default.cfm?page=351.

Pritchard, Tim. *Ambush Alley: The Most Extraordinary Battle of the Iraq War.* New York: Ballantine, 2005.

Puar, Jasbir K. *Terrorist Assemblages: Homonationalism in Queer Times.* Durham, NC: Duke University Press, 2007.

Pyle, Ernie. "Battle and Breakout in Normandy." In *Reporting World War II, Part Two: American Journalism, 1944–46,* edited by Samuel Hynes, Anne Matthews, Nancy Caldwell Sorel, and Roger J. Spiller, 461–70. New York: Library of America, 1995.

Rabinowitz, Peter M. "Noise-Induced Hearing Loss." *American Family Physician* 61, no. 9 (2000): 2749–56.

Rancière, Jacques. "Ten Theses on Politics." *Theory and Event* 5, no. 3 (2001). http://muse.jhu.edu/journals/theory_and_event/v005/5.3ranciere.html.

———. *The Politics of Aesthetics.* London: Continuum, 2005.

Reiss, A. J., Jr., and J. A. Roth, eds., *Understanding and Preventing Violence.* 4 vols. Washington, DC: National Academy Press, 1993.

Remarque, Eric Maria. *All Quiet on the Western Front.* Translated by A. W. Wheen. New York: Ballantine Books, 1987.

Ricoeur, Paul. *Memory, History, Forgetting.* Translated by Kathleen Blamey and David Pellauer. Chicago: University of Chicago Press, 2004.

Ritter, Jonathan, and J. Martin Daughtry, eds. *Music in the Post-9/11 World.* New York: Routledge, 2007.

Riverbend. *Baghdad Burning: Girl Blog from Iraq*. New York: Feminist Press at CUNY, 2005.

Rizzo, Albert, Jarrell Pair, Ken Graap, Brian Manson, Peter J. McNerney, Brenda K. Wiederhold, Mark Wiederhold, and James Spira. "A Virtual Reality Exposure Therapy Application for Iraq War Military Personnel with Post Traumatic Stress Disorder: From Training to Toy to Treatment." In *NATO Advanced Research Workshop on Novel Approaches to the Diagnosis and Treatment of Posttraumatic Stress Disorder*, edited by M. Roy, 235–50. Washington DC: IOS Press, 2006.

Rizzo, A. A., J. Difede, B. Rothbaum, J. M. Daughtry, and G. Reger. "Update and Expansion of the Virtual Iraq/Afghanistan PTSD Exposure Therapy System." In *Future Directions in Post-Traumatic Stress Disorder*, edited by M. Safir, H. Wallach, and A. A Rizzo, 303–328. New York: Springer, 2015.

Roads, Curtis. *Microsound*. Cambridge, MA: MIT Press, 2001.

Robben, Antonius C. G. M., ed. *Iraq at a Distance: What Anthropologists Can Teach Us About the War*. Philadelphia: University of Pennsylvania Press, 2009.

Robinson, Heaton Bowstead. *Memoirs of Lieutenant-General Sir Thomas Picton*. 2 vols. London: Richard Bentley, 1836.

Rogerson, Sidney. *Twelve Days, 1930*. Norwich, UK: Gliddon, 1988.

Rosen, Leora N., Kathryn H. Knudson, and Peggy Fancher. "Cohesion and the Culture of Hypermasculinity in U.S. Army Units." *Armed Forces and Society* 29, no. 3 (2003): 325–51.

Ross, Charles D. *Civil War Acoustic Shadows*. Shippensburg, PA: White Mane, 2001.

Russolo, Luigi. *The Art of Noise*. Translated by Robert Filliou. New York: Something Else Press, 1967 [1913].

Sachs, Curt. *The History of Musical Instruments*. New York: W. W. Norton, 1940.

Sack, Robert. *Human Territoriality: Its Theory and History*. Cambridge, UK: Cambridge University Press, 1986.

Said, Behnam. "Hymns (Nasheeds): A Contribution to the Study of the Jihadist Culture." *Studies in Conflict and Terrorism* 35, no. 12 (2012): 863–79.

Samuels, David W., Louise Meintjes, Ana Maria Ochoa, and Thomas Porcello. "Soundscapes: Toward a Sounded Anthropology." *Annual Review of Anthropology* 39 (2010): 329–45.

Sarhan, Afif and Caroline Davies. "Iraqi Artists and Singers Flee amid Crackdown on Forbidden Culture." *Guardian/ Observer*, May 10, 2008, http://www.theguardian.com/world/2008/may/11/iraq.

Scarry, Elaine. *The Body in Pain: The Making and Unmaking of the World*. New York: Oxford University Press, 1985.

Schafer, R. Murray. *The Soundscape: Our Sonic Environment and the Tuning of the World*. Rochester, VT: Inner Traditions, 1994.

Schank, Robert C., and Robert P. Abelson. *Scripts, Plans, Goals, and Understanding: An Inquiry into Human Knowledge Structures*. Hillsdale, NJ: L. Erlbaum Associates, 1977.

Scheper-Hughes, Nancy. *Death without Weeping: The Violence of Everyday Life in Brazil*. Berkeley: University of California Press, 1992.

Seierstad, Asne. *A Hundred and One Days: A Baghdad Journal*. Translated by Ingrid Christopherson. New York: Basic Books, 2005.

Selz, Peter Howard, and Susan Landauer. *Art of Engagement: Visual Politics in California and Beyond*. Berkeley: University of California Press, 2006.

Shehadi, Fadlou. *Philosophies of Music in Medieval Islam*. Leiden and New York: Brill, 1995.

Sheppard, W. Anthony. "An Exotic Enemy: Anti-Japanese Musical Propaganda in World War II Hollywood." *Journal of the American Musicological Society* 54, no. 2(2001): 303–57.

Shildrick, Margrit, with Janet Price. "Openings on the Body: A Critical Introduction." In *Feminist Theory and the Body: A Reader*, edited by Janet Price and Margrit Shildrick, 1–14. Edinburgh: Edinburgh University Press, 1999.

Shiloah, Amnon. *Music in the World of Islam: A Socio-Cultural Study*. Detroit: Wayne State University Press, 1995.

Silverman, Kaja. *The Acoustic Mirror: The Female Voice in Psychoanalysis and Cinema*. Bloomington: Indiana University Press, 1988.

Simmel, Georg. "The Metropolis and Mental Life." In *Social Sciences III: Selections and Selected Readings*. Vol. 2. 14th ed., 324–332. Chicago: University of Chicago Press, 1948.

Smith, James, and James Billingsley. "Abbreviated Test Report for Blue Force Communications Electromagnetic Compatibility (EMC) with WARLOCK-Green, WARLOCK-Red, and Self-screening Vehicle Jammer Systems, (FOUO)." Aberdeen Proving Ground, MD: US Army Developmental Test Command, May 2004. http://wikileaks-press.org:81/file/blue-force-comms-emc-warlock-test-results-2-2004.pdf.

Smith, Mark M., ed. *Hearing History: A Reader*. Athens: University of Georgia Press, 2004.

Smith, P. D. "Blast Walls for Structural Protection Against High Explosive Threats: A Review." *International Journal of Protective Structures* 1, no. 1 (2010): 67–84.

Snyder, Bob. *Music and Memory: An Introduction*. Cambridge, MA: MIT Press, 2000.

Soza, Samuel. "Shooter-Detection 'Boomerangs' Helping in Iraq." *Official Homepage of the US Army*, December 17, 2009. http://www.army.mil/-news/2009/12/17/32029-shooter-detection-boomerangs-helping-in-iraq/index.html.

Spears, E. L. *Prelude to Victory*. London: Jonathan Cape, 1939.

Stahlberg, Alexander. *Bounden Duty: The Memoirs of a German Officer, 1932–1945*. Translated by Patricia Crampton. London: Brassey's, 1990.

Stanyek, Jason, and Benjamin Piekut. "Deadness: Technologies of the Intermundane." *TDR* 54, no. 1 (2010): 14–38.

Sterne, Jonathan. *The Audible Past: Cultural Origins of Sound Reproduction*. Durham, NC: Duke University Press, 2003.

———. "Enemy Voice." *Social Text 96* 26, no. 3 (2008): 79–100.

Steuter, Erin, and Deborah Wills. "'The Vermin Have Struck Again': Dehumanizing the Enemy in Post 9/11 Media Representations." *Media, War & Conflict* 3, no. 2 (2010): 152–67.

Sutherland, John, Rick Baillergeon, and Tim McKane. "Cordon and Search Operations: A Deadly Game of Hide-and-Seek." *Air Land Sea Bulletin* 2010, no. 3. http://www.alsa.mil/library/alsb/ALSB%202010-3.pdf

Swedenburg, Ted. "Prisoners of Love: With Genet in the Palestinian Field." In *Fieldwork Under Fire: Contemporary Studies of Violence and Culture*, edited by Antonius C. G. M. Robben and Carolyn Nordstrom, 25–41. Berkeley: University of California Press, 1995.

Szendy, Peter. *Listen: A History of Our Ears*. Translated by Charlotte Mandell. New York: Fordham University Press, 2008.

Taber, Katherine H., Deborah L. Warden, and Robin A. Hurley. "Blast-related Traumatic Brain Injury: What Is Known?" *Journal of Neuropsychiatry and Clinical Neurosciences* 18, no. 2 (2006): 141–5.

Tanielian, Terri, and Lisa H. Jaycox, eds. *Invisible Wounds of War: Psychological and Cognitive Injuries, Their Consequences, and Services to Assist Recovery*. Santa Monica: RAND, 2008.

Thompson, Emily. *The Soundscape of Modernity: Architectural Acoustics and the Culture of Listening in America, 1900–1933*. Cambridge, MA: MIT Press, 2002.

Throop, C. Jason. *Suffering and Sentiment: Exploring the Vicissitudes of Experience and Pain in Yap*. Berkeley: University of California Press, 2010.

Thucydides. *The History of the Peloponnesian War*. Edited by Sir R. W. Livingstone. Oxford: Oxford University Press, 1968.

Tripp, Elise Forbes. *Surviving Iraq: Soldiers' Stories*. New York: Olive Branch Press, 2008.

Turkle, Sherry. "Introduction: The Things that Matter." In *Evocative Objects: Things We Think With*, edited by Sherry Turkle, 3–10. Cambridge, MA: MIT Press, 2007.

Turse, Nick. *The Complex: How the Military Invades Our Everyday Lives*. New York: Metropolitan Books, 2008.

Ullman, Harlan K., and James P. Wade. *Shock and Awe: Achieving Rapid Dominance*. Washington DC: National Defense University Press, 1996.

Vernon, P. E. "Psychological Effects of Air-Raids," *Journal of Abnormal and Social Psychology* 36, no. 4 (1941): 457–76.

Virilio, Paul. *War and Cinema: The Logistics of Perception*. London and New York: Verso, 2000 [1989].

Walker, E. H. "Air Raid Sirens," *Musical Times* 81, no. 1173 (1940): 458.

Weinberger, Norman M. "The Cognitive Auditory Cortex." In *The Oxford Handbook of Auditory Science: The Auditory Brain*, edited by Adrian Rees and Alan R. Palmer, 440–77. Oxford and New York: Oxford University Press, 2010.

Weisbard, Eric, ed. *Pop When the World Falls Apart: Music in the Shadow of Doubt*. Durham, NC: Duke University Press, 2012.

Wheatcroft, Andrew. *The Ottomans: Dissolving Images*. New York: Viking, 1993.

White, Hayden. *The Content of the Form*. Baltimore: Johns Hopkins University Press, 1987.

Wieviorka, Michel. *Violence: A New Approach*. Translated by David Macey. London: Sage, 2009.

———. "Violence and the Subject." *Thesis Eleven* 73, no. 1 (2003): 42–50.

Wilson, Clay. "Improvised Explosive Devices (IEDs) in Iraq and Afghanistan: Effects and Countermeasures." Washington, DC: Congressional Research Service, 2007. http://fpc.state.gov/documents/organization/57512.pdf.

Winthrop-Young, Geoffrey. "Drill and Distraction in the Yellow Submarine: On the Dominance of War in Friedrich Kittler's Media Theory." *Critical Inquiry* 28, no. 4 (2002): 825–54.

Wong, Edward, and David S. Cloud. "U.S. Erects Baghdad Wall to Keep Sects Apart." *New York Times*, April 21, 2007. http://www.nytimes.com/2007/04/21/world/middleeast/21iraq.html.

Wurtzler, Steve J. 2008. "One Future of Sound Studies Fits into the Palm of Your Hand." *Music, Sound, and the Moving Image* 2, no. 2 (2008): 169–73.

Xenophon. *The Persian Expedition*. Translated by Rex Warner. New York: Penguin Books, 1949.

Yates, Christopher. "Introduction." In *Philosophy and the Return to Violence: Studies from this Widening Gyre*, edited by Nathan Eckstrand and Christopher S. Yates, 1–12. New York: Continuum, 2011.

Žižek, Slavoj. *Violence: Six Sideways Reflections*. New York: Macmillan, 2008.

Index

9/11, 9, 166, 184, 220, 289n9
abjection, 20, 122, 207, 225
Abu Ghraib, 8, 166, 194, 225
acoustemology, 19, 98, 287n52
acoustic territories, 20, 125–7, 188–212
   of/in the body, 207–10
   and cultural anesthesia, 198
   displacement in, 190–91, 201–2
   emplacement in, 188–90, 201
   encompassing the body (helmets,
      hooding), 206–7
   interacting with auditory regimes and sonic
      campaigns, 210–12, 215, 219, 277
   interpellation into, 200–1, 211
   and Iraqi music, 269–70
   perforation of, 203–4, 255, 269
   persistence of, 200
   radiant, 193, 199–201
   relation between macro and micro, 190, 208
   resonant, 193, 201–210
   transplacement in, 191–2, 201–2, 307n12
   virtual, 193–9
acoustic weapons, 180–2, 322
adhan, 37, 57–61, 73, 179, 212
aesthetics (*see also* music; violence, aestheticization
   of), 5, 23, 58–61, 126, 199, 277

affect, 6, 17, 20, 26, 87, 101, 148, 162–3, 189, 209
   fight, flight, or freeze, 42, 78, 148–50, 199
   leakage of, 173, 195
   pre-hermeneutic terror, 157–8, 179,
      186, 313n20
   technologies of, 154
agency
   human, 16, 41, 62, 121, 159, 164, 168, 174–6,
      243, 277
   musical, 258
   technological, 228, 247
al-Askari mosque, 166, 204
al-Maliki, Nouri, 148–50
al-Qaeda, 183–4, 195–7
al-Qaeda in Iraq, 204, 256–7, 264–6, 306
al-Rassam, Hussam, 37, 261
al-Sadr, Muqtada, 51, 53, 179, 211
al-Saher, Kazem, 37, 256, 261
al-Sahhaf, Muhammad Sa'id, 177, 305n41
al-Zarqawi, Abu Musab, 185–6
Apocalypse Now, 135–7
ashura, 61–2, 292n52
audible inaudible, zone of, 77–80, 137, 149–50,
   211, 293n6
audition (*see* listening)
auditor, definition, 22–3

auditory regimes, 19, 123–4, 127,
128–158, 297n11
and aural acuity, 144–6
British vs. American, 139–41
difficulty of entering, 157
difficulty of exiting, 157–8
of Iraqi civilians, 147–58, 276–7
oblique indoctrination into, 141–2
and post-traumatic stress, 157–8
relation with acoustic territories and sonic
campaigns, 210–12, 215, 219, 277
and situational awareness, 142–147
Stop-Look-Listen-Smell (SLLS), 105, 143
auscultation, 34, 95, 130, 131–5, 288n1
Awakening, Iraqi, 195–7

Ban Ki-Moon, 148–50
Bataille, George, 23–4
belliphonic (*see also* sounds; weapon sounds)
and audionarratives, 80
contrasted with peacetime, 164
definition, 3–5
drowning out other sounds, 37–8
theory of listening, 16
Bennett, Jane, 175
Berg, Nick, 184
Bernstein, Robin, 150–1
Bijsterveld, Karin, and Trevor Pinch, 5,
133, 299n10
bin Laden, Osama, 184–5, 196, 306n61
blast walls, 35, 201–3, 205, 209–10, 256
blast waves, 94–5, 162, 185, 190, 295n29
bodies
as acoustic filter, 78
and displacement, 190–91
and emplacement 188–90
forced into vibration by sounds, 164–5, 170
homo geographicus, 189–90
indoctrinated, 102, 122, 128–158
inflecting the terms "auditory," "sonic,"
"acoustic", 122–7
microterritories within, 20, 189–90, 207–12
suffused with chemicals, listening, 78, 99,
109, 137
and transplacement, 191–3, 201–2, 277
vulnerability to belliphonic sounds, 5, 26,
92–5, 102, 162–6
Bourdieu, Pierre, 129–30, 166
Boyden, Jo, 12

Bush, George W., 164, 176–7, 184–5, 240–1,
305n41, 306n61
Buzzell, Colby, 6, 231–3

Calhoun, Craig, 129
call to prayer (*see* adhan)
Caruth, Cathy, 7, 285n21
Casey, Edward, 188–9, 190–1, 307n6
Casablanca, 131–2
casualties, 39–40, 97, 273, 283, 301n36
communications (*see also* incommunicability;
mishearing; voice), 43, 47–56, 79, 84,
144–5, 175, 195, 199, 220, 234, 240,
241–4, 290n24
complex personhood, 21–23, 270, 273
Connor, Steven, 5, 160, 303n25
contractors, 43–4, 53, 64, 142, 147, 180, 228, 236
Copper Greene, 224–5
Csordas, Thomas, 101
culture (*see also* war culture; auditory regime)
conventional understanding of, 17
differences in listening practices between
Iraqis and US troops, 95–8
fragility of, 18–19, 57
relation of sound and listening to, 6–7, 41, 59,
108, 123–7, 298n11
in relation to soundscape, 122
Cusick, Suzanne, 6, 95, 164–5, 169, 175,
209, 240–1

Daniel, E. Valentine, 7, 23–6, 285n23
Das, Veena, 15
Deer, Patrick, 98, 295n35, 306n56
Deleuze, Gilles and Félix Guattari,
307n14, 310n43
Denora, Tia, 238, 314n28
drones, 195

echolocation, 88, 129–30, 150, 161, 170–3, 202
ethics
in the audible inaudible zone, 79–80
and inaudition, 111–18
in other zones of audition, 95, 101–2
and scholarship, 25–6

Feld, Steven (*see also* acoustemology), 6, 98,
188, 287n52
Feldman, Allen, 7, 25–6, 198–9, 274, 285n23
Forkscrew Graphics, 224–5

George, Raed, 258, 261–3, 269
Gilman, Lisa, 229, 246, 311n3
Gittoes, George, 141, 227
globalization, 18, 169, 186–7, 194–5, 198, 207, 224, 269
Goodman, Steve, 6, 162, 169, 208–9, 313n20
Gordon, Avery, 21, 270
Green Zone (*see* International Zone)

Hair, Ayad, 265
hearing loss (*see also* shooter's ear), 5, 29, 68, 72, 92–4, 144–5, 150, 162, 167, 172–3, 182, 204, 208, 294n23, 295n27, 300n24, 310n47
hearing protection, 43, 92–4, 128, 145–6, 153–4, 210, 294n23
Heartbreak Ridge, 132–3
house raids, 55–6, 110–18
Howes, David, 6, 287n44
Hussain, Ismail, 260–1
Hussein, Saddam, 9, 60–2, 66–7, 110, 149, 152–3, 176–7, 186, 191, 255, 260, 263–4
Hussein, Uday, 260–1, 319n18
hyperalertness/hypervigilance (*see also* post-traumatic stress), 97, 99–100, 105, 129, 158, 209, 212, 215

images of the war, 194, 221–5
improvisation, 107–8, 128–30, 153, 228
inaudition (*see also* audible inaudible; silencing), 19, 101–2, 124, 130, 150–1, 153, 156–7, 322
close/hypermasculine, 111–18, 135–7, 148–50, 157
traumatic, 95
in the zone of the audible inaudible, 77–80, 211
incommunicability
of meaning, 53, 56, 60–1
of pain, 167
of a state of vulnerability, 46
International Zone, 11, 67, 69, 191, 211, 255
interrogation (using sound within), 166, 206, 240–1, 317n69
intersensoriality (*see also* scopic regimes), 40–5, 69, 83, 92, 156, 163, 204, 212
iPods (*see also* music), 9–10, 219–247, 257
as ambiguous technology, 228, 247
and ballistic calculation, 244–5

costs and benefits, 234–6
and crowd dispersal/interrogation, 240–1
and interpellation, 243
and PSYOPS, 238–40
and translation, 241–3
Iran-Iraq war, 28–9, 38–9, 65, 152, 262
Iraq
Baghdad neighborhoods
Adhamiya, 55, 309n33
al-Binouq, 275–7
Green Zone (*see* International Zone)
Kadhimiya, 61
Mansour, 202
Sadr City, 40, 53, 179, 203, 239, 265, 275
Saydiya, 255–6
Zayouna, 28, 37, 39–40, 289n6
Cities
Balad Ruz, 266
Basra, 266
Fallujah, 166, 179, 241, 267
Haditha, 68
Karbala, 61
Kirkuk, 252
Latifiya, 72–3
Mahmudiya, 72–3
Mosul, 68
Ramadi, 70–2, 268
Samarra, 166, 204
Tikrit, 229, 268
Ulwan al Khalf, 268
Yusufiya, 72–3
music
current challenges for, 269–70
emos, 266–7
first wave of violence toward, 263
history, 259–61, 263–4
Muslim attitudes toward, 263–4, 319n17
nashid, 268
post-invasion challenges for, 261–270
power of, 275–7
sectarian violence toward, 263–7
US forces targeting, 267–9

Jabry, Youssef, 266
Jackman, Mary, 167–8, 170, 174
Johnson, Jenny, 95, 162

Kimmitt, Brigadier General Mark, 46–7, 156–7

Labelle, Brandon, 5, 193, 298-9n17
listening (*see also* sounds)
  against the grain, 157, 212, 273–4, 275–7
  criminalization of, 183
  and dehumanization, 26, 59, 79–80,
    156, 291n45
  distinct from hearing, 134–5
  and empathy, 61–2, 131, 154
  as ethical practice, 15, 95, 101–2
  and fear, 44, 46–7, 56, 87, 101–2, 131, 139, 154,
    180, 201
  and hypermasculinity, 130–1, 135–9, 148–5
  and incommensurability, 148, 151–8
  literacy, competence, virtuosity, 150–151
  ontology of, 18–19, 123–6
  outer threshold of, 101, 207–9
  and performance, 155
  sociocultural variables, 41, 58–61
  stereotypes in film, 131–9
  technological surrogates for, 146–7
Long-Range Acoustic Device (LRAD), 52,
  181, 240
loudspeakers, 51–53, 60, 162, 175, 178–9,
  200, 234

media
  global reach of, 186–7
  and sonic campaigns, 176–8
  and sonic verisimilitude, 198
memory
  and acoustic territories, 189–90, 200,
    209–10, 289n8
  and countermemories, 274–7
  of peacetime Iraq, 36–8, 256
  of previous wars, 38–9
  traumatic/haunting, 35, 40, 99–100, 162–3,
    253, 271, 273
methodology, 12–18
milblogs, 14, 33, 284n3
military installations, U.S.
  Abu Ghraib (*see* Abu Ghraib)
  Camp Balad, 42
  Camp Echo, 67
  Camp Victory, 11, 51, 89, 162, 280
  Loyalty Base, 142
mishearing, 50, 56, 59, 91–2, 145, 213–15, 276
Mowitt, John, 142
music (*see also* Iraqi music) 11, 20, 107–9,
  248–257,

aestheticizing violence, 232, 236, 246
  as an assertion of control over sensory
    environment, 230
  battle playlist, 231–3, 249–50
  as calming force, 108–9, 226
  as communication, 226
  creating normalcy, 229, 230
  and crowd dispersal, 240
  as evidence for detention, 267–8
  as *haram*, 256–7, 263–4
  in the history of combat, 225–7
  and interrogation, 240–1
  invigorating the troops, 226, 229
  at Iraqi weddings, 265–6
  jamming radio broadcasts of, 260–1
  limits of the efficacy of, 261–2
  military regulations governing, 233
  in sonic campaigns, 179
  at US military memorial services, 237–8, 253
  as victim, 258–70
  and violence/conflict, 6, 20, 258, 318n1
"music program," the (*see also* interrogation),
  166, 240–1
narrational zone of audition, 80–88, 211, 276

Neimeyer, Robert, 15
noise
  from generators, 4, 11, 39, 55, 57, 89, 91, 201,
    251, 262
  paradoxical status of, 33–4, 168
  reported in military documents, 213–15
  from vehicles, 10, 41–3, 55, 89, 145, 202–3
  from weapons (*see* weapon sounds)
Nordstrom, Carolyn, 7, 15, 18, 19, 166, 285n23

O'Brien, Tim, 23–4
O'Callaghan, Casey, 160–2, 163, 169
Operation Desert Fox, 38, 152
Operation Desert Storm, 28, 38–9, 48, 65, 152,
  249, 260

phenomenology, 16–17
  intersensoriality as, 83
  of sound/listening, 76–102, 160–5
  of violence/combat, 26, 63, 165–70
Pieslak, Jonathan, 6, 229, 232, 246, 311n3
Poole, Oliver, 34–5
post-traumatic stress, 5, 7, 26, 40, 73, 98–100,
  253, 296n40, 304n37

and acoustic territories, 209–10
and auditory regimes, 157–8
and omnidirectional sound/violence, 174, 182
Powers, Kevin, 162–3
Pratt, Mary Louise, 17, 243
PSYOPS, 52–3, 176–9, 234, 238–40
PTSD (*see* post-traumatic stress)

Qais, Daoud, 263

Rancière, Jacques, 156, 157, 212
Rapid Dominance (*see* shock and awe
operation)
Red Badge of Courage, 138–9
Ricoeur, Paul, 14–15
Riverbend, 1, 2, 44–5

Sagebiel, Jason, 6, 103–9, 162
Samuels, David, Louise Meintjes, Ana
María Ochoa Gautier, and Thomas
Porcello, 122
Saving Private Ryan, 198
Scarry, Elaine, 285n21, 303n20
Schafer, R. Murray, 60, 121–3, 293n6
Scheper-Hughes, Nancy, 7, 13, 286n33
scopic regimes, 156, 297n11
scopic territories, 194–5
shock and awe operation, 3, 28, 39, 154, 172, 212,
255, 283n1
sensorium
armoring of, 157–8, 293n6
as distributed system, 50, 79, 207
impoverishment/attenuation of, 83–8,
190, 205
overwhelmed by sound and other stimuli, 20,
69, 91–2, 212
shooter's ear, 29, 94, 172–3
silence, 16, 78, 183, 187–8, 195–6, 201, 237–8
silencing, 182–186, 269
killing as, 184–6
Simmel, Georg, 293n6
sirens, 4, 28, 39, 44, 51, 141, 151, 154,
262, 290n25
situational awareness, 92, 142–7, 158, 206
soldier's creed, 131, 299n7
sonic campaigns, 20, 124–5, 127, 159–187
and amplification, 176–9
Hussein regime's, 261
Iraqi insurgency's, 179

music within, 179–80
relation with acoustic territories and auditory
regimes, 210–12, 215, 219, 277
relationship of sound and violence
within, 160–74
sounds (*see also* belliphonic; weapon sounds;
listening)
acousmatic, 34, 53, 68, 80–2, 142, 172
of civilian life, 56–63
and exhilaration, 137–9, 141–2, 154, 184
exposure to, 94–5, 100, 154, 156, 199, 207–9
forcing bodies into vibration, 162, 164, 175
indeterminacy of, 3, 84, 101
and indexicality/narrativity, 4, 34, 43, 45, 47,
154, 157, 180–2, 191–2, 199, 215, 230, 232,
271, 276
and leakage, 171–3, 203–4, 206
as manifestation of violence, 4, 160–174,
207–10, 271
of nature, 62–3, 125
omnidirectionality of, 171–2, 183, 271–3, 279
ontologies, 123–6, 160–3, 210
and positionality, 76–98, 152–3, 156, 193
and scarification, 208–9
and territoriality, 192–3, 207
of vehicles, 41–7
and violation, 165
of weapons, generally, 3–4, 63–74, 129–30
soundscape, 121–3, 126, 210, 219
Soundtrack to War, 227
Stanyek, Jason and Ben Piekut, 199, 203, 308n21
stealth, 103–7
Sterne, Jonathan, 5, 143, 184, 288n1
suicide bombers, 34, 69, 166–7

tactical zone of audition, 88–92, 139–41
testimony, 14–17, 182, 286n38
Tong Soon Lee, 58
translation and interpretation (*see also*
vulnerability), 53, 54–6, 155–6, 241–4
trauma zone of audition, 92–95, 139, 207–10
traumatic brain injury (TBI), 94–95,
207–10, 271

victim, victimhood
commonalities among, 18
commonalities with combatants/
perpetrators, 19, 167, 173
as discursive category, 22

victim, victimhood (*Cont.*)
    music as, 259–70
    of sonic violence (*see also* hearing loss, TBI,
        post-traumatic stress), 20–1, 95, 168,
        207, 209
    subject position of, 4–5, 17, 168, 200
    unequal distribution of, 5
videos
    amateur, 59, 70–2, 110–18, 142, 179, 184–5,
    professional, 65–7, 148–9, 185–6, 196–7
violence
    aestheticization of, 25, 139, 141–2, 246
    distinctions with sound, 169–70
    as forced change to a system, 170–1
    as hot or cold, 186
    and intersubjectivity, 167
    naturalization of, 186–7, 295n35
    omnidirectionality of, 170–174, 183,
        271–3, 279
    ontologies, 160–74
    self-inflicted (*see also* suicide bombers), 166
    and spectacle, 23–6, 169
    spectrum of application of, 166, 271–2
Virilio, Paul, 36
Virtual Iraq, 11, 285n28
voice (*see also* silencing), 4, 11, 40, 47–61, 111,
    139, 155–6, 184–5, 195, 273
vulnerability, 44–7, 162–5, 201–2, 206, 212

    of civilians, 155, 209
    of musicians and music listeners, 260–70
    of terps, 54
    of troops, 56, 155

Walter Reed Army Medical Center, 9–10
war culture, 18, 101, 154, 277
weapon sounds
    improvised explosive devices (IEDs), 35, 50,
        63, 69–73, 82, 84–6, 92–4, 139, 146, 151,
        163, 181, 186, 197, 200–2, 207–8, 210,
        214, 229–30
    incoming, 4, 81, 89–91, 140–2, 152
    mishearing anodyne sounds as, 213–15
    mortars and rockets, 34, 51, 63, 67–69, 186,
        198, 211, 235, 255
    small arms, 35, 64–67, 81, 150, 162, 175, 180,
        181, 186, 201, 256, 276–7
    within sonic campaigns, 180–2
    weaponization of, 180
weapon-in-use, 181–2
Wieviorka, Michel, 7, 166, 186
Williams, Kayla, 76

Yates, Christopher, 166
Yehia, Seif, 266

Žižek, Slavoj, 168–9